# The Emerging Network

# The Emerging Network

## A Sociology of the New Age and Neo-pagan Movements

*Michael York*

ROWMAN & LITTLEFIELD PUBLISHERS, INC.

ROWMAN & LITTLEFIELD PUBLISHERS, INC.

Published in the United States of America
by Rowman & Littlefield Publishers, Inc.
4720 Boston Way, Lanham, Maryland 20706

3 Henrietta Street
London WC2E 8LU, England

British Cataloging in Publication Information Available

**Library of Congress Cataloging-in-Publication Data**

York, Michael
The emerging network : a sociology of the New Age and neo-pagan
movements / by Michael York.
p. cm.
Includes bibliographical references and index.
1. New Age movement. 2. New Age movement—Great Britain. 3. New
Age movement—United States. 4. Paganism—History—20th century.
5. Paganism—Great Britain—History—20th century. 6. Paganism—
United States—History—20th century. 7. Great Britain—
Religion—20th century. 8. United States—Religion—1960—
I. Title.
BP605.N48Y67 1995  306.6'9993—dc20  94–43545  CIP

ISBN 0–8476–8000–2 (cloth: alk. paper)
ISBN 0–8476–8001–0 (pbk.: alk. paper)

Printed in the United States of America

⊖™ The paper used in this publication meets the minimum requirements of
American National Standard for Information Sciences—Permanence of
Paper for Printed Library Materials, ANSI Z39.48–1964.

# Contents

v

## 8  Conclusions: Evaluating Church-sect Theory, Its Modifications, and Replacements in Application to the New Age and Neo-pagan Movements          315

# List of Tables

# Preface

The purpose of the present undertaking is to arrive at some understanding of what the New Age Movement is; how it is formed; who is involved, who its leading spokespersons are; and in particular how it differs from, is similar to, and overlaps with what is simultaneously emerging as the Neo-pagan Movement. Though I have endeavored to develop an intuitive or subjective comprehension of the movements as a whole and through their particular expressions in the groups I have interacted with on a participatory/observational basis, I have nevertheless attempted objective application of ideal-types to the material forthcoming. This last has depended on a careful scrutiny of the church-sect typologies, their expansions and replacements in order to assess both their terminological precision and conceptual clarity as well as relevancy and utility to such largely amorphous and quasi-ephemeral manifestations as New Age and Neo-paganism. Following its introductory chapter delineating the subject and my methodology, the work proceeds on a chapter-by-chapter basis to outline the New Age Movement; the Neo-pagan Movement; the similarities, contrasts, and relationships between the two movements; observed practices within both New Age and Neo-paganism; survey profiles of particular groups within the movements; discussion of the church-sect and related typologies as a sociological tool; and finally an assessment of the use of this tool in application to the two movements in question.

# Acknowledgments

Though I accept full responsibility for the assertions, material and conclusions of this enterprise, this paper itself would not have been possible without the guidance, support and encouragement of my supervisor, Dr. Peter B. Clarke, King's College lecturer in the Sociology and History of Religion, and director of the Centre for New Religions. My debt of gratitude for his provocative questions, probing discussion, careful criticism and skillful shaping of form and content has been and remains immeasurable.

I would also like to thank the Revd. J.S. Keith Ward, professor of history and philosophy of religion at King's College, for his initial suggestions and orientations. Several significant beginning recommendations were also provided to me by Dr. Pennell Rock. King's College's lecturer on the psychology of religion and social psychology, Dr. Catherine M. Lowenthal, has never flagged in her generous encouragement and advice on my behalf, and Professor William Davenport of Northwood University has done me a great service through a careful scrutiny and judicious commentary on an early draft of the work.

I would also like to express my appreciation to my many American colleagues who continue on my behalf to retrieve relevant material on New Age, Neo-pagan and New Religious Movement happenings throughout the United States. Among these to be mentioned in particular are Lynne Eggers, Donald Lippe, Mary Tradowsky, Tom Sadowsky, Fred Profeta, Mary-Ann Haynes, and Senator Myrth York, with special thanks to Mr. and Mrs. William McKee, Lois Drake Messer, Thomas S. Woodruff, Irwin G. Epstein and the reception staff of Columbus, New Mexico's City of the Sun Foundation, William and the late Mary-Jane Switzler. Further appreciation is to be extended to Revd. Leslie Phillips and Linda Pinti, CUUPS editors of *Pagan Nuus*, to Revd. Cara-

Marguerite of the Lyceum of Venus of Healing in Ayer, Massachusetts, and to UCSB Professor Emeritus Howard Fenton and his wife Jean. Additional thanks are to be extended to Dr. J. Gordon Melton of the Institute for the Study of American Religion as well as Dr. James R. Lewis and Evelyn Dorothy Oliver from the Association of World Academics for Religious Education. Not to be overlooked for invaluable advice and suggestions especially concerning indexing is Dr. K. Jay Wilson. Lois Drake Messer has been particularly helpful in assisting me with the final preparation of the manuscript text.

I would like also to acknowledge my appreciation to the staff of Rowman and Littlefield Publishers and in particular to Jonathan Sisk, Julie E. Kirsch, Lynda S. Hill and Jennifer Ruark. Melissa McNitt, as Production Editor, takes central stage in this expression of gratitude.

Here in Britain, the numbers are too great to enumerate fully, but I would like to mention in particular Glascow's John Wilson, Manchester's *Hoblink*'s Gordon MacLellan, *Religion Today* and *The Journal for Contemporary Religion*'s Elisabeth Arweck, Thorsen's Liz Puttick, King's College's Beverly Clack, Alternative's Dr. William Bloom and Sabrina Dearborne, and especially Shan, High Priestess of London's House of the Goddess, who allowed me and encouraged an access to the Neo-pagan world of London I doubt I would have otherwise been able to attain. Dr. Eileen Barker (LSE) has helped me gain important insights on several fronts. Roger Gann, London Fields Studios' TP Group Ltd., has been instrumental in the technical conception and production of the dissertation. Along with this last I must thank as well Gordon Gallager and and David Powell from the Computer Centre of King's College London. Monica Canizares has also been of supporting assistance.

A final round of appreciation must be given to my parents, Mr. Otto H. York and Mrs. Myrth York, to my patient wife, Nancy, and to my ever encouraging sister-in-law, Pat Wilbarger. I could not conclude, however, without expressing my deepest gratitude for the perpetual assistance of Jennifer Dunscombe and Caroline Pyke and, above all, for the endless support and inspiration of Mr. Richard Lee Switzler.

# Abbreviations

| | |
|---|---|
| COG | Children of God |
| DLM | Divine Light Mission—now called Elan Vital |
| *est* | Erhard Seminars Training—now called The Centres Network |
| HPM | Human Potential Movement |
| ISKCON | International Society for Krishna Consciousness |
| *JSSR* | *Journal for the Scientific Study of Religion* |
| NA | New Age (Movement) |
| NP | Neo-paganism |
| NRM(s) | New religious movement(s) |
| PMO | Political movement organization |
| RMO | Religious movement organization |
| SMO | Social movement organization |
| SPIN | Segmented polycentric integrated network |
| 3HO | Yogi Bhajan's Sikh Dharma or Healthy-Happy-Holy Organization |
| TM | Transcendental Meditation |
| UC | Unification Church |

# Chapter 1

# Introduction and Overview

During the 1980s, the New Age Movement emerged to present a religious or semireligious option for the spiritual market consumer or metaphysical seeker. As a label if not a viable sociological expression, 'New Age' has caught the attention of the media and has more or less ridden the same bandwagon on which the human potential movement has become known and available to the layman/laywoman interested in spiritual innovations. At the same time, and as expressed by general consensus at, for instance, the International Seminar on New Religious Movements: The European Situation held in Lugano, Switzerland, on April 20–21, 1990, 'New Age' has become a reference term of frequent usage by sociologists of religion as well.

The purpose of the present undertaking is to arrive at some understanding of what the New Age Movement is; how it is formed; who is involved; who its leading spokespersons are; and in particular how it differs from, is similar to, and overlaps with what is simultaneously emerging as the Neo-pagan Movement. Although New Age has several antecedents in the American metaphysical tradition and even American Transcendentalism, in Theosophy, in Spiritualism, in Swedenborgianism, New Thought, and other European nonmainstream developments as well as Eastern religious philosophies and practices, it is distinct from its predecessors in its own self-consciousness as a new way of thinking, as part of the so-called 'quantum leap of consciousness' that is thought to be part of and in part the cause of an imminent new age—often referred to as the Age of Aquarius. New Age is doubtlessly an umbrella term that includes a great variety of groups and identities—some of which may also consider themselves pagan or Neo-pagan, but it is the expectation of a major and universal change being primarily founded on the individual and collective development of human poten-

1

tial that is what links together the disparate components identified as New Age.

As a new religious movement (NRM), New Age is chiefly American in origin—although its subsequent development may be said to have occurred as much on British as it has on American soil. To a lesser extent, New Age developments are also to be found on continental (primarily Western) Europe as well as in Australia and New Zealand. These same areas have also witnessed the growth of the Neo-pagan Movement. The two are by no means easily distinguishable developments—if indeed they can be separated at all. I shall explore their more specific identities later, but for the moment there are two salient features or inclinations about which the respective orientations may differ. Where New Age per se pursues a transcendent metaphysical reality, Neo-paganism seeks an immanent locus of deity.[1] Second, New Age is innovative in the sense that it does not feel beholden to any particular tradition or traditions but may borrow eclectically from any or all of them. In other words, New Age thinks of itself as a *new* and distinct religion or religious orientation. Neo-paganism, on the other hand, stresses instead its links to the past and its continuities with earlier traditions. Whereas New Age is self-styled as an *awakening*, Neo-paganism thinks of itself more as a *re*-awakening.

I have chosen this investigation into the New Age/Neo-pagan corpus of thought and social expression because I believe that together they represent a theological perspective with particular sociological consequences, which has been largely absent from or ignored in the Judeo-Christian hegemony dominating the West. Under the strains of our consumer-oriented, technological, and industrialized society of role-playing as opposed to communities of interpersonal relationships (e.g., Wilson, 1982; Wallis in Barker, 1982), the New Age/Neo-pagan perspective shows signs of momentum and growing acceptance that might be interpreted as part of the broader social attempt, albeit limited, toward counterbalancing the prevailing tendencies. It is likewise in part a response to a dissatisfaction with more orthodox religious institutions to meet the challenges of growing impersonalization in our secularized and increasingly bureaucratic society.[2] It also stems from what might be termed the rising 'ecological panic' of our times. But for whatever reasons, the New Age/Neo-pagan format is a phenomenon that *is* occurring, and that in itself requires an effort toward its understanding by the sociologist of religion.

Because of the 'newness' of both New Age and Neo-paganism, however, the available literature on the relevant material is both scarce and often incomplete. This has offered a certain constraint on my methodology, and I have as a result had to rely more heavily on media coverage, participant observation, interviewing, and questionnaire sampling than on unavailable or nonexistent academically published research and analysis. In particular, in my methodological approach of direct observation, I have taken my cue from Robert Balch (1985:32) who argues that "Immersion in the day to day flow of group activities tends to give researchers greater insight into the way members perceive reality." In obtaining the basic descriptive data or ethnographies of a group or orientation, participant observation allows one to become sensitive to internal conflicts, factions, geographic variations, etc., as well as possible or actual changes in a movement. Nevertheless, as Balch admits, the very volatility of NRMs—including both New Age and Neo-paganism—makes cataloguing on the basis of any anthropological model difficult at best.

However, use of primary source material and sociological methodology can only be viable if the analysis occurs within an investigative framework free from terminological confusion and ambiguity. It is for this reason that my effort toward understanding the New Age and Neo-pagan movements has simultaneously focused on typological assessment. I have endeavored to develop an intuitive or subjective comprehension of the movements as a whole and through their particular expressions in the groups I have interacted with on a participatory/observational basis *and*, at the same time, come to an objective recognition through application of ideal-types to the material forthcoming. This last has depended on a careful scrutiny of the church-sect typologies, their expansions, and replacements in order to assess both their terminological precision and conceptual clarity as well as relevancy and utility to such largely amorphous and quasi-ephemeral manifestations as New Age and Neo-paganism.

## Available literature

There is as yet relatively little available sociological material on the New Age Movement per se when compared to the literature on some of the other NRMs (e.g., the Unification Church, Children of God, ISKCON, Scientology, *est*/The Forum, etc.). What does exist ranges from such finer if limited explication as Bednarowski (1989), Barker (1989), or Melton (1986b) to such indirect, partial, or dated surveys as Moore (1986), Wagner (1983), or Needleman (1970) to the more

questionable sociological assessments in terms of value-neutrality taken
by Basil (1988) et al., Hexham and Poewe (1986), Gardner (1991), or
Peters (1991).[3]

More important comments on the New Age—either directly, inciden-
tally, or by allusion—occur within some of the more professionally
oriented works that have become available (e.g., Harris 1981; Snow and
Machalek 1984; Beckford 1985a, 1985b, 1986; Robbins 1988; Anthony
et al. 1987; Nelson 1987; Richardson 1983; again Barker 1989 and Melton 1986b), which focus instead on the broader area of NRMs or some
other aspect of sociological or advisory concern in general. An overview of the North American NRM situation is provided by Wallis
(1988), which delineates both origins and typologies of the human potential movement (HPM) as well as the New Age Divine Light Mission
(DLM), est, Silva Mind Control, Rajneeshism, etc. Heelas's coverage
of "Self-Religions" (1988) sketches HPM and New Age developments
for Western Europe. One of the better presentations of the HPM and the
Esalen center in California (which, in turn, have helped to spawn both
the New Age and Neo-pagan movements) remains Gustaitis (1969).
More recently, pertaining to New Age itself, Gordon Melton, Jerome
Clark, and Aidan A. Kelly have published a *New Age Encyclopedia*
(1990) and a *New Age Almanac* (1991), which delineate beliefs, concepts, terms, people, and organizations comprising the movement. See
further, Streiker (1990).

Then too, in the literature that is currently available on the New Age,
there is a category of material that either uses the term 'New Age' in
its title (e.g., Bailey 1944, 1954, and 1955, Orr and Ray 1983, Montgomery 1986, Crowley 1989, Bloom 1991) or is written—usually from
an insider's point of view—about a particular interpretation or promul-
gating framework. In general, this group of material has been written
by those marketing their own brand of the New Age vision—e.g., Trevelyan (1977/1984), Russell (1983), MacLaine (1987), Argüelles (1987),
Bloom (1990) (which manages studiously to avoid any mention of
'New Age') or even the more reflective and balanced outputs of Spangler (1976, 1977, 1984) and Ferguson (1987).

## Pluralism of contemporary society and
## the New Age movement

The situation that prevails within today's pluralistic operatives in
which each viewpoint struggles and competes to establish itself as the

'official voice' of a still inchoate and highly flexible environment of spiritual ferment is much akin to a similar situation in early imperial Rome where an official religious orthodoxy was on the wan (despite Augustus's attempt to revivify the city's ancient faith and religious institutions) as a vast intrusion of cults and foreign sects, each contended to install their own particular authority in the resultant power vacuum. Whether our own times will produce a new religion that might achieve a success ratio similar to that of nascent Christianity in the Roman empire is a question only time can answer.[4] My statement may suggest at least that for present-day Christianity, any attempt to rescue its declining fortunes through appeal to a more puritanical re-presentation of itself may be of little durability in the long-run when faced with the large-scale and largely depersonalizing changes of sociological conditions in Western society, but for what might come to take its place—if anything—it is still much too early to say. In other words, if the question remains at present open regarding what movements shall yet emerge 'on the scene' to market themselves, New Age is itself still largely an open-grab field as various schools of thought and religious leaders struggle to present what each hopes will become the accepted version of the New Age.

## Church-sect typology as an investigative tool

The contemporary search for spiritual alternatives in the West today might at the very least be a product of people's disenchantment with an increasingly disenchanted society. As Goodman (1988:171) expresses it in terms of humanity's biological propensity for experiencing both ordinary and alternate reality, "In the long run, . . . humans cannot tolerate ecstasy deprivation." If the New Age and Neo-pagan movements, as part of the broader NRM explosion, are manifestations of this 'intolerance,' they are nonetheless viable sociological expressions if not formal organizations into which the sociology of religion discipline must extend its on-going inquiry. It is for this reason that, in my presentation and examination of these movements, I wish also to investigate the church-sect formulation and expanded typologies to which it has given rise in order to appraise whether, *as a tool*, these furnish ideal-types through which we might assess these particular NRMs. If the tool is found wanting or inappropriate, then we must consider others that might provide a better means for analytic research.

## Sociology of religion and relevant sociological studies

For the sociology of religion, Hill (1973), Wilson (1982), and Nelson (1987) among others provide overviews of its growth as a cogent field of research and the current issues with which it is concerned as well as the progress of the church-sect typology and its modifications within the discipline's overall development. Key sociological questions concern methodology and issues of secularization, social disillusionment, religious pluralism, religious experimentation, the role of ritualization, cult controversy, and recruitment/conversion/adherence/disaffiliation. Studies of individual groups or orientations that could be identified as New Age and/or Neo-pagan include Wagner (1983), Prebish (1978), Mosatche (1984), Luhrmann (1989), Juergensmeyer (1978), Bednarowski (1989), Needleman (1970; 1982), and King (1970).[5]

Among the various theoretical frameworks to emerge in sociological analysis that could have elucidating potential for New Age and Neo-paganism, there is Anthony and Robbins's distinction between dualistic and monistic religion, in which the former tends "to affirm the contrast between concrete exemplars of good and evil as a metaphysical principle," whereas monistic religions, "on the other hand, tend to interpret their own conceptualizations of space as symbolic" and recognize an unlimited number of "Centers" (1978:93f). Along with Ecker and Wilber, Anthony (Anthony et al., 1987) extends the earlier metaphysical/ethico-salvational monistic-dualistic typology formulated by Anthony and Robbins to include a "technical-charismatic" dimension and, more importantly, a "unilevel-multilevel" interpretive dimension. The former, distinguishing between whether techniques (such as chanting, yoga, etc.) or direct grace through a religious leader form the basis for spiritual transformation, is the least satisfactory. Contact or relationship with a charismatic leader may itself be considered a kind of "salvational technique."

Another potential typology of NRMs is presented by Bainbridge and Stark (1980) and Stark and Bainbridge (1985), which distinguishes between the "audience cult," the "client cult," and the "cult movement." They have here expanded upon their theory of religious compensation (e.g., 1979, 1983) in which people settle for specific or general compensators in the absence of scarce but desired rewards. The sociologists deny the reality of secularization since "only by assuming the existence of an active supernatural can credible compensators be created" (Stark and Bainbridge, 1985:7)—hence, religion is always a necessity.[6]

More empirically, Hargrove (1978:257f) considers that

The entire phenomenon [of NRMs] has been an unexpected reversal of the process of secularization which many scholars still consider to be the overwhelming pattern of our culture, at least its public manifestations. . . . In sum, it would seem appropriate to apply the term 'new' to any religions whose ties to the society's recognized organized religion are problematic, in that they (1) are based on religious forms of another culture, (2) present a radical shift or reversal of cultural trends, or (3) offer a unique combination of elements which in themselves may be familiar.

For Hargrove, "new" means "unusual or exotic," i.e., cultural borrowing, eclecticism, or adaptation of borrowing. "New" refers to "the unexpected, to a change in direction or emphasis, to some kind of reversal of trends." From a different perspective, however, Melton (1987:47f) and Melton and Moore (1982) present a view that attempts to deny alternative religions of the 1970s as "a new event in Western culture" and understand them instead as "a continuation of the flowering of the occult mysticism and Eastern thought that began in the nineteenth century." While a case for historical antecedents can certainly be made, it is the social impact of NRMs in present-day society that exemplifies their 'newness' and their popular, media, and occasionally sociological perception as sudden and unprecedented developments.

Another typological approach is that of Beckford (1982, 1985a) who, like so many others, is also unsatisfied with the "church," "sect," "cult," etc. categories—particularly in the search for a designation of "marginal religious movements" (Harper, 1982), "alternative" or "unconventional religious movements" (Tipton, 1982b), or "post-movement movements" (Foss and Larkin, 1976). He settles on "new religious movement" (NRM) as the least objectionable and most value-free term—although in many cases any particular movement identified within the category may not be all that recent. He would prefer the generic singular of "*the* new religious movement," which allows that separate groups may not be new but nonetheless "their collective impact is novel." Nevertheless, Beckford (1985a:1) implies that the NRM is still essentially a "cult," that is, one of several "relatively small, new, and unconventional religious groups which grew rapidly in the 1960s and 1970s."

Like Beckford, Wallis had come to eschew the "church," "sect," and "cult" constructs, although earlier (1974, 1975a, 1975b, 1976) he developed a typology of ideological collectivities based on the features of legitimacy (unique: church and sect; pluralistic: denomination and cult) and respectability (church and denomination) or deviance (sect and cult) (e.g., 1976:13). The central aspect of the cult for Wallis (1975b:91) is its "epistemological individualism" in which there is "no clear locus of final authority beyond the individual member," and heresy therefore becomes a concept without valid application. In his later works, however, Wallis (1979c, 1984) found the church-sect-cult typology largely inappropriate for post-1960 religious groups and developed instead a typology based on whether they reject, affirm, or accommodate themselves to the world. I shall examine Wallis's modes-of-insertion analysis as well as the church-sect typologies—including Wilson's sectarian typology (e.g., 1959, 1969, 1973, etc.)—in more detail at a later point (see Chapter 7).

## Sociological light on the New Age/Neo-pagan phenomenon

For now, I wish to mention some of the salient points raised by various sociologists that appear to have shed some light on the New Age/Neo-pagan phenomenon and orientation. One important aspect of these movements—especially New Age—is the concern with healing and holistic emphasis. In this, both movements may be seen in part as developments of and outgrowths from the broader human potential movement (HPM). Describing NRMs in general, Beckford (1984) finds those in which "holistic" themes are frequently common, i.e., "holistic movements," tend to relativize such established institutional boundaries that normally exist between religion and psychiatry, etc., even when they are not communally totalistic. Along with healing, Bird (1979a) finds initiatory and meditation rituals to be prominent in cults—especially "charismatic cults." Rituals authorized by charismatic leaders are practiced in an attempt to achieve well-being and for followers to absorb the leader's charisma as well.

For Beckford, the appeal of symbolic mystiques and movements that stress holistic conceptions of self caters to people fragmented into diverse functionally specific social roles, that is, people suffering from a diffusion of personal identity. This idea is also to be found in the writings of Roszak (e.g., 1969, 1977, 1978a, 1978b), who has emerged as a leading formulator of New Age ideas. He is sharply critical of the dehumanizing process resulting from secular humanism, which eschews the ancient route of "vision and rhapsodic utterance" for the skepticism and instruments of social revolution designed "within the strictly desacralized worldview of modern science" (1978b:55). For

Roszak, the new religions and psychotherapies, though dealing with the anxieties of guilt and inner terror, are not obsessed with them and rest instead on Oriental imports that teach ''our inherent divinity.''

Wallis (1985), too, understands the Growth Movement following the mid-1960s as founded on both humanistic psychology (as developed by William Reich, Otto Rank, Kurt Lewin, Abraham Maslow, Carl Roger, and Fritz Perls) and anti-authoritarian transpersonal psychology, which focuses on experiencing mystical and spiritual states,[7] but he rejects the Stark-Bainbridge reward-and-compensation theory of religion and denies that the increased spirituality coming to be part of the HPM is sought as a substitute for this-worldly eventuality. Instead, religious goals are becoming sought *in addition to* the practical consequences of the HPM—being encouraged further through its diffuse and epistemologically individualistic belief system. One clear instance presented by Wallis of a successful transformation of clients into followers is the Bhagwan movement of Rajneesh. But not all if even most New Agers could be classified as ''followers'' or, to use Bird's terms (1979b, 1978:184), ''devotees'' and ''disciples,'' for, as Wallis (1985:30) himself says for the HPM—words that apply equally to the New Age Movement, ''It consists of a congeries of individual groups, leaders, media of communication, etcetera, which display no common structure of authority or membership, with divergences of purpose and practice, yet recognising that they share in common a commitment to the attainment of personal growth by self-directed means.'' In fact, the anti-authoritarianism of the New Age identity is among its dominant features—as strong if not stronger than any of the more guru-oriented groups (e.g., Bhagwan, Transcendental Meditation [TM], Divine Light Mission [DLM], Johannine Daist, Meher Baba, etc.) that identify with it.

The role of transpersonal psychology, along with Western structural-developmental theory and Vedantic philosophic derivatives, is considered by Wilber (1983) to foster ''the psychic, subtle, causal and ultimate levels of transcendence and comprehension,'' which culminates a sequence of personal, organizational, and/or historical progression from the archaic, magical, and rational to the transrational/transpersonal. This typological formulation of religious experience and social interaction suggests for Wilber that the contemporary growth of secular rationalism and decline of mythic worldviews do not represent degeneration but a necessary, phase-specific step toward an emergent transrational structuralization.

Along with Wallis, the other authors in the same volume (Jones, 1985) examine relationships between religious sectarianism and marginal medicine and how each reveals the struggles involved with establishing a dominant ideology. Coupled with questions of the relationship between psychoticism and/or neuroticism and religiosity, Jones points out that healing movements correspond to Bryan Wilson's (1970b) categories of manipulationist and thaumaturgical sects—with medical sects generally considered as a "sub-classification within the manipulationist category."[8] Quackery approximates to the concept of "cult" through its temporality of association and access to an ephemeral gnosis, while marginal medicine (e.g., homeopathy, osteopathy, etc.) is likened more to that of the "sect." Nevertheless, Jones (1985:122) feels that "religious sects emerge during times of rapid social change and upheaval." Moreover, "their appeal is predominantly to the urban, structurally alienated population." For an alternate approach, see Beckford's essay in this volume.

Gary Easthope (Jones, 1985:53) investigates "impression management" by marginal healers of their public personae, i.e., as "personally disinterested, sympathetic and caring, knowledgeable and authoritative." In situations of uncertainty, the "placebo effect" operating through the "aura" of trust and authority by the healer can result in real—not fictitious—healing of the patient. But Jones argues that the very socio-cultural context itself structures the experience—creating not only the illness's form but presumably also its cure. Tanice Foltz (Jones, 1985:153) perceives this process operating as well within the healing sect itself. In particular, student/instructor "feedback exercises become ritual methods of socialising apprentices into a range of desired behaviour and the appropriate mind-frame with reference to the group's worldview and practices."

It is Frederick Bird (1978:173), however, who has emphasized NRMs' tendency to stress cultic rituals (e.g., initiation, meditation, healing) over "more sectarian or ecclesiastic rites—such as those for the stages of life or seasons of the year or for confession and penance." He feels that modern etiquette along with primitive rituals "establishes and orders social relations" while the ritual of new religious movements inclines practitioners with a sense of self-worth and allows them to "feel prepared for the dramas of life." For Bird, the aim of the "new" religious movements is to promote the realization of self-transcending, self-authenticating experiences.

The question of ritualization is important in any discussion of Neopaganism where ritual is overtly stressed as part of its normal practice. But even New Age activities, though comparatively more informal, are ritualistic—especially according to Bird's 'broad definition' of ritual activities that includes the enactment of various liturgies, ceremonies, therapeutic techniques, games, etiquettes, social conventions, and even exercises. From Bird's (1978:175) position, "Generally defined, 'rituals' are a family of stereotyped, stylized, repeated, authoritatively designated, and intrinsically valued activities." But he makes the methodological contention that wherever parallels among religious ritual and ceremonies and games, therapeutic techniques, etiquette, and social observation have been observed, "attention is focused on conformation to an already stereotyped, objectively given form of acting rather than on the consequences of that acting." I would contend, however, that at the end of the day, it is the self-improvement and self-growth orientations of New Age and Neo-paganism that constitute the *raison d'être* behind their rituals.

In drawing on the Montreal area study of Protestant and Catholic Charismatics, francophone and anglophone Spiritualist groups, ISKCON, Nicheren Shoshu Academy, Divine Light Mission, Shri Chinmoy followers, Montreal Zendo, Montreal Dharmadhatu, the Integral Yoga Institute, the Institute de Yoga Sivananda, Transcendental Meditation, Subud, Tai Chi, Silva Mind Control, the Self Realization Fellowship, Scientology, and Arica, Bird (1978:188f.) questions the monism of Anthony and Robbins.

> There may, in opposition to Anthony and Robbins, be a basis for arguing that these ['new' religious] groups express a gnostic dualism, which views everyday existence as being predetermined by fate and/or chance and encourages an enlightened detachment, a Gurdjieffian mindfulness, about everyday exigencies.

Nevertheless,

> Three kinds of ritual enjoy prominence in most of these movements: (1) various therapeutic rituals for healing or purification; (2) a range of meditation rites, which may be practiced both alone and within a group setting; and (3) rites of initiation, which may be performed either on a single occasion or as a series of occasions. (Bird, 1978:177f.)

In contrast to other contemporary movements in Catholic and Protestant Christianity, these movements make little or no appeal to cognitive understanding in meditation rituals (chanting, silent repetition of a sound or word, breathing exercises, stylized body posturing or movement) aiming toward connection with sources of peace and power. Instead of the vernacular, they employ (1) foreign or ancient languages (Hare

Krishna, Nicheren Shoshu, Shri Chinmoy, Zendo), (2) glossolalia
(Charismatics and Subud), (3) non-verbal body language (Tai Chi, Gur-
djieff, Yoga), or (4) avant-garde science fiction language (Scientology,
Shakti).

Greater emphasis is placed on group meditation when the higher reality is conceived of as transcending individual persons—e.g., Hare
Krishna, Divine Light Mission, and Charismatics. Individual meditation
is emphasized when the higher reality is considered to be within one—
e.g., Transcendental Meditation, Dharmadhatu, and Nicheren Shoshu.
Bird also distinguishes according to whether: (1) the goal is a still, quiet
state of mind as an end in itself (Zendo, Integral Yoga, Transcendental
Meditation), (2) the goal is a more trance-like state of mind as an end
in itself (Subud, perhaps Divine Light Mission), or (3) meditation is not
seen as an end in itself but as a means to achieving other ends (Silva
Mind Control and Arica).

> Except for the International Society for Krishna Consciousness, which ar-
> gues that Krishna is ultimate reality, these movements do not necessarily
> assign ultimacy or exclusive preeminence to these otherwise unacknowl-
> edged realities. Rather, they view these realities as powerful life-enhancing
> but neglected dimensions of self and world. . . . These movements in
> general do not propose clear alternatives to the dominant spectrum of cul-
> tural values, which honor personal success and happiness. Rather, they
> propose that by meditation, adherents will come into contact with ne-
> glected dimensions of reality which may well enhance their chances, if not
> for success, then certainly for happiness. (Bird, 1978:181)

These assorted meditation rituals reinforce "a sense of selfhood connected with one's intrinsic dignity as an anonymous human being."

Bird observes that only initiation rituals feature as a rite of passage
by these new movements: the symbolic metaphors center on awakening
from sleep or gaining sight after blindness; for the Jesus groups, "being
born again."

> In summary, the initiation process, which may be more or less formally
> stylized, introduces potential practitioners to the central ritual activities,
> assigns adherents to a special, personal, yet private status, and licenses
> them to re-enact these rites in the appropriate fashion. (Bird, 1978:182)

## The Human Potential Movement

While admittedly Bird's broader NRM focus takes in such related
areas as Oriental mysticism and the HPM, his analyses appear to be

fully applicable to New Age and Neo-paganism. The easy overlap between all these areas is such that it could well be counterproductive to attempt to separate them. Consequently, such investigations into the HPM as Prebish (1978), Robbins and Anthony (1981), Tipton (1979), Wallis (1985), Westley (1983), and Wuthnow (1985) delineate features that belong to New Age as well. For instance, Wuthnow (1985:46) finds that various esoteric religiotherapeutic movements (e.g., Transcendental Meditation, yoga, guru, and therapy groups as well as ISKCON) "bear the distinctive imprint of the prevailing technological worldview." This spiritual technicalism, he argues, is not incongruent with mainstream values and tendencies but represents a substantial continuity— regardless of the NRM's declared position—with the cultural emphases by which the movement is surrounded. In other words, the "technical" approach to empirical-experiential immediacy characteristic of various mystical occult, human potential, and charismatic groups "echoes suppositions characteristic of the culture at large." For Wuthnow (1985:53), the new religions (which would include New Age) are "exploiting techniques having immediate consequences and adopting consequentialist reasoning in support of their practices."

The broad HPM is also seen by Prebish (1978) as an outgrowth of the American psychedelic heritage as reflected in such seminal literatures as William James's *The Varieties of Religious Experience*, Aldous Huxley's *The Doors of Perception*, and Alan Watts's *The Joyous Cosmology: Adventures in the Chemistry of Consciousness*. However, "The landmark work of Abraham Maslow, Fritz Perls, and others was to coalesce in the 1960s under the rubric [of the Human Potential Movement]. Encompassing a wide variety of techniques and therapies, the Human Potential Movement was symbolized by Esalen Institute, where many of the superstars of the movement came to offer seminars and programs" (Prebish, 1978:164).

For a look into the religious and quasi-religious groups that contributed to the counterculture of the San Francisco Bay Area, see Glock and Bellah (1976). In the same work, Wuthnow suggests social attitude differentials between Oriental and neo-Christian cultists and thereby challenges the often-made assumption that Hindu-Buddhist cults and Jesus sects are equally exchangeable consumer items in the contemporary spiritual market. His data support the contention that "monistic" Eastern mysticism and "dualistic" neo-fundamentalism appeal to different types of individuals in the present-day spiritual and moral crisis. These are not interchangeable. On the broader level, Yinger (1982) considers the role of countercultures in society and the ways they influence or contribute to social change. While their direct influence may be insignificant, Yinger sees the growing acceptance of pluralism, of emotions over strict rationalism, of escape from unmitigated scientific methodology, and of conceptual changes in understandings of well-being resulting from the effects of countercultural phenomena in maintaining a balanced view of society.

The chief criticism leveled against Human Potential is one frequently made for New Age as well, namely, charges of narcissism.[9] Benton Johnson (Robbins and Anthony, 1981:61) would distinguish between the new religions and the new therapies—claiming that the former avoid the "narcissistic and atomizing regimens" advocated by the latter. The new religious movements, unlike the new therapies, stress the experience of transcendence, a commonness of purpose and motive, and group support. Bound by a common regimen and moral code, "Most of the new religions provide a reliable community of fellow adherents. . . . Most of the new therapies do not."

In the same work, however, the attribution of narcissism itself is disputed for the new human potential therapeutic movements by Donald Stone. For instance, with *est*, "the best known and most controversial" of these, its founder, Werner Erhard, explains that "When people become free to acknowledge their real needs at a deeper level of awareness, . . . their apparent self-interest becomes transferred into concern for others as well" (Robbins and Anthony, 1981:23). According to Stone, the critical arguments are often linguistically circular or tautological: "since human potential enthusiasts are concerned with 'self,' they must be 'selfish', and so forth" (Robbins and Anthony, 1981:24). The fundamental problem may stem from the fact that "Social science lacks a concept for motives that produce service out of a sense of satisfaction" (Robbins and Anthony, 1981:224). Moreover, there is no empirical testing of the critics' basic assumptions. On the other hand, Robert Wuthnow's data indicate that persons attracted to new mystical religions are more likely than others to become involved with political protest and activism—not less. In Stone's words, "Wuthnow found that people reporting mystical and peak experiences were less materialistic, less status-conscious, and more socially concerned" (Robbins and Anthony, 1981:227; cf. 233). Both the survey and interview evidence does not indicate that awareness group participants are less sensitive to social forces and the lot of the disadvantaged. This conclusion presumably applies to the broad range of HPM groups including gestalt, encounter, *est*, Zen, Aikido, Transactional Analysis, and Transcendental Meditation and, by extension, New Age and Neo-paganism.

## Boundary maintenance and "conversion"

A key distinction between the wide area of New Age/Neo-paganism and some of the charismatic-leader-dominated or totalitarian groups that belong to it is to be found in the question of boundary maintenance. For this issue, see Griel and Rudy (1984), Kanter (1968), Robbins (1988b), and Travisano (1970), among others. Boundary maintenance is intimately tied up with the process of conversion or other forms of socialization. Griel and Rudy, for instance, distinguish between groups characterized by "role-discontinuity," "communal totalism," and "deviant stigmatization" (e.g., ISKCON and fundamentalist or neo-Christian movements such as the Unification Church [UC]) and those characterized as more "open" and revealing less evidence of converting prior "seekers" and eliminating extra-group attachments (e.g., DLM, Nicheren Shoshu, UFO groups, etc.).

In his discussion of conversion, commitment, and disengagement, Robbins refers to A. D. Nock's 1933 distinction between *conversion* "to the intolerant faiths of Judaism and Christianity" and *adhesion* to the cults of the Roman Empire. Robbins (1988b:71) finds that

> In general the literature on conversion processes in contemporary NRMs has been dominated by two models: the brainwashing model (not really a single model), and the early causal process model developed by Lofland and Stark (including the ultimately derivative social network research).

He feels that intellectual and experimental conversions may be increasing in contemporary Western society while revivalist conversions are becoming fewer. Groups,

> which are not highly stigmatized and do not drastically transform the social roles of converts, are able to recruit new members from pre-existing social networks. Conversion of prior 'seekers' and neutralization of extra-cult attachments are manifested less by such groups than by communal groups . . . which are perceived as highly deviant and involving a radical discontinuity of social roles. (Robbins, 1988b:83)

Although some broader models of "thought reform" and "coercive persuasion" do apply to many cults, Robbins (1988b:76) refers to Robert Lifton's dismissal of the brainwashing connotations as "an all-powerful, irresistible and quasi-magical technology for gaining total control over human beings." Instead, "A number of reports have emphasized the key significance of *ritual* in creating or reinforcing commitment'' (Robbins, 1988b:84).

Kanter (1968) defines commitment through the willingness of individuals to give their energy and loyalty to a social system. ''Continuance commitment'' is based on cognitive orientations which perceive the ''cost of leaving'' the system to be higher than the ''cost of staying.'' ''Cohesion commitment'' relates to effective bonding ties to the group solidarity. ''Control commitment'' is based on the individual's positive evaluation of the norms of the group that demand obedience.

Each form of commitment (all of which the successful organization seeks mechanisms to ensure) has a negative and positive component. For continuance, the negative mechanism is ''sacrifice''—the higher the price, i.e., cost, of membership, the more valuable it is perceived; the positive is ''investment''—whether in financial terms or those involving time or energy.

Cohesion commitment depends negatively on ''renunciation'' of external attachments. Its positive factor is ''communion'' by which the individual becomes ''part of the whole'' through communal sharing, working together, group meetings, ritual, and other mutual activities. Control operates through ''mortification'' techniques that reduce the individual's self-esteem and self-identity so that he can ''surrender'' to the new identity imposed by the group authority, which he has come to accept.

Kanter finds a higher survival rate among communes that employ these various commitment mechanisms. Her analysis applies, however, more to authoritarian NRMs than to those of the human potential type or various New Age movements that do not maintain a high degree of boundary maintenance. Moreover, a classificatory vagueness emerges when one considers the high cost of training programs in such movements as *est*, Scientology, or the British-based I Am movement. These would appear to conform more to the ''investment'' mechanism despite the fact that, when compared for instance to costs for Neo-pagan seminars, etc., these fees are clearly also based on the sacrifice principle that the higher the cost (which may likewise include the renunciation of alcohol, tobacco, or sex) the more meaningful it becomes.

For Travisano (1970), conversion is defined as ''a radical re-organization of identity, meaning, life.'' By contrast, ''alternation'' involves a *less* radical and complete transformation. This last refers to transitions that the individual's ''established universe of discourse'' allows. Conversions, by contrast, are proscribed by the person's former meaning-value system. While in the ideal-type of conversion, one ''embraces a negative identity," Travisano's concept of "alternation" fits the 'religious market consumerism' characteristic of the New Age and human potential movements. Consequently, the questions revolving around "exiting" or disengagement from an NRM enter into the discussion of conversion, adhesion, alternation, and boundary maintenance as well. On these, see in particular Beckford (1985a:135–48), Robbins (1988:88–99), and Bird and Reimer's concept (1982) of "conversion careering" in which many NRM adherents readily move from one group to the next.

Richardson, van der Lans, and Derks (1986) suggest a "typology of disaffiliation modes": *exiting*, in which the disaffiliation process is self-initiated by the member; *expulsion*, in which the organization itself initiates the process; and *extraction*, in which disaffiliation is initiated by an external party (e.g., family or counselor) either coercively or non-coercively. Richardson et al., in describing exiting from the non-communal group, claim that departure may be followed by participation in a succession of different groups. This amounts to the "denomination switching" or the religious market consumerism characteristic of the diffuse New Age and human potential movements.

## The occult metaphysical tradition

Apart from the broader look at NRMs and sociology of religion, several scholarly writers have specific things to say about the occult or metaphysical tradition in general and about the New Age and/or Neopagan movements that have come out of it. For the former, see in particular Ellwood (1973 and 1978), Fichter (1983), Greeley (1972/1985), Harris (1981), Judah (1967), Kerr and Crow (1983), Melton (1982), Tiryakian (1974) and Webb (1974 and 1976). Harris, for instance, examines the socioeconomic mobility that is sought in terms of increased wealth and power as well as healing efforts. These are perceived as actively aided by Jesus in the evangelical NRMs or achieved through self-responsible mind-imposition in such human potential movements as *est* or Silva Mind Control. The chanting of mantras, faith in Jesus, and/or "psychological training" techniques characteristic of these esoteric religiotherapeutic movements from the 1970s Harris sees as representing a "revival of magic." In the book edited by Kerr and Crow on American occultism, Galbreath denies that the occult can simply be equated with the irrational and argues that it must be seen as a cultural phenomenon instead.[10] Melton focuses on astrology as the largest of the cultic milieu followings. In the volume he edited, Tiryakian argues that the "cultic milieu" is a legitimate and necessary focus of sociological inquiry—one with specific social import as well.

Tiryakian posits that "new systems of social action" and emergent processes of social change may result from modern occult practices that are not in themselves simply "atavistic throwbacks" stemming from "modernization breakdowns." In this light, the most significant groups currently would be the magical-occult, i.e., those collectivities within "esoteric culture" that focus on a covert and exclusive gnosis seeking to manipulate concealed natural forces. The author emphasizes the potentially creative and transformative role of the "cultic milieu." He proposes that "esoteric culture, and groups of actors mediating esoteric to exoteric culture, are major inspirational sources of cultural and social innovation" (Tiryakian, 1974:273).

Meanwhile, in America and now, by extension, in Britain and the Western world in general, Greeley (1972/1985:160) finds the "neosacred" manifesting even in the supposed bastion of the secular campus:

> The communes, rock music (particularly as presented by such groups as the Jefferson Airplane, The Doors, and The Grateful Dead), hallucinogenic drugs, the *I Ching*, tarot cards, astrology, witchcraft, the Meher Baba cult, etc. are an attempt to reassert meaningful community in ecstasy in a rationalistic hyperorganized world which had assumed, in keeping with the tenets of the conventional wisdom, that man could dispense with all these elements.

What Greeley here delineates is the occult and countercultural traditions that have given birth to the New Age movement. Elsewhere he says, "I would contend that the rock-music enthusiasts, the drug addicts, the hippies, the communitarians, the witches and warlocks, the protesters, the radicals, the Weathermen, are all but the tip of the iceberg" (Greeley, 1972/1985:260). For Greeley, these are young people without a faith, and it is this "broken myth" of the orthodox mainstream in the West that in turn allows, now for all age ranges in society and not just the young alone, competing mythopoeic world outlooks or interpretative schema to emerge beside those of the Judeo-Christian tradition. Perhaps the growing profile of Neo-paganism and New Age phenomena is evidence that there no longer exists an *a priori* accepted religious and existential truth, and, consequently, the field has become open to alternatives in an unprecedented manner.

## New Age comments by sociologists

For specific sociological comments on the New Age phenomenon or specific New Age groups, see Ellwood (1979), Gilkey (1978), Lofland and Skonovd (1983), McGuire (1986), Nelson (1987), Raschke (1980), Robbins (1988b), Robbins and Anthony (1981), Roszak (1969; 1977, 1978a, 1978b), Smith (1978), Snow and Machalek (1984), Straus (1979), and Wagner (1983). For instance, in the book edited by Robbins and Anthony, there is in particular Robbins and Anthony's essay on Meher Baba,[11] D. Stone's on Human Potential and *est*, as well as Wuthnow's data on involvement in social causes by participants in the Human Potential groups. In her contribution, which largely precedes the period in which the 'New Age' concept achieved media notoriety, Wagner (1983) investigates the Spiritual Frontiers Fellowship (SFF). As portrayed by Wagner, the SFF is clearly a part of what is coming to be termed ''New Age Christianity.''[12] From a different slant, in a plea that strikes to the core of the New Age Movement and sociological study of it, Smith (1978:215) exclaims that

> When white scholars ignore racism, they legitimate covert violence in a racist society and contribute to problems of interpretation in the study of predominantly white new religious movements.

''Recruits to the new religious movements tend to be urban white youth, well-educated and from middle- and upper-class families'' (Smith, 1978:212). This applies equally to the New Age and Neo-pagan movements in the United Kingdom.

On the other hand, Snow and Machalek's understanding (1984:170) of conversion as entailing ''the displacement of one universe of discourse by another or the ascendency of a formerly peripheral universe of discourse to the status of a primary authority'' allows them to summarize among its effective indicators a person's biographical reconstruction, his or her subscription to a ''master attribution scheme,'' suspension of reasoning by analogy, and overt acceptance of the ''convert role.'' Although not part of the authors' explicit intentions, their summary provides a yardstick against which to compare ''conversion'' or ''commitment'' to non-authoritarian or non-totalistic New Age and pagan belief-systems as well.

Along this line, Straus (1979) delineates two models of conversion. The passivist model, which doubtlessly conforms to the active recruitment efforts by most NRMs, posits the individual as determined more by social or psychological factors—with little or no control over his own behavior. The activist model, on the other hand, conceives of conversion as a negotiating process toward achieving an understanding of reality. Here the individual actively seeks and adopts a new interpretation of reality—one that is significantly different from that which he held previously. This last approximates Travisano's concept of "alternation" as well as the "religious market consumerism" characteristic of the New Age and human potential movements.

Some of the other writers again unintentionally sketch aspects of the New Age—e.g., McGuire (1986) in discussing the "precarious organizational forms" of cults,[13] Raschke (1980) in his application of the term "gnosticism" to modern systematized views that criticize industrialization,[14] and Gilkey (1978), who, focusing on Eastern religions, considers the discovery of the self as the "initial gift of Oriental religions of meditation" to the West. Ellwood (1979), too, in his concern for alternatives to the Judeo-Christian mainstream religions in the form of the personal and subjective experience of small groups, foresees what later emerged as the New Age phenomenon.

The most specific statements on the New Age movement, however, are to be found in Robbins (1988b) and Nelson (1987). Robbins (10, 62) refers to "the 'New Age' constellation of the mid 1980s" which, following Diane Salvatori in the July 1987 issue of the *Ladies Home Journal*, he cites as appealing predominantly to middle-aged adults and to women.[15] Though the post-World War II science fiction subculture has influenced Scientology and its offshoots, Robbins (1988b:26) finds that the earlier "harmonical" and occult ideas embraced by Christian Science and Theosophy "display continuity with the symbolic universe of 'New Age' and human potential groups" (see also Bednarowski, 1989). In fact, "Currently the HPM appears to have been assimilated to the broader 'New Age' subculture" (Robbins, 1988b:126f), but the author sees the loose networks characteristic of various contemporary 'New Age' and mystical groups resulting in an "ineffective mobilization" that does not augur promisingly for these collectivities' continuing success.

Along with 'witchcraft-satanist groups', there is also a frequent attack on 'New Age' movements by contemporary televangelical presentations, which include denunciations of the entry of 'New Age' practices and thought into "educational, business and even military institutions." But for Robbins "product diversification" within instrumentalist New Age movements appears to be part of its human potential movement legacy, which seeks "worldly" material and social benefits rather than strictly "expressive and ecstatic emotional release." And yet along with this increasing commercialization, there is also an increasing supernaturalism that is associated with the New Age subculture. Robbins cites the "commercialized mediumistic practice of "channeling'" as "a key instance," and he considers that Stark and Bainbridge's concept of the "audience," and "client" cults along with the spiritual supermarket consumerism notions developed by Wallis and Bruce may provide analytical frameworks for understanding the New Age movement (Robbins, 1988b:127). In particular, Robbins (1988b:155) finds Wallis's concept of the "cult" in his church-denomination and sect-cult typology to apply to many New Age, Human Potential, and spiritualist groups including Vedanta, astrology, Silva Mind Control, 3HO, Rosicrucianism, American Zen, and UFO groups.

On the other hand, because for Nelson (1987:157) religion is the institutionalization of supersensory experience, sensate systems that deny that very experience are "inherently unstable." ". . . not even the arid rigidity of the organisational structures can destroy the spontaneous expression of man's need for the divine, or his ability to experience the presence of the spirit world." In the consequent exhaustion of "sensate culture," the field has become ripe for the development of idealistically oriented new religious movements. Among these he considers witchcraft and traditional occult movements, those of Eastern origin (Divine Light Mission, ISKCON, Transcendental Meditation) or such "pseudoscientific cults" as Scientology or the "Flying Saucer movement." However, though Nelson (1987:158) states that "the West is now moving into a period of sacralisation which is the process which promotes idealistic values and beliefs," he does not specify that these last necessarily include acceptance of the supernatural.

When examining the functions of NRMs, Nelson turns to Robbins and Anthony's 1978 theoretical classification of these as socially integrative, socially disintegrative, socio-culturally transformative, or socially insignificant. Stressing that the NRM category is not a unitary one—some cults being integrative while others are disintegrative or transforming—Nelson clearly favors the thesis that new religions (seen more as products of social disintegration processes rather than their cause) function as agents of socio-cultural transformation. In particular, the counterculture movements of the 1960s had been seen as the foundation for a new socio-cultural system. But

By the mid-1970s the counterculture had largely disappeared, and the hope for a transformed society seemed to have faded, at least in the short term.

However, by the 1980s the counterculture has been replaced by the New
Age movement which encompasses a wide variety of social movements
and cults, some of which have survived from the 1960s but many of which
have developed on the foundation laid by the counterculture. (Nelson,
1987:183)

According to Nelson, the New Age movements are basically either personal (being concerned with individual transformation) or social (concentrating on social, collective, and global problems). The foremost example of the latter Nelson specifies as the Green movements, which
reject the same set of values belonging to the dominant tradition as did
the counterculture. Whereas the personal movements focus on individual awareness and its expansion (varying "from secular encounter
groups to meditation groups"), for Nelson the Green movement is
"clearly the movement of the future" regardless of the length of time
involved with the socio-cultural transformation it seeks.

## Sociological comments on Neo-paganism

The 'green' concern is likewise an integral part of the ecological
orientations of the Neo-pagan movements. If viable sociological literature is largely absent for New Age, the situation is even more problematic for Neo-paganism. There are, however, a limited number of fine
works—both by sociologists (Bednarowski in Kerr and Crow [1983],
Culpepper [1978], Ellwood [1973], Luhrmann [1989], Melton [1986b],
Miller [1974)] Truzzi [1972], etc.) and by Neo-pagans themselves
(Adler [1986], Jones and Matthews [1990], Starhawk [1979])—that delineate overviews of the movement or at least aspects of particular
groups or orientations within it. A comprehensive bibliography covering material relating to both anthropological studies of witchcraft and
contemporary forms of Wicca in the West is provided by Luhrmann,
1989:357–73. Good bibliographies of works written by figures prominent in the area of modern witchcraft (Wicca, the Craft) are to be found
in both Farrar (1984:330–34) and Green (1987:217f). The most thor-
oughgoing study and presentation of witchcraft and paganism in general for North America is that of Adler (1986). Crowley (1989) introduces the Wiccan perspective—both Alexandrian and Gardnerian—of
Great Britain, and Jones and Matthews (1990) is a compilation of articles by people from different traditions within the Neo-pagan movement of the United Kingdom. See further, Skelton (1988).

While Bednarowski (Kerr and Crow, 1983) explores the tensions between feminism in nineteenth-century spiritualism, American theosophy and present-day feminist witchcraft with the dominant religious structure in "Women in occult America," as a counterbalance to the traditional patriarchal trend, Culpepper (1978) recognizes three main streams of feminine-oriented religion or new religious development: (1) Feminist Witchcraft and Worship of the Goddess, (2) Woman-identified Culture, and (3) Woman-identified Chronicles, Philosophy, and Theory. Since Neo-paganism as a whole has occasionally been identified with contemporary Witchcraft,[16] it behooves us to consider what Culpepper (1978:222) says about it. She herself quotes Morgan McFarland:[17]

> Witchcraft is a religion. It is the Worship, not of the Christian Satan, but of the Great Mother, the Supreme Creatrix, the Primum Mobile. It is the celebration of the Goddess.

Culpepper adds that Witchcraft "is perhaps the most conventionally organized (in the sense of having initiation procedures and a hierarchical membership) form of feminine spiritual interest." The common theme which unites "most practitioners of the Craft" is the recognition of matriarchal forms of social organization. These are seen as part of the original history of human beings but also as the form most conducive to living in attunement with both nature and each other.

Culpepper cites the following works as particularly expressive of or helpful for an understanding of the Craft: J. J. Bachofen [1815–87], *Myth, Religion, and Mother Right* (1967); James Frazer [1854–1941], *The Golden Bough* (1911–15); Robert Graves, *The White Goddess* (1948); Esther Harding, *Women's Mysteries* (1955); Margaret Murray, *God of the Witches* (1933) and *Witch-Cult in Western Europe* (1921); and Erich Neumann, *The Great Mother* (1963) as well as Anne Kent Rush, *Moon, Moon* (1976) and Merlin Stone, *When God Was a Woman* (1976). These works have encouraged the emergence of such key realizations of feminism as accepting one's self as female and use of women's thinking and lifestyle to transform "the reigning androcratic social order."

Luhrmann (1989) undertakes a social anthropological analysis of a British magical community in the 1980s. Working on the assumption that magic is "the romantic rationalist's religion," she concludes that the members of the "Hornsey" group she studied, although "rebellious, spiritual, intelligent, intense, self-absorbed and concerned with the hidden exercise of power," were not of a particularly unusual dispo-

sition. This work, the published result of her Ph.D. research, is frequently favorably reviewed in Neo-pagan newsletters and magazines
(e.g., *The Cauldron, The Wiccan,* Skoob's *Occult Review,* etc.) but nevertheless criticized for the academic concessions one perceives that
Luhrmann was forced to make on the basis of an exclusively material-
ist-individualist psychology in which such "transpersonal" experiences of the group mind, precognition, and telepathy are rejected out of
hand as heuristic and/or actual possibilities.

In his work, with a chapter entitled "The Edenic Bower," Ellwood
(1973) investigates the broader area of Neo-paganism in general. He
begins with the Shinto faith of Japan and argues that polytheism in that
country has operated as a binding and structuring system countering an
increasing multiplicity. Historically, Ellwood argues, polytheism has
played an imperialistic function—allowing the cults of the opposition
to be essentially monotheistic: the mystery religions, Christianity, and
the new religions of Japan. In developing his perspective of contemporary Western paganism, Ellwood criticizes David Miller for giving "our
revitalized heritages in Celtic (Yeats), Nordic (Wagner), African (LeRoi
Jones), and Amerindian (many names) polytheistic religions short
shrift."

Nevertheless, although admitting the sincerity and even "reality" of
Neo-pagans' experience in America, he sees the modern revivalist Neo-
pagan groups as unstable and inadequate responses to the needs im-
pelled by human alienation. With polytheism putting "a severe strain
on group formation and continuity," it can only work subjectively and
through terms of "an intensely personal vision." Consequently, each
resultant group as Ellwood sees it remains "tiny, struggling and probably ephemeral."

Ellwood's criticism of Neo-paganism extends to its inability to play
a causal role. Instead it merely forms the background against which
various causes have moved. Considering the major spiritual problem of
today to be the necessity of "dealing with multiplicity," polytheism in
general is thought to lead to "anchorless feelings," which, with regard
to generalized life styles, will only precipitate backlashes such as the
"One Way" of the Jesus Movement or other new monotheisms. Despite
these criticisms, Ellwood's writings on the Neo-pagan movement remain among the more accurate to have been formulated by an academic
outsider to the movement itself.

In contrast to Ellwood, Miller (1974) takes the increased interest of
today's students in the variety of mankind's religious traditions as evidence that, despite the former dominance of monotheism in the West,

we live now in a pluralistic society. According to him, the "Gods and Goddesses" are being reborn through the re-discovery of classical Greek myths. These deities "free one to affirm the radical plurality of the self, an affirmation that one has seldom been able to manage because of the guilt surrounding monotheism's insidious implication . . ." (Miller, 1974:*ix*).

Miller, who teaches classical Greek religion at Syracuse University, uses polytheism to describe the pluralistic religious and social environment comprehending a range of values and organizational patterns. Polytheism, in its theological, psychological, and philosophical ramifications, "is a feeling for the deep, abiding, urgent, and exciting tension that arises when . . . one discovers that a single story, a monovalent logic, a rigid theology, and a confining morality are not adequate to help in understanding the nature of real meaning" (Miller, 1974:11). If pluralistic society sanctions a multi-value system, and if, *à la* Richard Niebuhr, gods are value centers, the modern world legitimates many different gods.

A further emphasis that Miller makes, however, is on narrative myths. These appeal to people in ways that formal theology and philosophical abstractions cannot. Myth as story automatically suggests the phenomena of time and process, and these, in turn, imply that the gods are real and living beings rather than merely value projections. In this provocative volume, the author establishes himself as a leading academic contributor to the emerging Neo-pagan movement. However, Adler (1986:31), though recognizing that Miller sees emergent polytheism as a contemporary affirmation of diversity, questions his exclusive use of a Greco-Roman framework.

## Methodology

In the preceding paragraphs, I have tried to furnish an overview of sociological perspectives on NRMs in general and on the New Age and Neo-pagan movements in particular. For the most part, the available literature is sketchy, incomplete, and sometimes biased. It is for this reason that I have endeavored to undertake an investigation into New Age and Neo-paganism in an attempt to alleviate some of the lacunae in a proper and more comprehensive sociological assessment that is focused specifically on this area. An insider's presentation of the New Age itself is furnished by Bloom (1991)—an anthology of writings considered expressive of various facets of the movement from New Age identity, the idea of an inner voice, healing, human potential, Gaia, and New Age pragmatics. Based on the British Channel Four Television series broadcast in six parts from the end of January 1991 and entitled "The New Age," Bloom (1991:223–29) also furnishes a profile of New Age figures as well as an introductory bibliography (231–34). Although most of my research and writing was done before the appearance of this work, Bloom's overview conforms with many of my own conclusions concerning the salient features of the New Age orientation.

In general, my methodological techniques and constraints comply with the empirical investigative model delineated by Barker (1984:17–37). There are, of course, important differences between the Unification Church of Sun Myung Moon and the New Age/Neo-pagan movements that have affected my research. There is for one no recognized hierarchy or bureaucracy that speaks for either New Age or Neo-paganism as a whole. Consequently, there are no membership lists. At best, certain "centers" or groups may have mailing lists, but even here the suspicions and fears of potential persecution toward pagans prevents access to such to even the most sympathetic of observers. On the other hand, neither New Age or Neo-paganism formulate any clearly expressed idea of religious or organizational boundaries to be maintained. Membership apart from formal initiation into a witches' coven is not a concept entertained by either movement. Adherents in both may 'drift' between a range of meetings, workshops, lectures, or ceremonies. Even the concept of a New Ager itself is vague: on the one hand, there is no formal initiation; and on the other, is someone who attends a *t'ai-chi ch'uan* workshop or a talk by Peter Russell on creative management automatically a New Ager?

This last broaches the point that there are no doctrines, creeds, or belief-systems to be collectively endorsed by those who identify themselves as New Agers and/or Neo-pagans. Within either grouping, one encounters theists, pantheists, agnostics, and atheists alike. And although I am in full accord with Barker's contention (1984:36) that "social scientists are useful only in so far as they communicate information which corresponds to the object of their study rather than colouring, distorting, confusing or over-simplifying an already messy and complicated reality with the addition of their personal beliefs and values," I also entertain the possibility expressed in Hadden's question (1977:308), "Why shouldn't natives, compassionately committed to their culture, be trained to do sociological observation?"

Nevertheless, Stone (1978b) raises problems concerning the gathering of adequate but objective information on NRMs that I have endeavored to keep in mind. Although acknowledging that knowledge about new religious groups is situational and is produced by the interaction of the researcher with the focus and object of study, Stone argues that there is always an interpretation, and this becomes even more problematic when concerned with religious and transpersonal areas. Stone (1978b:142) calls for an interdisciplinary psychology dealing with "the varieties of personal bias and how they might be controlled."

Specifically, "If a researcher does not carefully examine his attitudes toward the purported truths of a religion, the analysis may be full of unconscious hedging" (Stone, 1978b:143). Remaining "suspicious" of any research accounts that do not pay attention to "the possible issues of bias," Stone demands a variety of vantage points including psychoanalysis of the ethnographer, collaborating research, journalistic research, inclusion of instructive autobiographical detail, letting the subject under study review the findings, and inclusion of objections to interpretation in the research report. Wherever possible, I have incorporated these suggestions into my inquiries into the New Age and Neopagan movements.

This use of multiple research methods and, ideally, investigators, Stone terms "triangulation." This last should include "theoretical triangulation" and "investigator triangulation" because participant observation does not readily clarify the meaning of actions nor application of generalization to actions not directly observed, and survey interviews themselves tend to frame information in the researcher's categories rather than the respondent's. Moreover,

> any accounts of new religious movements that does [*sic*] not take note of [mystical experiences or altered states of consciousness provided by the group] misses what is perhaps *the* essential feature that they all share in common. The provision of intense religious experience is what characterizes the new religious consciousness. (Stone, 1978b:147)

By suggesting entry into the state being studied, Stone notes the value of "state-specific research."

Bearing such criticisms in mind, and to gain as much of an overview of the respective movements as possible in preference to an in-depth survey of only a few specific groups within them, I have relied more on participant observation than on interviews but have nevertheless employed both techniques where feasible. For participant observation itself, I have followed Barker's *verstehen* sequence of passive, interactive, and active stages (1984:20). In an effort to develop a multidimensional picture, though concentrating on a few groups, I have attempted nevertheless to observe as many different venues, workshops, events, and assemblies within the New Age and Neo-pagan categories as possible in the physical constraints of time. Furthermore, to gain a perspective of the respective movements each as a whole, I have resorted to questionnaire sampling of certain New Age and Neo-pagan groups as well as control groups for comparative purposes.

## Presentation

The specifics of my methodological approach are discussed at the beginning of Chapter 6, in which I focus on New Age and Neo-paganism as observed in practice. This is preceded by an overview of the two movements with particular focus on their respective leaders (Chapters 2 and 3). Chapter 4 examines the similarities, contrasts, and relationships or overlaps among the movements themselves. In Chapter 5, I present the findings of my own surveys as well as those by Adler, the Sorcerer's Apprentice, and *Body, Mind, Spirit* magazine. The penultimate chapter consists of a discussion of the church-sect and related typologies developed as potential tools for the sociological understanding of NRMs. In Chapter 8, these are evaluated in application to New Age and Neo-paganism, and a replacement model is suggested.

## Notes

1. This last perhaps overlaps with what Ernst (1978:44) refers to as "this world religiosity." By contrast, much but certainly not all New Age might be said to focus on "other world religiosity."

2. For instance, with the collapse of institutional frameworks within traditional religion, Daniel Bell (1977:443) argues that "the search for direct experience which people can feel to be 'religious' facilitates the rise of cults." Nevertheless, he considers that the current magical belief-based cults offer merely ephemeral responses and will not survive. All the same, Bell counters the fashionable sociological concept of secularization that predicts the diminishing or eclipse of religion since religion per se is an inevitable response to the sociocultural milieu. From a different perspective, Stone (1978a) sees ecstatic religious experience having a popular attractive appeal that is nevertheless fully compatible with contemporary secularization.

3. See also Lewis (1991).

4. See also Shepherd (1979), who, on the basis of "serial adhesion" (peo-

ple's facile transfer from one specific religious commitment to a different one) and "polysymbolism" finds a basic similarity between the religiosity of the Greco-Roman world and that of contemporary America.

5. See further such contributions dealing with such broader loci of change as the counterculture "Youth Movement" (Foss and Larkin, 1976), "new religious consciousness" (Stone, 1978), "new religiosity" and the displacement of church religion (Campbell, 1978), religious evolution according to Durkheim's predictions (Westley, 1978), and "the different layers of moral meaning that make up social life" (Tipton, 1982). Foss and Larkin (1978) examine loss of causality among followers of Maharaj Ji.

6. See further Hammond (1985) on the question of secularization. Many of the essays in this volume, which includes contributions by W. S. Bainbridge, E. Barker, J. D. Hunter, B. Johnson, M. B. McGuire, W. Pruyser and D. Capps, R. Robertson, W. C. Roof, A. Shupe and & D. G. Bromley, R. Stark, and R. Wuthnow are direct or indirect critical responses to Bryan Wilson's secularization hypothesis (Wilson, 1976). NRMs, utopian communities, re-emergent American fundamentalisms are here interpreted as counter-secular developments to Wilson's "model of secularization [which] is concerned with the operation of the social system—it is the *system* that becomes secularized" (Hammond, 1985:19)—suggesting that as a social phenomenon controlling and influencing institutional policy-making, religion is becoming peripheralized despite its possible importance still felt by the individual. Nevertheless, many contributors in this volume are also aware of the current accommodating trend toward secular modernity. Most call for more research and caution in determining whether there is a re-sacralization process now underway or whether there is need for a "post-secular theory." See also Nelson (1987:184), who, in answer to Wilson's view that NRMs are marginal and irrelevant, claims not only contrary evidence for this contention but argues that Wilson "fails to see that the most important achievement of 'secularisation' was to break the monopoly of institutionalised religion." The question of secularization or resacralization in sociology of religion is far from being settled. For an overview of earlier arguments, see Hill (1973).

7. Goleman (1978:120) understands there to be an emerging "transpersonal" school of Eastern psychology that involves meditation and "offer[s] models of inner development over and above the psychoanalytic, behavioristic, or humanistic models of mental health." Though presenting a vision that coincides with visions pertaining to religion, "This vision of human possibilities is described in psychological, not metaphysical, language." For Goleman, the transpersonal school has become the West's fourth and most recent branch of psychology.

8. Tina Posner considers TM as "manipulationist" in that it is an association of like-minded persons seeking salvation in terms of realizing "the good things of the world" through short-cut transcendental means. She follows Wallis in describing TM as a "more general cult of meditation" with a "millennial sect as its core."

9. Delineating contrasting critical outlooks on the new religious movements, Needleman (Needleman and Baker, 1978) states that the negative response, instead of viewing the transformation of the individual as a positive
development, sees the "new narcissism," self-indulgence, and retreat from
community commitment as expressions of pseudo-mysticism, superstition, and
anti-rationalism. Needleman himself questions the use of Eastern religious techniques to strengthen "the sense of social personality or ego" when these methods were "originally meant to weaken or destroy" the self. A careful reading
of the earliest *Brâhmaña*, however, reveals that the discipline known as yoga
belonged first to the rajas or warriors as a means for attaining physical strength
and invincibility *before* these techniques were taught to the brahmans or priests
with whom they became subsequently associated as a method leading toward
self-extinction. Cf. the *Aitareya Brâhmaña* 7.29.4 as well as *Kâthaka Samhitâ*
28.5. For the Brahmans learning from the Râjanya, see also *Brihadârankya
Upanisad* 2.1 and *Chândogya Upanisad* 5.3–10. Indeed, this very issue is also
an archeological point relating to an Indo-European, proto-Indo-European, or
even pre-Indo-European setting, that is, not even indigenously to be associated
*just* with the Orient, since early depictions of a man in yogic position are to be
found both on Mohenjo Daro seals and in pre-historic Ireland.

10. Webb (1976), on the other hand, approaches his construct of the "occult
establishment" on the premise that the occult equals irrationality. In this work,
he attempts to delineate how the cultic milieu—traditionally underground—is
influencing, and beginning to emerge into, the religious mainstream of twentieth-century American and Western European political and social life through
various anti-rationalistic institutions (e.g., astrology).

11. Citing Bruyn (1966), Anthony and Robbins in their investigation into the
Meher Baba movement point out that in a participant observation or "anthropological" approach (emphasizing living within a culture until one assimilates its
meaning system), "The meaning system is presumed to have been acquired
when the investigator can participate in the symbolism, ritual, and patterned
interaction of the culture in a way that is deemed acceptable or correct by its
members" (p. 193).

12. "The 'New Age'—What is it?" *Omega News* 40 (Spring 1990).

13. McGuire (1986:121), in considering "Arica, Vedanta, astrology, flying
saucer groups, Silva Mind Control, 3HO, Rosicrucianism, and American Zen,"
virtually comprehensively covers the amorphous New Age movement as a
whole.

14. Raschke's interpretative flexibility is significant when compared to an
increasing utilization of such expressions as "new gnosis," "new age gnosis"
or "pagan gnosis" within the collective New Age/(Neo-)pagan movement. The
author finds specific gnostic elements in Romanticism, Gurdjieff, Jung, New
Thought, and the Divine Light Mission as well as the Hare Krishna movement.
Compare Shepherd (1979).

15. However, on page 45, Robbins observes that " 'New Age' groups are

said to appeal largely to middle-aged people, while 'cults' are now increasingly targeting women and the elderly.''

16. E.g., Melton (1984:464). According to Melton (1986b:213), the non-Wiccan Goddess worshippers were first dubbed ''Neo-Pagans'' by Tim Zell, the founder of the Church of All Worlds. However, in general usage, Neo-paganism, although definitely including Goddess-spirituality, cannot be identified with it.

17. Morgan McFarland, ''Witchcraft: the art of remembering,'' *Quest* 1 (1975):41.

*Chapter 2*

# The New Age Movement

Both New Age and Neo-paganism are manifestations of the Western occult tradition—specifically, of what is often termed the American metaphysical tradition.[1] Although Neo-paganism has a wider base of origin, one that in particular includes Britain, both movements may be thought of as largely American in inception. More broadly, both are expressions of what Campbell (1972) terms the "cultic milieu"—the New Age in fact being possibly an attempt to unify to some extent the great diversity and amorphousness which is that milieu and bring its related tenets and activities under a single label and organization; in a word, to bring the "cultic milieu" together as a new religious movement.[2]

J. Stillson Judah (1967) identifies the "American metaphysical movement" in the likes of Spiritualism, Theosophy, the Arcane School, Astara, New Thought (e.g., the International New Thought Alliance), the Divine Science Church, the Church of Religious Science, the Unity School of Christianity, Christian Science, the Association for Research and Enlightenment, and the Spiritual Frontiers Fellowship. The original impetus for this movement in the United States is to be found in the New England transcendentalists (Emerson, Thoreau, Alcott, Margaret Fuller, etc.) Salvation is considered obtainable through discovery of the divine inner self. Though many metaphysical groups are Christian, few accept the idea of sin—especially 'original sin'. Evil is an illusion of the mind. Nearly all groups, however, whether ostensibly Christian or not, accept Jesus Christ as the 'way-shower' par excellence. Through Theosophy, the Oriental ideas of reincarnation and communication with spiritual masters were first incorporated into this metaphysical tradition founded upon the ideas of Swedenborg, Mesmer, and the transcendentalists. In the wake of Theosophy, additional Eastern concepts (e.g., those of karma, auras, chakras, and astral projection) have continued to arrive in the West. According to Anita Manning,[3] spokesmen for the movement developed from ideas first taught thirty years ago by Maharishi Mahesh Yogi to the Beatles and the Beach Boys claim that Transcendental Meditation "spawned the human potential movement of the 1960s and 1970s, the 1980s new age movement and the fitness and holistic crazes."

This last is illustrative of the fact that without a central authority, the New Age movement is subject to the conflicting claims of the many contenders within the contemporary spiritual supermarket.[4] This conflict extends to various claims over the New Age spiritual leadership as well. For instance, ISKCON's Tripura Swami sees "that general category of people loosely defined as the *new age* group" as his target clientele.

> The new age is really just a theory at this time. It consists of people who are looking for alternative solutions and are open to alternative ways of thinking. It's seeking to define itself, and we want to be within it, giving our definition of what it is or what it should or could be. And the new age allows a format for that kind of discussion.[5]

Tripura Swami's 'spiritual opportunism' would include promotion of both sectarian Gaudiya Vaishnavism[6] over secular humanism and theism over monism. At times, the 'New Age battlefield' can be seen as a far cry from the gentle network and peaceful dissolution/re-coalescement envisioned by Ferguson (1987:213ff).

New Age is a blend of pagan religions, Eastern philosophies, and occult-psychic phenomena. The Euro-American metaphysical tradition and the counterculture of the 1960s together constitute the occult underground or what Campbell refers to as the "cultic milieu." At the same time, New Age itself is an outgrowth of the Haight-Ashbury flower power expression and the broader occult-metaphysical tradition (of the United States in particular). Melton (1986b:116), in fact, explicitly considers the New Age Movement "an updating of the longstanding occult and metaphysical tradition in American life." The 1960s' musical *Hair* did much to popularize the idea of a coming "Age of Aquarius"—not only brought about by dedication to psychic phenomena, the occult or spiritual techniques but also concerned with ecological restoration, new understandings of education, citizen diplomacy missions, decentralist empowerment politics, and holistic thought. In short, this concern is what may be thought of as pragmatic efforts toward social change.

The "first recognized national exponent of New Age consciousness" in America was Baba Ram Dass (a.k.a. Richard Alpert)[7]—a former Harvard psychology professor who established renown through the psychedelic experiments he conducted with Timothy Leary. Ram Dass, following a discipleship period in India, became the earliest of a series of Western gurus, often leaders of various NRMs, who emerged as symbols of the New Age. However, apart from the Aquarian Age expectations based on the astronomical phenomenon known as the "precession of the equinoxes" and the popularization of the concept through the efforts of Ram Dass, Kirpal Singh, Yogi Bhajan, Pir Vilayat Khan, etc., the term "New Age" was coined reputedly first by Alice Bailey, the medium-founder of the Arcane School.[8] In America, the Esalen Institute in Big Sur, California is more or less recognized as the "mother church" of the New Age movement. The "Esalen" of the United Kingdom is the Findhorn community on the north coast of Scotland, which in turn recognizes Alice Bailey as "a prophet of the movement."

With no central authority, New Age is not doctrinaire and consequently means many things to many different people. David Spangler, for instance, a co-director of Findhorn in the early 1970s and subsequently founder of the Lorian Association, a New Age community near Madison, Wisconsin, feels that "The New Age deals with issues of planetarization and the emergence of an awareness that we are all one people living on one world that shares a common destiny."[9] Another figure who holds a primary social commitment to the New Age is Marilyn Ferguson, who, as editor of both the *Brain/Mind Bulletin* and *Leading Edge Bulletin*, has maintained a high profile in establishing an image of the New Age as a humanitarian and ecological movement that seeks a "global consciousness."[10] Like Spangler's *Revelation, the Birth of a New Age* (San Francisco: The Rainbow Bridge, 1976), her *The Aquarian Conspiracy* is a popular statement of the movement's goals and perspectives.

A popular instructional book for New Agers is *A Course in Miracles*, published by the Foundation for Inner Peace in 1975. Although channeled over a seven-year period via Helen Schucman with the encouragement of Bill Thetford, both colleagues of the psychology department of Presbyterian Hospital at Columbia's College of Physicians and Surgeons in New York, neither wished to be publicly associated with the work, and instead such figures as Judith Skutch, Robert Perry, Tara Singh (the Foundation of Life Action in Los Angeles), Mike Saedlo, and Dr. Susan Trout (the Washington Center for Attitudinal Healing) have been thrust into the New Age limelight as Course explicators.

Spawning hundreds of study groups across the North American conti-
nent, the Course employs a metaphor of "miracles" that is essentially
a restatement of New Thought metaphysics pertaining to the almost
limitless power of the human brain and its relationship to an ultimate
universal energy. The nearly 1,200 pages of the book itself comprise
three parts: a long text, a workbook of 365 daily lessons, and a manual
for teachers. Nevertheless, as Robert Perry explains, the Course has
something to offend nearly everyone.

> For a secular age, it is too spiritual. For those into alternative spirituality,
> it is too Christian. For Christians, it is too Eastern. For those into self-help,
> it is too emphatic about helping others and being helped by God.[11]

In fact, the Course teaches that forgiveness is the primary purpose for
man being on earth. It in turn gives rise to healing and counteracts the
very ego that keeps one asleep to the fact that everything is illusion.
The Holy Spirit is seen as the bridge to true reality from our illusion of
it. According to Bloom (1991:42), despite its Christian devotional style,
*A Course in Miracles* "is thought by many to be the most powerful
transformatory course currently available."

## New Age's social, occult, and spiritual dimensions

Nevertheless, if Ram Dass, Spangler, and Ferguson represent what
might be termed the "social camp" of New Age service—one that
additionally includes such names as Patricia Sun, George Leonard, Jean
Houston, Norman Shealy, Irving Oyle, and Sam Keen, apart from *A
Course in Miracles*, the "occult camp" is expressed through the likes
of Shirley MacLaine, Ruth Montgomery, and José Arguëlles. The understanding of New Age by these thinkers includes contact with spirit
guides, channeling, use of crystals, and interpretation of the legacy of
past cultures. If MacLaine is more self-oriented and closer to the human
potential idiom of self-help and self-growth, Montgomery and Arguëlles are more apparently suggestive of using the esoteric as an aid toward
social change and New Age consciousness. What unites the leaders in
this "camp" is the acceptance of the supernatural as real—even if
rooted in the deep recesses of the self—and the effort to employ this
element in the furtherance of the New Age goal, which seeks a quantum
leap in consciousness. Other names associated with this "supernaturalistic" approach within New Age are legion and include Edgar Cayce,

Alice Bailey, Arthur Ford, Ruth Montgomery, Jane Roberts (channeler of Seth), Jach Pursel (channeler of Lazaris), J. Z. Knight (Ramtha), Ellwood Babbitt, and Kevin Ryerson.

The "spiritual camp" occupies what might be considered a middle-ground between the service and esoteric extremes of New Age. Here we find a preponderance of names of Eastern gurus but also a few Western teachers as well. Foremost are perhaps Maharishi Mahesh Yogi (TM), Bhagawan Rajneesh, Swami Muktananda (Siddha Yoga), Pamahansa Yogananda (Self Realization), Guru Maharaj Ji (Elan Vital, formerly DLM), Swami Rama, Swami Amar Jyoti, Trungpa Rinpoche (Naropa), Oscar Ichazo (Arica), and Meher Baba. Prominent Western figures include Arthur Ford, Carlos Castaneda, Sun Bear, Da (Bubba) Free John (Johannine Daist), Stephen Gaskin, John-Roger Hinkins (Movement for Inner Spiritual Awareness), Reb Zalman Schachter-Shalomi, and Rabbi Joseph Gelberman. Also related to this last are the more purely human potential developments such as those inaugurated by Werner Erhard (*est*), Terry Cole-Whittaker, Shakti Gawain, or even Krishnamurti Jeddu. The spiritual camp of New Age centers on self-discipline as a means toward experience of or union with divine or ultimate reality. Its techniques are essentially those of human potential without the supernatural intervention characteristic of the "occult camp." And, unlike the "social camp" of New Age, its primary focus is toward individual development rather than social change.

## New Age healing

Another important area within New Age—one that relates to a preponderance of cultic effort in general—is that of healing. Much of the New Age and human potential effort is concerned less with global ecological concerns than it is with personal health. In this connection, it is worth mentioning the emphasis on self-healing (Bernie S. Siegel, Norman Cousins, Meir Schneider, Onslow H. Wilson, Kenneth R. Pelletier, Louise L. Hay, and the magazine *Medical Self Care*, etc.) as well as such therapy techniques as acupuncture, acupressure (shiatsu), biofeedback, body cleansing, bodywork, chiropractic therapy, flower essence therapy, herbology, homeopathy, macrobiotics, polarity therapy, reflexology, reiki, rolfing, visualization and imagery, and yoga.

But increasingly, "New Age" is becoming recognized as a 'generic term' for the exploding re-interest in the 1960s counterculture concerns of ecology and all things alternative—mystical religion, mind expan-

sion, meditation, and healing. In part, it partakes of the nature of Bryan
Wilson's "conversionist" sect as seen in Ari Goldman's explanation
that

> New Age is an amalgam of therapies and philosophies aimed at a holistic,
> or complete, approach to healing individuals and, through them, the planet.
> The movement employs such strategies as astrology, hypnotism and belief
> in reincarnation, paganism, ritual and mysticism to achieve what adherents
> call wellness.[12]

Katie Saunders adds that "Basically, the New Age person is into consciousness-raising, caring and green politics."[13] She argues that the
movement is a revival of Sixties mores and a revolt against the hedo-
nism and "selfish bingeing" of the 1980s—a "hanging loose" but
without a "dropping out." Despite the hundreds of ideologies that fall
under the New Age umbrella, "Really dedicated New Agers believe
they are all plugged into the same source of spiritual power which will
unite the whole world by 2000." Meanwhile, old-fashioned hippie values are being used to combat the stress of yuppie life.

Part of the bedrock of the New Age experience is complementary
medicine. This is an area that is facing its own problems and controversy—such as in Britain, for instance, which had to conform to European Economic Community guidelines by 1992. From Trinity University in San Antonio, Texas, Meredith McGuire, conducting a four-year
study of alternative healing beliefs and practices among middle-income
people in northern New Jersey, finds the diversity of alternative healing
systems falling into roughly five broad types: Christian healing groups,
Eastern meditation and human potential groups (e.g., TM, Tibetan Buddhism, rebirthing, est, and Arica), traditional metaphysical groups (e.g.,
Christian Science, Unity, and Religious Science), psychic and occult
groups (e.g., Eckankar, Great White Brotherhood, and Spiritual Frontiers Fellowship), and manipulation/technique practitioners (e.g., shiatsu, iridology, acupuncture, reflexology, rolfing, Alexander and
Feldenkrais methods, homeopathy, naturopathy, organotherapy, etc.).[14]
For Christian healing groups, McGuire found sin being perceived as a
major cause of illness. Metaphysical thinkers translate this into "the
individual's incorrect ways of thinking and speaking," that is, without
connection to the Divine Mind or Truth within. Likewise, psychic/oc-
cult healing groups place emphasis—here the strongest—on individual
responsibility for both disease and other misfortunes. By contrast, Eastern and human potential groups tend to place more stress on "social

and individual lifestyle factors'' than on individual responsibility as the cause for illness.

In all healing groups, McGuire notes a general predominance of women, mostly white though sometimes racially mixed, usually middle class. Metaphysical groups have more often an elderly membership; Christian and psychic/occult, usually middle-aged; practitioners, clients of all ages; Eastern and human potential, generally a younger membership ranging between twenty-five to forty. With the exception of the Christian groups, the remaining four of McGuire's "broad types" fall within the New Age identity. However, McGuire's classification cuts across Judah and Wagner's understanding of the "American metaphysical tradition." While admitting that the groups spawned by the early twentieth-century metaphysical movement hold many beliefs in common with psychic and occult groups, she argues that the former are organized more like denominations—maintaining church buildings and controlling religious teachings. The latter are "the most diverse and difficult to categorize." But both the metaphysical and psychic/occult groups emphasize the potential of individuals to gain power and control in their lives—with the former stressing a generally non-sectarian continuity with Christian traditions; the latter—along with the meditation/ human potential groups—being much more eclectic. While Eastern meditation and human potential groups remain open to other forms of healing, they tend to view their own as superior. Psychics and occultists, on the other hand, consider that only people who are "spiritually attuned, psychically developed or adept in special occult knowledge" have access to the great internal reservoir of divine power and can channel it to others.

## The New Age vision

New Age is a decentralized movement—one built around not doctrines or particular belief systems but an experiential vision. In fact, the visionary ideal or goal is the *sine qua non* of New Age identity. Adhering to that expectation is a whole spectrum of individuals and groups who hold mutually contradictory opinions and beliefs. What unites all New Agers, however, is the vision of radical mystical transformation on both the personal and collective levels. In fact, the awakening to the potential abilities of the human self—one's individual psychic powers and the capability for physical and/or psychological healing—is the New Age springboard for the quantum leap of collective consciousness, which is to bring about and constitute the New Age itself. In other words, "The essence of the New Age is the imposition of that personal vision onto society and the world" (Melton, 1986b:113).

In Spangler's "conversionist" terms, the New Age—at least externally—grounds on the efforts "to implement holistic and planetary values." Inwardly,

> it is a rebirth of our sense of the sacred, an inner impulse to understand and express our own divinity in cocreation and synergy with the divinity within creation and with the Source of that divinity. . . . (ibid.)

Spangler claims that many New Age activities are neither involved with the paranormal or are specifically religious, and he denies equating the "New Age movement" with psychic phenomena, the occult, or a specific form of spirituality whether pagan, Eastern, or other. And rather than seeing the New Age as a future or transforming event, he accepts the designation and concept as a metaphor "for the expression of a transformative, creative spirit."

Part and parcel of the process of transformation that Spangler, Ferguson, and virtually all New Age spokespersons recognize at the heart of the New Age vision are the facilitating organizations and businesses as well as individuals that have arisen to assist this process. These include those teaching various transformational techniques ranging from yoga and meditation to the martial arts, those teaching or practicing various healing techniques (psychological and/or body therapies, alternative medicine), and those marketing any of many New Age products (health foods, natural vitamins, macrobiotic cookware, meditation cushions, yoga mats, crystals, related books, New Age music tapes, incense, Oriental art, etc.). These tend to proliferate in Western metropolitan areas—often being assisted by local and frequently ephemeral organizations that serve as points of contact (e.g., Alternatives at St. James, Piccadilly, London). And although many New Age businesses tend to present themselves as models employing New Age ethics, a potential conflict arises in that many New Agers envision the future world along more socialistic, economically egalitarian lines, while others are equally adamant that the capitalistic profit motive is fully compatible with New Age ideals (e.g., Leonard Holihan of London's Advanced Energy Research Institute).[15] Consequently, a tension exists in New Age between socialistic egalitarianism and capitalistic private enterprise.

For New Age itself, apart from the techniques often taught by Insight, the Forum (i.e., *est*) and Life Training within the premises of large corporations in both Britain and the United States, a chief institutional form is the "New Age center." Other than the Omega Trust, Esalen in Big Sur, California ("the granddaddy of the movement"),[16] and Findhorn in Scotland, such centers include the Naropa Institute in Boulder, Colorado; Interface in Newton, Massachusetts; Holly Hock Farm off Vancouver in Canada; the Omega Institute for Holistic Studies in Rhinebeck, New York; the Wrekin Trust in West Malvern, Worcester, the United Kingdom; and the Skyros Centre on the Greek island of Skyros. The Omega Institute is typical and offers a summer camp of courses in the Hudson River Valley. Offerings in 1989 included "The Mythical Quest," "Crystals, Magnets and Vibrational Healing," "Cooking as Spiritual Practice," "Aromatherapy," "Kabbalistic Astrology," "The Joy of Self-Loving," and "Know Your Car: Basic Automobile Preventive Maintenance."

Communal organizations are another prominent feature of—at least early—New Age efforts. Already established communes were among the first groups to identify with the New Age label and its preference for cooperation over competition. Among these are the Lama Foundation of New Mexico, the Renaissance Community of Massachusetts, the Stelle Community of Illinois, and Stephen Gaskin's The Farm in Tennessee. Several Eastern teachers also promoted communes within their religious organizations (e.g., Pir Vilayat Khan's Abode of the Message in the Sufi Order—New York; Swami Kriyananda's Ananda Cooperative Community—California; etc.).

## Statistics

McGuire's study noted above shows that American suburbanites have, like their city counterparts, "come to use health, illness and healing as expressions of their concerns for meaning, moral order and individual effectiveness and power in their daily world" (*Psychology Today*, Jan./Feb. 1989:58). In other words, through perceived shortcomings of the mainstream medical system, spiritual concerns and social strains come more clearly into focus. One's state of health becomes a means to gauge one's spiritual understanding and development—with healing metaphors grounding on a holistic concept of self that comprehends the physical, mental, and spiritual dimensions of human life. McGuire's data lend support to Beckford's contention (1983c) that new religious movements may be perceived by adherents as sources of personal empowerment. The American *Body, Mind & Spirit* magazine

(May/June 1989) reports its survey results taking a random sampling of 600 questionnaires drawn from a pool of 4,000 responses from its readers.[17] This undertaking provides a profile of various New Age experiences that are thought to generate meaning and strength for the individual—including psychic healing, spirit channeling, psychic/intuitive experiences, out-of-body experience, contact with a deceased friend or relative, or even attendance at a spiritual seminar or workshop.

This survey, organized by Frederick G. Levine (author of *The Psychic Sourcebook*, Warner, 1988), determined that 79 percent of the American magazine's readers responding to the questionnaire feel there is a distinction between religion and spirituality—only 40 percent admit to being religious, whereas 94 percent consider themselves spiritual. Conforming to the national average, 95 percent believe in God (57 percent in heaven, 24 percent in hell), but only 36 percent currently belong to a church, synagogue, or temple—though more than 60 percent attend services at least occasionally.[18]

To suggest some idea of numbers for the New Age movement, a 1976 Gallup poll reported that, with 4 percent of those questioned having engaged in TM, 3 percent practicing yoga, and 1 percent indicating an involvement in an Eastern religion, more than 10 million Americans are involved with just a few of the alternative religious movements. Through his annual religious surveys, George Gallup, Jr. concludes that "most forms of mysticism are on the rise." Wuthnow's 1973 San Francisco Bay Area study indicates an even higher percentage of participants vis-à-vis the national average: nearly 8 percent in *est* alone and 1.1 percent in Scientology. Andrew Greeley, using the University of Chicago's National Opinion Research Council's data, estimates that close to 20 million Americans now report profoundly mystical experiences, including healing.[19] Greeley adds that over a recent eleven-year period, the proportion of adults who say they have been in touch with the dead has risen from 27 percent to 42 percent. In addition, 14.3 percent of all adults surveyed in a statewide poll in Virginia claimed to have been healed by prayer or a divine source.

To date, the New Age movement is especially an American-Canadian-British-Dutch-West German-Australian-New Zealand phenomenon. There is also a growing presence in both France and Italy as well as within Scandinavia.[20] It has become visible in every major metropolitan complex in the United States. Nevertheless, in answering a questionnaire handed out 23 September 1989 in the New York metropolitan area during a collective fiftieth birthday celebration for a suburban high school class reunion, out of forty-eight respondents (of which forty live within the U.S. East Coast area), only eleven admitted that they were familiar with the New Age Movement.[21] The same question put to a group of eleven San Francisco Bay Area lawyers vacationing together in the South of France a month earlier drew four affirmatives, with one respondent answering "marginally."[22]

For the United Kingdom and Europe in general, statistics are even more difficult to come by. Clarke (1987:11–14) gives some rough figures of total membership claimed by or estimated for such New Age movements in Britain as TM (100,000 +/− 20,000), Rebirthing (11,250), *est* (8,000 +/− 500), Exegesis (6,000), and Rajneesh (4,000). Figures for TM in other European countries are Holland (50,000), Italy (30,000), Sweden (70,000), Switzerland (6,000–10,000), and West Germany (35,000 full time—100,000); for Rajneesh: Holland (15,000), Italy (16,000), Sweden (1,300), Switzerland (6,000–10,000), and West Germany (6,500 full time—41,000). Other full-time figures for West Germany include from the same source: *est* (5,200), Divine Light Mission (800), and Eckankar (600).[23] For a rough estimate of possible attendance to the more 'non-denominational' New Age venue of St. James Piccadilly in London and its Monday evening program, Alternatives, co-director Sabrina Dearborn informed me on January 28, 1991, that 12,000 programs are printed tri-monthly. Of these, 4,000 are included with *Human Potential* magazine, 1,000 are mailed to individuals, 2,000 are posted to various centers, and the remaining 5,000 are distributed from the church itself.

The difficulty in estimating the numbers of people attracted to the New Age phenomena stems in part from the diverse range of activities with which the movement is identified. For instance, a *Wall Street Journal* article (January 8, 1989) draws attention to the number of "New Age" training programs used by various consulting, management, and sales firms, which, although they "eschew the New Age label, which they say conjures up notions of cultism and the bizarre," combine traditional management training methods in communication and cooperation with use of meditation and hypnosis. Moreover, although much Eastern mysticism and positive thinking techniques identify with New Age, there is much that does not. The line of differentiation is often not clearly drawn. Nevertheless, as the *WSJ* reports, lawsuits are emerging over workers' rights and the contention that such training programs conflict with an individual's religion or constitute "a forced religious conversion."

## External perceptions and responses

Another response to the New Age movement arises amid the vociferous Anti-Cult Movement (ACM). As this last becomes more profession-
alized in its approach (see Bromley and Shupe, 1987), it also provides
another perspective from which to surmise any delineation of the New
Age Movement itself. In its August 1978 journal, the fundamentalist
Berkeley Christian Coalition (sponsor of the Spiritual Counterfeits
Project) expressed concern over the New Age incorporation of Eastern
mysticism and non-Christian doctrine, the belief of a God within, and
humanistic psychology and secular humanism as parts of the new
movement's corpus of ideas. According to Ferguson, the B.C.C. places
the chief blame for the rise of New Age spirituality on the diffidence of
the Christian church in the United States. According to the ACM, the
religious point of view embodied in the holistic health movement is an
integral part of the mystical worldview that is making a coordinated
thrust into every aspect of our cultural consciousness—one that is fundamentally hostile to Biblical Christianity.[24]

On the other hand, in a survey done on local clergymen by *The Providence Journal-Bulletin* (January 26, 1989) in Providence, Rhode Island,
the most outspoken critic proved to be the senior minister of the First
Unitarian Church in Providence. Although he has many New Agers in
his congregation, the Rev. Tom Ahlburn believes the New Age to be
simply a fast remedy for people who are too impatient for traditional
religious disciplines.

> My own personal theory about this is: These are people who missed, or
> miss, the sixties. . . . [Buddhism—Ahlburn himself practices Tibetan Bud-
> dhism—would not be embraced by New Agers because] they're not disci-
> plined people. It's a faddy kind of thing. It's loads of fun for a lot of
> people, and especially some merchants.

Such external perceptions of the New Age phenomenon must, of
course, be balanced by how adherents and leaders of the movement
describe it from their own vantage points.

Despite the accusations against the New Age movement as a whole
for its "cranky reputation," its "buy yourself spirituality" approach,
its high cost and compatibility with "the hard face of hierarchical capitalism," and the use of neurolinguistic programming (NLP) along with
hypnosis in business contexts, Kieran Foley, a computer systems proj-

ect manager investigating New Age manifestations, expresses a growing consensus within the movement:

> There's a lot of bullshit about the New Age; a lot of airy-fairy waffle which disguises the underlying kernel of truth. For example, channelling—why say "this is a 4,000 year old discarnate entity" when it may be just part of a person's cortex, purely more intuitive thought linkages? It's a shame because it devalues intuition. More and more studies are showing that, say, top executives are extremely intuitive in their decision-making. People who argue against the New Age are missing out on a lot of powerful new processes. I loathe a lot of the packaging around but let's not throw the baby out with the bath water, even if there *is* a lot of very frothy bath water. (In Alexander, 1989:21)

Graham Wilson (organizer in 1977 of the Festival of Mind, Body, Spirit—"the best-known and longest-running of the New Age fairs") perceives the New Age as one about fundamental change rather than consumer faddism.

> It's a shift in consciousness which manifests itself in our being more aware about what we eat and what we are doing to our bodies on a physical level and, on a mental level, about being more conscious about other people and caring for the planet. . . . Things build up to a certain level and then there's that quantum leap. I think we've about reached that level and we're going to see very rapid change over the next five to ten years. (In Alexander, 1989:21)

Jane Alexander (1989:20) admits that critics consider the whole New Age phenomenon along with magic, ouija boards, and bonfire leaping as "pure hocus pocus . . . but while much of Occult teaching has a direct bearing on New Age philosophy it's fair to say that the overwhelming majority of New Agers would consider themselves neither magicians or witches."

There is additionally the growing media and academic perception of the New Age movement as a whole. In a recent compilation edited by Robert Basil, *Not Necessarily the New Age: Critical Essays* (1988), various scholars perceive a reputedly tenuous relationship between New Age spirituality and the scientific understanding of the world. Because of the "scientism" or pseudo-scientization characteristic of much New Age metaphysics, Gordon Melton (p. 51) argues that the cogency of the New Age Movement will soon self-destruct. He feels that, through continued self-revision, science "is already moving beyond concepts

from which the New Age Movement has constructed its world view.''
In the same volume, Paul Edwards lampoons the concept of reincarnation through the mathematical calculation that the size of the present
world population would entail that anyone who had ever once been
alive on this planet must now be alive today and even then the totality
of past human populations is still insufficient for soul replacement when
measured against the number of persons currently comprising the
human race.[25]

The defense of the New Age Movement against the criticisms raised
in Basil's volume center on the question of how closely the New Age
is to be identified with faddish superstition or any particular scientistic
metaphysics.[26] The long tradition stemming from Swedenborg, Mesmer, Spiritualism, and Theosophy on which New Age thought rests is
arguably unlikely to cease simply because current scientific concepts
will change. As scientific metaphor develops, so too is the non-doctrinaire and flexible New Age outlook likely and able to transform. Moreover, a consensus in the ''Body, Mind and Spirit Spirituality Survey''
considers both religion and science as ''equally rigid, dogmatic and
closed-minded'' (*Body Mind Spirit*, June 1989:83). Los Angeles pub-
lisher Jeremy P. Tarcher reflects that media coverage has been accurate
in reporting New Age interest in reincarnation, extraterrestrial contact,
channeling, psychic phenomena, crystals and ''even in earning a good
living from the various products and activities associated with them''
but has completely missed ''the core of New Age thought''—the efforts
toward personal and social transformation based on a commitment to
what Aldous Huxley termed the Perennial Philosophy (Tarcher, undated).

At the heart of the New Age is what Wagner (1983) has identified as
''the American metaphysical tradition'' with its core ideas of the divine
spark within each individual, the power of the mind, and Swedenborg's
principle of spirit-matter correspondences between all parts of the universe. These are viably adaptive religious concepts unlikely to be affected by either conceptual changes in science or by what many would
consider simply to be the more superficial and transient aspects of New
Age fads and superstition. The ''metaphysical tradition'' is the obvious
springboard for what Tarcher (undated) specifies as the New Age worldview:

1. The everyday world and our personal consciousness is a manifestation of a larger, divine reality;

2. Humans have a suppressed, or hidden, Higher Self that reflects, or is connected to the divine element of the universe;
3. This Higher Self can be awakened and take a central part in the everyday life of the individual, and
4. This awakening is the purpose or goal of human life.

The "Aquarian, or New, Age is generally believed to herald a period of metaphysical awareness, the Spiritual Revolution" (in Alexander, 1989:20). Apart from becoming one of the buzzwords of the '90s along with anything prefixed "Green, . . . for more and more people it's becoming a way of life or, at least, an intrinsic *part* of life."

## The Church Universal and Triumphant

From the public view, however, controversy frequently adheres to various groups within the New Age movement as well as to the movement as a whole. For the former, there are the narcissistic allegations of *est* and other human potential groups. Maharishi Mahesh Yogi's Transcendental Meditation, Bhagwan Rajneesh's Rajneesh Foundation International, and Guru Maharaja Ji's Divine Light Mission have all been attacked as deceptive, brain-washing cults despite their non-totalistic position vis-à-vis such other groups as the Unification Church, Children of God, Scientologists, etc. More recently, with the arrest of Vernon Hamilton, a member of its Cosmic Honor Guard security force, the Church Universal and Triumphant has attracted controversial media attention.

As an amalgam of Christianity, Hinduism, and Buddhism, the Summit Lighthouse was founded by the late Mark L. Prophet in 1958. Being a development of ideas and iconographic symbolism found in Theosophy and the "Mighty I AM" movement of Guy and Edna Ballard, Prophet's New Age teachings include belief in reincarnation, the role of "ascended masters," the idea of a divine spark within the individual, and the ultimate goal of reuniting the godly part of each person with God.[27] With Prophet's death in 1973, he was succeeded by his wife, Elizabeth Clare Prophet, both as the living messenger of the "ascended masters" and as the leader of the movement renamed the Church Universal and Triumphant. In 1978, CUT relocated its headquarters—now known as Camelot—to Malibu, California. As the Ascended Master Lanello, Mark Prophet joins the coterie of El Morya, Gautama Buddha, Jesus Christ, the Virgin Mary (as the primary representation of the Divine Mother), William Shakespeare, Christopher Columbus, and St. Germain (as the "messiah of the New Age of Aquarius").

CUT's stance is strongly patriotic; it also condemns abortion, drug use, alcohol, tobacco, child pornography, extramarital sex, terrorism, nuclear warfare, and world communism. But even before Hamilton's arrest on 7 July 1989 for the illegal possession and transportation of weapons and ammunition, the organization's communal life style at various centers, the charges of indoctrination and brainwashing, and the practice of hypnotic, high-speed prayer chanting called "decrees" for hours each day using portable stereo headsets while both working and meditating had already engendered a degree of media and public antagonism. Mrs. Prophet, known by followers as "Mother" and "Guru Ma" and alleged to be the reincarnation of Marie Antoinette and Queen Guinevere, predicts that a great Armageddon is to occur on earth between 2 October 1989 and the year 2000.

> Our calling . . . is to fulfil the teachings of Jesus because people need them to go on into the New Age. (Lattin, 1989a)

As a result, CUT has undertaken an extensive construction program of underground bombshelters at the Royal Teton Ranch in Montana (its Inner Retreat—also known as Glastonbury) and elsewhere, the establishment of a food-processing plant on the ranch to stockpile dried vegetables and macrobiotic meat substitutes, and, it is now alleged, the stockpiling of firearms and weapons. In short, Mrs. Prophet's prophecies see the change from the Age of Pisces to the Age of Aquarius as a "dark transition." Her movement, mostly white and middle class and estimated to comprise between 10,000 to 25–30,000 members, expresses a reactionary and militaristic interpretation within the overall New Age movement.[28]

## New Age spokespersons

### Marilyn Ferguson

Mrs. Prophet, however, is an atypical figure. Among the leading New Age spokespersons—speaking more or less for the movement as a whole—we find Ram Dass, Marilyn Ferguson, and David Spangler. Here we find views that are more illustrative of New Age in general.

Gordon Melton (1986b:111) cites Ferguson's *The Aquarian Conspiracy* (first published in 1980) as "the most commonly accepted statement of Movement ideals and goals.'' Ferguson herself tends to eschew the designation ''New Age,'' presumably in part because she endeavors to explore not only the spiritual aspect but rather the wider parameters of New Age as a social movement concerned with the conscious transformation of society itself. During his Alternatives talk (April 6, 1990), Spangler went so far as to deny that there is any such thing as ''the New Age movement.'' He sees instead a wide spectrum of people who do not agree but instead support different methods and visions of healing, etc., in our society. New Age is, according to Spangler, ''a mnemonic device far more than a prophecy.''

Borrowing from Thomas Kuhn, Ferguson's central concept is that of the ''paradigm shift'' involving both the transformation of individual consciousness and major cultural evolution. Tracing from both the American Transcendental movement and, more immediately, the counterculture of the 1960s, Ferguson (1987:19) refers to the New Age harbinger as the ''Aquarian Conspiracy'':

> after a dark, violent age, the Piscean, we are entering a millennium of love and light—in the words of the popular song, ''The Age of Aquarius,'' the time of 'the mind's true liberation'.

This ''paradigm shift'' described by Ferguson is to be a distinctly new way of thinking about old problems. The change involved is different from that which occurs by exception, that which occurs ''incrementally,'' or that which occurs ''pendularly.'' It is true transformation, the harmonizing of new ideas into a powerful synthesis, ''a sudden shift of pattern, a spiral, and sometimes a cataclysm'' (Ferguson, 1987:73). She describes its root in virtually shamanic terms as the deep inner shift of personal consciousness that can occur through ''disciplined contemplation, grave illness, wilderness treks, peak emotions, creative effort, spiritual exercises, controlled breathing, techniques for 'inhibiting thought', psychedelics, movement, isolation, music, hypnosis, meditation, reverie, and in the wake of intense intellectual struggle'' (Ferguson, 1987:31).[29] The term ''psychotechnologies'' applies to ''systems for a deliberate change in consciousness'' (Ferguson, 1987:87)—those that are employed for psychological liberation and for breaking the ''cultural trance''; that is, ''the naive assumption that the trappings and truisms of our own culture represent universal truths or some culmination of civilization'' (Ferguson, 1987:103).

Ferguson, Ram Dass, and Spangler are united in explaining that because of the inseparability of self and society, self-transformation implies social action. In other words, beyond personal evolution is the collective paradigm shift—one that is rooted in the former but represents a consensus that occurs "when a critical number of thinkers has accepted [a] new idea" (Ferguson, 1987:28). It is this current, almost millennial, expectation of the Aquarian Age, the New Age, which is what unifies the various movements, cults, sects, groupings, and individuals identified within the New Age Movement. This very transformative vision, in fact, gives the Movement its name.

Ferguson's new paradigm is seen in part as a result of the stress of our times. A repeated theme she emphasizes is that conflict and struggle lead to transformation. If individuals within a society experience anomalies and conflicts that become socially too intense or focused to be suppressed, "a revolution eventually occurs in the form of a *social movement*" (Ferguson, 1987:197). The Aquarian Conspiracy is such a movement, and, as such, it is both the goal itself and the process leading toward it. The sought-after transpersonal perspective aims toward a cognitive level in which the perception of normal linear causality is superseded by a holistic or unitary pan-causality that can best be conveyed through paradox, meditation, and mystical experience (Ferguson, 1987:372).

Ram Dass (*Whole Life Times*, May 1990:6) admits that on infrequent occasions he still uses psychedelics since, "as a responsible researcher of human consciousness, they are a profound method." Ferguson too does not deny that for many the experience with psychedelic drugs constituted their incipient access to paradigmatic shift, and she subscribes to Stanislav Grof's claim that psychedelics as catalysts or amplifiers of mental processes seem to facilitate access to the holographic domain described by Karl Pribram and David Bohm. The individual may experience himself as a field of consciousness rather than as an isolated entity; he may experience multidimensional and limitless space, matter as patterns of energy, past events, microcosm, macrocosm, archetypes, and deities. (Ferguson, 1987:375). But though one cannot overestimate the historic introductory role of psychedelics "non-drug psychotechnologies offer a *controlled*, sustained movement toward the spacious reality. The annals of the Aquarian Conspiracy are full of accounts of passage: LSD to Zen, LSD to India, psilocybin to Psychosynthesis" (Ferguson, 1987:89–90).

The overall experience of alternate states of consciousness within the New Age perspective is understood as a quest for meaning and spiritual experience. Though the New Age Movement has implications for and aspirations toward the domains of science, politics, health, education, and vocation, as a new religious movement and focus for the sociologist of religion, it is primarily the emerging belief system that becomes our immediate concern. This includes the New Ager's encounter with the realm of paradox, the transcendent aspects of reality, and the planetary consciousness. But the pervasive cultural bias against seemingly introspective indulgence had produced such former pejoratives as 'the new narcissism' and 'the Me Decade.' New Age beliefs are also critiqued as self-annihilating, elitist, and irrational.

In rebuttal, New Age argues that "a major task of the Aquarian Conspiracy is to foster paradigm shifts by pointing out the flaws in the old paradigm and showing how the new context explains more—makes more sense" (Ferguson, 1987:151). The key principles within this emergent belief system center on the concepts of flow and wholeness. The ideas of movement and completion are opposed to those of struggle and brokenness. These are, however, not perceived in such traditional or Christian ethical terms as good and evil but rather in those of a universal spiritual metaphor, namely, light and darkness, or light and the absence of light. "Always, the vision of evolution [is] toward the light . . . the oldest and most pervasive metaphor in spiritual experience" (Ferguson, 1987:385). This last is a key point to keep under consideration when we come to compare New Age with Neo-paganism.

Ferguson captures the essential theme behind most prominent New Age thinkers when she contends that the uniqueness of our times is that never before has the innate human capacity for mystical experience been explored by people in large numbers as is now occurring. In contemporary America, the East no longer represents a culture or a religion but has become instead a liberating methodology. "Quite suddenly in *this* decade, these deceptively simple [psychotechnological] systems and their literature, the riches of many cultures, are available to whole populations, both in their original form and in contemporary adaptations" (Ferguson, 1987:31).

Whereas Wuthnow ((1976) speaks in terms of traditional American theism and "rugged individualism," Ferguson (1987:120) sees the latter in terms of two major foci that constitute the basis of New Age spirituality. One is the concern for material well-being and practical, everyday freedoms; the other is the search for psychological liberation. As Ferguson points out, nearly all participants in the emergent spiritual tradition come from the comfortable social classes—having already achieved the first measure of (material) freedom. It would follow from this assertion that whatever are the motivations an individual might have for identifying with the New Age Movement, these are less likely to include that of economic deprivation. One question that therefore arises in this context is that concerning how much the New Age Movement is a so-called Yuppie phenomenon and how much it might be broader than this sector within contemporary society.

If there is a distinction to be made between the New Age Movement and the Aquarian Conspiracy, the former is to be seen more specifically as a religious expression; the latter, as a more broadly faceted social movement—one that includes the former but more clearly focuses on the social transformation necessary for the new age. In that both perspectives consider the radical paradigm shift as imminent, sudden, and dependent on an altered state of collective consciousness, they may be considered essentially one and the same. Both rely primarily on the techniques and resources of the human potential movement, and even where New Age may be seen as more inclusive of the supernatural per se (as opposed to the humanistic) through its emphasis on channeling, reincarnation, multiple concepts of the godhead, and so forth, the New Age shift is still viewed and expected primarily as the achievement of human endeavor. In this, it may be likened to Wilson's understanding of the ''reformist'' sect.

The chief criticism of Marilyn Ferguson and *The Aquarian Conspiracy* relates to an observation made by Gordon Melton (1984:461–62) when considering the psychic/new age family of modern alternative religions in the West:

> The psychic groups share a common relationship to science, in that they believe that psychic phenomena demonstrate 'scientifically' the truth of their religious perspective. They look to parapsychology for a verification of their religion, and have grown as the recognition of psychical research has grown. They might be said, however, to have an attitude better labelled 'scientism', that is, they have a love of things scientific but little knowledge, or appreciation, of science and scientific methodology.[30]

This observation applies to many if not most New Age leaders and adherents. Blanket statements and non sequitors are frequent in New Age writings and talks. Apart from these, interest in, and study of, psychic phenomena remains a major component of New Age preoccupation, and if *psi* designates the unknown in both physics and parapsychology, Ferguson (1987:175, 434) reports that the ''Aquarian Conspirators surveyed reported an extremely high level of belief in psi''—with the mean percentage of those accepting telepathy, psychic healing, precognition, clairvoyance, synchronicity, psychokinesis, and cosmic intelligence being 88 percent.

For the New Age outlook as a whole, *The Aquarian Conspiracy* remains perhaps its most comprehensive statement. It provides a detailed picture of its adherents' understanding of such central concepts as "collective need" and "evolutionary leap," their belief that paradigmatic shifts are sudden and nonlinear, and their viewpoint that instability is the key to transformation—that new order is created by perturbation. In other words, "the creative process requires chaos before form emerges" (Ferguson 1987:166). Melton (1986b:111) refers to Ferguson's work as the most commonly accepted statement of New Age ideals and goals and cites her, after Baba Ram Dass, as the most prominent spokesperson for the Movement.

## Ram Dass

If Ferguson might be considered representative of the New Age "social service" camp, Ram Dass is the most prominent person in recent times to have set the spiritual groundwork upon which Ferguson's vision rests. He, too, has concerned himself with social efforts and has founded several service organizations, including the Seva (Sanskrit for "service") Foundation in Missouri and the Hanuman Foundation in New Mexico. Apart from promoting education, raising and distributing funds, publishing and recording, Ram Dass and his organizations stress the spiritual well-being of members and others as their primary concern. Ram Dass's spiritual guru in India was Neem Karoli Baba, and the central aspect of the disciple's teachings has become the practice of meditation.

Meditation for Ram Dass has proved to be the 'best way' to approach one's inner being directly, to find a more permanent answer than that which one might gain through experimentation with LSD and other psychedelics. Employing or testing many different techniques from various philosophies and religions, Ram Dass argues that meditation is a means for achieving integrity of self and for permeating each moment regardless of the situation with "space, peace, equanimity, joy and lightness." To the question "Why meditate?" Ram Dass (1978:5) replies, "To live in the moment. To dwell in the harmony of things. To awaken." In the multiple versions of reality in which we live, meditation is recognized by Ram Dass as the device by which we can awaken from any single reality and understand its relative nature. As a consequence, his effort has become one of exploring and teaching practices in which the meditative moments in a person's life increase until one's entire life becomes "meditation-in-action." The gradual shift to a vege-

tarian diet, fasting, the setting aside of a special place in which to meditate, regularity, satsang, etc., are additional techniques suggested by
Ram Dass as meditational aids.

In the development of his thought, Ram Dass draws on the teachings
of many spiritual teachers—ranging from Lao Tse, Chogyam Trungpa,
Mahmud Shabistari, Divani Shamsi Tabriz, Ramakrishna, Ramana Ma-
harshi, Meher Baba, and Shunryu Suzuki in the East to Simone Weil,
René Daumal, Thaddeus Golas, William Law, William Blake, Meister
Eckhart, and St. John of the Cross in the West. The range of meditation
forms suggested include karate or kung fu, t'ai chi, still contemplation,
vipassana, singing, chanting, and Sufi dancing. Although the techniques
of meditation are akin and/or fundamental to what is more broadly
known as the human potential movement, the goal of Ram Dass's spiritual path is different. For him, meditation that aims to relieve psychological pain, increase pleasure, or enhance power is simply strengthening the ego. Instead, he seeks to realize that one is more than the
ego—for only this leads to an awareness that is totally free, to a being
that does not cling to anything and is therefore liberated. Ram Dass's
motive is clearly spiritual, and in his emphasis liberation supersedes the
more limited development of human potential.

Ram Dass's early high profile coupled with the American repeal of
the Asian immigration exclusion acts in 1965 paved the way for the
increased missionary thrust by Eastern religions in the West. Eastern-
oriented NRMs that have subsequently emerged in the West and that
may be at least loosely identified with the "spiritual camp" of the New
Age movement include Trungpa Rinpoche's Naropa Institute of Tibetan
Buddhism, Maharishi Mehesh Yogi's Transcendental Meditation, Bhagwan Rajneesh's Rajneesh Foundation International, Swami Muktananda's Siddha Yoga Dham of America, Pamahansa Yogananda's Self Realization Society, Guru Maharaj Ji's Divine Light Mission, Yogi
Bhajan's Sikh Dharma (3HO), Kirpal Singh's Ruhani Satsang, Pir Vilayat Khan's Sufi Order, Oscar Ichazo's Arica Institute, and Meher
Baba's Friends of Meher Baba.[31] Each of these has been centered
around a charismatic leader, but other Oriental religious expressions in
the West's New Age movement include both Tantric yoga groups and
expressions of Zen Buddhism as well as the relatively older Vedanta
Society of Ramakrishna and Vivekanada. Non-imported Eastern spiritual NRMs that have arisen in the West itself might include the Johannine Daist Community of Da (Bubba) Free John, the Movement for
Inner Spiritual Awareness of John-Roger Hinkins, and Stephen Gaskin's The Farm.

There is no denying the important role Eastern mysticism has played in the inception and growth of the New Age and human potential movements in the West. Many of the individual groups, such as TM and 3HO, stress their commitment to social service as well. Stripped of the effort to transcend the ego, however, the employment of Eastern techniques has spawned the ''personal growth'' movements that dominate a large portion of New Age journals, newsletters, and workshops. If these are not as directly concerned with social service in some cases, the New Age collective vision is nevertheless ''conversionist'' and thought to rest on personal transformation: as the individual perfects and develops his or her potential, so too does the universal New Age become more imminent for all.

## *Werner Erhard*

A leading instigator of the HPM has undoubtedly been Ron Hubbard's Church of Scientology, which, although not included by Melton under the New Age rubric, does now advertise in such New Age publications as *Body, Mind and Spirit* (e.g., August, 1989:97).[32] More immediately New Age and HPM is the Erhard Training Seminars (*est*) founded by Werner Erhard.[33] Although there are a host of similar movements, such as I AM in Britain, the Institute of Noetic Sciences in California, the Rebirthing movement, and Silva Mind Control,[34] *est*—now known as The Forum (sponsored by the broader congeries known as The Network or The Centres Network or The Society for Contextual Studies and Educational Seminars)—is perhaps among the most extensively documented. It is also typical of the kind of developmental psychotechnology that constitutes the HPM backbone of the New Age movement.

The Forum's founder, Werner Erhard, variously studied Eastern mysticism including Zen and yoga, cybernetics, business, psychology, and Scientology. Other influences include those from Alan Watts and Ram Dass. Among Western psychologists, the most influential on Erhard's developing ideas have been Abraham Maslow (Self-Actualization), Fritz Perls (Gestalt therapy), and Roberto Assagioli (Psychosynthesis). Though I have not found it attested per se, one could suspect a possible Gurdjieffian influence as well. He was eventually led to a ''direct experience of himself'':

It meant that I no longer identified myself with my body or my personality or my past or my future or my situation or my circumstances or my feel-

ings or my thoughts or my notion of myself or my image. . . . I have to tell
you that I realized immediately that verbalizing it was irrelevant. What I
considered relevant was being it. (Bry, 1976:155)

Continuing his study of various humanistic, psychological, and Eastern
systems including Mind Dynamics, brain function study, and hypnosis,
Erhard was led more and more into Scientology. However, when he
began *est* as a combination of Zen, Gestalt, and Psychosynthesis as well
as business management in 1971, he was automatically expelled from
the Church of Scientology for becoming involved in another discipline.
Roy Wallis (1988:917) pictures *est* as a product of Scientology, Gestalt
therapy, and the Silva Mind Control offspring of Mind Dynamics; Silva
Mind Control being itself based on New Thought and Couéism.

The *est* program (now modified) consisted of a sixty-hour training
experience for 250 people spread over two successive weekends with,
in 1976, a cost of $250 per person.[35] Despite the predominant "verbal
flagellation" involved, the essential thrust was to open for the individual an additional dimension of living to his awareness; that is, to transform the level at which one experiences life so that the life process
itself becomes one of expanding satisfaction.[36] The aim is still to have
people dis-identify completely from themselves for objective self-ob-
servation.

Those who have been attracted to the *est* training process are described as "young and old, confused and confident, divorced, married,
professionals, housewives, students, rich, not-so-rich (but rarely poor)"
(Bry, 1976:31). For Young (1987:142), "The 'est' movement seems to
attract a Liberal and intellectual class of North Americans and Western
Europeans." The appeal to these various people is explained as a search
for satisfaction in lives otherwise evaluated as successful. As Erhard
explains, satisfaction is not the concern of hungry people. His maxim
is that if life were three feet long, being freed from having to fulfill
basic physiological and psychological needs as we are in contemporary
Western technological society, one is allowed to concentrate on "that
last quarter inch called satisfaction" (Bry, 1976:197). One's belief-system is condemned as a myth that is created by knowledge or data without experience. For Erhard, even people's believing in *est* is a failure of
*est*. In place of belief, *est* stresses observation—what yoga refers to as
witnessing and Castaneda's Don Juan as "stopping the world."

The Human Potential notion of self-development directly relates to
the recurrent New Age notion of self-responsibility. This last pervades
every aspect of the *est* training and The Network's The Forum, which

rests on the maxim that "we are each the cause of our own experience and responsible for everything that happens in it." The mind and body are seen to be one. Illness does not just happen. In Scientological terminology, "getting clear" is accepting life exactly as it is; that is, exactly as we experience it with the acknowledgement that we are ourselves responsible for the way it is experienced despite our beliefs, expectations, and desires. In HPM terms, each one of us is "God" in his universe.

Although properly speaking not a theocentric movement, *est* sees itself as a new experience of self, body, and God in which God and the self are inseparable. Developing the traditional Eastern concept that is recognized in the West as "the God of the 70s"—the God within—*est* finds the mystic/feeling/inner experience as the means to cosmic consciousness. Young (1987:135) describes The Network as a "world-affirming quasi-spiritual movement." Nevertheless, as with any belief-system from the *est*-ian perspective, "God believed is a lie." It is *experiencing* God that matters and constitutes true religion.

In *est*-ian terminology, feeling "all right" because God is going to save me is salvation, but feeling the same because nothing is going to save me is enlightenment. As a belief system, *est* does not qualify as a religion, but it does have its own language and shares in common with traditional Western religion a sense of service, mission, and a definition of a way of being and experiencing. For Erhard, the core of *est* is spiritual people, because spirituality/God is everywhere—including the "business jungle," which is where Erhard himself claims to have learned about spirituality.

Nevertheless, the chief criticisms of *est* are that it is either fascistic, minimalistic, narcissistic, or simply a brainwashing technique. But against former Esalen president Richard Farson's denouncement of *est* as totalitarian, defenders argue that *est* training has no creed and that people are free to choose and accept or break agreements and leave at any point. While with brainwashing new beliefs are substituted for the old ones destroyed, in *est* simple "epistemological alternatives" are said to be offered without any predisposition toward anything in which to believe. As far as being too short-cut for any durable effect, Erhard has concluded through his own observations that the sixty-hour training program is "what works." Nevertheless, in 1984, the *est* training program was modified to eliminate some of its harder edges and rechristened The Forum.

The charge of narcissism, that is, the deification of the isolated self, is one that is leveled against Human Potential and New Age groups frequently (Marin, 1975; Wagner, 1983).[37] But *est*/The Forum counters with the argument that the experience of self encourages one to serve others in the world. Erhard himself affirms that what people really want to do with their lives is to make a contribution to the well-being of others. Consequently, within the *est* organization, people clamor to volunteer.[38]

In addition, there is *est*'s philanthropic Foundation, which concentrates on making grants not only to more specifically consciousness-related activities (in research, education, and public communication as well as human potential and transformational areas) but also in the form of donations to hospitals and pediatric centers for child development and in the form of scholarships to clergy and recently released convicts (Bry, 1976:158f). Nevertheless, "The Network . . . has moved away from the exploration of the 'inner self' and the attendant emphasis on introspection to a concern with community-orientated activities which seek wider social change" (Young, 1987:138).

More recently, *Time Out* (13–20 December 1989:9) reports that *est* (i.e., The Forum) has launched a new community project entitled Youth at Risk, which, under its Coordinator Rebecca de Souza, is being exported from America to London. Aimed at young people facing problems with drugs, prostitution, homelessness, and general helplessness, the project presents itself as extending Erhard's philosophy of "making the most of yourself as an individual" to "making the most of the community." The £250,000 ($400,000) scheme is attempting to persuade London youth agencies into participating in a series of three weekend workshops, but several agencies have objected to "the project's evangelical, hard-sell tactics."

In defense of *est*, it must be noted that it presents itself as simply *a* way but *not* the *only* way. It is typical of New Age groups in that it offers a consumer option, a technique, rather than a comprehensive system. The stress is laid in identifiable New Age terminology on the here and now of experience, the here and now of experienced experience in which "You see you *are*, not as a thought but as an experience" (Erhard in Bry, 1976:134). In the *est*-ian training, "the attempt is to bypass the mind so that the self can experience itself being." In this way, one comes to experience *aliveness*. Dissatisfaction, confusion, emotional pain, and physical distress are accordingly transformed into health, happiness, love, and full self-expression. In common with other New Age consciousness groups, *est* endeavors to get large numbers of people in touch with their own experience.[39] Since this particular goal has been achieved with greater success by Transcendental Meditation, through which expanded consciousness is no longer seen as the private preserve of "the avant garde and relatively isolated gurus," *est*/The Forum has concentrated instead on effecting alteration in people's experience of their belief systems. In this way, the movement firmly takes its place within the "consciousness revolution" of the New Age Movement, that is, the "beginning of the New Age, a time in mankind's evolution which has been prophesied for centuries and which is both an end and a beginning; a critical point in history in which man and his planet are undergoing vast transformation" (Bry, 1976:21f).

Nevertheless, the key point to keep in mind with *est*, its offshoots such as Lifespring, Actualizations, and Insight (Wallis, 1988:917), or virtually any of the Human Potential groups, is that they all comprise extensions and developments of one or more of the various meditative techniques outlined by Ram Dass (1978:47–103): concentration, mantra, contemplation, devotion, visualization, movement, mindfulness, meditation in action, and meditation without form. But whereas "psychic powers, astral travel and even power on other planes"—which can develop out of any or all these—are considered "traps" by Ram Dass, the HPM recognizes the same as legitimate means toward legitimate ends. For Ram Dass (1978:153), "Power entraps even when it is used to do good" because it still involves the ego. With Human Potential, on the other hand, psychic powers become helpful tools for military efficiency, business acumen, or political and economic management.

## Edgar Cayce

Ram Dass (1978:151), however, raises another understanding that has implications for what I have termed the "supernatural or occult" branch of New Age thinking. He cautions that "there are planes where beings exist other than the physical."

> If in meditation you enter other states of consciousness, you may meet such beings who seemingly come to instruct or guide you. At first, they are awesome. They seem to exist either in disembodied states or with luminous or transparent bodies that appear and disappear at will. They do not exist for normal vision.

He warns that these beings are not necessarily wiser despite their good intentions. On the other hand, some might in fact be masters who come from "higher, more conscious realms" to impart instructions during a critical period in the individual's life. His advice is to be open but judge personally the relevancy of such an encounter. If the "feeling" is right, work with the entity until it is time to proceed alone. The discarnate realm, however, appears to be the prime concern of the "occult camp" within the New Age movement—one associated with such names as Edgar Cayce, Alice Bailey, Ruth Montgomery, and José Arguëlles.[40]

Edgar Cayce (1877–1945), from a self-induced, hypnotic, sleep-like state, produced what have become known as the Edgar Cayce "readings" prophesying the future, recalling the past, describing distant events, or diagnosing illness.[41] Following William James, Ram Dass considers that Cayce had available to him "the discontinuity of two states of consciousness."

Because the gist of Cayce's message is the necessity for the individual to relinquish his self-oriented spirit and turn instead toward work, application, and service, his philosophy and teachings might place him closer to the social or spiritual aspects of what has emerged as New Age rather than to its concern with the occult. In Ram Dass's words,

> it is difficult because of the sort of shucky nature of the organization that got going around [Edgar Cayce] often to hear the wisdom of the message in there and to hear the real stuff in there. But there certainly is a lot of real stuff in there. There's no doubt about it. (Ram Dass, 1974:56)

The first premise for Cayce is "the oneness of all force," and this he identifies with "Life," "Love," "Light," "Law," or "God." The mystical experience then becomes defined as experiencing the awareness of oneness. It is contrasted with the "occult," which in Cayce's understanding is "the use of the mind's powers without respect to purposes" (Puryear, 1982:200). In this sense, even visualization or positive thinking when done without consideration of the "spiritual law" or the need of others becomes occult practice. It differs from psychic activities, which are those of the soul—the manifestation of the One Spirit through the individual.

But though Cayce eschews occultism, he has laid the foundation in America for much of the present belief in the supernatural and the existence of many different spirit realms or dimensions. Within the body of God there are said to be many "consciousnesses" or beings—incarnate, discarnate, and angelic. He acknowledges telepathy, clairvoyance, precognition, astral projection, and communication with dead relatives, spirit guides or even archangels, but if this becomes one's prime focus rather than seeking "attunement" to God alone, one risks idolatry and possibly the risk of possession. Likewise, Cayce recognizes the ability of prayer, projected thought, psychokinesis, and distant healing as the manifestation of the mind's ability to mediate between "the One force" and physical things, but if this is done without reference to an evaluating ideal, that is, without spiritual motivation, it is condemned as "occultism."

In the learning opportunity that exists on the earth plane, all necessary information, guidance, and healing are gained by "listening to the Spirit within."[42] For Cayce, this is accomplished primarily through the practice of silent meditation. Like Ram Dass, meditation is a device for attuning the physical and mental to the spiritual, but unlike Ram Dass, who employs meditation as a means for centering into the here-and-now of reality, for Cayce we are "imprisoned in the here and now" (Puryear, 1982:10), and meditation becomes the means to become liberated from this imprisonment. In a word, Cayce's path is close to the New Age ideal of seekership.

The "Sleeping Prophet's" readings are invariably "Christ-centered" and are expressive of what might be termed "New Age Christianity" or "Christian New Age." Cayce always considered himself a devout Christian and read the Bible from beginning to end every year of his life. His teachings differ from traditional Christianity, however, in their acceptance of the concept of reincarnation. This alone allows God to be truly equable and provides man opportunities for constructive self-development. Moreover, man's spiritual fall from a state of being co-creator with God—the result of pride and the desire to be separate from God—has brought about humanity's three-dimensional manifestations in the earth plane. Despite God's omnipotence and omnipresence, Cayce states that "Having given free will, then . . . it is only when the soul that is a portion of God chooses that God knows the end thereof" (Cayce reading 5749–14). Matter is not perceived as evil; instead what is evil are our own separative thought forms and self-oriented desire patterns. This religious philosophy is thoroughly monistic rather than being one that views dualism as an elevation of evil into a second reality with the good. There is no evil force, but only a product of rebellion. God's mission is not one of overcoming evil but of reconciliation with his children with an emphasis on theological universalism—all souls will eventually be saved and brought into oneness with the One Force.

Cayce's Christianity emphasizes 'helping' rather than 'converting'. Though he maintains that

> the Master, Jesus, even the Christ, is the pattern for every man in the earth, whether he be Gentile or Jew, Parthenian or Greek. For all have the pat-

tern, whether they call on that name or not; but there is no other name given under heaven whereby men may be saved from themselves. (3528–1)

Cayce nevertheless suggests a pluralism of religion,[43] inclusiveness over exclusiveness, and the comparative study of religion.[44] And though religion is contrasted with spirituality, that is, form with spirit, both are considered to be necessary for spiritual growth in the earth plane. Religion allows contact with a spiritual heritage, long-term growth in a spiritual community with others, opportunities for fellowship, and opportunities for one's children to learn both formally and informally. The Cayce readings 'confirm' a hierarchy in the spirit world—though one's orientation should be directly to God.

Edgar Cayce founded the Association for Research and Enlightenment, Inc., in 1931. This organization is headquartered in Virginia Beach, Virginia, but consists today of hundreds of open study groups throughout the United States and other countries for people interested in the teachings deriving from Cayce's work. The focus of the A.R.E. Study Group is seekership, and the text employed is *A Search for God*, Books I and II. These groups are nondenominational and avoid ritual and dogma. "Their primary purpose is to assist the members to know their relationship to their Creator and to become channels of love and service to others" (Puryear, 1982:248). Their maxim is that "Man may not have the same idea. Man—all men—may have the same IDEAL" (3976–8). The ideal is the qualitative and motivational standard by which we measure our decisions and actions. It is to be dwelt upon in daily meditation since "the most important experience of this or any individual entity is first to know what *is* the ideal—spirituality" (357–13). For Cayce, this ideal is total love of God and of one's neighbor as oneself. In a thought that has subsequently become the hallmark of Ruth Montgomery's message as well, the Christ within—the mind—is said to be able to transform us only through dwelling on loving thoughts and acting in loving ways toward God and our fellow man.

The Director of Research Services for the A.R.E., Herbert Puryear, in his work *The Edgar Cayce Primer* (1982:85, 211, and 236), makes several references to New Thought or New Age thinking in terms of other dimensions, other spirit beings, and individual spirit guides. Cayce's description of the ancient civilization of Atlantis and the "law of one" developed over 12,000 years ago as the harbinger of "a whole new order and a new age" that present-day re-alignment may bring about in our time as well, his predictions concerning "major geological, economic, social and spiritual changes for the latter half of this century," and his declaration that "A little leaven leavens the whole lump" (an exponential concept subsequently incorporated into Maharishi Mahesh Yogi's Transcendental Meditation) delineate key issues that have today become identified with the New Age movement. The originality of Cayce's contribution, however, may be questioned by Gordon Melton (1986c:55), who states that "Cayce's teaching closely resembles Theosophy, which Cayce slowly absorbed from the people around him, and emphasizes karma and reincarnation." This does not of course deny the role Cayce has played in the dissemination of these ideas as part of the "cultic milieu." In this context, another influential figure in the present New Age movement to emerge from a Theosophical background is the medium Alice Bailey (1880–1949).

## Alice Bailey

The English-born Bailey rose to prominence within the Theosophical Society in California as the editor of its periodical, *The Messenger.* Disagreements with the organization, however, over Bailey's claim to be in contact with the ascended master Djwhal Khul (the Tibetan) led to the separation from the movement of both Alice and her husband-to-be, Foster Bailey (died 1977). By 1922, Alice Bailey had completed three books—two dictated through her by the Tibetan and another her own. The first was *Initiation: Human and Solar* (1922). In all, nineteen books were dictated— perhaps *The Reappearance of the Christ* (1948), reflecting in part Bailey's Anglican background, being the most popular. With her husband, she founded the Lucis Trust in 1922 to publish her works including a magazine, *The Beacon.* The Lucis Trust has remained the legal recipient of the royalties accruing from the Bailey books. The following year, the Arcane School was instituted. This was augmented in 1932 with the founding of the New Group of World Servers to foster a coming world civilization through union of people of goodwill.

The Lucis Trust was first incorporated in the United States and afterward in the United Kingdom, the Netherlands, and Germany. Today it has "representatives and banking facilities in many other countries" and is headed by an international board of trustees. Under its auspices are included the Lucis Publishing Companies, the Arcane School, the Men of Goodwill (since 1950 known as World Goodwill), Triangles, and the various "Units of Service." Triangles constitutes one of the basic sociological units of the Lucis Trust—consisting of a group of three people not necessarily in the same locality who link through "creative meditation" (not necessarily synchronized) for a few minutes each day. The daily practice of the Triangles meditation is mandatory for each participant or group member. A Lucis Trust pamphlet entitled "Triangles" states that the purpose of each triangle is to

invoke the energies of light and goodwill, visualise these energies as circulating through the three focal points of each triangle, and pouring out
through the network of triangles surrounding the planet.

Workers of each group keep in touch through personal contact or correspondence. When this "activity" was inaugurated in 1937 by using the
already existing Arcane School as an anchoring channel, it was not
considered connected with any of the world's great religions but rather
as a universal spiritual project that includes men and women of all
faiths. "In fact, today the vast majority of Triangles members, who
exist in practically all the countries of the world, are not students in the
Arcane School" (Bailey, 1978:1). The Triangles network is claimed to
be found in at least 103 countries worldwide.

The key Theosophical ideas that Bailey incorporated into her Arcane
School philosophy include beliefs in a spiritual hierarchy, karma, reincarnation, and the existence of a divine plan for the world. Like Edgar
Cayce's teachings, there is a reiterated emphasis on goodwill and world
service. The Arcane School also continues the Theosophical idea of a
religious union between the East and the West (e.g., *Light from the Soul*,
1927). Bailey's most famous piece, however, used frequently throughout occult circles as well as all Arcane School gatherings, is known as
"The Great Invocation":

> From the point of Light within the Mind of God
> Let light stream forth into the minds of men.
> Let light descend on Earth.
>
> From the point of Love within the heart of God
> Let love stream forth into the hearts of men.
> May Christ return to Earth.
>
> From the centre where the Will of God is known
> Let purpose guide the little wills of men—
> The purpose which the Masters know and serve.
>
> Let Light and Love and Power restore the Plan on Earth.
>
> OM   OM   OM

This "world prayer"—repeated during the daily triangular link and visualization among meditating Triangles members—is said to express
acceptance of a basic intelligence (i.e., God), that there is a "divine
evolutionary plan" motivated by love, that there is a "great individuality" or World Teacher whom Christians call the Christ but others Lord

Maitreya, the Imam Mahdi, the Messiah, etc., and that "only through humanity itself can the divine plan work out."

At best, Bailey's teachings are only slightly more universally Christ-centered than Edgar Cayce's. As with Cayce, there is a triune formulation of key ideas such as divinity—here expressed as spirit, soul, and body; that is, life, consciousness, and appearance. On the other hand, there are *four* "seeds" of all right service: "loving relationship; conformity to the *idea* not to the ideal, for that is incidental [a semantic reversal to Cayce]; perception of reality; and creative manipulation" (Bailey, 1978:3). The theosophical underpinnings of Arcane teachings focus on a cosmology that parallels the six descending chakras of the human body: (1) Shamballa/Sanat Kumara (the highest energy center within the planet, "the centre where the will of God is known," (2) the spiritual Hierarchy, (3) "the Christ at the heart of Hierarchy" ("equivalent to the heart centre", also "where the love of God is known"), (4) the new group of world servers, (5) men and women of goodwill everywhere, and (6) the physical centers of distribution (i.e., London, Darjeeling, New York, Geneva, and Tokyo). Three "Buddhas of Activity" in Shamballa are linked to the three "departmental Beings" in Hierarchy. The Nirmanakayas link Shamballa and Hierarchy while "the new group of world servers," in turn, link Hierarchy and humanity. In this way, the Spiritual Triad is connected via "a lighted path of energy communication" with "the soul-infused group personality."

Another Lucis Trust cooperative activity is the network of Units of Service, focusing on activities that range from running schools for children to various fund-raising events. These are groups or individuals who have been inspired by the teachings contained in the twenty-four books by Alice Bailey to "share a common vision of the plan and a commitment to do something to help in the work of bringing that plan into manifestation" (*Units of Service Forum*, Issue No. 5, December 1988:1—Introduction). This network functions in association with World Goodwill and Triangles. Most units hold group meditations during the full moon, with the key Arcane 'festivals' being the full moons of April, May, and June (Easter, Wesak, and World Invocation Day); that is, the periods of maximum lunar light between the vernal equinox and midsummer solstice (Bailey, 1948:155f). World Invocation Day was originally called the Festival of Goodwill. Group meditations comprise the directing of thought energy and follow a general format. In the "Yoga of Synthesis," the sequence consists of alignment, higher interlude, affirmation, meditation, precipitation, lower interlude, and distribution. In "Letting in the Light," the order proceeds from group fusion, alignment, and higher interlude through meditation and precipitation to lower interlude and distribution. This last always entails the group voicing of the Great Invocation.

In his talk entitled "What on Earth Is the New Age?" given March 20, 1989, at St. James, Piccadilly, as part of the Alternatives program, co-director William Bloom said,

> In actual fact, the phrase 'New Age', I think, I can't find another source for it, the phrase 'New Age' was initiated in the form that it is used in the New Age movement by Alice Bailey who from the 1920s onwards published about fourteen books in which she acted as secretary for a Tibetan teacher called Djwhal Khul. These books, in blue covers, are quite long—about five or six hundred pages; they're 'heavy going'. Nevertheless, nearly all of them have been through ten, twelve, thirteen, fourteen, fifteen reprints, and if you pick up any of those books and look at the index in the back and look for 'New Age', you will find up to sixty references per book.

Alice Bailey, the Arcane School, Triangles, World Goodwill, etc., have undoubtedly played and continue to play an influential role in the New Age movement and the establishment of some of its parameters. Although there is an emphasis on service and tangible efforts toward betterment of the physical and spiritual lot of humankind, there is also a strong theosophical/metaphysical or occult contribution to New Age thinking that runs through Bailey's teachings. The spiritual hierarchy and, in particular, the inhabitants of the lower echelons that are closest to the earth plane of human beings, the devas, have been receiving increased prominence in the emergence and dissemination of New Age ideas.

> The *devas* do not suffer pain as does mankind. Their rate of rhythm is steadier although in line with the Law. . . . They grow through appreciation of and joy in the forms built and the work accomplished. The *devas* build and humanity breaks and through the shattering of the forms man learns through discontent. (Bailey, 1944:677)

The delineation of a world of discarnate spirits, spirit guides, devas, and/or angels is the hallmark of the supernatural wing of the New Age movement. Following in this tradition of Edgar Cayce, Alice Bailey, and the American medium Arthur Ford is Ruth Montgomery, "the First Lady of the Psychic World."

### Ruth Montgomery

Coming from a Methodist upbringing in small midwestern American communities, Montgomery had what she terms a natural doubt concerning the occult. As a Washington, D.C.-based news reporter, she attended a series of darkroom séances in pursuit of an assignment. These included sessions with Ford. As a result of these encounters she became curious about automatic writing. After several attempts in holding a pencil lightly on a sheet of paper, on one occasion "the pencil began to race around the page, drawing circles and figure-eights with wild abandon." Before long, Montgomery began "receiving" written messages from various "guides": ". . ."we" referred to whatever mysterious force propelled the pencil" (Montgomery, 1966:48). She would devote no more than fifteen or twenty minutes a day to automatic writing—usually after first meditating and preferably at the same time each day. Eventually, at her guides' prompting, she substituted a typewriter for the pencil. Her "best seller," *A Search For The Truth* (1966), is the result of the "messages received," but it also includes several chapters recording synchronistic events or "psychic communications" to numerous other people as supporting evidence for the validity of occult phenomena.

The essential thrust of the "spirit messages" as Montgomery reports them is the insistence on oneness with God, the unlimited capacity within ourselves, and, especially, the belief that the good we do here is what advances our souls' progression. "The greatest thing in life is the aid that you extend to others, in order to help them upward and onward" (Montgomery, 1966:90). In fact, "Without helping others, we fragmentize into tiny units. Together we are all-powerful in our quest for perfect union and Oneness with God" (Montgomery, 1966:139). As a commentary on the ideas she transmits, Montgomery (1966:88) states,

> Those thoughts are too deep for me. I did not originate them, nor did I compose their phraseology, but I set them down here as a mere reporter who has been assigned a specific task.

Repeatedly she learns that she can have no higher mission than to pass on to others the truths she learns from the spirit guides.

"The only part which matters is how well you prepare yourself for the next stage of life by making the most of your time while [on the worldly plane]. We want you to help others through our teaching" (Montgomery, 1966:85). The guides explain that the time spent on earth is merely preparation for the next phase—that of the spirit guides themselves. The faster this conversion of earth-souls into "transfigured spirits" occurs, the more rapid will be the progress toward "a fusion of the whole." The promised land is the infinite plane beyond "the Golden Door through which none must return to serve further penance" (Montgomery, 1966:87).

The psychic world-picture Montgomery presents is firmly grounded within a Christian framework. In fact, quoting biblical passages, the author (1966:126) claims that Christians must own up to the implications of their faith.

> Throughout the Bible we encounter a world of spirit beings. Therefore, how does a minister explain the transfiguration of Moses and Elijah before Christ and the three disciples, if he does not accept psychic experience? How does the Holy Spirit speak to us, except through psychic awakening? The early Christians knew psychic experience, and took it for granted. Somewhere along the way, the church lost touch with this God-given faculty, but an awakening seems to be at hand.

The psychic origins of the church have subsequently come to be branded "superstition" through the influences of "scientific materialism and philosophical rationalism" (Montgomery, 1966:131). In fact, however, the Judeo-Christian religion remains the logical realm for pursuing psychical study (p. 246). Though the psychic experience is part of every culture, through Christianity it has taken on "an ethical coloration" for the first time. Moreover, "The concept that men have free will is the major contribution of the Christian religion" (p. 187).

The psychic experience is fully compatible with the essential message of Montgomery's spirit guides that material things are utterly unimportant, that one's body plays only a brief part in the soul's upward climb during the millennia yet to come in the progression toward eternal truth and "Oneness with God." But since temptations lie in wait for every mortal, the earthly experience is a hard test. By contrast, "Because the Son of God was able to reject those temptations, He is able to return to the earth again and again, without any of its hampering limitations of time and space and body" (Montgomery, 1966:94). In other words, "The Man of Nazareth was the most holy of all saints . . . indeed the Son of God. Because of His perfection He ascended directly to His Father, without the intermediary steps" (p. 174). It is the "intermediary steps" with which Montgomery's message is concerned—in particular, with this plane and the one immediately following, i.e., that of the spirit guides themselves.

As her guides explain,

> We occupy the earth, as well as the sky and the heavens. We are striving to break our ties with the earth, to free ourselves for the next phase; yet we cannot sever the tie until we have completed the good tasks that we should and could have done on your plane. (Montgomery, 1966:98)

Unlike many New Age channeled entities, however, Montgomery's guides remain reluctant to speak of their earthly identity—explaining that worldly successes are of no possible use in the next phase. Had they truly been successes, they could have moved to "an earth-free existence in a still higher phase of our progression" (Montgomery, 1966:99). In fact, despite her family's opposition to "spirit writing," the guides refused to supply evidential material—or, if requested, often gave incorrect information.

Beside the influences of Arthur Ford and his seminars on behalf of the Spiritual Frontiers Fellowship, Montgomery has also pursued an interest in Edgar Cayce and the Edgar Cayce Foundation in Virginia Beach as well as in the Association for Research and Enlightenment headed by Cayce's son, Hugh Lynn Cayce. She considers prayer to be a psychic experience closely related to both meditation and dreams.[45]

Montgomery remains at the core of the New Age movement— especially with the proclamation that

> There is no Death. Let this be the crux of the story. The world is ready for it now, as it struggles to cope with a universe gone mad with power and fear. (1966:140)[46]

She explains—or it is explained through her—that upon creation each entity immediately seeks re-union with its "Maker," "but along the way the temptations proved too strong for all of them" (Montgomery, 1966:94). In contrast to the human potential movement per se, however, Montgomery admonishes that "To live for self alone is to destroy one's self" (p. 96). Instead, Montgomery's Christian slant requires "loving one another; by helping others, one helps himself advance." Nevertheless, a humanistic danger inherent or criticized as inherent in much New Age/human potential thinking remains in such recorded statements as "The hungry ones are not nearly as pathetic as those who starve for spiritual goods and fail to grasp the light" (Montgomery, 1966:97). Earthly advancement is presented as unimportant. In seeking to pass through the Golden Door, progress depends on the individual, not on God, who has given all equal opportunity.

> Those who are born with physical deformities chose those bodies deliberately. . . . by overcoming the difficulty of a deformity they are advancing their souls more rapidly than otherwise. (Montgomery, 1966:241)

Everyone here on this plane has chosen to be here. Angels and saints, however, "have overcome temptations to such a degree that they need not wear the earthly form that suffers such temptations" (p. 243).

Belief in reincarnation is a concept frequently associated with the New Age movement. At first, Montgomery's guides appear reluctant to speak about it. Subsequently, however, they admit that it is "not far from the mark" but that the great misunderstanding is that no personality is completely re-born. Nevertheless, in one of several apparent contradictions, the author also states that Christianity made it clear that everyone can duplicate the resurrection experience of Jesus—namely, *"the survival of the complete personality with the same character*, and with memory, and with the freedom to make a choice" (Montgomery, 1966:186; italics mine). Another contradiction appears in contrary statements concerning time: "Time is the indestructible quality that exists throughout eternity" (ibid.:98), and yet "the over-all plan for this universe is so immense that it is tragic to waste even the minutes that it takes to adjust to a new form of existence here. Time is the most precious commodity in life" (Montgomery, 1966:86). The time that is wasted in one's soul's development can never be regained.

Although *A Search For The Truth* does indeed hint at reincarnation, it was not until after Montgomery's subsequent experiences with hypnotic prenatal regression that she affirms her belief in a succession of lifetimes through her 1968 book *Here and Hereafter*. Reincarnation

> explained the apparent inequities of life and the purpose of living, erased fear of death, and placed the obligation of 'judgment' squarely on the shoulders of each of us, respecting our free will to learn and grow and atone for our mistakes. We can't blame God for our present circumstances. We chose them ourselves—to learn. (Montgomery and Garland, 1986:126)

This idea is also stressed by Britain's "grandfather of the New Age Movement," Sir George Trevelyan. During a St. James' Alternatives talk (February 2, 1990), Trevelyan's main thrust was his "absolute certainty" that "the I AM means there can be no death. . . . Since we are all part of the one great conscious being which is humanity, we do not need to be frightened of change or death.'' Montgomery has here accepted what has become a common New Age notion: namely that we choose our own hardships since 'spiritual growth' is the purpose of life. Coupled with this concept that we have chosen our own gender, race, locale, parents, etc., there is additionally 'group karma', that is, the tendency for clusters of souls to reincarnate together in cycles in order to work out mutual problems left unresolved in previous lives.

A further New Age idea concerns the possibility of life on other planets. Montgomery's guides suggest that

> Perhaps as those in the earth phase progress in intellectual advancement, they will find it possible to communicate with powers higher than ours, and these will perhaps be able to tell them of other life forms which they have encountered from different planets and orbits; but this is beyond our own ken at this stage. (Montgomery, 1966:172)

In this way, Montgomery has left the door open for much of the extraterrestrial channeling and experiences claimed within many New Age circles.

Despite some inconsistencies to be found with *A Search For The Truth*, Montgomery has compiled what might be termed a Christian New Age vision of the New Age Movement. She includes in this work a short glossary of terms used in psychic study, and if her ideas are not fully coherent, they nevertheless conform to what is becoming recognizable as a New Age world-outlook. Indeed, because of her pioneering volume and her ongoing work with automatic writing and continuing publications of these ''messages,'' Montgomery has emerged a leading contributor and leader of the New Age Movement.

In 1968, Montgomery published *Here and Hereafter* in which she explores the concept of reincarnation in ways believed to be compatible with Christianity, Judaism, and Eastern philosophy. Here she stresses the therapeutic value of understanding past lives as the hidden causes of irrational phobias or puzzling attitudes. *A World Beyond* (1971), based on messages received from Arthur Ford (died January 4, 1971), focuses on life beyond the grave in the astral plane. Here, Montgomery incorporates the Caycean idea that we are co-creators with God (the core of the universe, truth and energy, matter and spirit, the essence of our being, total awareness, the All). In this book too is the first mentioning of the coming planetary axis shift.

*Born to Heal* (1973) covers ''magnetic healing.'' *Companions Along the Way* (1974) is about Montgomery's own past lives with Arthur

Ford. The world's history is presented in *The World Before* (1976)—
including the lost continents of Lemuria/Mu and Atlantis as well as
further predictions of the catastrophe for the earth at the end of the
present century.

Montgomery's twelfth book, *Strangers Among Us* (1979), introduces
the concept of the Walk-in—"an entity who is not born as an infant but
takes over (always with permission) the body of one who wishes to
depart." These "people" are "superior but not perfected souls," having already gone through many earthly lives but having earned the right
to avoid childhood and return to earth directly as adults. They inherit
the memory bank of the Walk-out. Through the process of soul transfer-
ral, Walk-ins—of whom there are already "tens of thousands"—are
expected to play an increasingly significant role as the earth approaches
the "New Age of Aquarius."[47] Various case histories of Walk-ins are
presented in *Threshold to Tomorrow* (1982). Some are working to improve people's health through greater understanding of herbs and sound
nutrition, some aim to help dispel the fear of death in others, some
are establishing self-reliant communities without electricity and modern
technology, some are fostering human interaction, etc. In addition,
"The Walk-in concept . . . is taken seriously by a growing segment of
the psychiatric medical community" (Montgomery and Garland,
1986:213).

In *Aliens Among Us* (1985), Montgomery stresses that earth is part
of an intergalactic universe-federation. Here she explores the concept
of extraterrestrials visiting or living on earth to help humankind prepare
for the New Age. These comprise space visitors materializing throughout the world (with or without UFOs or machines), space Walk-ins,
space channelers and "a vast orbiting watchful fleet." Much of the
evidence is gathered through Dr. R. Leo Sprinkle of the University of
Wyoming who has interviewed and/or hypnotized hundreds of people
who have seen UFOs, have been troubled by dreams of space aliens, or
have suffered unexplained loss of time. Many of these refer to themselves as "Contactees." Sprinkle has held annual summer conferences
since 1980 for contactees to relate their stories to each other.

It is Montgomery's latest book, co-authored with Joanne Garland,
*Ruth Montgomery: Herald of the New Age* (1986), a retrospective ac-
count of Montgomery's life, that squarely deals with the concept of the
New Age and also squarely identifies it and the prelude to it with the
prophesies in the Book of Revelations. Montgomery's version of the
New Age is strictly millennialist—preceded by a final battle between
Satan/the Antichrist ("now an American boy in his early teens") with

his forces of evil ones (largely reborn Atlanteans) and the rest of humanity including many of the more spiritual reincarnated Lemurians along with the assistance of Walk-ins and extraterrestrials. As the earth approaches its axial shift (variously attributed to an imbalance caused by ice build-up or the "warming trend that could reduce the size of the polar ice caps quickly enough to raise sea levels drastically throughout the world"),

> The satanic influences are pervading all strata of society throughout the world. Never in many centuries has there been such fertile ground for the spread of evil influences, as people dip into the occult for nonspiritual purposes, using the demonic powers that they learn in this way to influence others. They are selling dope, taking dope, and employing black witchcraft that had all but died out during the Dark Ages. Evil is rampant. (Montgomery and Garland, 1986:261)

Prior to the global catastrophe, the earth will experience "violent alternations in weather patterns," earthquakes, plagues (e.g., AIDS), famine, and possibly world wars. With the planetary shift itself (perhaps "in the very last months of the century"),[48] the world's population will be decimated, commerce halted, and cities destroyed. Large parts of Hawaii, the west coast of California, Florida, England, Holland and the lowlands of Europe, Japan, and many island nations will cease to exist through submersion.[49]

Montgomery has drawn on the various prophesies of Nostradamus, Edgar Cayce, and Levi Dowling (*The Aquarian Gospel of Jesus the Christ*, 1907). Although the imminent cataclysm will "force its survivors to establish an interaction of helpfulness, love and mutual respect"—inaugurating "a golden New Age of peace," the Antichrist too will survive in the chaos that immediately follows, but once he "tries to assert dictatorial authority, the people will turn on him and put him to death"—while many of the Atlantean terrorists "will be swept into the seas or otherwise disposed of during or shortly after the event" (Montgomery and Garland, 1986:264f.).[50] Some of the "good souls" will be lifted off the earth temporarily in the spaceships of the extraterrestrials.

After a period of reconstruction, the New Age will emerge as a paradise on earth. It will be

> a time of love and understanding, of consideration and compassion, and of a joyous awakening to the reality that we are all one. . . . [There will be] the joyous fellowship that will occur whether in body or in spirit, for

communication in that New Age will be simplicity itself between the physical and the etheric vibrations. It will be a time when men's eyes are opened to the Universal Truth—the eternal truth that there is no death and that love is the unifying force of the cosmic world. . . . direct communication with the astral and etheric planes . . . will be rather commonplace. . . . (Montgomery and Garland, 1986:268)

Things will once again be made by hand, neighbors and friends will cooperate, and people will be allowed to die with dignity without artificial extension of life. And "in that golden time, it will be understood that to be Catholic or Presbyterian, Southern Baptist or Jewish, Muslim or Hindu or whatever is an arrogance of mind that has no place in religion." Moreover, "The Christ spirit will enter a perfected person within some twenty to thirty years after the earth has restabilized" (Montgomery and Garland, 1986:270).

Montgomery's message appears at times to be pure Cayce. It follows as well the pyramidal hierarchy characteristic of the Arcane School. New Age consciousness is thought to consist of many paths to the mountain's single top, i.e., God. "All paths which lead upward in spirituality will eventually reach the pinnacle, the return to the Creator" of whom our souls are cast off sparks. Montgomery paraphrases Cayce in declaring that there is one God indivisible and that love for one's fellow man is what religion is all about. Nevertheless, despite her literalistic interpretation of Revelation, she attempts to distinguish herself from Christian fundamentalists, although she does appear like them to link "today's cults and satanic influences" (Montgomery and Garland, 1986:260f.). Recognizing the fundamentalists' "sincere effort to stem the progress of evil," she considers them all the same as "ignorant, with closed minds and little education," as lost unless they realize there are many paths, that Christ's teachings and Eastern religions are in accord, that we are one.[51] In its spiritual implications, Montgomery's teachings are monistic, but her millenarian vision of the New Age conforms ethically more to the moral absolutism characteristic of what Anthony and Robbins (1978) describe as "dualistic religion."[52]

### Shirley MacLaine

Like Ruth Montgomery, another major New Age contributor is Hollywood actress Shirley MacLaine. Beginning with *Don't Fall Off The Mountain* followed by *You Can Get There From Here*, MacLaine investigates candidly and humorously her background, her public career, and private life as well as her political activism, involvement with the women's movement and life-changing excursion to the People's Republic of China. It is, however, her third in the series, *Out On A Limb* (1983), in which the actress begins her inner voyage in search of her spiritual self and what she refers to as "the connection between mind, body and spirit." In her early forties, the author encounters what was for her a world that had formerly belonged only to science fiction or the occult. *Dancing In The Light* (1985), begins with MacLaine's fiftieth birthday celebration and proceeds to explore the actress's childhood as well as, with the help of her spirit guides, her past lives. *It's All In The Playing* (1987) is the latest in this series of autobiographical explorations into her life and spiritual quest, covering the period of her life during the filming of her earlier book *Out On A Limb* in which the actress plays herself for the television mini-series.

Undoubtedly, Shirley MacLaine has emerged as a leading spokesperson for the New Age Movement. She uses the term no less than fifteen times in her *Out On A Limb* narrative, and she circumscribes all the phenomena that have, at least in the popular understanding, become associated with the New Age Movement: karma, reincarnation, spirit guides, higher self, meditation, holy spots, talismans, and magic. "The New Age awakening of the spirit" is seen as part of the emergence of yin (female) energy but not simply to end the old traditional patriarchal system in favor of matriarchal values but to assert an equality between the two, a balance between yin and yang (MacLaine, 1987:207).

> The domination of masculine energy represented the Old Age, the old way of operating. We had seen that male domination and female submission as a way of life had brought us to the brink of ruin. The dominion of yin energy was built on loving, nurturing—the New Age energy with roots deep in the very ancient worship of the mother-image, the Goddess aspect of the God-force. (MacLaine, 1987:231)

In short, the New Age is perceived as "a spiritual shift in consciousness which will benefit humankind" (p. 326).

Like Montgomery, MacLaine also finds New Age references in the Bible, though she emphasizes especially its teachings about "the Kingdom of Heaven existing within each one of us," an idea about to be attested in "a New Age of recognition." But the energy of this new era means an acceleration as well in our life and times, its pressures, and the accompanying events of international world wars, plagues, and famines. Many individuals would opt out of the process—using "karmic workouts to leave the body."

The world was so difficult to live in. There was so much harsh and volatile interaction occurring everywhere, as though millions of people, including myself, had decided to clear up their karmic debris before the New Age arrived. Or maybe the cleaning up was what would actually herald the New Age. (MacLaine, 1987:228)

In MacLaine's perception, a "giant *clean-up*, a cleansing, is in process on the planet" in which old karmic patterns are being cleared, and each event has a reason for being (pp. 136f.).

The concepts with which MacLaine constructs her spiritual odyssey are those that have become frequently associated with New Age beliefs: out-of-body experience, meditation, the higher self, reincarnation, karma, spirit guides, etc. During a spiritual channeling session in the actress's home, the question was put to the contacting discarnate spirit regarding AIDS. The disease was explained as an indication of the role consciousness plays in illness. "The disease has appeared, in your social order, to focus on the problems of stress upon the immune system." It is a direct ratio to the homophobia in our social order and a result of socially disinvested individuals unable to maintain healthy immune systems due to the stress of isolation (MacLaine, 1987:37f).[53] (The pattern of AIDS in Africa is not mentioned or explained.)

As in *est*[54] and other Human Potential movements, there is an almost insistent emphasis on self-responsibility. With MacLaine, this idea is strongly connected to the idea of karma and reincarnation. As a spirit guide explains,

"What we cause, good or bad, will have an effect—on *us*" is karma. Karmic justice is the extension of cause and effect, so that the seeds we sow in one lifetime may not be reaped until a much later lifetime. Hence, Karmic Cosmic Justice. (MacLaine, 1987:24)

MacLaine cites Matthew 16, verse 13 among several biblical references to the concept of reincarnation that had not been "discarded" before the final formulation. As a result of the actress's beliefs, she and her 'followers' have focused much attention on searching out past-life recall—through channeling or such techniques as spiritual acupuncture.[55] Nevertheless, although the media has done much to popularize this aspect of so-called New Age belief, it should be noted that whereas in Marilyn Ferguson's Aquarian Conspirators survey (1987:434) most respondents indicated a high belief in psychic phenomena (96 percent in telepathy, 94 percent in psychic healing, 89 percent in precognition,

88 percent in clairvoyance, 84 percent in synchronicity, 82 percent in psychokinesis, 86 percent in cosmic intelligence, and 76 percent in consciousness that survives bodily death), only 57 percent affirmed a belief in reincarnation.[56]

But reincarnation forms only a part of MacLaine's belief system. She places as much emphasis on what has also become a hallmark of New Age conviction, namely, the idea of God within, the self as God. Accordingly, the fundamental lesson we are receiving from extraterrestrials is "that each human being *was* a god, never separated from the God-force," but whereas they accept that they are gods, we remain largely ignorant of this reality and consequently unable to assume our full responsibility (MacLaine, 1987:69). All the same, we and the God-force are one and the same; our souls have the same divine characteristics as God. In fact, "the reality of God and Divine intention exists and begins *within* us" (p. 337).

MacLaine contends that our present age of spiritual ignorance has caused a "particularly destructive form of fundamentalism" in which each faction intolerantly believes that their God is the only one "because they couldn't accept anyone else's God, much less that God was within each of us" (MacLaine, 1987:304f.). But it is this very "deep internal spiritual belief in the God within each of us which would be the salvation of mankind" (p. 312). MacLaine wonders in regard to herself whether

> this was why I had created a role for myself this time around whereby I would be at the forefront of the New Age spiritual movement, heralding *the* giant truth that one individual is his or her own best teacher, and that no other idol or false image should be worshipped or adored because the God we are all seeking lies inside one's self, not outside. (MacLaine, 1987:172)

Like the *est*-ian assertion, we alone are responsible for what is. "What you believe is what will occur" (p. 283). There are no accidents. Combining the doctrine of self-responsibility with that of reincarnation, MacLaine can conclude that each of us chooses the life we have as well as all the lives we have had and will have in the future. Expressing the freedom which exists within our lives, the author contends, "I could alter the very fiber of my existence by knowing that I had the choice to do it" (p. 111).

As events occur in life, "we should examine how *we* might have created the reality of things going wrong to begin with" (MacLaine,

1987:162). Our anger is simply the soul's recognition for its own responsibility for what is. "And the most difficult aspect to admit is that
we do it in order to learn" (ibid.) Yet MacLaine takes this belief in self-
responsibility to its furthermost limit. During what might be described
as a New Age ceremony in which twenty people sat around an oval
table on New Year's eve and, as a crystal was passed around, each
person then expressed what s/he would like to manifest in their lives for
the following year, MacLaine declares that "since I realized I created
my own reality in every way, I must therefore admit that, in essence, *I
was the only person alive in my universe.*" She expresses her "feeling
of total responsibility *and power* for all events that occur in the world
because the world is happening only in my reality."

> *And* human beings feeling pain, terror, depression, panic, and so forth,
> were really only aspects of pain, terror, depression, panic, and so on, in
> *me*! If they were all characters in my reality, my dream, then of course
> they were only reflections of myself. . . . If we each create our own reality,
> then of course we are everything that exists within it. Our reality is a
> reflection of us. . . . But whether anyone else was experiencing the news
> *separately* from me was unclear, because *they* existed in my reality too.
> . . . My purpose in mentioning this on New Year's Eve was to project a
> hope that if I changed *my* conception of reality for the better in the coming
> year, I would in effect be contributing to the advancement of the world.
> . . . How do we change the world? By changing ourselves. (MacLaine,
> 1987:173–75)[57]

MacLaine's solipsism becomes the underlying message of her book.
She returns to it constantly. She sees two levels of simultaneous consciousness: the earth-plane physical level on which we experience pain,
difficulty, and joy as realities; and the spiritual level, "which in its
infinite wisdom is loving enough to guarantee us that *it* is the reality,
everything else an illusion. The lesson of each? We create them both"
(MacLaine, 1987:333). At another point she states that if it is true that
we all create our own reality, the "creative technology of perceiving
alternative realities is a quantum leap in the progress of mankind" (p.
335). This shift is part of touching and trusting the "Christ" consciousness within, then knowing that "we actually effected a physical force
which collectively could alter the course of mankind."

> *We* were responsible for creating everything. Now we needed consciously
> to align ourselves with the Divine intention of the universe so that our
> forces could work together. (MacLaine, 1987:337)

At times, MacLaine's subjective idealism or mentalism seems at variance with what she or her spirit guides otherwise describe as God. For instance she quotes a benediction from an entity named John of Zebedee who uses Kevin Ryerson as his instrument:

> there are many souls, but only one God. Each of you is a thought and creation within the universal mind which you call God. Walk in this the father-mother God's light. God bless you. Amen. (MacLaine, 1987:39)

MacLaine (1987:282) herself can refer to the higher self's direct contact to "the Divine Universal Energy Source." Moreover, she declares,

> Religion doesn't necessarily have anything to do with spirituality. Each religion thinks it has a hot line to God. When the truth might well be that we are *all* attached to God. We are all part of God. (MacLaine, 1987:122)

"Or, as Lazaris would say, we are all part of God-Goddess All There Is" (p. 232).

Media notoriety has brought into prominence the New Age preoccupation with extraterrestrial beings—both those in physical bodies using UFOs or various spacecraft as vehicles for transportation, and those discarnates who usually use mediums as instruments (MacLaine, 1987:322). One class, for instance, are known as "Apunian angels." These are space beings from a star called Apu who have been visiting the Andes mountains for centuries. MacLaine, who at one point invokes "all you invisible guides and teachers and Gods around me" (p. 265), has much to say about these entities and the pragmatics of channeling. We learn that the spiritual beings live in the ethers (which is as well "our natural habitat, not the earth"—p. 232), that they "can see our vibrational light frequencies better when electricity doesn't interfere with the medium's own eyes" (hence the injunction to turn down the lights for a seance—p. 29), that because life for them does not exist in linear measurement but all time is simultaneously hologramic, they do not always communicate through transmediums correctly—especially when it is a question of time and mathematical figures (p. 20), and that there is a strong sense of competition among them ("the battle of the Gods"—p. 62).[58] On the practical level, however, she assesses the correctness for mediums to charge for their services.

> In my opinion, when metaphysical practitioners render a service of spiritual value they should receive remuneration just as anyone does who renders a service of value. (MacLaine, 1987:21)

The clarity of the message becomes the control on a channeler's motivation. If he succumbs to a materialistic greed incommensurate with his activities, the transchanneled information will be clouded with static.

All in all, the essential message that is received through spiritual entities and space beings pertains to the recognitions of each individual as well as all of us collectively as a "masterpiece of spiritual potential," of the earth as the locus for spirit-matter interaction being a "learning center," of the physical being, itself a product of conscious intention and capable of change if and when we change our consciousness, and of all physical and nonphysical guides as siblings of the cosmos-embracing companion intelligence systems continually interacting with us whether we are aware of them or not.

> . . . the purpose of the space beings and the nonphysical beings was to help us expand our conscious awareness so that we could radiate from within on a level that was more in keeping with our power and spiritual expression in the human experience. (MacLaine, 1987:326)

Nonetheless, MacLaine's formulation of the New Age thought system is not purely transcendental. Though she speaks primarily about such things as spiritual evolution, cosmic union, and the relativity of evil, she also accepts a pagan framework that is typical of much of the New Age Movement's grounding. For instance, she explains talismans as working

> in human understanding because we ascribe magic to them. And magic works wonders. The loss of magic is the denial of unlimited possibility. (MacLaine, 1987:243)

The talisman is essentially a "reminder." It would be akin to the earth's holy spots such as Cuzco ("a holy city, a place of pilgrimage," "the navel of the earth"—p. 246) or the Great Pyramid at Gizeh ("a Bible in stone, that . . . stands at the epicenter of the earth's land mass"—p. 128). Moreover, she explains the Andes mountains of South America as "the gateway of the feminine energy on the planet; the Himalayas, the gateway for the masculine" (p. 242). Consequently, MacLaine's mentalism must be balanced with her appreciation for the physical immanence of sacred power—a common feature of a pagan worldview.

In explaining religious history, MacLaine (1987:334) claims that

> The concept of an afterlife took on abstract reality when it became codified by the formal religions. Dogma and ritual created both good and bad afterlives—Paradise or Hell—using mankind's urgent need to believe in *some-*

thing beyond this world as a mechanism through which to amass and exploit power.

Nevertheless, our spiritual capabilities are vastly more developed now than they have been in the past, and this fact alone "is a testament to the spiritual and mental progress of the human race" (MacLaine, 1987:334). Through her work *It's All In The Playing* and the several books that preceded it as well as her television film *Out On A Limb*, her workshops, and her constant involvement with the spiritual quest on both the personal and collective levels, actress Shirley MacLaine has placed herself at the vanguard of the New Age Movement as one of its leading spokespersons but without the millenarian colorings that have become characteristic of Ruth Montgomery.

## *José Argüelles*

Another leading spokesperson for the New Age Movement, one closer to MacLaine than to Montgomery, is José Argüelles. In his book, *The Mayan Factor* (1987), he has laid a groundwork for a New Age worldview, the evolutionary timetable leading to it, and a description, albeit radically idealistic, of the form this post-technological world will take. His model assumes three stages: pre-history = pre-technological, history = technological, post-history = post-technological. He asks (p. 132), "Could the New Jerusalem, New Heaven, and New Earth, be the same as the entry into the unimaginable realm of the new cycle, the post-galactic synchronization following A.D. 2012, Mayan calendar date 13.0.0.0.0?" The Second Coming, the specter of Armageddon, i.e., the final conflagration of extinction, is seen as an avoidable event in "the Christ-based time frame that now dominates the world."

Argüelles speaks of "the Armageddon by-pass" that is possible if we reject the scientific-materialistic worldview and expose the inner contradictions of our dominant paradigm bounded by its own beliefs. In other words, we must end the planetary political power plays undertaken by the ruling white, male, neo-Protestant priesthood in defense of its scientific "objectivity." If we are successful—and the Mayan timetable on which these predictions are based, it is argued, support this likelihood—in the New Age that follows,

> Instead of going to a job at nine o'clock every morning, we shall prepare each day for the celebratory task of ritual sensory attunement to solar galactic pulsations. Through sensory fusion—bringing together of various

senses into the experience of synaesthesia—we will realize a synergistic amplification of energy and enjoyment.

The leisure for so doing will be the natural result of having divested ourselves of an unnecessary military economy and the production of wasteful and even toxic consumer goods that were in total disregard of the reality of the light body. Nourishing ourselves as simply and as locally as possible, we shall turn our surplus wealth into the research, education, and artistic production necessary for the establishment of a healthy collective organism in resonant attunement with the Sun and, through the Sun, with the galactic core, Hunab Ku. (Argüelles, 1987:190)

But Argüelles adds to this—as a direct challenge to a leading trend within the New Age Movement, "Rather than dredge up dreary past-life archetypes announced in pseudo-spooky voices, we will channel the stars directly."

Seminal influences on Argüelles that he acknowledges in his book include Ouspensky's *Tertium Organum* and the teachings of Chögyam Trungpa Rinpoche of Tibetan Buddhism's Naropa Institute based in Boulder, Colorado. But in addition to these, Argüelles has also been shaped in his thinking by Sylvanus Griswold Morley's *The Ancient Maya* (1956) and by Native Americans Tony Shearer and Sun Bear. As a result, he has come to recognize the Mayan sacred calendar (the Tzolkin) and the 5,125-year "Great Cycle" with which it corresponds as the key to the meaning of human history. As he explains, the Mayan Great Cycle is a galactic synchronization beam through which the earth has been passing (Argüelles, 1987:111), while the Tzolkin or harmonic module consisting of thirteen numbers and twenty symbols is

the simplest possible mathematical matrix to accommodate the largest possible number of harmonic transformations, transmissions, and transductions—a veritable periodic table of galactic frequencies. (Argüelles, 1987:57)

This galactic gauge, which comprises an effective means by which mankind can link himself to a galactic community of intelligence, is the hitherto overlooked Mayan Factor. More precisely, and as it reputedly indicates, "we are at a point in time 26 years short of a major galactic synchronization. Either we shift gears right now or we miss the opportunity" (Argüelles, 1987:41).

Argüelles never uses the term "New Age" directly, but his description of galactic intelligence(s) and harmonic synchronization is certainly New Age language. His interpretation of the new era is decidedly anti-technological with "the purpose of the Mayan Factor to lead us to the path beyond technology [as well as] through . . . the transformation of matter which technology has induced" (Argüelles, 1987:148). Argüelles argues that twentieth-century technological comfort along with the suburban automobile-and-television existence close off our perceptions and sense fields. In turning to gadgetry through our fatal fascination/ infatuation with our technological/material inventiveness, we have developed a contemporary blindness to the Sun as an intelligence and have disregarded our own potential as universal co-creators (p. 178). He cites cancer and AIDS as typical Late Industrial Age diseases resulting from radical blockages in our collective bio-electromagnetic field. Their cure lies

> in a radical shift in disposition accompanied by the development of a genuine bio-electromagnetic medicine that accounts for the power of the mind, the reality of the light body, and the natural, organic restoration of intrinsic resonance as key factors in healing. (Argüelles, 1987:182)

Nevertheless, despite his post-technological stance, Argüelles sees the future in terms of globally disseminated information and education through a single computer-video network.

Other New Age features of Argüelles's vision (1987:170) include the imminent returns of Christ, Quetzalcoatl, and all the gods and goddesses, heros and heroines of human imagination; that is, of the resonant structure of the mind. Moreover, he recognizes what is called "the etheric geomagnetic grid of the earth." A common pagan/New Age understanding envisions the erection of temples, ziggurats, pyramids, cathedrals, pagodas, mosques, palaces, and houses of parliament as well as more recently airports and power plants at the nodal points of this grid (cf. p. 155). But almost in contrast to the frequent New Age emphasis on the individual as sole creator of his or her own destiny, Argüelles (1987:154) cautions that "We are not the sole authors of our experience, but *players* in a galactically amplified field whose principle character is Earth herself" (emphasis mine).

Using what is cited as the "Goodman-Martinez Hernandez-Thompson correlation of Mayan and Christian chronology" completed in 1927, Argüelles (1987:45) locates the start of the Mayan "Great Cycle" between the 6th and 13th of August in 3113 B.C. and its conclusion (i.e., the repetition of the same inceptive Mayan date of 13.0.0.0.0) on the 21st of December, A.D. 2012. In other words, Argüelles has located a date for the beginning of the New Age. Though he has been seminal in the founding of the First Whole Earth Festival at Davis, California (1970), behind the staging of Trungpa Rinpoche's Dharma Art projects in Los Angeles (1980) and San Francisco (1981), and in founding the Planet Art Network (1983), Argüelles's most recent and noteworthy New Age task has been in promoting the notion of the Harmonic Convergence (cf. Argüelles, 1987:32, 145, 148, and 159). This last was recognized as "the resonant frequency shift of 1987" occurring on the 16th and 17th of August. Although the final archetypal period of the "Great Cycle" spans 1992 to 2012, the Harmonic Convergence is perceived as preceding this as

> the first Mayan-return entry point, a temporal planetary Tollan at which time their presence will be perceived by some as an inner light and by others as feathered serpent rainbow wheels turning in the air. Accompanying the resonant frequency shift, the luminous wave-forms of Quetzalcoatl will re-enter the atmosphere. (Argüelles, 1987:169)

In an afterword to *The Mayan Factor*, Argüelles (221) states that the Harmonic Convergence "depends upon self-empowered individuals creating rituals, celebrations, and joyful events expressing their feelings of peace and harmony with the Earth and with each other."

In evaluating Argüelles's contribution to the New Age Movement and his understanding of "the Mayan Factor," one is confronted once again with a form of scientism. There is an abundance of technical, quasi-scientific terminology, and, in referring to the fundamental postulate of the Mayan Factor ("what light is to life, so the 260-unit Tzolkin is to the 64-unit DNA"), Argüelles (1987:151) makes the questionable assertion that "This postulate *defines* radiogenesis" (emphasis mine). Nevertheless, in so much as any system must be coherent internally and upon its own terms, I would argue that Argüelles's presentation of the Tzolkin's complex design and mathematical intricacy along with its chronological application to human history as well as its correlation with both the I Ching and the DNA genetic code does stand on its own. The real difficulty as I see it, however, lies with its linkage to equivalent Gregorian dates. For instance, the Harmonic Convergence itself is not based on the Mayan calendar but on that of the Aztecs—relating to the arrival of Cortés on Good Friday in 1519. So far, fine, but unfortunately the whole question of Mayan and Aztec intercalation has sharply divided the academic community that has examined it. There are as many scholars who argue that it was ignored by the Central American peoples as there are those who consider that it was practiced. On such an impor-

tant question, however, Argüelles (1987:210) waits until the penultimate paragraph of his fifth and last appendix to include the statement
that "On leap years, there are six instead of five Vayeb" (i.e., extra
days). Even if this were the case, there are internal difficulties that then
apply to the functioning of the Aztec calendar itself.

Nevertheless, almost single-handedly, Argüelles engineered the
worldwide celebration of the Harmonic Convergence (e.g., at Glastonbury Tor in Britain a large crowd including Sir George Trevelyan assembled for "the birth of the New Age"); and, vis-à-vis the New Age
Movement as a whole, Argüelles has emerged as a leading shaper of
thought. He recognizes the role played in the current "awakening" by
the counterculture's "renewed interest in psychic phenomena, UFOs,
psychedelic drugs, interspecies communication, and the ecology movement" (Argüelles, 1987:158). And he sees the "emergence of the psychically unified, media-connected, locally operative planetary society"
(p. 161) as the offspring of the future—one in which there will be semi-
annual, planet- wide Solar/Earth-Day celebrations. "Functioning again
within the context of a greater natural hierarchy, our life will merge the
shaman's environmental resilience with the pageantry of medieval
court life . . . a kingdom in liege to the Sun, and the entire Earth its
single realm" (p. 192). Consequently, despite the questions relating to
the empirical application of Argüelles's analysis, he himself must be
seen as a major formulator of an emerging and popular New Age vision.

## New Age and Christianity

In the broad-spectrum New Age outlook, conventional Christianity
has little place. A transcendental deity separate from mankind is replaced by the immanent God/Goddess/All That Is—found throughout
nature and within each individual. Evangelical Christians, however, see
the New Age God as "a manifestation of Satan" (e.g., McGuire, 1988).
Nevertheless, as Phillip Lucas, religion researcher for the center for the
study of new religious movements at the University of California at
Santa Barbara, points out, both the New Age movement and the Pente-
costal/charismatic revival may be part of the same "Great Awakening"
of spiritual fervor.[59] Both seek guidance from spirits and a direct experience of the sacred, both see the world on the edge of a radical spiritual
transformation, both stress spiritual and physical healing outside medical science, and both arose outside the mainline churches but are now
influencing beliefs and worship within the religious establishment (Lat-

tin, 1989). One interesting observation that McGuire (1988) makes is that although women predominate in the membership of all healing groups, men tend to prevail in the leadership of the Christian groups alone. She also points out that Eastern meditation and human potential groups attract more men than do most other groups, although some psychic/occult groups do have a "substantial proportion of men."

Although conventional Christianity finds little place within the New Age spectrum, Christian ideas and orientations are to be found.[60] We have already noted New Age's metaphysical inheritance of the concept of Jesus Christ as the 'way-shower'. Moreover, its millenarian outlook, especially in the 'teachings' of Ruth Montgomery, Edgar Cayce et al., have been highly colored by ideas contained within the Book of Revelations. More specifically, centers such as the Omega Order and Trust operating from Tunbridge Wells, Kent, in the United Kingdom and founded in 1980, which functions as "both a Contemplative and a teaching Order, operating at a point of intersection between 'the faith once delivered to the Saints' and the essential unity of all Mystics,"[61] seeks to relate "the widespread spiritual awakening"—also known as "New Age Spirituality"—with "the essence of the Catholic faith." Largely administered by clerics, the Order endeavors to develop the "Omega Vision" in terms of the Cosmic Christ and to reconcile within a framework of Christianity the traditional exclusivism of Christian salvation to the growing inclusivistic inclinations toward humanistic holism. Another New Age program is sponsored by St. James Church in Piccadilly, London, and is entitled Alternatives. St. James' rector, the Reverend Donald Reeves, speaks of the need to refer to God as Mother, Friend, and Lover to counteract the stifling years of patriarchal thinking generated by considering God exclusively as a distant, male Father-Judge (lecture, June 19, 1989). These Christian elements in New Age thinking find their greatest champion in the Jesuit priest Pierre Teilhard de Chardin (1881–1955), whose evolutionary philosophy and visionary prophecy have become bedrock ideas of the movement.

The alliance between Christian and New Age thought is an uneasy one at best. Matthew Fox, the Dominican priest and "self-appointed Roman Catholic emissary to the New-Age movement," was officially silenced by the Vatican for a year beginning December 15, 1988. Fox had founded the Institute in Culture and Creation Spirituality in Chicago in 1978. This was moved to the Holy Names College in Oakland, California, in 1983. Strongly influenced by the ideas of Meister Eckhart—if not Teilhard de Chardin as well—Fox's "creation spirituality" teachings are a blend of Christian mysticism, feminism, and environmentalism. Faculty members of the Institute have included a certified masseuse, a yoga instructor, a Zen Buddhist, and the Wiccan leader Starhawk. Fox and other Christian New Age figures like him are seen to be "opening up . . . some churches to the Eastern mysticism and modern paganism of the New-Age movement."[62]

Another prominent Christian New Age figure is, in 1994, the seventy-nine-year old American Catholic monk, Father Thomas Berry, who stresses the sacred and conscious nature of the natural universe. Berry calls for a reverence of all creation and all living creatures—in a word, for a belief in "divine immanence." He rejects the dualistic Biblical view of nature as one of dominance and exploitation. He writes,

> The natural world is the larger sacred community to which we all belong. . . . From its beginning in the galactic system to its earthly expression in human consciousness, the universe carries within itself a psychic as well as a physical dimension.

Berry also criticizes the Judeo-Christian-Islamic emphasis on "redemption out of this world through a personal Savior relationship that eclipses all concerns with cosmic order and process." He furthermore rejects any exclusivistic use of the Bible that does not also find value in the sacred scriptures of Hindus, Buddhists, and Taoists. Religions are complementary, he argues, and each creates its cultural niche in world societal evolution (*Hinduism Today* 11.8, August 1989:3).

## Teilhard de Chardin

In Marilyn Ferguson's survey of "Aquarian Conspirators," Teilhard de Chardin was "the individual most often named as a profound influence" (1987:50). But unlike Matthew Fox, Teilhard fused his modernistic ideas—though still suspect by the Vatican—with a doctrinally pure Christianity.[63] More specifically, he attempted to interpret what he saw as the "ultra-human cosmic future" through an understanding of Christ in an all-embracing total world position structured in terms of evolution and convergence. In Teilhard's vision of anthropogenesis, the resulting neo-humanism consists of one in which love of the world and love of God are fully united and centered on man's earthly tasks.

For Teilhard, the evolution of the cosmos is a movement oriented to a central apex—the Omega point of science, the Christ of Christianity. "Cosmic and Christic consciousness," however, are not viewed as separate but as converging through a fundamental unity and cohesion—culminating in a "divine, personal Omega." For Teilhard, as for many within the New Age movement, there is no conflict between universal evolution and affirmation of a personal God. But the seminal New Age idea to be found in the Jesuit's writings pertains to the evolution of an organic universe in which all its entities are interconnected. Teilhard traces the cosmic eventualizing process of matter, life, and mind as stages in which the "biosphere" or band of life that comes to envelop the world emerges from the "geosphere," which is superseded in turn by a second "envelop"—that of mind (the "noosphere")—which arises from the biosphere. In other words, in Teilhard's "cosmogenesis" of increasing complexity and increasing consciousness, the history of the universe comprises a linear ascent in the build-up of matter, its vitalization, and the hominization of life. But man, through socialization and unification, becomes the turning point in which progress changes from one toward further differentiation to one toward greater unity and concentration. However, whereas Teilhard's Christian New Age vision pictures the whole history of the world in the terms cosmogenesis, biogenesis, noogenesis, and Christogenesis, there are many New Agers who would substitute the last with something like 'theogenesis' and see the cosmic eventualizing process not as convergent and something closed or akin to the American metaphysical tradition's 'return' of the individual divine spark to its Creator, but as 'multivergent' and eternally expansive. Psychic healer Geoff Boltwood calls this last "the infinite journey" ("Spoonbending is a Spiritual Lesson"—lecture given for Alternatives, St. James Church, Piccadilly, London, January 22, 1990).

### Living earth and the worldwide communications network

Apart from the healing aspects of the New Age movement and its American metaphysical inheritance of the idea of the inner divine spark or being, there are two other key elements behind both its belief system and its organizational structure. Both are to be linked with ideas contained in chemist James Lovelock's "Gaia Hypothesis" (Lovelock, 1979). With his conjecture that the planet Earth is a complete and self-regulating system and, along with its inhabitants, comprises a single, living organism, the key idea of New Age holism is established. In addition, current chaos and quantum chaos theories are thought to reinforce the notion of evolution in conscious intelligence. This parallels, according to Lovelock, the evolution of technology: telecommunication networks, and information processing. William Bloom, in his St. James March 20, 1989, talk, refers to this last as "an information age, the beginning of a planetary network, . . . an age of synergy." He considers that this will become "as profound, as dynamic, as anything that happened in the industrial revolution or pastoral revolution." With the world network growing at an unprecedented rate ("worldwide computer power doubles every three years and will continue to do so until about 2000"—*i-D* 75, Nov. 1989:21), a technical basis alone is being established for the expected and extreme shift in consciousness that comprises the New Age with its millennial overtones.

## Conclusion

To conclude this chapter on the New Age, much of the foregoing can be found summarized in William Bloom (1991:xvi-xvii), who sees the phenomenon as "a mass movement" of people who are reasserting their "right to explore spirituality in total freedom." For Bloom, the New Age consists of recognizing "an invisible and inner dimension to all life"—with the task before us as individuals and collectivities of exploring this "inner reality." He sees four major fields comprised by the movement: (1) "New Paradigm/New Science," from which emerges the concept of an interconnection among all life as well as a new assessment of health and the human body, (2) "Ecology," which, through interdependence and interpenetration, accepts responsibility for the total planetary state, (3) "New Psychology," which stresses, through releasing the unconscious, the "supraconscious," and the "transpersonal," that "*all* people are capable of becoming integrated, fulfilled and completely loving human beings" (xvii), and (4) "Spiritual Dynamics"—a product of honouring all esoteric, mystic, and religious wisdom traditions including gnostic Christianity, the Jewish Qabalah, Sufi, Zen, and other Buddhist meditation techniques as well as such native traditions as that of the North American Indian, Australian Aborigine, African medicine people, and Celtic Europe (both Wiccan and Druidic).

Bloom's picture of the New Age is that which is most cogently expressed in Britain through the Alternatives Programme of St. James' Piccadilly, the Findhorn Community, the Lucis Trust, and the Open Gate,[64] but he stresses the freedom of the individual to trust himself/herself and his/her intuition in exploring the inner reality. Claiming that New Age attitudes are the antithesis of fundamentalism, Bloom argues that a common theme to be found in all inner awareness is the dawning of a "New Age" in which human consciousness is to undergo a cosmically significant transformation. He sees that "the New Age movement in all its various facets, gives us maps, insights, friends, techniques, inspiration and strength in our exploration of the inner world" (Bloom, 1991:xviii).

Finally, Lowell Streiker (1990:10) pictures two kinds of New Age phenomena: the "left hand" or "ecstatic" New Age of gurus, channelers, psychics, Witches, crystal healers, and other visionaries; and the "right hand" or "social transformationist" New Age "of ecology, social conscience, feminism, responsible investing, and compassion for all creatures." Although the media and the ecstatics have tended to preempt the "New Age" term as suggestive of a fad, Streiker feels it is something more than this despite a possibly eventual rejection of the expressions "New Age" and "Aquarian" as viable labels. The orientation that Streiker has come to understand as New Age includes spiritual ecology, reflection, androgynous balance, ecstasy, life-affirmation, and death-denial, tolerance both of the mainstream and of itself (including its own con artists and manipulators), pantheism instead of theism, transformation instead of reformation, and xenophilia instead of xenophobia (Streiker, 1990:51–54).

## Notes

1. This usage contrasts with the more restrictive definition of the American metaphysical tradition used by Judah (1967), Wagner (1983) et al. For the distinction between the *paramount reality* of the common-sense world with its set of various mental subuniverses and the "exotic paramount reality" of the various worlds of occult lore in which "the world of common sense becomes a limited truth or an illusion to be overcome," see Stupple (1975a). New Age tends to oscillate between both positions, or, rather, various factions within New Age appear to exalt one position over the other.

2. The background sources for New Age thinking are to be found in such works as Bailey (1948), Brooke (1976), Burr (1972 and 1975), Das (1966), Dowling (1907), Hall (1937), Heline (1943), Parker and St. John (1957), Sinclair (1984), and Vaughn (1967). See further, Judah (1967).

3. "Meditation on 30 years of TM," *USA Today*, August 17, 1989.

4. Various New Age proponents and themes are to be discerned through the following works: Academy of Parapsychology (1972), Allen (1978), Arguëlles (1987), Bartley (1978), Castaneda (1968), Clark (1972), Dass (1971, 1976, 1978, 1979), Dezavalle (1976), Ferguson (1980/1987), Funderburk (1977),

Gaskin (1974, 1976), Grad (1970), Haglet (1978), Inglis (1969), Joy (1978), Keyes (1972/1975, 1982), Kirpalvand (1977), Krishna (1971), Lande (1976), MacLaine (1987), Mann (1976), Meyer (1976), Motoyama (1981), Nofziger (1976), Orr and Ray (1983), Oyle (1976), Perkins (1976), Perrone (1983), Popenoe and Popenoe (1984), Rama et al. (1976), Regush (1977), Rosenblum (1974, 1976), Rudhyar (1975, 1983), Satin (1979), Spangler (1975, 1976, 1977), Tart (1972, 1975), White (1972), White and Krippner (1977), and Wilber (1977).

5. Tripura Swami in *"Clarion Call,* a Classy New Journal from S. F. Gaudiyas," *Hinduism Today* 10.9 (October 1988):13.

6. The Gaudiya Vaishnava Society (GVS) is a breakaway movement from ISKCON proclaimed by Tripura Swami sometime after 1975 (see ibid.) Its center is in San Francisco. Gaudiya Vaishnavism itself is the Hindu sampradaya or school of thought founded by Chaitanya (1486–1534 C.E.), focusing on Krishna and a theistic interpretation of divine reality.

7. *Be Here Now* (San Christobal, N. M.: Lama Foundation, 1971); *The Only Dance There Is* (New York: Jason Aronson, 1973); *Grist for the Mill* (1976); *Journey of Awakening* (New York: Bantam, 1978); *Miracle of Love* (New York: E. P. Dutton, 1979); *How Can I Help?*(New York: Knopf, 1985).

8. E.g., *Discipleship in the New Age*—Vol. I (1944), Vol. II (1955); *The Reappearance of the Christ* (1948) ["During the coming century, . . . the new age will begin to reveal its deep purpose and intention" (p. 22)]; *Education in the New Age* (1954); etc. However, earlier appearances of the term are also known. Since approximately 1900, the Supreme Council, 33 degrees, Ancient and Accepted Scottish Rite of Freemasonry of the Southern Jurisdiction has published a monthly journal entitled *The New Age Magazine.* In 1940, occult writer Corinne Heline founded her quarterly magazine, the *New Age Interpreter.* See Jay Kinney's "The New Age: Is it really so new after all?" in *The San Francisco Chronicle* (March 15, 1989).

9. David Spangler, "Defining the New Age," *The New Age Catalogue* (New York: Doubleday, 1988).

10. Other works by Spangler include *Festivals for the New Age* (Forres, Scotland: Findhorn Foundation, 1975), and *Towards a Planetary Vision* (Findhorn Foundation, 1977).

11. In Sandra Matuschka, "A Course in Miracles: Panacea for Mankind?" *Body, Mind, and Spirit* (August 1989) p. 187.

12. Ari L. Goldman, "Searching for the Holy Grail at an Adult Healing Camp," *The New York Times* (August 21, 1989) p. B1.

13. Katie Saunders, "All You Need Is Self-Love," *The Sunday Times* of London (October 29, 1989) p. F1.

14. McGuire (1988), extracted as "The new spirituality: healing rituals hit the suburbs" in *Psychology Today*, January/February 1989:57–64. McGuire identified more than 130 different groups of healers and then, through participation-observation, intensively studied some groups within each of the five broad

healing types for ten to eighteen months, visiting others occasionally. Two hundred fifty-five sessions in thirty-one groups were observed and recorded in total. This was supplemented through more than 300 one- to three-hour open-ended interviews of leaders, healers, adherents, and clients as well as "a number of non-adherents selected from comparable neighborhoods and matched for gender and age" (p. 58).

15. See further, John Harricharan's article "Spirituality and prosperity," in *Body, Mind & Spirit*, August 1989:26, 28, and 47, which states that "we are all spiritual beings conceived with the inalienable right to be prosperous." Citing Foster Hibbard, "Peter, the Magic Man of Mystic Mountain" as well as Sanaya Roman and Duane Packer (channelers of entities entitled Orin and DaBen), Harricharan mentions guilt, fear, and lack of self-esteem as prime reasons for experiencing a lack of money.

16. However, during an interview that took place at Big Sur on May 14, 1991, Esalen manager Brian Lyke admitted that he was "much more comfortable" with the suggestion of Esalen as the "granddaddy" of the HPM than of New Age.

17. Responses were located geographically as 22 percent Northeast, 20 percent Southeast, 23 percent North Central, 9 percent South Central, 7 percent Mountain, and 19 percent Western. Other results from this survey are included in Chapter 6.

18. For comparison purposes, according to *Religion in America 1971*, Gallup Opinion Index, April 1971, Report No. 70, 98 percent of Americans believe in a God. On the other hand, 85 percent of Americans believe in heaven; 65 percent in hell (Gallup Opinion Index, February 1969).

19. T. George Harris, "Mysticism Goes Mainstream," *Psychology Today* (Jan./Feb. 1989:64).

20. In its listing of ninety-three New Age newsletters/magazines, the 1986/87 edition of *The Whole Again Resource Guide* edited by Tim Ryan and Patricia J. Case (Santa Barbara, Calif.: SourceNet [Capra Press]), sixty-seven are U.S. publications (twenty-seven of these originating in California), eight are British, four Australian, three West German, two Canadian, two Argentinian, and one each from New Zealand, Denmark, Sweden, Italy, Switzerland, Spain, and Mexico.

21. When asked on the basis of whatever the individual knows about *New Age*, how would he or she characterize it, nine respondents described it as generally positive; eight as generally negative.

22. Five people described New Age as generally positive; one said "neither" positive or negative; two answered with a "don't know"; and three ignored the question altogether.

23. In comparing these to American figures, note that Wuthnow (1976:31) in 1976 gave what he considered "highly unreliable estimates" for those trained in TM (over 350,000), those processed by 3HO (200,000), and Meher Baba followers (approximately 7,000).

24. For a range of conservative New Age movement critics, see Alexander (1978), Burrows (1984–85), Cumbey (1983), Halverson (1984–85), Hunt (1983), Kaslow and Sussman (1982), Michaelson (1982), and Reisser, Reisser, and Weldon (1983). See further, Lewis (1991).

25. For the growing use of the 'new age' label in a biased, derogatory sense, see Duncan Campbell's article entitled ''The rise of the new age pill pushers'' in *The Correspondent Magazine* (3 December 1989), p. 18. The New Age concept is also becoming an increasing target for theatrical satire. For example, the performance of *Gland Motel* by the Bloolips in London's Drill Hall Arts Centre (January 9–February 3, 1990) includes the 'astral plane' as its location along with such characters as Madame Blavatsky and Twirly McLaine.

26. On the other hand, Eugene Lin (in ''Quantum Leaps,'' *Body, Mind, Spirit*, August 1989:24, 48f) argues that contemporary quantum theory actually supports the mind-body dualism, which is required for the existence of psychic phenomena.

27. Stupple (1975b:901) mentions that other ''neo-theosophical groups'' deriving essentially from Blavatsky's Theosophy, beside I AM, include ''Alice Bailey's Arcane School, Robert and Earlyne Chaney's Astara Foundation, Dr. M. Doreal's Brotherhood of the White Temple, George King's Aetherius Society, and Mark and Elizabeth Prophet's Summit Lighthouse.''

28. See in particular Melton (1986b:135–40) and Stupple (1975b). Also various media articles such as Chance Connor ''Montana Cult Makes Neighbors Uneasy,'' *USA Today* (August 11, 1989); Michael P. Harris ''Paradise Under Siege,'' *Time Magazine* (August 28, 1989).

29. Peter Clarke, in personal communication, sees this description conforming to a cross between Wilson's revolutionist and reformist sects.

30. See further Melton's ''A History of the New Age Movement'' in Basil (1988). See also Melton, Clark, and Kelly (1990:xxx).

31. Other Eastern meditational movements in the West that are not identified as New Age—either by themselves or others—include ISKCON, Ananda Marga, the Shri Chinmoy Center (New York), Swami Satchidananda's Integral Yoga Institute, the Sathya Sai Baba organization, the Sivananda Yoga Vedanta Center in Canada, and Nichiren Shoshu (Soka Gakkai).

32. Ron Hubbard's earlier *Dianetics: The Modern Science of Mental Health*, reprinted in 1985 by Bridge Publications (Los Angeles), is advertised in the 1988 edition of *The New Age Catalogue*.

33. According to Young (1987:133), the *est* Training developed by Erhard ''may be referred to as 'consciousness raising' and is considered to be part of 'The New Age' movement, or The Human Potential Movement, although participants do not generally refer to these terms, nor do they appreciate categorization.''

34. Young (1987:132) assigns *est* to ''a family in which Arica, Assertiveness Training, Actualizations, Gestalt Therapy and several other psychologically oriented groups belong.'' These, as well as Lifespring, Relationships, Self-Trans-

formations, the Church of the Movement for Inner Spiritual Awareness/Insight and others, are what Paul Heelas terms "self-religions." For an investigation and analysis of Exegesis, an *est* derivative, see Heelas (1987).

35. The *est* Training was discontinued in 1984 and replaced a month later by The Forum, which is less structured, and now lasts only fifty hours, and stresses intragroup spontaneity in identifying specific social, cultural, and environmental problems (Young, 1987:141). The Forum was introduced at a cost of £465 ($750).

36. See also Simon (1978), who observed among his patients 61 percent who evidenced some positive response to *est* in terms of "predefined psychodynamics and treatment goals." He concludes that "where motivation and readiness for change are present in a patient with good ego strength, est appears often to assert a strong influence toward a psychotherapeutic type of movement" (p. 691).

37. According to Monica Sjoo, "Some Thoughts About the New Age Movement," *Wood and Water* 2.28 (Summer 1989), p. 6, "With incredible smugness and cynicism, New Age white Americans, who live in the world's most powerful and exploitative imperialist and warmongering nation, say that people dying in the Third World from hunger and diseases chose to do so because this is the lesson they needed to learn in this life. According to this 'logic' a Black child in detention in South Africa created the reality of Apartheid and women living in patriarchal societies chose to be raped, physically abused and oppressed. . . . The Rebirthers even say that if one becomes ill or dies this is a 'sin against God'."

38. Bry (1976:109) explains that "people give their best efforts to *est*, . . . out of the intense focus, discipline, and caring of staff and volunteers has come an incredibly tight, efficient, and effective business." She also points out "the directness characteristic of *est*-ers (a graduate can be known by his direct eye contact)" as well as the attention to detail that has been a significant factor in *est*'s success (101f).

39. In 1978, Simon (1978:691) could report that over 125,000 people had completed the *est* training. Young (1987:132) claims that more than a half million people (including 6,000 Britons) have completed at least "The Basic Training, The Communications Workshop, or The Forum." She adds that "If all groups under the auspices of The Network are accounted, Erhard's enterprise has a following of over one million people." Young identifies Area Centers in most American states, in Canada, Mexico, Brazil, the United Kingdom, Ireland, France, The Netherlands, (West) Germany, Israel, Nigeria, Kenya, India, and Australia.

40. Another name that might be associated with the 'occult' might be the Spiritual Frontiers Fellowship's co-founder Arthur Ford. However, "People may be attracted to SFF or to a study group initially because they are interested in the psychic, but their interest usually shifts to spiritual growth." In fact, Wagner (1983:143) finds that people who are only interested in occult/psychic phenomena will soon 'drop out' of the SFF study group.

41. The A.R.E., Inc. in Virginia Beach, Virginia has available for study 14,256 copiously indexed and cross-indexed readings "consisting of 49,135 pages of verbatim psychic material plus related correspondence."

42. Likewise, "All healing comes from the divine within, that is creative. Thus, if one would correct physical or mental disturbances, it is necessary to change the attitude and to let the life forces become constructive and not destructive. Hate, malice, and jealousy only create poisons within the minds, souls, and bodies of people" (3312–1). As the "father of holistic medicine," Cayce's preoccupation with healing is revealed in that nearly 8,000 of the more than 14,000 readings (often referred to as the "physical" readings) relate to the subject of diet, disease, and preventive medicine. In the 'Caycean' system of thought, before a cure is attempted—including the opening of the seven glands or motivational centers of the endocrine system (identified as the seven spiritual centers as well as the seven seals of Revelation) — one must first set the spiritual ideal before any application of drugs, hypnosis, breathing exercises, or other specialized meditation or inner awareness techniques.

43. "As he has given, it will ever be found that Truth whether in this or that schism or ism or cult—is of the One Source. . . . Then, all will fill their place. Find not fault with *any* . . ." (254–87).

44. "Coordinate the teachings, the philosophies of the East and the West, the oriental and the occidental, the new truths and the old. . . . Correlate not the differences, but where all religions meet—THERE IS ONE GOD! 'Know, O Israel, the Lord thy God is *ONE!*' . . . Christ is not a man; Jesus was the man, Christ the messenger. Christ in all ages, Jesus in one, Joshua in another, Melchizedek in another" (991–1).

45. In SFF terminology, "Prayer is talking to God. Meditation is listening to God" (Wagner, 1983:48).

46. This idea is also stressed by Britain's "grandfather of the New Age Movement," Sir George Trevelyan. During a St. James' Alternatives talk (February 12, 1990), Trevelyan's main thrust was his "absolute certainty" that "the I AM means there can be no death." "Since we are all part of the one great conscious being which is humanity, we do not need to be frightened of change or death."

47. To my knowledge, there has been no acknowledged influence from Scientology on Montgomery's thinking.

48. Or "it may occur in July, September, or October of 1999" (Montgomery and Garland, 1986:233).

49. On the other hand, Australia, New Zealand, and the Bahamas will greatly increase in size. The 'relatively safe areas' include the large land masses away from the sea in the United States (save for the area between the Great Lakes and the Mississippi River), Canada, Russia, Siberia, Africa, and China.

50. "True, some will survive who are not fit to exist in the New Age, but . . . they will soon die off . . ." (p. 268). Otherwise, the guides assure Montgomery that the evil souls will be 'overcome, subdued and banished from polite society'.

51. The psychic astrologer Frederick Von Mieners considers that Ruth Montgomery, like the "great Yogi-Christs of India," has popularized the sacred ideals of universal religion, i.e., the message of the East among Western peoples (Montgomery and Garland, 1986:12f).

52. In Anthony's revised and extended typology (Anthony, Ecker, and Wilber, 1987:355), Montgomery's New Ageism would be classified as 'unilevel monism'. Referring to "the great 'Aquarian Conspiracy'," the authors claim that the unilevel monist groups "continue the covertly dualist strategy of basing their revolutionary status upon their claim to be the natural antithesis to the hegemony of mainstream objectivism" [the externalistic values of the "cultureof role"] which in fact is "a hegemony that no longer exists."

53. Compare the answer given by Ruth Montgomery's guides about the current epidemic of AIDS: "As for AIDS, it is one of the seven ancient plagues of the testaments, and has returned to devastate the population of the earth. It is a virus that has been brought back into being by man's evil ways and discordant thought, and until humanity reverses its downhill plunge, it will continue to infuse and plague the population. . . . AIDS will still be around until the shift cleanses the earth and humankind" (Montgomery, 1986:259).

54. In presenting a capsule summary about a spiritual entity called Lazaris (channeled through the San Francisco trance medium Jach Pursel), MacLaine delineates a basic *est*-ian stance as well: Lazarus "taught that the universe is an extremely successful place—it is man whose perceptions have veiled the truth. Lazaris taught that mankind's natural proclivity was to be in harmony . . . that just to *be* was the goal and secret to happiness. That was why nature was the ultimate teacher" (p. 18).

55. This part of MacLaine's beliefs and pursuits, however, has generated a large degree of controversy. One former fan with whom I spoke had read all her works until *Dancing In The Light* in which, for him, her credibility rating dropped totally. "She has always been a princess," he explained, "never simply a peasant."

56. Montgomery (1986:232) cites a 1981 Gallup poll "surveying the religious attitudes of adults in the United States [which] indicated that 23 percent embraced the concept of reincarnation, and among Catholics the rate was 25 percent. This would mean that at least thirty-eight million American adults hold such a view, many incorporating it within their own religious faith."

57. This attitude is similar to the conversionist response to evil. See e.g., Wilson, 1969:364f., 1967:15f and 1973:22f.

58. "And because I was in the eye of the hurricane of the rapidly developing metaphysical movement, I and my endorsement would be a prized trophy. It was indeed a lot like Hollywood studios. Each was creative, knowledgeable, accomplished, and useful, *and* each dealt with the stuff dreams are made of. There was no way to choose. I loved them all" (MacLaine, 1987:62f).

59. In this connection, Wuthnow (1976:196) appears to argue for a link between evangelical fundamentalism and liberal New Age thought when he says

that "The uncertainties inherent in times of unrest and experimentation and the costs inevitably associated with bringing about social improvements provide powerful incentives to the emergence of reactionary nostalgia and to compulsive loyalty to any symbol of strong unifying leadership no matter how retrogressive such leadership may prove in the long run." Nevertheless, from the obsolete vantage point of 1976, Wuthnow (212) added further that "The grand vision of community at a national or even international level that was so important to the early Puritans or even the Social Darwinists is not a part of the current counter-culture, except perhaps in some vague notions of a miraculous Aquarian Age."

60. One example of the fusion of Christian and New Age ideas is to be found in the short-lived *The Eye of Gaza: A New Age Journal* with strong links to Glastonbury. In its first issue (1.1. n.d.), editor Greg Branson argues that while many people will work within "lost traditions" such as the Greek mysteries, Solomon's Temple structure, or Druidic forms, "Some people for karmic reasons will choose to work within existing structures, the orthodox Christian tradition for example." In fact, "The papacy will be one focus for the channelling of the power that can transmute the cross of Jesus that man might know the spirit and material as one" (pp. 2f.). He calls upon Pope John Paul II to "open up the way for the New Age Pope who will follow, the last in the line because the church as we know it will become redundant in some fifty or so years."

61. From the "Omega Residential School of Spiritual Studies: September 1988–June 1990," p. 3.

62. See the articles by Don Lattin, "Vatican Gags New-Age Priest From Oakland" (October 18, 1988) and "Showdown Between Vatican and Priest" (October 19, 1988) in the *San Francisco Chronicle*. According to Daniel Cohen (*Wood and Water* 2.27, Spring Equinox 1989:3), "The English contact for [Matthew Fox's] approach is at St. James's Church, Piccadilly, London." Cohen adds that "His views, though not necessarily the details of their expression, are likely to appeal to pagans. . . ." Fox gave four talks at St. James' on the 1st, 2nd (part of the Alternatives program), 4th, and 5th of July, 1990.

63. See N. M. Wilders, *An Introduction to Teilhard de Chardin* (London: William Collins Sons & Co., 1968)—especially pp. 18f., 24f. *et passim.*

64. The Open Gate: 6 Goldney Road, Clifton, Bristol BS8 4RB (tel. 0272–734952). The Lucis Trust is headquartered in the United Kingdom at Suite 54, 3 Whitehall Court, London SW1A 2EF (tel. 071–839 4512). The address for the Findhorn Community is The Park, Findhorn, Forres IV36 0TZ, Scotland (Cluny Hill tel. 0309–72288); that for St. James's Piccadilly is St. James's Church, 197 Piccadilly, London W1V 9LF (tel. 071–734 4511).

*Chapter 3*

# The Neo-pagan Movement

Interconnecting with the New Age movement is the contemporary Neo-pagan movement. Many New Agers do not consider themselves Neo-pagan, and likewise, not all Neo-pagan groups identify with the New Age. Nevertheless, there is an emerging overlap between the two phenomena, and increasingly paganism is becoming recognized along with both Eastern mysticism/human potential and the theosophical-occult/spiritualist-psychic/new thought metaphysics mix as one of the main constituents within New Age (e.g., Spangler, 1988:*xi*). However, the modern Neo-pagan movement, which is to be found in many of the same countries as the New Age movement is perhaps at least as eclectic and heterogeneous as the New Age.[1] A lucid and comprehensive account of the movement as a whole is furnished by Margot Adler (1986).

## Neo-pagan representatives

### Margot Adler

When asked the question, "What advice would you give a newcomer in Paganism if s/he asked you for counsel on 'getting started' in Paganism?" the fifty-seven respondents participating in the Pagan Spirit Alliance Newsletter, issue 32 (Winter 1988–89) edged Margot Adler's *Drawing Down the Moon* over Starhawk's *The Spiral Dance* (eight times to seven) as the most frequently suggested book to read. Currently among the most popular texts about pagan religions, in particular Neo-paganism in America today,[2] this book is "easily understood" and is "particularly valuable because it is the only extended description of groups generally ignored." Through use of questionnaires, interviews,

correspondence, and extensive visiting of pagan groups across the
United States, Alfred Adler's granddaughter investigates modern Neo-
paganism and Witchcraft as expressions of a "radical polytheism"
("the view that reality is multiple and diverse") and related theologies.
The author discovers these religions as contemporary Western attempts
to create highly ritualized but almost invariably non-authoritarian and
non-dogmatic religions. Through the use of ceremony as well as ecstatic
techniques, Neo-paganism and Witchcraft differ from such other anti-
authoritarian faiths as liberal Christianity or Unitarianism.

In Adler's understanding, the modern pagan movement does not include Eastern religious groups, Christians, or Satanists. It does include
the feminist goddess-worshippers, new religions inspired by the imagi-
nations of science-fiction writers, the surviving tribal religions, and the
revivalist attempts to re-formulate the ancient European religions (those
of the Norse, Celts, Romans, Greeks, etc.). The various groups that have
evolved from this heterogeneous movement

> are often self-created and *homemade*; they seldom have 'gurus' or 'mas-
> ters'; they have few temples and hold their meetings in woods, parks,
> apartments, and houses; in contrast to most organized cults, money seldom
> passes from hand to hand and the operations of high finance are nonexis-
> tent; and entry into these groups comes through a process that could rarely
> be called 'conversion'. (Adler, 1986:3)

Despite their many differences from one another, these religious groups
invariably regard each other as belonging to the same religious and
philosophical movement.

Using a definition of religion as "any set of symbolic forms and acts
that relate human beings to ultimate conditions of existence, cosmic
questions, and universal concerns," Adler (1986:11) suggests that the
religious movement which includes people designating themselves as
Pagans, Neo-Pagans, or Witches often inescapably intersects with the
ecology movement, the feminist movement, the libertarian tradition, the
visionary tradition, and the artistic tradition as much as it does with
"occult" phenomena themselves. With regard to this last,

> Many Neo-Pagan Witches, and Neo-Pagans generally, see themselves as
> modern-day heirs to the ancient mystery traditions of Egypt, Crete, Eleu-
> sis, and so on, as well as to the more popular peasant traditions of celebra-
> tory festivals and seasonal rites. (Adler, 1986:11)

In fact, these groups are "occult" often only insofar as they are concerned with "hidden or obscure forms of knowledge not generally ac-

cepted,'' while many groups pursue a celebratory path more than a magical or occult one.

Adler (1986:4f) perceives that the 1960s counterculture and its accompanying psychedelic movement has largely given way to authoritarian and ascetic but well-financed religious groups such as the Unification Church or ISKCON, but the original ''visionary, 'neo-sacral', 'neo-transcendental' movement which joined a mystic view of the cosmos to a counterculture life style and worldly politics'' has instead resurfaced in the Neo-pagan movement. The religious framework of this last, being pluralistic and thereby allowing differing perspectives and ideas to co-exist, may be most generally characterized as animistic (viewing vitality inherent in all things), pantheistic (viewing the divine as inseparable from and immanent in nature), and—especially— polytheistic (viewing reality as comprising multiplicity and diversity) (Adler, 1986:25).

Adler considers various analyses of paganism ranging from those of Theodore Roszak (if there is an idolatry, it is ''the religion of the single vision''), James Hillman (a Jungian proponent of ''polytheistic psychology''), David Miller (the ''death of God'' concept is an expression for the end of one-dimensional ''monotheistic'' domination of Western culture and thought; polytheism is an affirmation of ''the radical plurality of the self'') to William Hamilton (''the gods'' are ''to be used to give shape to an increasingly complex and variegated experience of life'') as well as such critics as H. Richard Niebuhr (a social polytheism is the central problem of modern society that entertains such conflicting value centers as money, power, and sex), Harold Moss (Greco-Roman polytheism is not a suitable framework for today), and Robert Ellwood (polytheism is fundamentally antipolitical and antisocial, unable to foster social cohesion or increase multiple options except privately).

Adler (1986:33) counters the critics by admitting that ''Certainly one would have to agree that Neo-Paganism is a minority vision, struggling amidst the major trend toward authoritarian cults,'' but though its structures may change, the basic pagan community remains. In striking similarity to the New Age movement's structure or lack of structure, ''practicing Neo-Pagans'' ''say that communities formed for mutual aid and sustenance should break apart when those needs no longer exist, or are met in different ways.'' Adler contends that the only real question is whether such loosely based communities can survive for more than one generation, though she acknowledges a recent trend within the movement toward establishing legal recognition for various institutionalized pagan organizations. Nevertheless, Adler (1986:220) confirms that ''academics . . . have judged, rightly, that the Neo-Pagan scene is even more fluid than the general situation pertaining to 'cults'.''

As a "tentative conclusion," Adler (1986:37) suggests that Neo-pagans are "an elite of sorts . . . those few who, by chance, circumstance, fortune, and occasionally struggle, have escaped certain forms of enculturation." She cites Alison Harlow's comment that the "recognition that everyone has different experiences is a fundamental keystone to Paganism" (p. 36). In fact, polytheism is said always to include monotheism, although the reverse is not true, and within the pagan movement, Witchcraft (Wicca, the Craft) might be more accurately described as a form of 'duotheism' with its almost exclusive focus upon the Goddess and her consort, whereas feminist Witches (e.g., the School of Wicca, Sharon Devlin) are often simply monotheists. This last also applies to followers of the Church of Aphrodite, whereas adherents to the Sabaean Religious Order espouse a henotheism as the culmination of a sequence that progresses through atheism, pantheism, polytheism, and monotheism before beginning all over again.

A general conclusion Adler appears to reach, however, is that for many contemporary Neo-pagans, belief is an incidental aspect of their religion that comprises instead techniques and practice and, most of all, an attitude toward life—a way of living. It is a religion based on what is *done* rather than what is *believed*. Accordingly, a basic and informal anarchism prevails in Wicca and Neo-paganism in general. Truth is never more than a metaphor. One can worship the gods or the Goddess without believing in them. Especially in Witchcraft and related forms of pagan shamanism, experience prevails over belief or belief-systems, and this experience centers on "altered states of consciousness" as well as intense feelings of ecstasy and joy. In short, "most Witches and Neo-Pagans do not link 'magic' with the 'supernatural' . . . Those who do magic are those who work with techniques that alter consciousness in order to facilitate psychic activity" (Adler, 1986:154). In her researches, Adler (p. 106) finds that "Most Witches stressed that the goal of the Craft was helping people reclaim their lost spiritual heritage, their affinity with the earth, with 'the gods', with the infinite." This objective could be experiential, pragmatic, self-developmental, or ecological, but within the Neo-pagan movement as a whole there nevertheless exists an implicit agreement to disagree.

A significant clarification made by the author through tracing the evolution of modern Neo-paganism via the works of Margaret Murray, Charles G. Leland, Robert Graves, Gerald B. Gardner, and Doreen Valiente is that "Today most revivalist Witches in North America accept the universal Old Religion more as a metaphor than as a literal reality" (Adler, 1986:86). In other words, the Murrayite thesis that Witchcraft is a religion dating to paleolithic times and founded upon worship of the god of the hunt and the goddess of fertility—a religion that went underground in the Middle Ages with the persecutions fostered by the Roman Catholic Church—is largely a fiction, albeit a strongly influential one in stimulating the contemporary revival of Wicca. In fact,

> Modern Wicca, while retaining the use of such terms as *esbat, sabbat* and *coven*, bears no resemblance to the European witchcraft that the scholars have discussed. There are no beliefs in Satan, no pacts, no sacrifices, no infanticide, no cannibalism, and often not even any sex. (Adler, 1986:56)

And in discussing the Craft version promulgated by Gardner, which sees Witchcraft as "a peaceful, happy nature religion," Adler presents the views of Aidan Kelly (a founder of the New Reformed Orthodox Order of the Golden Dawn), which dismiss as unimportant whether or not Gardner had "traditional information" or instead borrowed various concepts through his extensive readings. These concepts were transformed "so thoroughly that he instituted a major religious reform—that is, . . . he founded a new religion . . ." (Adler, 1986:81).

The participation figures behind this "new religion" or "new religious movement" founded essentially by Gardner is difficult to assess. "Since the Craft is so decentralized, since each coven is autonomous, there is no way to compile accurate statistics" (Adler, 1986:107f.).[3] Adler concludes that in the United States probably no more than 10,000 people identify with the broad Neo-pagan phenomenon, which includes subscriptions to its journals and newsletters or affiliation to its covens, groves, and other groups.[4] Nevertheless, there may be many other groups and individuals who have no formal links with the Neo-pagan movement.

Adler (1986:311) also contests J. Gordon Melton's claim that most Neo-pagans are ex-Catholics and, secondly, ex-Jews. Melton had postulated that the high use of ritual in Neo-paganism appealed to both the Jew and Catholic whose original traditions are strongly ceremonial, but for Adler "in my own experience in the Neo-Pagan movement, there are equal numbers of ex-Catholics and Protestants, with a smaller number of Jews. I also found many who had been deprived of any religious rituals as children."

Perhaps more important than the questionable accuracy concerning the numbers who identify as pagans and witches or the mainstream traditions from which they come is Adler's delineation of the various sects or modern Craft traditions. These may be understood as "traditionalist Wicca'' (e.g., Welsh, Scots, Irish, Greek traditionalist); Gardnerian (covens using Gardnerian rituals; or United States covens, which descend in a line of ''apostolic succession'' from Gardner's Isle of Man coven); Alexandrian (descending from the coven established by Alex Sanders in the United Kingdom); Algard (a combined Gardnerian-Alexandrian tradition instituted in the United States by Mary Nesnick); NROOGD (the New Reformed Orthodox Order of the Golden Dawn, which presents recreations of the Eleusinian Mysteries); Georgian (an eclectic revivalist tradition founded by George Patterson of Bakersfield, California); Dianic (essentially monotheistic Goddess worship that includes both feminist Craft and Morgan McFarland's Dianic Covenstead tradition, which does not exclude men from the worship); and the School of Wicca (worshipping one deity without gender).

Adler also uses Isaac Bonewits's breakdown of ''classical'' witches (the traditional witch), ''neo-classical'' (today's equivalent of the ''classical'' witch and identified through use of magic, divination, herbology and extrasensory perception with little regard for religion per se), ''gothic'' (''a Church fiction'' covering those persecuted between 1450 and 1750—perhaps including contemporary Satanism inasmuch as it descends from the gothic witchcraft created by Christianity), ''familial'' (the family traditions) as well as ''immigrant,'' ''ethnic,'' ''feminist,'' and ''neo-pagan.'' Bonewits estimates that approximately 70 percent of the American witches are in fact ''neo-classical.'' Adler prefers the term ''Neo-Pagan''—''the revival, or re-creation, or new creation (depending on your viewpoint) of a Neo-Pagan nature religion that calls itself Witchcraft, or Wicca, or the Craft, or the Old Religion(s)'' (Adler, 1986:42). She nevertheless concedes that ''each coven radiates its own identity, which often has nothing to do with the supposed 'tradition' it follows or with the particular rituals it performs'' (p. 113). Moreover, in 1986, an anti-fragmentation trend appeared well under way in which many English traditional covens (e.g., Gardnerian, Alexandrian, Algard, Georgian, Kingstone, Majestic, and Silver Crescent) were beginning to join together. One such fused English traditional Wicca group is the New Wiccan Church.

''Outside of the various Witchcraft traditions, the most prevalent forms of Neo-Paganism are groups that attempt to re-create ancient European pre-Christian religions'' (Adler, 1986:233). Adler discusses a large selection of these pagan reconstructionists: the Church of Aphrodite (the first U.S. reconstructionist Neo-pagan organization, established in 1938), Feraferia (a doctrinal mystery religion based on the processes of nature worshipped as ''a family of Gods issuing from a cluster of

Goddesses''), Dancers of the Sacred Circle (a Feraferian offshoot), the Sabaean Religious Order (focusing on "ritual art" as a fusion of Basque, Yoruba, Sumerian, and Babylonian traditions), the Church of the Eternal Source (a federation of Egyptian cults), and the Norse paganism groups (the neo-Nazi and largely political Odinist Fellowship; the more religious but still patriarchal and conservative Asatru Free Assembly; the more spiritual, ecological, and open Heathen Way in San Francisco, etc). The author (1986:308) also includes chapters on the futuristic, perhaps New Age, Church of All Worlds, which, "like Feraferia, sees Neo-Paganism as a response to a planet in crisis''; the religions emerging from the "paradox and play tradition'': the Reformed Druids of North America; the New Reformed Druids of North America; Isaac Bonewits's *Ar nDraiocht Fein*; and the Discordian Society and its offshoots, the Paratheoanametamystikhood of Eris Esoteric and the Erisian Liberation Front; and men's spirituality in the forms of Brothers of the Earth and the Radical Faeries. In her update of her original 1979 edition, Adler (1986:282) states that

> Wiccan organizations have come to the foreground as the primary form of Neo-Paganism in America, [nevertheless] the reason the Pagan movement in the United States is so rich and varied and presents such a unique perspective to the world is primarily because of the non-Wiccan influences that were so dominant in earlier years.

Beside including several appendices—one reporting on the author's 1985 questionnaire, another reproducing five rituals, and a third on resources (capsule descriptions of 135 current newsletters and journals, seventy-five groups, and thirty-seven basic books)—Adler cites the growth of ecological consciousness, networking, collective pagan festivals, and shamanism (Shamanic Wicca, Shamanic Craft, and Wiccan Shamanism, and such related groups as the Church of the Seven Arrows, the Athanor Fellowship, Circle, the Earth Song Community, etc.) as well as the establishment of nature sanctuaries, legal recognition, and institutionalization as among the most important changes to be taking place since the original publication of her book in 1979. She also points out the increasing scholarship within the movement itself. Another development is the formation of CUUPS (the Covenant of Unitarian Universalist Pagans) within the Unitarian Universalist Association (UUA).[5]

The striking aspect about Neo-paganism as Adler perceives it is the assumption that human beings can become gods either through the notion that "we *are* the gods" or that "we are the gods in *potential*" (1986:166).

> In general, Neo-Pagans embrace the values of spontaneity, nonauthoritarianism, anarchism, pluralism, polytheism, animism, sensuality, passion, a belief in the goodness of pleasure, in religious ecstasy, and in the goodness of *this* world, as well as the possibility of many others. They have abandoned the 'single vision' for a view that upholds the richness of myth and symbol, and that brings nourishment to repressed spiritual needs as well as repressed sensual needs. "Neo-Pagans," one priestess told me, "may differ in regard to tradition, concept of deity, and ritual forms. But all view the earth as the Great Mother who has been raped, pillaged, and plundered, who must once again be exalted and celebrated if we are to survive." (Adler, 1986:179f)

In basic affinity with "what little we know of the Mysteries," the Craft at its best today emphasizes "*experience* as opposed to *dogma*, and *metaphor* and *myth* as opposed to *doctrine*, . . . initiatory *processes* that lead to a widening of perceptions. Neither [the Mysteries nor the Craft] emphasizes theology, belief, or the written word. In both, participants expect to lead normal lives *in* the world, as well as attain spiritual enrichment" (Adler, 1986:441).

### Starhawk

As Adler makes clear, contemporary Wicca has come to dominate the current Neo-pagan milieu. This is reflected in use of the Gardnerian identification of elements with the cardinal directions in creating "sacred space" as well as celebration of the eight Wiccan sabbats or festivals.[6] A leading expounder of contemporary American Wicca is known throughout the Neo-pagan world as Starhawk.

In her book, *The Spiral Dance: A Rebirth of Ancient Religion of the Great Goddess* (1979), Starhawk (Miriam Simos) has produced the most comprehensive presentation and description of the modern movement of Witchcraft (also known as Wicca and the Craft), which includes over sixty exercises and forty rituals (chants, invocations, spells, etc.) as well as detailed, no-nonsense, and down-to-earth explanations of the reasonings and implications behind these various ceremonies, consecrations, and meditations. Starhawk imbues her work with a steady pragmatic grounding on all occasions ("It is simpler to lock your door than to protect your house with psychic seals;" "A job spell is useless unless you also go out and look for a job" [p. 113]; "It is more romantic and exciting (and probably truer) to see ["trance entities"] as at least partly external; it is psychologically healthier and probably wiser to see them as internal" [p. 142]). She insists, however, that witches are "extremely reluctant to hex anybody." Magic is not a device for securing power over others but is part of the broader discipline of developing "power-from-within." In fact,

> Love for life in all its forms is the basic ethic of Witchcraft. Witches are bound to honor and respect all living things, and to serve the life force. (Starhawk, 1979:11)

On another level, "The sense of wonder, of joy and delight in the natural world is the essence of Witchcraft" (p. 25). Pursuing techniques that center on the spiritual value of ecstasy, Witchcraft is seen as a shamanistic religion.

The underlying respect for "the sacredness of all living things" stems from the model of the universe that pictures the Goddess as immanent in nature. Starhawk borrows the idea of Mary Daly (1973:13) that the more traditional Western model of the universe, which posits a male God as ruling the cosmos from outside, is one that legitimates male control of social institutions. Instead of continuing the age-old oppression of women, Starhawk sees Witchcraft providing "feminine spirituality," a needed balance or rectification of the dominant patriarchal orientation of Western society. In the Craft, all people are considered manifest gods, and honor becomes a guiding principle. The Goddess is the primary symbol for "That-Which-Cannot-Be-Told." Nevertheless, "The view of the All as an energy field polarized by two great forces, Female and Male, Goddess and God, which in their ultimate being are aspects of each other, is common to almost all traditions of the Craft" (Starhawk, 1979:26).

Contemporary Witchcraft is a religion based on metaphor—not doctrine or "sacred truths"; one comprising will rather than belief; a religious model founded on poetry—not theology. Starhawk (1979:138) advises, "If some other metaphor works better for you, use it!" She recognizes the role the East-West dialogue currently plays in "the evolution of a new world view." Witchcraft is seen in many ways as similar philosophically to Eastern religions with their non-anthropomorphic God and their experiential rather than intellectual approaches to *becoming* God in place of simply *knowing* God. But from a woman's viewpoint, she asks of Eastern philosophy, "What's in it for *me*?"

Before I toss [my ego] out into the collective garbage heap, I want to be
sure I'm getting something in return. I don't feel qualified to discuss the
way Eastern religions function within their own cultures. But if we look at
women in the West who have embraced these cults, by and large we find
them in bondage. An ecstatic bondage, perhaps; but bondage nevertheless.
(Starhawk, 1979:193)

Likewise, there appears to be a large overlap of Witchcraft with the
New Age "growth" movements and human potential movements. Starhawk provides, for instance, an exercise for "sensing the aura" of the
kind one might find in New Age itself, and the essential thrust of Witchcraft as she presents it is both self-development as well as ecological/
environmental concern. But she stops short of fully embracing the abso-
lutist concept that "I create my own reality." Recognizing her own
white, middle-class background, she denies emphatically that those of
other races and/or of lower economic strata have chosen their misfortunes, their malnutritions and disabilities, the violences that occur to
them.

Sexism, racism, poverty, and blind accident do shape people's lives, and
they are not created by their victims. If spirituality is to be truly life serving, it must stress that we are all responsible for each other. Its focus
should not be individual enlightenment, but recognition of our interconnectedness and commitment to each other. (Starhawk, 1979:194)

In other words, "Night will follow day, and there's not a damn thing
you or I or Werner can do about it" (Starhawk, 1979:195). Instead, in a
Goddess-oriented outlook, even the dark becomes a positive experience
through risk, courage, the freedom to make mistakes, and the will to be
our own authorities. Consequently, Starhawk eschews the "Great
Man" model of spirituality (Jesus, Buddha, Krishna, Moses, etc., as
well as Freud or Werner Erhard) "who knows more about ourselves
than we do." "A feminist religion needs no messiahs, no martyrs, no
saints to lead the way" (ibid.) Validation and integrative wisdom come
from within as well as from without. Likewise, in what might be seen
as a differentiating contrast with New Age emphases, the author claims
that "There is nothing amorphous or superficial about love in Goddess
religion; it is always specific, directed toward real individuals, not vague
concepts of humanity" (Starhawk, 1979:83).

Nevertheless, several additional features of Starhawk's Witchcraft reveal similarities with New Age ideas. Foremost perhaps is the concept
of reincarnation. Like New Agers, most Witches are acknowledged as

believers in some form of reincarnation—though this is non-doctrinal and instead closer to a "gut feeling" based on the cyclical round of nature that is at the pulse of the Wiccan/Neo-pagan perception. Death is followed by rebirth, but

> Not all Witches believe in literal reincarnation; many, like Robin Morgan [1977:306], view it as "a *metaphor* for that mystically cellular transition in which the dancers DNA and RNA immortally twine themselves." (Starhawk, 1979:98)

As a point on an ever-turning wheel, death is a transformation rather than a "final end."

A further link with New Age thinking is the emphasis within Witchcraft on a "religion of ecology." In serving the life force, the Witch and the New Ager alike are working to preserve the rich diversity of natural life and combat both environmental pollution and species destruction. With its goal of harmony with nature and its deity model as one embracing and including all manifestations of life, Witchcraft is clearly ecological and intimately involved with the planetary well-being and promotion of organic balance. As Starhawk (1979:12) explains,

> Meditation on the balance of nature might be considered a spiritual act in Witchcraft, but not as much as would cleaning up garbage left at a campsite or marching to protest an unsafe nuclear plant.

Moreover,

> Witchcraft strongly imbues the view that all things are interdependent and interrelated and therefore mutually responsible. An act that harms anyone harms us all. (Ibid.)

Starhawk identifies her 'brand' of Witchcraft as belonging to an unelucidated "Faery Tradition"—presumably based in large measure on ideas formulated by Evans-Wentz (1966). Nevertheless, she acknowledges that many of her interpretations are not necessarily accepted academically or as scientifically verified but are instead illustrative of "oral Craft traditions of our history." Within this heritage, the conscious mind is referred to as "Talking Self"; the unconscious as "Younger Self." The former "corresponds roughly" with the Freudian and Jungian concepts of "ego" but also the "superego"; the latter with Freud's concept of the "id" and with Jung's concept of the personal and collective unconscious. The Talking Self is understood by Starhawk as linked to the functioning of the left hemisphere of the brain, which deals in terms of linear vision, verbal, and analytic awareness. Younger Self relates to the right hemisphere of holistic awareness, emotions, sensations, intuition, image memory, diffuse perception, and basic drives. Classical psychoanalysis is concerned with understanding the speech of Younger Self, but Witchcraft goes beyond this and "teaches us how to speak back to Younger Self" (Starhawk, 1979:21). Its rituals are designed toward this end. And finally, the Faery tradition is said to entertain a third, non-psychological concept that Starhawk identifies as the High Self or God Self—the "Spirit Guide"—which is linked to Younger Self but is not connected directly with the Talking Self.

Nevertheless, late in her book, Starhawk (1979:144f.) presents the occult concept of the Guardian or Shadow on the Threshold, which "squats in the doorway between Younger Self and Talking Self, refusing to let us pass until we have looked it in the face and acknowledged our own essential humanness." Initiation in Witchcraft involves this process of confronting the Threshold Guardian. "Magical training," though it varies greatly from one tradition to the next, from coven to coven, always has the same purpose—namely, opening the contact with and through the right hemisphere consciousness—and the development of the same basic abilities: relaxation, concentration, visualization, and projection. The danger in this training and with magic in general is not inherent in the Shadow or from anything external but stems "from our own defense strategies, which can be intensified and rigidified by trance and magic as they can by drugs or fanaticism" (p. 145).

A defense strategy favored by many 'spiritual' people is an elaborate form of denial, an assertion that the individual has 'gone beyond' the shadow qualities of sexuality, anger, passion, desire, and self-interest. Many religions cater exclusively to this strategy. Priests, ministers, gurus, and 'enlightened masters' who adopt a posture of transcendent superiority have great appeal to people with similar defense systems, who are able to escape their personal confrontations by identifying as members of an elite, 'enlightened' group. Thus are cults born and perpetuated. (Starhawk, 1979:145)

But this kind of strategy of avoidance masks a vulnerability to the shadow fear that may lead to desperate but spurious attempts of masochism, self-sacrifice, or self-embraced martyrdom. Starhawk cites the case of Jim Jones and the People's Temple as the classic example of this strategy taken to its extreme. She equally rejects such alternate strategies of avoidance as interpreting shadow qualities as physical or mental illness or projecting them externally onto another person or group.

Starhawk is at her best when she explains that control is the essence of trance technique, that is, "to change consciousness at will" (Dion Fortune). She cautions that "Mind-altering drugs are *not* used in magic (at least, not by the wise), because they destroy that control" (Starhawk, 1979:147). Instead of forcing a confrontation with the Guardian, a drug risks stripping away one's defense prematurely. Although true shamans and priestesses structure their religio-mystical experience along mythological lines, ". . . we do not live in a traditional society. We live in a society based on commodities, in which even enlightenment can purportedly be encapsulated and bought and sold" (ibid.) Although magical ritual and technique are likened to the trance produced by marijuana or the ecstasy of LSD, they go infinitely further, are more subtle, more sublime, and yet teach one how to return as well.

On a sociological level, Starhawk offers various insights into Witchcraft as a NRM. At its center is the coven: "a Witch's support group, consciousness-raising group, psychic study center, clergy-training program, College of Mysteries, surrogate clan, and religious congregation all rolled into one" (Starhawk, 1979:35). Its structure ("cellular, based on small circles whose members share a deep commitment to each other and the Craft") is what differentiates Witchcraft from the organization of most other religions. Today especially, many new, self-initiatory covens are emerging without the background of formal Craft training. Moreover,

> As the group grows more unified, certain interpersonal conflicts will inevitably arise. The very cohesiveness of the group itself will make some members feel left out. Each person is part of the whole, but also an individual, partly separated from the rest. Some people tend to see the group as a solid entity that completely enfolds everyone else, while they alone are partly left out. Sexual attraction often arises between coveners, and, while the first bright flush of love will draw power into the group, a quarreling couple will cause disruption. If the two break up, and no longer feel they can work in the group together, a real problem arises. A coven leader who is strong and charismatic often becomes the focus of other members' projections . . . It is always tempting for her to believe these flattering images . . . ; but if she does . . . Sooner or later, she will fumble and the image will be shattered; the results can be explosive. (Starhawk, 1979:45f.)

Although some covens hold open classes or study groups, others expand through their initiates taking on individual apprentices. Witches do not proselytize. Some make contacts with potential recruits through giving classes at Open Universities or metaphysical bookstores. There are, according to Starhawk, no fees for initiation—this being considered a "breach of ethics." Moreover, coven membership is not isolating. Individuals maintain external contacts and close relationships outside the group.

Starhawk also decries the popular media's perpetuation of associating "Witchcraft and Goddess religion with horror and sacrifice." Though there is no universal creed, there is within Witchcraft agreement avoiding any form of ritual murder, torture, or human sacrifice. Anyone who does, according to Starhawk, is not a Witch but a psychopath. As a contemporary Western religion, Witchcraft is one that values life and freedom. The cost of this last is measured in terms of discipline and responsibility. "Those who would be free must also be willing to stand slightly aside from the mainstream of society, if need be" (Starhawk, 1979:19).

The chief criticism of Starhawk comes from her feminist stance and implicit double standards. Although she calls for a radically new (or very ancient) theonymic metaphor through which femininity can break free of the cultural attributions of inferiority and degradation it has so long endured, in referring to men embracing a matrifocal understanding, she allows that "While individuals may not escape external authority in their own lives, they see it for what it is: an arbitrary set of rules to a complex game" (Starhawk, 1979:102). Women, on the other hand, must apparently change the rules altogether.

Admittedly, "The pull to burst beyond the limits of the socially conditioned mind seems to be a deep-seated human need" (Starhawk, 1979:141), and whether this occurs within the framework of Wicca or feminism, it rings close to humankind's inevitable "religious creativity" as described by Geoffrey Nelson (1987). For Starhawk, the real sources of discomfort are our invisible and underlying mind sets which she terms "the scabies of consciousness." Nevertheless, as Jungian psychoanalyst Ian Baker once told me, argument from a minority position inevitably sounds like 'preaching', and Starhawk, by totally identifying Witchcraft and the feminist movement, has assumed the double onus of making her case from two minority viewpoints. Recurringly, an uncomfortably strident and beleaguered posturing mars the balance that might otherwise be perceived in her delineation of a significant neopagan movement. Her characterization of "patriarchal culture" and what "it expects" never varies from a pure black-and-white reductionism.

On the broader level, the writer sees a multifaceted religion of the future growing out of many traditions (e.g., cults of the Virgin Mary, the Hebrew Goddess, Native American and Afro-American traditions, Eastern religions, etc.) in which Witchcraft is included as one among several others (Starhawk, 1979:196). However, Starhawk's expression of Wicca implicitly raises the question as to why paganism has been as universally condemned as it has. Virtually every major religion or religious culture has in some way endeavored to devalue the animistic and multi-valent orientation toward an immanent Godhead, whether it be the Judeo-Christian-Islamic hostility toward idolatry and early polytheism; Zoroastrian Parseeism's elevation of the *Ahuras* over the *Daevas*; Brahmanic Hinduism's rejection of Lokayata; Tibetan Bon Po's replacement by Buddhism; or the emergence in China of Confucianism, Taoism, and Buddhism over the nativistic but non-intellectual "Classical" religion. Judging superficially from *The Spiral Path*, one might consider that Starhawk's explanation for this almost ubiquitous anti-pagan phenomena stems from the world's lengthy subjugation to patriarchal domination and its insistence on the separation of spirit and matter, but upon a deeper analysis of the author's ideas, this attribution is too simplistic and does not, among other things, explain why one realm—namely the spiritual—is exalted over the other. Instead, Starhawk's emphasis on self-responsibility and the individual as final arbiter for the meaning and direction of life is more suggestive of an answer to our question. Priesthoods must be exclusive if they are to have any *raison d'être*, and for many of the traditionally indoctrinated, it is more immediately comfortable—at least in the absence of any officially sanctioned alternate perspective—to shift the burden of responsibility to some external cause or condition beyond one's own self-control.

### Circle Network's Selena Fox

Although self-responsibility is a key idea of New Age thought—especially its oriental mysticism and human potential wings—within Neo-paganism this stance is equally central. At the inaugural meeting in Britain of the Pagan Federation[7] (originally the Pagan Front) on 1 May 1971, founder-member Doreen Valiente proclaimed in her opening address:

We rejoice in being heretics, because a heretic means 'one who chooses'. That is, we choose our own way, to live, to think and to worship; not only because it pleases us, but because we believe that human society needs the old pagan wisdom to restore it to health and sanity, in what people are increasingly recognising as a very sick world.[8]

Another example of the centrality of self in pagan thought might be found in the (American) Pagan Spirit Alliance's "Pledge to Pagan Spirituality" in which at least three of its thirteen separate affirmations refer to self-determination.

> I am a Pagan and I dedicate myself to channeling the Spiritual Energy of my Inner Self to help and to heal myself and others.
> May I always be mindful that I create my own reality and that I have the power within me to create positivity in my life.
> May I always take responsibility for all my actions, be they conscious or unconscious.[9]

The Pagan Spirit Alliance (PSA) is a special pagan friendship network sponsored by the broader Circle Network organization based in Mt. Horeb, Wisconsin. According to its brochure, "PSA is comprised of Pagans attuned to positive (helping/healing) magickal [*sic*] ways." It publishes both a newsletter and a directory.

Among the more prominent Neo-pagan organizations to emerge with a high public profile, Circle is headquartered on Circle Sanctuary Land—a 200-acre nature preserve and herb farm—in the hill country west of Madison, Wisconsin. According to its introductory pamphlet,

> Circle is a Wiccan Church serving Wiccans and other Nature religions practitioners around the world. Founded in 1974 and incorporated as a non-profit religious organization in 1978, Circle is one of the few Wiccan groups in the world today that has legal recognition as a Church on state and federal levels of government. Other legal names for Circle are Circle Sanctuary, Inc. and the Church of Circle Wicca.[10]

Circle is headed by a High Priestess and a High Priest. The latter is currently Dennis Carpenter—replacing Jim Alan; the former, Selena Fox—one of the co-founders. The Circle Network, which Circle coordinates, is described as "an international information exchange and contact service for practitioners of the Wiccan religion and related paths which honor the spiritual dimensions of Nature." Membership extends throughout the United States and Canada and more than two dozen additional countries.

> Circle Network connects individuals, groups, and centers representing a wide variety of spiritual paths and includes Wiccans, Neo-Pagans, God-

dess Worshippers, Shamans, Druids, Seers, Eco-Feminists, Native American Medicine People, Norse Religionists, Gnostics, Mystics, Hermetic Magicians, Pantheists, and others. Circle uses the words 'Pagan' and 'Nature Spirituality' interchangeably as general terms for Nature-oriented religions and philosophies which are the focus of Circle's networking ministry. The Wiccan religion is a type of Paganism which is also known as 'Wicca', 'The Craft', 'White Witchcraft', and 'The Old Religion'.[11]

Membership in Circle Network is free. The Network publishes the *Circle Network Bulletin* with information concerning gatherings, workshops, books, recordings, etc. The quarterly *Circle Network News*—"the voice of Circle Network"—is available to members by subscription. It contains articles submitted by Network members relating to rituals, invocations, meditations, artwork, herbcraft recipes, photographs, reviews, news, etc. Circle Network also publishes the *Circle Guide of Pagan Resources*, a directory with names and addresses of groups, centers, stores, artists, musicians, and other affiliated contacts. Apart from PSA, which has its own quarterly, the *PSA Newsletter*, a forum for members to share personal experiences and ecumenical views, Circle Network also sponsors the Pagan Strength Web—a "network of Pagan religious freedom activists."

Selena Fox has described her own path as "Wiccan Shamanism," which, although it draws on "the Old," blends this with "the New" to better fit present times. Emphasis remains on European symbolism and traditions but is nevertheless multi-cultural. And yet, "at the heart of this spiritual approach is the idea that each person must seek their own connection with the divine, within their own Self." As Fox (1984:15) explains, "This is not a path of a leader with followers, but a path where each becomes their own leader."[12] There is also an ecological dimension to Wiccan Shamanism as there is to most forms of Neo-paganism.

> What I am concerned about is the survival of the human race—will we annihilate ourselves and many of the life forms around us, or will we wake up in time to see the larger picture, find and implement creative solutions to the world's problems, and enter a New Age of expanded consciousness? (Fox, 1984:15)

To these ends, Fox and Carpenter do counseling and therapy (dream work, past life regression, tarot readings, and creative visualization), hold various workshops and lecture tours, do public education through local, national, and international media, conduct training and study

groups (Wiccan spirituality, priestess education, etc.), sponsor environmental events, and perform various ministerial rites (weddings, child
blessings, funerals, dedications, inner vision quests, etc.)[13]

Circle Sanctuary "is not open to visitors on a drop-in basis." Visits
must be arranged in advance. This includes attendance at the New Moon
Healing Circles as well as most of the seasonal sabbat festivals. Full-
moon ceremonies are open only to Circle Sanctuary residents and in-
vited guests. The largest and most open gathering Circle sponsors is the
International Pagan Spirit Gathering held each year near the summer
solstice. This "week-long magical retreat and festival" has an ecumenical slant which attracts individuals and groups from various forms of
paganism across the United States and beyond.

### *Shan of London's House of the Goddess*[14]

In London, Selena Fox's equivalent is known as Shan, House of the
Goddess Clan Mother,[15] who maintains a prominent public profile both
through the media and the various events that she sponsors. Like Fox
but with a different emphasis, Shan describes her path as "Shamanic
Craft." For the Wiccan tradition in general, Shan explains that "The
Craft which has emerged from the reclamation project [following "the
christian persecutions"] is an earth centred, self centred, life affirming
tradition, with several growing branches" (Jayran, 1986:4). These last
are identified as hereditary and traditionalist Witches (who are "private
and seldom meet"); ceremonial Magicians, Gardnerians, and Alexandrians; Celtics, Nordics, and Saxon/Seax (founded by Raymond Buck-
land); Dianics (spread by Hungarian-born Zsuzsanna Budapest) and the
feminist intuitive Witches; and Shamanic Crafters ("Pagans pure and
simple"). Shan considers Dianic as

> my own original tradition, which I see as an important option for all
> women. While few would wish to dedicate themselves as Dianics for life,
> most women need or want recourse to women's mysteries at some time in
> their lives. (Jayran, 1986:35)

Nevertheless, "I began as a Dianic, and I still work in coven with
women. But the rest of my life as a Witch is now Shamanic." Shan
identifies the origins of Shamanic Craft as "shamanism, Green politics,
feminism, humanistic psychology and the essence of the Craft."

The House of the Goddess is a temple room appended to Shan's
residence in South London.[16] Shan is currently the most public of Brit-

ish Witchcraft priestesses. Through her, the House of the Goddess sponsors each Thursday evening an open "Pagan At Home" alternating with "Pagan Paths." For the former,

> We gather in the Temple, exchange a little gossip, then fill the circle with chanting and energy. We pass a well filled Chalice by candlelight. We work simple healing and celebration, honouring the Dark and the Light in our lives. (House of the Goddess 1989 brochure; see also, Jayran, 1986:35)

For Pagan Paths Evenings, Shan explains that

> After an opening circle we hold discussion on a chosen topic. We complete with meditation or trancework. This meeting honours the many different ways we can be Pagan.

In addition to these weekly meetings, Shan conducts four annual extended versions known as Pagan Energy Days (in 1989, these were held on May 13, July 15, September 9, and November 11), a Darklight Retreat (e.g., Friday, September 1 to Wednesday, September 6, 1989) and a Pagan Hallowe'en Festival (held at the Commonwealth Institute, Kensington High Street, London W8 on October 28–29, 1989; attendance is usually over 2,000 people). Moreover, until the autumn of 1989, Shan ran from her home The Magical Teahouse five days a week. This served as an open means for beginners in the occult tradition to network and make initial contact. Though this service has been suspended, the Pagan At Homes are still open to all who wish to attend.[17] Like Selena Fox, Shan also gives workshops ("Circlework" and other courses/groups), personal counseling (Tarot, individual study), and help with handfastings, funerals, etc.

### Vivianne Crowley

Shan captures the eclecticism of contemporary Wicca in the phrase: "not so much Witchcraft, as Bitchcraft." Whereas the U.K. occult figure Marion Green—centered in Bath—is more focused on the broader magical tradition, within witchcraft, Shan's foremost local rival is Vivianne Crowley, who presents not only a more 'up-market' or 'yuppified' image, but also a different version of the Craft itself.

Vivianne Crowley, in *Wicca: The Old Religion in the New Age* (1989), considers Wicca to be "at the forefront of the neo-pagan revival" and, with similar aims to the more spiritually oriented psychotherapies of the human potential movement, it is also capable of serving "the religious needs of many in the Aquarian Age" (p. 242). Moreover, although

> Christianity with its worship of the sacrifice of the self was the religion of the Piscean Age, . . . We have now entered the Age of Aquarius, the age of humanism, in which the divine as God and Goddess will be found in all men and women, not just in one perfect man now long dead. (Crowley, 1989:16)

Wicca therefore provides a religious framework in which "ritual and celebration can reveal to us the place of humanity in the cosmos" being fully compatible with the New Age discovery of the divine within humanity rather than outside it. Yet, in the necessity to create gods in our own image, Wicca is "the only religion of the West which worships the Goddess." Moreover, its Horned God—a combination animal-human-God archetype—represents an embodiment of harmonious integration toward which humanity must aspire. The present-day awakening within many individuals to the call of pagan gods and goddesses is a result of what Jung terms the individuation need emerging within the psyche of humanity. However, besides being a form of worship and a spiritual system operating in terms both of metaphysical truth and psychological truth, Crowley's Wicca provides a means for developing and employing psychic and magical power. It teaches concentration.

In Crowley's understanding, Wicca traces its origins to the paleolithic/neolithic fertility cult, the pagan mystery religions of late antiquity, and the occult tradition in general with its own antecedents in Neoplatonism and Stoic philosophies. With the repeal in Britain of the Witchcraft Act in 1951 and the publishing of Gerald Gardner's *Witchcraft Today* in 1954, a renewed possibility for the co-existence of pagan and mainstream religions came into being for the first time since the edicts of the Emperors Constantine and Justinian. Between the monopolistic triumph of Christianity and the greater openness of occultism within the pluralism characteristic of the latter half of the twentieth century, there is the long-standing magical tradition associated with the likes of Michael Scot, Masilio Ficino, Pico della Mirandola, Cornelius Agrippa, Reginald Scot, Thomasso Campanella, Giordano Bruno, Francis Barrett, etc. Nevertheless, as Crowley contends,

> The Paganism which stimulated the magical revival was not the Paganism of the witch-cult, with its emphasis on the Horned God and the ecstatic,

Dionysian side of Paganism, but the Apollonian Paganism of the Neoplatonists with their emphasis on the practice of magic as a system of spiritual development. (Crowley, 1989:39)

This particular spiritual system is to be traced in such magical societies as the Martinists, the Illuminati, the Rosicrucians, the Freemasons, and the Golden Dawn as well as in the philosophical teachings of the Theosophical Society. According to Crowley, Rosicrucian and Masonic ceremonies are themselves derivatives of ancient Egyptian rites of Isis and the Eleusinian Mysteries of Greece.

Although the contemporary forms of Wicca owe something to the influence of Margaret Murray, the key names associated with their recent historical developments are those of Charles Leland, Gerald Gardner, and George Pickingill, along perhaps with those of such ceremonial magicians as S. L. MacGregor Mathers and Aleister Crowley.

This revamped version of Wicca was more likely to appeal to the educated spiritual seekers of the fast-approaching Aquarian Age. Wicca was steering a middle course between magic and religion, between Dionysian and Apollonian Paganism, and between formalized ritual and creative spontaneity. Another aspect which was likely to appeal to New Age men and women was the emphasis on equality between the sexes and a strong emphasis on the worship of the Goddess. (Crowley, 1989:49f.)

As "the Old Religion in the New Age," contemporary Wicca is seen by Crowley as a combination of Apollonian paganism (the mystery religions, temple worship, and Neoplatonism), "the more Dionysian ecstatic and shamanistic practices of less sophisticated forms of paganism" (that of the woods and groves), and the tradition of magic. As an esoteric religion with an initiatory religious and magical system akin to the Eleusinian and Isiac mysteries, "Wicca differs from other forms of Paganism which have open rituals and meetings and can be termed exoteric rather than esoteric religion." In fact, while there are some witches who simply practice sympathetic magic and yet are Christians or atheists, "all Wiccans are Pagans, but not all Pagans are Wiccans" (Crowley, 1989:55f.).

Crowley's own form of Wicca is Alexandrian—essentially an offshoot that developed through the reforms of Gardnerian witchcraft instituted by Alex and Maxine Sanders in the early 1960s. Although she acknowledges the existence of some hereditary covens as well as Robert Cochrane and Dianic branches, Gardnerian Wicca is described as "Low Church" and Alexandrian as "High Church" with a greater interest in ritual magic than in folk paganism. Crowley herself combines her "High Church" Wiccan tradition with a therapeutic training in Jungian psychology. The God and Goddess are understood in terms of psychological archetypes and as part of the human psyche.[18] She considers, for instance, the traditional expression used in magic, "as above, so below," to have been largely replaced by Jung's more modern term of "synchronicity."

For Crowley, Alexandrian and Gardnerian Wicca are "part of the same tradition." Differences between the two are largely ones of emphasis.

> Gardnerian covens tend to be much more sensation/feeling/intuitive and Alexandrian covens much more thinking/intuitive. Gardnerian covens are usually much more oriented to sympathetic magic and healing than Alexandrian covens, but they do little teachings. Alexandrian covens tend to be more intellectual than Gardnerian covens and more oriented to ritual magic and, because there is less emphasis on developing the feeling side, the covens are sometimes more short-lived. (Crowley, 1989:138)[19]

These differences are reflected in the books written by members of the various traditions—e.g., the Gardnerian Doreen Valiente's *Natural Magic* (1975) vs. Janet and Stewart Farrar's Alexandrian *Eight Sabbats for Witches* (1981), which exclusively concentrates on increasing ritual content for the seasonal celebrations. Nevertheless, both the Alexandrian and Gardnerian traditions—as do others within the overall Wiccan movement—speak directly to intuition and imagination through their orientation to myth and ritual. Moreover, "The rounding of the personality is one of the major aims of Wicca and of all systems of magical and spiritual development" (Crowley, 1989:142).

Crowley's description of Wicca conforms to the presentation made by other leaders in the movement. There is no unique monopoly of truth nor a received bible.[20] The one "meta-rule" is expressed in "An it harm none, do what you will." The Wiccan self-image is of a non-exoteric religion that is unsuitable for the many. This is reflected in the status accorded to adherents. In Wicca, one is initiated into a priesthood. Its membership is comprised therefore of priests and priestesses. Although Wicca accepts non-material reality, it does not hold it to be in any way superior to the material. Physical incarnation is perceived as a gift from the gods. Consciousness, however, is not considered dependent on the body but is capable of extending beyond the limits of the sensory world. In general, with Wicca,

Other than a very simple belief in the life force and the powers of the human psyche, all that is required is that we accept the framework of ritual and symbolism in which Wicca operates as containing age-old truths which are not literal but which are hidden and whose truth will unfold over the years as we integrate them into our own lives. (Crowley, 1989:16)

"In Wicca each person is free to come to their own views based on their own inner experiences and revelations and it is these which must ultimately determine our beliefs" (Crowley, 1989:158).

Unlike Starhawk's almost exclusively feminist brand of Wicca—one in which the male god is seen as a subordinate emanation of the Goddess—Crowley's Alexandrian persuasion clearly emphasizes the male and female balance necessary within its image of the divine. To focus on either the Goddess or God alone, Crowley contends, produces both social and individual spiritual imbalance. For though the divine may be ultimately one, within the divine consciousness Wiccans relate to a duality. Crowley's interpretation of this duality of Goddess and God parallels psychic symbols imbedded within humanity through its pagan past and focuses on "the Triple Goddess (Virgin, Lover/Mother, and Hag) and the Dual God (Lord of Light and Lord of Darkness)."[21] These are accepted as expressions of the divine within humanity but also as divine forces operating in the universe. It is the individual's own inner experiences that determine whether these aspects reflect an impersonal life force or cosmic beings with individuality. Most Wiccans take the divine as immanent throughout the universe. Others, including Crowley herself, consider the divine in addition to be transcendent. She feels that the idea of metempsychosis corresponds to the concept of immanent divinity whereas a transcendent concept of divinity tends to be accompanied by the idea of reincarnation.[22] Natural phenomena are also seen to possess forms of consciousness. For these, Crowley employs the term "devas" or "nature spirits" and recognizes them as "elemental forces" rather than as "divinities."

Alexandrian and Gardnerian Wicca comprise three degrees of initiation. The first degree initiate becomes a witch and priest or priestess. This conforms to the preliminary vows of the novice and the Probationer stage of the Arcane School. A year and a day must elapse between the first- and second-degree initiations. During the latter, the postulant is bound for life and becomes a High Priest or High Priestess comparable to Alice Bailey's Accepted Disciple. The second degree is conferred when the individual is competent to instruct first-degree witches as well as conduct rituals; that is, run a circle and raise, control and direct "the cone of power" within it. The third degree, conferring the rank of Magus or Witch Queen, can be taken together with the second degree (the Alexandrian preference) or separately (the usual Gardnerian practice). This degree is generally given to couples who are thereby considered competent to run a coven and take responsibility for initiating others into Wicca. At this stage in Wicca, one no longer has any higher authority than him- or herself.[23]

Despite her highly ceremonial approach, Crowley, through her book *Wicca: The Old Religion in the New Age*, presents a sensible and more balanced form of Wicca than many of her, especially American, contemporaries. She has fused a grounded psychological understanding with the concepts and practices of a magically based religion. Here, unlike even many non-feminist forms of Wicca, there is a strict emphasis on male-female balance. Covens and circles should if possible consist of alternating members of the opposite sex. While the working space for all Wicca rites, the witch's sacred circle, must be created anew for each occasion, interaction, including initiation, within the Alexandrian ceremonial circle always takes place from woman to man or from man to woman and never between members of the same sex. And like much of Wicca in general, barring unfavorable weather conditions, rites are usually performed naked since clothing is believed to absorb "etheric" energy. Crowley has consequently developed a picture of both Wicca in general and Alexandrian Wicca in particular. She stresses, however, that

> Any book about Wicca can only be the personal view of the individual priestess or priest. . . . Other and sometimes opposing views will be equally valid and right for those who hold them. (Crowley, 1989:19)

In Crowley's view, Wicca does not take payment for its working of magic. Instead, as responsible practitioners of magic, the process must coincide with "spiritual development and the growth of self-knowledge and inner wisdom." Unlike many other pagans including Clan Mother Shan of London's House of the Goddess or the eco-pagan feminist Monica Sjoo, Vivianne Crowley clearly recognizes the role of Wicca and paganism in the New Age and the link between Neo-paganism and the New Age movement.

## Neo-pagan criticisms of New Age (Monica Sjoo)

The fusion of Neo-paganism with the New Age movement is to be witnessed on many fronts. In 1989, the Australian ecology magazine

*Simply Living* presented an article by Neville Drury explaining the New Age and occult overlap (*Circle Network News*, Summer 1989:4). On Sunday, 2 July 1989, Selena Fox co-facilitated a public interfaith worship service in Madison, Wisconsin with Kenna del Sol—a practitioner of Native American medicine, Sufism, and New Age spirituality. "The ritual included chanting, dancing, Divine invocations from a variety of spiritual traditions, a Lakota song to the Directions, a Wiccan blessing with the Elements, an invocation of Mother Earth, and prayers for planetary peace and healing" (*Circle Network News*, Summer 1989:4).

On the other hand, much criticism of New Age emerges from the Neo-pagan movement. Shan considers it "airy-fairy." She echoes a common Neo-pagan complaint that New Age consciousness is not "grounded."[24] Monica Sjoo is even more vociferous against New Age. In an article entitled "Some Thoughts About The New Age Movement" for the "goddess-inclined eco-pagan magazine" *Wood and Water* (Summer 1989:2–6), she lampoons the prevalent patriarchal and politically reactionary views in New Age, "using patriarchal terminology of man-he, mankind-he, etc.," "the blatantly male gods, Fathers and sons, emphasis," and its spiritual approach in terms of the "Brotherhood of Man," the "White Brotherhood of Light," etc. Moreover,

> In the New Age thinking there is a great emphasis on a supposed cosmic struggle between the 'Forces of Darkness and the Forces of Light' in which the New Agers are to fight diligently on the side of the Forces of Light in a scenario taken straight from Tolkien. . . . Darkness is unquestionably identified as 'evil' and to be defeated; the Mother Dragon is to be yet again slain . . . this time by solar-obsessed New Age knights in shining cybernetic armour."

Sjoo explains to the contrary that darkness is necessary—for without it, life could not be born in the dark womb, nor the seed germinate within the dark soil. And "it is in the dark night that we dream Lucid dreams when the Ancestors and Spirits speak with us and take us to their realms."

For Sjoo, most of the New Age movement is colored by "godfather and Sun/son religious thinking." This allows a comfortable distancing from economic and political reality to become "a kind of spiritual Yuppiedom or even Thatcherism." She cites Peter Russell's *The Awakening Earth: the Global Brain* (1982), which assumes that spirit and consciousness are not properties of the earth itself "but are somehow imbued into earth/Gaia from a male transcendent Spirit Mind." This type of spiritual thinking, she contends, has nothing to do with life on this planet because, for the New Ager, " 'Spirit' is disembodied, pure, 'uncontaminated by Matter', never born of the Mother and always male." "New Agers seem to want to escape into an eternal Light-existence divorced from the Dark Earth and womb. . . ."[25]

Sjoo's critique of the New Age extends to criticism of its capitalistic aspects as well. Having watched a grown son succumb rapidly to cancer once he became involved with "rebirthing" techniques, she feels that Rebirthers are "amongst the most dangerous as well as the most reactionary, irresponsible and mercenary of the New Age therapies." She also finds repugnant New Age therapeutic talk about money as "just an energy" that someone may or may not attract to himself. "The 'you create your own reality'—catch-phrase of the New-Age-speak does in no way take into account the collectively created 'Karma' accumulated by the generations before us and that we now have to live with." However,

> What I find most worrying is that some of the thinking of the New Age connects back to some very reactionary and pro-fascist religious views— via the Theosophists and the medium Alice Bailey writing in the 30s—of secret elite 'Masters' who through hidden/occult means somehow control world-events and human minds—and who are attempting to bring about an Aryan 'superrace' on this Earth. Such technological/scientific developments as nuclear power, space exploration and even 'the Bomb' were welcomed by 'the Master' speaking through Alice Bailey, who herself was obsessed with imagery of Light and Fire. She has, through the Findhorn community—or 'Light centre'—in Scotland, become a prophet of the movement.[26]

When I mentioned this to Alternative's William Bloom, he explained that pro-fascist accusations are frequently leveled against any spiritual discipline that employs a "spiritual hierarchy" terminological framework. Nevertheless, racist and fascistic allegations can be made among groups within the Neo-pagan movement itself.

## Nordic paganism

Shan (Jayran, 1986:34) refers to the "racialist overtones" sometimes apparent in Nordic Craft. Margot Adler (1986:273), in her discussion of "Norse Paganism," speaks of some "groups clearly using Odinist symbols and mythologies as a front for right-wing and even Nazi activities.'' With its stress on family, courage, loyalty, honor, and warrior virtues, Odinists are largely more conservative than most Neo-pagans.

> In general, Odinism attracts people who are more politically conservative than the majority of Neo-Pagans. They are uncomfortable with feminism, anarchism, and diversity in sexuality and life style. . . . there's less vegetarianism and more alcohol as opposed to other mind-altering methods. There's a stress on martial arts and on warrior values. (Adler, 1986:279)[27]

Odinists and Norse Pagans are also among the most polytheistic of the Neo-pagans. Though their rituals are frequently less elaborate than those of Wicca, their gods serve as examples and models— "inspirations and self-aware personifications of natural forces." On another level, they are considered "numinous logic-defying reality, something apprehended only by means of symbols" (Stephen McNallen, founder of the Asatru Free Assembly, in Adler, 1986:276).

Along with the AFA in the United States, Norse and Teutonic forms of paganism manifest in San Francisco's Heathen Way, the Odinist Fellowship, the Odinist Committee in England, and the Asatruarfolks in Iceland. In its newsletter, *The Odinist*, the Odinist Fellowship, based in Crystal River, Florida, maintains that they are "non-dogmatic." Although opposed to "domestic Marxism, liberalistic cosmopolitanism and usury capitalism,"

> Odinism is not a cult. A cult by definition is dogmatic, authoritarian and regimented. Odinism is non-dogmatic; our basic religious views lend themselves to a wide variety of doctrinal interpretations and working applications; we in fact encourage creative heterodoxy. Odinism is non-authoritarian; we have no leader or leadership which dictates to 'followers'; individual Odinists and Odinist groups function autonomously. (*The Odinist*, No. 122, 1989:1f.)

The Odinist Fellowship also denies that they are satanic, Nazi, "rightwing," or "rightist" ("'Rightism' is a political position expressing opposition to change and support for conservative or authoritarian views"), advocators of religious hatred (maintaining they are anti-Christian only in a philosophical sense), or promoters of racial hatred or "anti-Semitism."

> We believe that every racial group and subgroup, every folk, is a unique, non-repeatable biological-historical phenomenon that should be preserved . . . At the same time, we reserve the right to expose, criticize and defend

ourselves against any ethnic interest group that threatens and attacks our Folk; this is the basis, e.g., for our stance against Zionism. (Ibid.)

Building on Jean-Paul Sartre's affirmation that "existence precedes essence," Odinists maintain that "ethnos precedes existence."

Although every race and ethnic group is threatened by cosmopolitanism and homogenization, our chief concern must be for our own Folk, an endangered minority. We support the awakening of racial consciousness for all peoples as a bulwark against assimilation. (*The Odinist* 123, 1989:4)

In its stance for neo-tribalism, Odinists recognize their link with Islamic fundamentalism. In the West, this attitude isolates them not only from other Neo-pagans, but from mainstream society as well.[28]

The pre-packaged answers being peddled today just don't suffice: judeo-christianity incites man to war against his instincts and common sense; the cult of the consumer leaves man bored, empty and yearning for something more; ideologies of compulsory collectivism stifle his individuality; philosophies of egoism violate his 'We-feeling'; 'New Age' spiritualisms outrage his rationality. (Ibid.)

In their introductory brochure, *Odinism and The Odinist Fellowship*, Odinism is explained in terms generally in keeping with Neo-paganism at large: teaching the non-separation between material and spiritual existence; use of myth as "the language of the Gods"; stress on freedom, self-determination, and self-reliance; holistic naturalism and an understanding of the universe as an interdependent whole in keeping with formulations of modern physics; the non-use of intoxicants and hallucinogenic drugs; non-dogmatism; and non-missionary zeal. In all these, Odinism is little different from other forms of Neo-paganism, its chief contrasts being instead its emphasis on "the family unit and the extended family" as well as on "racial purity." In this brochure, it is stated that "we have no direct connections with Wicca or Witchcraft although they are fellow-pagan organizations."[29] *The Odinist* stresses Odinism's links with Zen Buddhism, Shinto, and many native American nations—including "love of nature" (e.g., 125, 1989:10). However, following a survey, the magazine's staff stated that "It . . . came as a surprise that few Odinists are interested in ecology" (117, 1988:1).

In Britain, a loosely identified "Northern Tradition" is emerging, which stands in contrast to the more conservative and racially oriented forms of Odinism or Asatru. At the Second Pagan Federation Conference held in Conway Hall, University of London Union, on November 24, 1990, Nigel Pennick—a leading spokesman for this development—gave a talk on "The Unity of the Northern Tradition: Celts and Vikings." He recognizes "the old, indigenous, nameless tradition" (which "tends to be away from the tradition which is popular today")—that of the "cunning man and wise woman." Pennick sees Hinduism as the Eastern tip of European paganism, and he entertains the possibility that Western paganism may come to be recognized as a member of the World Hindu Congress. He is careful to distinguish the Northern Way from the monotheistic tendency of the Goddess-oriented religions. Other figures associated with this emergent Northern Tradition include Bernard King, who gave a lecture on "The Viking Magical Tradition" for the Talking Stick on January 1, 1991, and the rune specialist Freya Aswynn.[30]

## Animism

Delineating Norse Paganism and its contrast with Wicca, however, helps to describe the other manifestations of Neo-paganism—especially the "Pagan Reconstructionists." These last—and as portrayed by Adler (1986)—represent revivals within the traditional religious frameworks of the ancient faiths of Egypt, Greece, and the Celtic world, among others. Welsh religious revivalism in particular, based largely on the *Mabinogion*, often overlaps with Wicca and has played a formative role in development of Gerald Gardner's thinking. Beneath the philosophies and mythologies of most Neo-pagan cults is, as Adler (1986:25) makes clear, the assumption of an animistic reality.

> *Animism* is used to imply a reality in which all things are imbued with vitality. . . . At some level Neo-Paganism is an attempt to reanimate the world of nature; or, perhaps more accurately, Neo-Pagan religions allow their participants to reenter the primeval world view, to participate in nature in a way that is not possible for most Westerners after childhood. The Pagan revival seems to be a survival response to the common urban and suburban experience of our culture as 'impersonal', 'neutral', or 'dead'.

In an article for *ORE* magazine, P. C. Johnson links this pagan animism with the New Age thought complex as well. She describes Roman religion as animistic, "springing from a belief in an enlivening life-force to be found in every natural thing—stone, pool, tree as well as rivers, groves and cities."

This is precisely the view which is gaining credence again today, nurtured through the centuries by northern paganism, and seen in the New Age recognition of devas and nature spirits, and the discovery that every atom has a memory bank.[31]

She denies the traditionalist "tag" that labels animism as "primitive" in comparison with the concepts of polytheism and monotheism and feels instead that it may represent "the highest flowering of religious awareness, as well as the earliest and most ancient."

## Neo-paganism and Christianity

In contrast to New Age, however, Neo-paganism exhibits much less of an overlap or compatibility with Christianity. Nevertheless, even here there are to be found some links which are not otherwise immediately apparent. For instance, even within such an anti-Christian formulation as Odinism, in line with one of its "Nine Principles"—namely, "the seeking of wisdom is the highest virtue," The Odinist Fellowship states that "We even acknowledge whatever wisdom is to be found in the lives and teachings of sincere holymen esteemed by Judaism, Christianity and Islam" (*The Odinist* 123, 1989:7). Selena Fox puts it even more succinctly: "My practice of Wicca includes following Christ's teachings. I love my fellow man and try to be a good neighbor."[32]

From a different point of view, the *Aquarian Arrow*'s editor, Zachary Cox, argues that despite the "vigorous debate" between occultists and pagans with the Christian Establishment, "no-one wants to stone anyone to death over it." Describing Kenneth Baker's new education act as a mechanism to reinforce "vertical social cohesions at the expense of the horizontal," Cox concludes,

To its great credit, the Church of England vigorously opposes this nonsense. Pagans take note: the battle lines are changing fast, and we should choose our friends on the basis of principle rather than of form.[33]

Personally, through his "Neopantheism," Cox finds all monotheism pernicious and flawed. He can accept monism philosophically and theism religiously, but when combined as monotheism, "you open the door to manipulative priestcraft" through finite minds defining the Divine Revelation of the Infinite in their own finite terms. Nevertheless, "Christianity has a few good ideas to contribute here—notably the concept of 'Men of Goodwill', which we would of course update to 'People of Goodwill' " (*Aquarian Arrow* 28:2). The real variance among Christians and Neo-pagans he sees as one over means rather than ends. Both stand opposed to "Fascists and Fundamentalists" who "have no contribution to make to a multiracial, multicultural plenum." For this reason, Cox is willing to dialogue with "monotheists of goodwill."

## Covenant of Unitarian Universalist Pagans (CUUPS)

Perhaps Neo-paganism's most public foray occurs at present through the Unitarian Universalist Association (UUA) church in the United States. Following a series of "Women and Religion resolutions" passed by the UUA General Assemblies in 1977, 1979, and 1980, William F. Schulz, four months before becoming elected president of the Unitarian Universalist Church, wrote a paper about the "religious revolution" in which he declared, "to put it in symbolic terms, Ashtar, the Goddess, had been issued invitation where formerly only Lord Jehovah dared to tread."[34] On June 24, 1987 in Little Rock, Arkansas, the Covenant of Unitarian Universalist Pagans (CUUPS) came into being with the adoption of the following statement of purpose:

> The Covenant of Unitarian Universalist Pagans is formed for the purposes of enabling networking among Pagan-identified UUs; providing outreach of Unitarian Universalism to the broader Pagan community; providing educational materials on Paganism for Unitarian Universalist congregations and the general public; promoting Pagan/Judaeo-Christian dialogue; encouraging the development of theo/alogical and liturgical materials based on earth and nature centered religious and spiritual perspectives; encouraging greater use of music, dance, visual arts, poetry, story, and creative ritual in Unitarian Universalist worship and celebration; providing support for Pagan-identified UU religious professionals and ministerial students; and fostering healing relationships with our mother the Earth and all her children.[35]

In its pamphlet "Unitarian Universalism and the Pagan Path: The relevance of modern neo-pagan spirituality for Unitarian Universalism," CUUPS suggests that the "Earth Religions"—with their emphases on experience over doctrine, immanence over transcendence, and the idea that there are multiple pathways to the divine—"share many religious truths, to be sure, with the Judaeo-Christian tradition that is generally held to be the principal source of the Unitarian Universalist faith." It is recognized that the name "Neo-paganism" is that which is often given to this resurgence of interest in religion based on harmony with the earth and her cycles "particularly as it manifests in the 'mainstream' culture in Europe and North America."

Writing in the *UU World* in February 1986, Schulz called for Unitarian Universalists "to serve as prophets of a global spirituality." He found that the resources for this new spirituality are to be found among "feminist theology, creation spirituality, inter-faith and inter-cultural bridging, and the re-enchantment of the world." Moreover, editors Linda Pinti and Lesley Phillips of CUUPS's newsletter, *Pagan Nuus*, declare that in keeping with the evolution of their religious tradition, "in 1985 we revised our statement of principles to include an affirmation of 'respect for the interdependent web of existence of which we are a part'."

> Our new statement also speaks of our enriching and ennobling religious pluralism and acknowledges that our living tradition is drawn from many sources, including direct religious experience, words and deeds of prophets past and present, wisdom from the world's great religions, Jewish and Christian teachings, and Humanist teachings. The time has come, we believe, to further our living tradition by directly acknowledging among the sources of our faith the spiritual teachings of native Americans and other native peoples who live in close relationship with the earth. ("Deepening Our Living Tradition," *Pagan Nuus* 3.1, Beltane 1989:1)

Within overall Unitarian Universalism, Phillips and Pinti argue that "the neo-pagan path needs to be recognized as another stream that is part of our radical religious pluralism."[36]

In a sermon given by the minister of both the UU Fellowship of Mobile, Alabama, and the UU Church of Jackson, Mississippi, Shirley Ranck identifies the revival and transformation of pagan traditions as of interest to Unitarian Universalists in three chief ways: the internalization of religion in which rituals awaken a sense of wholeness, selfhood, and human potential; concern for the well-being of the earth through recognition of the divine as immanent in all nature; and paganism's non-authoritarian attitude without creeds or scriptures. These are UU values as well and, according to Ranck, "make us kindred spirits with Witches and Pagans" ("Pulpit Voices," *Pagan Nuus* 3.2, Samhain 1989:6,8). The general thrust of CUUPS events and discussions appears to be "thealogical" and largely Wiccan. Starhawk and Margot Adler frequently appear at CUUPS functions and give CUUPS talks at UUA General Assemblies.[37]

As a legitimate organization within the established UU church, by the summer of 1988 there were eleven active CUUPS chapters along with a dozen additional local contact people plus enough others in virtually every metropolitan area to make starting a chapter feasible. By spring of the following year, there were at least fifteen CUUPS groups on the American West Coast alone.[38] To gain official recognition as a CUUPS chapter, the new group is expected to be in sympathy with the CUUPS Statement of Purpose, to include at least three dues-paying members of the CUUPS continental organization (increased in 1990 from $10 to $20), pay an annual chapter registration fee, and include the CUUPS continental headquarters on its chapter mailing list. However,

> There is no set format for the organization or programming of a CUUPS chapter, and those that are currently active vary from ritual groups to discussion groups to a combination of the two, and meet anywhere from weekly to monthly. (''CUUPS Chapter Update,'' *Pagan Nuus* 2.2, Litha/ Lammas 1988:6)

*Pagan Nuus* suggests for beginning chapters that at least the first meetings be held in UU buildings. Publicity ought to be sent one month to six weeks in advance to all UU societies within ''a reasonable driving area.''

## The external 'negative image' of paganism and witchcraft

If the growth of CUUPS and its local chapters represents a chief means by which Neo-paganism is fusing with an at least nominally Christian movement as well as gaining greater mainstream acceptance, there is nevertheless a burgeoning backlash and controversy arising in connection with the Neo-pagan and Wiccan religions as well. The anti-pagan sentiment may be spearheaded by Christian fundamentalists, but because of the deep-seated cultural bias against witchcraft and paganism, it is a more broadly based antagonism as well. This 'negative image' that Wicca and Neo-paganism share is reflected, for instance, in the topics of concern frequently raised for Pagan Spirit Alliance discussion: ''How have you dealt with anti-Pagan propaganda and/or actions in society?'' (*PSA* 15, 1984); ''What should Pagans do regarding slander, harassment, and other attacks on our religion by fundamentalist 'Christians'?'' (24, 1986); ''In the light of widespread variation and controversy regarding the meaning of the word 'Witch', what are your

views regarding the use of this word to describe your beliefs and practices?'' (25, 1987); ''How do your Pagan beliefs and attitudes translate
into ethical guidelines for your day-to-day actions?'' (27, 1987); ''What
are your thoughts regarding educating police forces and the public
about the differences between Paganism and Satanism? What, if any,
actions should be taken in this regard?'' (34, 1989).

The linking of modern witchcraft and paganism with Satanism by the
media and conservative religious factions is of particular concern
among Neo-pagans. Often the attitude of the public press is simply one
of amusement rather than harassment or hostility; however, the mere
noteworthiness of Neo-paganism vis-à-vis the society at large is in itself
significant. For instance, on 28 March 1989 the normally staid BBC
World Service during its News About Britain segment saw it fit to report that twenty people had registered for a class on witchcraft—and
possible initiation into a coven—given by a Mrs. Doc Griffiths in Milton Keynes, Buckinghamshire. Perhaps because of its stance for individuality and non-conformity, any neutral or non-reaction to Neo-paganism is precluded, but when this is coupled with such events as the
Charles Manson murders, the Matamoros murders[39] or the American
psychotherapeutic 'discoveries' of early childhood recollections by at
least 100 women patients connected to ''abuses they say they suffered
in satanic rituals,''[40] the chances of public hysteria being indiscrimi-
nately directed against all forms of Neo-paganism becomes increasingly
possible.

*The Miami Herald* newspaper in Florida reports on a seminar held in
the Hilton Hotel in Gainesville for teachers and police officers—
including priests and social workers—focusing ''on satanic cults and
religious practices similar to voodoo'' (''Cult movements pose threat,
experts warn,'' June 4, 1989). A particular emphasis was on how parents can tell if their children are leaning toward involvement in satanic
worship. The telltale symptoms were said to include:

(1) Obsession with fantasy role-playing games, (2) More than the usual
interest in books on magic and witchcraft, (3) A collection of objects, such
as candles and ropes, that can be used in rituals, (4) A collection of symbolic jewelry, such as an inverted pentagram or cross, (5) Drug use and
unexplained sudden paranoia, and (6) Extreme secrecy.

The 'experts' claimed that ''Children often learn about satanic rituals
through listening to heavy metal music.''

Apart from the validity or non-validity of 'Establishment' claims that magical practice invariably means satanic involvement and use of bloody rites, Neo-paganism is constantly wary of such headlines as "Black magic attack on church," "Devil worshippers return," and "Satanists in church raids for black mass." These were reported by Joy Melville in *The Guardian Weekly* (March 17, 1985) "after two north London churches were desecrated and the consecrated sacrament, essential for a black mass, was stolen." The article, "That old Black Magic," continues:

> Father Dominic Walker, of the Churches Exorcism Study Group, set up in 1972 to investigate occult incidents, counsels about 200 occult "casualties" a year. He considers that the occult, like the drug scene, has a hard and soft side. "At one end you begin with tarot cards, fortune telling, ouija boards; at the other are witches' coven groups, black magic and satanism."

This is countered by Chris Bray of the Sorcerer's Apprentice in Leeds who claims that the "People who are taking up witchcraft and paganism are the type who are interested in ecology. They tend to be slightly left wing, anti-nuclear, nature lovers, into saving animals."[41]

## The "Occult Census" and Satanism

The chronic fear among all Neo-pagans is the reinstitution of "the Burning Times," that is, the European Witch Craze that lasted from the fifteenth to the seventeenth centuries.[42] This historical event has doubtlessly restricted any rapprochement on the part of the pagan community toward the larger, predominantly Christian, mainstream society. This unease is reflected not only in traditional pagan secrecy but also in pagan attitudes toward Satan, which they inevitably see as a "Christian creation."[43] To counteract the automatic "lumping together under the media's 'Devil Worshippers' banner" of all hermeticists, Witches, or persons with any "alternative belief," Chris Bray undertook in 1989 "The Occult Census" (*OC1989*).[44] "The spin off of the OCCULT CENSUS is that we will have compiled the first real analysis of the sociological importance of Occultism in the history of the world," Bray claimed in his advertising circular for the census.[45] Aiming to dissipate the "Establishment view" that "Occultism consists of immature psychopathic illiterati with criminal and anti-social tendencies who emanate largely from lower socio-economic stratas of our society," Bray sought "Factual evidence [which] was needed to dispel the idea that all of occultism is dangerous and anti-social" (*OC1989*:3f.).

Although I shall defer discussion of the overall results of The Occult Census until later, the survey response indicated some salient distinctions between occultists and Satanists. While the average age of occultists in the complete sample was thirty-two years and that of committed Satanists was twenty-seven—with thirty-three being the average age for those with "a serious interest in Satanism,"

> The aspect of occultism which LEASTS [*sic*] interests those polled is Satanism. Three quarters of our sample said they had no interest whatsoever in Satanism. Of the remaining 25% of entrants 15% only had a curious or passing interest in Satanism. Only 4% of Occultists in our sample said they were Satanists. (*OC1989*:17; see further the SAOC interest table in Chapter 5 below.)

When asked the question whether one had ever worked magic for an evil purpose, only 14 percent of occultists said yes. This figure rose to 43 percent among Satanists. However, of those "who claimed to have worked evil magick over 10 times only two were committed Satanists" (*OC1989*:32). The average number of times the average occultist had worked evil magic was 3.3.

*The Occult Census: 1989* ends with a chapter entitled "Satanism Defined—By Satanists: A Proclamation by D. Lily."

> Now Satanists are once again being confused with the idiotic 'Devil Worshippers' spawned by tabloid press. We are accused of sacrificing babies and indulging in illegal sexual acts. People assume that we gain some advantage by doing so, though no-one has ever detailed how such acts could increase Knowledge, and Knowledge is what Satanists are seeking. . . . Freed from the tenets of orthodoxy its lies and its improbable placebos, we want to know what really happens when our mortal body ceases to function. We also wish to learn how to become more effective whilst on Earth, how to Achieve in many ways. Myths and legends do not interest us. We are concerned with Reality. WE WANT TO KNOW. Those four words summarise the Satanic quest. . . . Knowledge is achieved by learning, working, experimenting, experiencing and thinking. (*OC1989*:39)

Nevertheless, despite the more favorable image of Satanism that *The Occult Census: 1989* attempts to project, it is also clear that most occultists seek to distance themselves from the image of Satanism (see Chapter 5 below). Moreover,

WHO IS RESPONSIBLE FOR THE DIS-INFORMATION ABOUT OC-CULTISM? Of those polled 82% of occultists felt that NEWSPAPERS were most responsible . . . 68% of our sample also chose WRITTEN-MEDIA AND MAGAZINES but by far the greatest vote . . . went to the CHRISTIAN CHURCH. 85% of occultists in our sample believed they were most responsible. . . . A further 43% of our sample said that OTHER ORTHODOX RELIGIONS were to blame too. 57% of those asked thought that Broadcasts on Television and Radio were also guilty of misinforming the populace about the true facts of occultism and the Government polled 34% which was the lowest percentage of blame. (*OC1989*:28)

## Conclusion

In an article entitled "Modern Magic" (*Religion Today* 5.1 and 2 [undated]), T. M. Luhrmann considers that contemporary "ritual magicians" in Britain divide roughly into four groups: those who continue the Western Mysteries tradition first formulated by the Order of the Golden Dawn in the nineteenth century; the less organized and non-initiatory ad hoc ritual magicians who nevertheless usually take the Golden Dawn as their locus of inspiration; practitioners of witchcraft first inaugurated by Gerald Gardner in the 1930s and worshipping the "Goddess"; and a "catch-all category" of pagans whose rituals are undergirded by a non-Christian nature symbolism similar to that of witchcraft but "without the elaborate initiatory structure."[46] Comparing ritual magicians to various New Age individuals, i.e., psychics, crystal ball gazers, spoonbenders, tarot readers, and other occult practitioners observed at the Camden New Age Psychic Centre as well as occult fairs, Luhrmann finds that most magicians are from a comparatively higher socio-economic level. My own observations would support this conclusion for those associated with Vivianne Crowley but certainly not for those attending the House of the Goddess functions. Moreover, those who attend New Age events such as the Alternatives lectures at St. James, Piccadilly, may be as "sane and highly educated [as most magicians—leading] otherwise normal lives as civil servants, businessmen and computer analysts." Whereas Luhrmann's assessment of most psychic practitioners serving occult fairs may be correct, the same does definitely not apply to the more 'up-market' lecturers at both Alternatives and the Mind, Body and Spirit Festival, whose lucrative incomes place them on average higher along the economic scale. On the other hand, Luhrmann appears to be correct in her consideration that most New Agers "would not use the word 'magic' to describe their doings."

Figures for the Neo-pagan movement are even more difficult to obtain than those for New Age. Again there are no central registrars, and any records that are kept are not generally accessible for reasons of security. Estimates range as high as Chris Bray's (so-called) "conservative" figure of "over a quarter of a million occultists in the U.K."[47] These would comprise all four of Luhrmann's groups of British "ritual magicians" and not be restricted to Neo-pagans only. For the latter, a modest estimate might be gained from figures released by Vivianne Crowley at the Second Pagan Federation Conference held on November 24, 1990 for which 200 tickets were sold. Crowley explained that since its beginning in 1970/1971, membership for the Federation has remained approximately 200. The Federation's journal, *The Wiccan*, has currently a six-hundred copy print run, but "since many of these are couples, we are really into four figures."

In general, Neo-paganism may be summed up as comprising an animistic, pantheistic, and pluralistic religious orientation that is non-octrinaire but employs traditional pagan metaphors (myths, foci, and rituals) or modern reconstructions of them as a means of celebrating a this-worldly emphasis either on a solitary basis or with others of a like mind. It stresses self-responsibility, self-development, individual exegesis, and full freedom of self-determination, the experience of ritual and ecstasy, and an ecological preoccupation with the well-being of the planet regarded as a living entity. The interconnectedness of all life forms and the habitat is a central belief. Other concerns include tolerance, respect for diversity, healing, and the use of non-malevolent forms of 'magic'. Its ethics are pragmatic and grounded in the concept of honor.

Having now delineated both the New Age Movement and the Neo-pagan movement in general, I wish to proceed in the next chapter to examine more specifically the 'overlap' between the two as well their contrasts. Subsequently, I shall present the results of specific surveys to reach an understanding of how New Agers and Neo-pagans may be distinguished—if at all—from the public at large. In my sixth chapter, I shall present the meeting formats of a representative local group from each movement: Monday night at Alternatives, and a "Pagan At Home" in the House of the Goddess. Finally, in my last two chapters, we shall investigate the relevance of the church-sect continuum and sociological concepts of the cult to both the New Age and Neo-pagan movements. Do they apply? Are they helpful? What other concepts might be useful?

## Notes

1. For Witchcraft alone, Vivianne Crowley (1989:240) reports that "As well as the UK, there are thriving Wicca movements in the United States, Canada, Australia, New Zealand, Ireland, and also in Germany and the Netherlands."

2. "Starhawk's *The Spiral Dance* had sold about 50,000 copies by the end of 1985 and *Dreaming the Dark* had sold about 30,000 copies. *Drawing Down the Moon* had sold about 30,000 copies" (Adler, 1986:418f.).

3. Crowley (1989:240) says that "People often ask me how large Wicca is and I have to reply that I have no idea! Wicca has no central organization which can do a headcount, but it is certainly large and growing." The same statement applies equally to the more encompassing Neo-pagan movement.

4. Presumably due to the popular connotations with its heightened emotionality regarding the subject of witchcraft, this modest estimate ought to be compared with the following distortion appearing in an article by Paul Clancy, "Witch Ways OK by Air Force," *Newsline* April 25, 1989: "Margot Adler, author of *Drawing Down the Moon*, a popular book about pagan religions, says there are hundreds of thousands of followers, with quite a few in the armed forces."

5. A vague idea of American pagans might be assessed in the growth of CUUPS membership. In its Member Supplement (Spring 1990) issue, *Pagan Nuus* editors Lesley Phillips and Linda Pinti recall that "Just three years ago, when the first regular issue of PAGAN NUUS was produced, our total mailing list numbered only about 90. . . . Six months later, we had a mailing list of almost 500, with 60 dues-paying members. Six months after that (two years ago), our mailing list was approaching 900, and our membership was 230. And a year ago, these figures had become 1600 and 380 respectively. In the past year, our membership has again almost doubled, to just over 700, and the total mailing list is approximately 2350." Some 300 inactive names were being dropped as of the current mailing. In a letter to me dated May 20, 1990, Phillips states that "The membership currently stands at about 750, plus another 250 paid subscribers. Our total mailing list . . . is currently almost 2,500, with an estimated total readership for PAGAN NUUS of perhaps up to 4,000."

6. For instance, Serena Roney-Dougal, the first Briton to receive a doctorate in parapsychology, during a London workshop on alternate states of consciousness which I attended the weekend of January 20–21, 1990, evoked air as the guardian of the east, fire in the south, water in the west, and earth in the north. By contrast, the 'astrological associations' for the directions would be: fire-east, earth-south, air-west, and water-north; the traditional pagan outlook sees fire

with the east, earth with the south, water at the west, and air for the north. However, the Gardnerian associations are used in virtually all contemporary Neo-pagan celebrations and ceremonies. Many pagan leaders, however, deny these are Gardnerian—claiming instead they are 'natural'. When I asked during the Quest Annual Conference on March 10, 1990 about the origins of these particular alignments, no one could say.

7. In 1989, the PF president was Leonora James; its secretary, Vivianne Crowley; and its treasurer, Christopher Crowley.

8. Reprinted in *The Wiccan* 91 (February 1989:1). *The Wiccan* has been in existence since its founding in 1968. It subsequently sponsored the PF, for which it now serves as newsletter. Other pagan magazines in Britain include *Quest*, since 1970 (edited by Marion Green) and *The Cauldron* since 1976 (edited by Mike Howard). *The Wiccan* was preceded in 1964 by *Pentagram*—the magazine of the Witchcraft Research Organisation—which folded in 1972.

9. From a one-page form published by the Pagan Spirit Alliance (c/o CIR-CLE, Box 219, Mt. Horeb, Wisconsin 53572, USA) entitled "A Pledge to Pagan Spirituality" (undated). A photocopy of this pledge is on file with the Centre for New Religions, King's College London.

10. From a four-page brochure entitled "Circle" (undated) published by Circle (Box 219, Mt. Horeb, Wisconsin 53572, USA). A photocopy of this brochure is on file with the Centre for New Religions, King's College London. The quotation is found on the first page of the brochure.

11. Ibid.

12. Selena Fox, "Wiccan Shamanism," *Circle Network News* (Winter 1984:15).

13. More recently, however, Selena Fox has stated that "I am narrowing the focus of my magic and concentrating on Planetary Healing. . . . I no longer consider myself primarily a Wiccan priestess. I have founded a new religion and invented some new names. The name of this new Nature Religion is the Naturean religion also known as the Church of Nature, the Nature Mystic Movement, and the Mystic Nature Church. It is a spiritual environmental religion . . ." Fox explains further, "In addition to these changes, I also am changing my media image. I will still play Good Witch sometimes when I defend the Craft. However, I also will be appearing from time to time as the Fairy Queen of Circleland when I am defending Nature Religions of many varieties in addition to Wiccan" (*Circle Network News*, Winter 1989/90:5).

14. At the House of the Goddess and throughout the British pagan network, Shan is known only by her first name. Recently, however, she has been identified as "Shan Jayran" in the *Talking Stick Magazine* 1 (Summer 1990):37 and as "Shan Jehan" in *Pagan News* (Sept./Oct. 1990):3.

15. On June 9, 1990, during the monthly ULU Pagan Moon celebration, the ceremony included the investiture of a second "Clan Mother" (Suzanne) as well as two "Clan Consorts" (John and Barry).

16. 33 Oldridge Road, South Clapham/Balham, London SW12 8PN; telephone: 01–673 6370.

17. In the course of data collection, I have attended Pagan At Homes on a fairly regular basis since the fall of 1988. These are informal gatherings of usually fifteen to thirty people. There is a core group who are invariably present, followed by another set of people who appear only occasionally. There are in addition always new faces who have not been to a pagan function previously. The ceremony appears to be largely Gardnerian in inspiration.

18. "Identification with an archetype of a particular God or Goddess form is an aim of religious or magical rites" (Crowley, 1989:152). This identification is achieved through a ritual process of invocation. Evocation, by contrast, is the "splitting off" by the psyche of parts of itself to function autonomously as separate personalities. Evoked consciousness is " 'flung out' of the [witches'] circle by the will of the group and 'sent' to do its work" (see pp. 128f.).

19. Crowley (1989:95) also points out the greater importance in Alexandrian Wicca than in Gardnerian of symbolic gestures, which suggest the subordination of the intellectual world of the God to the spiritual and intuitive world of the Goddess.

20. The witches' closest equivalent, *The Book of Shadows*, is copied by hand from one's initiator and consists primarily of skeletal descriptions of rites, etc.

21. "Aradia is the principal name by which the Goddess is known in Wicca today" (Crowley, 1989:164). Among the many forms in which the God is worshipped in Wicca, the Horned God is primary. He is known as Cernunnos by Gardnerians and as Karnayna by Alexandrians.

22. "My own view leans towards reincarnation and a sense of an enduring Self which existed before, during and after physical incarnation." This reflects Crowley's "experience of the inner divinity; it is both immanent and transcendent" (Crowley, 1989:155).

23. Crowley (1989:54f.) points out that "Many traditional and hereditary groups do not have the system of three degrees, but instead have two senior people who run the coven, the Master and the Lady, and a third, the Summoner, who is subordinate to them and does much of the administrative work of the coven. These three positions are gained by election either on the part of the coven or by the individuals themselves who decide they are ready to run a coven." In contrast to Crowley's recommendation, both Doreen Valiente and Janet and Stewart Farrar suggest that people unable to contact a Wiccan group could practice self-initiation.

24. Shan tells the story in which she attended a large gathering presided over by the New Age healer Matthew Manning. During a group exercise he asked everyone to image an object or person the individual held in extreme dislike. Each was asked to allow the build-up of feelings of animosity to a peak level. Shan and her companions were not too popular, she explains, because of indulging in a particularly ostentatious chanting of "Hate! Hate! Hate!" When the emotional hatred reached a collective culmination, Manning then asked everyone to feel and express the emotion of love. To Shan, this was typical of dangers

inherent in New Age approaches. "You don't allow and encourage the creation of so much negative energy without giving it a proper release, direction or grounding!" she said.

25. William Bloom expressed a typical New Age concept from Monica Sjoo's point of view when, during his "Devas, Angels and Fairies" talk at the Wren Café, St. James, Piccadilly (March 15, 1990), he referred to Gaia as "an angelic consciousness *enfolding* the whole planet" (italics mine), i.e., still as something separate from the earth itself.

26. From a completely different if not fundamentalist point of view, Dr. Margaret Brearley of the Centre for Judaism, Selly Oak Colleges, Birmingham, came to much the same conclusion regarding the fascist orientations of Alice Bailey for New Age thought in a paper delivered at the Inform-sponsored New Age Seminar (April 28, 1990): "Aspects and Implications of the Aquarian Age."

27. Despite Odinism's anti-feminist position and stress on preservation of the racial gene pool, The Odinist Fellowship is against the anti-abortionists. ". . . the real issue regarding abortion is obvious, and it has to do with keeping women in a position of subservience, controlling their sexual habits, their bodies, their very lives. Such control has always been a priority for judeo-christianity" (*The Odinist* 118, 1988:8).

28. The quasi-racial bias of Nordic paganism was highly evident during the discussion which followed Eamon Brooks's talk, "Introduction to the Runes" (May 23, 1990) for the biweekly Wednesday evening meeting of the Talking Stick on "esoteric and occult-related subjects" held during the first half of 1990 in the upstairs of The Plough, Museum Street, London WC1. With the writer Freya Aswynn present, the consensus expressed was that runes could only properly be used by someone of Germanic descent. The suggestion that 'Germanic' could equally apply to one's cultural and linguistic rather than racial background was rejected.

29. In an article on "The Sexes" (*The Odinist* 117, 1988:7f), it is stated that Odinists do not "agree with Wicca with its strong adoration of the goddess, only giving the male the role of consort [which] seems to create an imbalance that is unhealthy. Men and women should not be seen as opposites in the sense of competitors, but rather as members of the community with equal responsibilities for the future of the folk."

30. Ms. Aswynn has published *Leaves of Yggdrasil*. She is a frequent attender at the Talking Stick venues and has in the past enunciated a more racial position—e.g., that only someone of Germanic/Nordic ancestry can develop a proficiency with the runes. After meeting a Black Caribbean during the summer of 1990 who demonstrated a skill in interpreting and working with the Nordic runes, Ms. Aswynn has publicly retracted her earlier position.

31. Patricia Cannon Johnson, "Elements of Roman Religion and the Lupercalia," *ORE* 37 (undated: 8). Ms. Johnson is currently the Conservator of Antiquities at the Nicholson Museum, University of Sydney.

32. Chris Martell, "We don't worship Satan, witchcraft priestess says," *Wisconsin State Journal*, Wednesday, 27 August 1986, Section 3. Likewise, many Neo-pagans and Wiccans express a non-hostility toward the teachings of Christ. For instance, in the *Pagan Spirit Alliance* (Issue 24, Samhain Quarter 1986) forum discussion on the topic: What should Pagans do regarding slander, harassment, and other attacks on our religion by fundamentalist 'Christians'? K. J., as part of her response, said "I acknowledge all prophets—Christ, Buddha, Muhammed, etc.—but I do not believe in them. They were wonderful human beings who taught some wonderful things." In the same issue, B. H. argued for forging bonds with other groups who, along with Pagans, come under attack from the fundamentalists. He names Jews, Buddhists, Taoists, Hindus, Moslems, Agnostics—"anybody who disagrees with the 'fundamentalist' doctrine"—including other Christians. In another *PSA* issue (number 18, Beltane 1985), L. J. claims that "My [pagan] beliefs have helped me to lead a truly Christian life style." However, in *PSA* 20 (Samhain Quarter 1985), Selena Fox states that "suspicions have been raised that Lurline, or someone with access to Lurline's Pagan mail, may be trying to infiltrate the Neo-Pagan Movement to channel information to born-again Christians." Meanwhile, L. R. (*PSA* 19) condemns "the incorporation of non-Pagan elements into Pagan worship (e.g., invoking Jesus as an aspect of the God)." But in answering the question regarding life after death, N. L. (*PSA* 28, 1987/88) feels that "Only when a person has learned life's 'lessons' do they become purely spiritual such as with Ghandi, Jesus Christ, Mother Theresa, etc."

In Britain, similar attitudes are expressed—e.g., during the ULU Pagan Moon celebration of November 3, 1990 in a forum entitled "Paganism and the Media" and including Jane Alexander as well as Nigel Bourne and Seldly Bate, HOG's Shan declared that the Craft was fully compatible with non-fundamentalist Christianity. Earlier, Shan represented "the Pagan faith" at the Student Christian Movement Conference and found the interchange mutually positive and gentle. She concluded that "people who respect the Spirit in the heart, rather than of the book, can transcend differences of religion even easier than Heart and Book can converse within the same religion" ("House of the Goddess Review 1989–1990"). On the other hand, from an integrative perspective, Caitlin Matthews, author and speaker (e.g. the Wrekin Trust's "Freeing the Feminine" conference at Regent's College October 27–28, 1990; Alternatives October 29, 1990), claims that her paganism does not conflict with her Roman Catholicism. She identifies Sophia, Goddess of Wisdom, as the female Christ.

33. *Aquarian Arrow* 28 (n.d.), p. 5. In another issue (no. 29:3), Cox states that "Runcie's Church may be losing ground in the old arenas of dogma and counter-dogma—but it is increasingly justifying its claim to a place at the Table Round and a hand in the shaping of the Holy Grail."

34. W. F. Schulz, "What the Women and Religion Resolutions Mean to Me," paper issued February 1985.

35. Article II of the Bylaws of the Covenant of Unitarian Universalist Pa-

gans, which were adopted in full on October 15, 1987, in Cambridge, Massachusetts, and ratified and amended June 19, 1988 in Palm Springs, California. The beginning of CUUPS is traced to a spontaneous summer solstice ritual held during the UU General Assembly of 1985 in Atlanta, Georgia. "CUUPS was formally founded in 1986, and accepted by the UUA Trustees as a UUA Affiliate Organization in October 1987" (letter to me from L. R. Phillips dated May 20, 1990).

36. The fusion of institutional Christianity, Unitarian Universalist theology and pagan practice is also reflected in letters to the editors of *Pagan Nuus* by individual CUUPS members. Two examples: "I believe paganism is a logical consequence of Universalist theology" (RC, Michigan; Beltane 1987:2); "The Church brings me a stability my Pagan groups never could, and seems to allow me space and support for my beliefs." (HK, Minnesota; Candlemas/Eostar 1988:4). Moreover, Phillips and Pinti gave a talk for the ULU Pagan Moon on September 8, 1990, which was billed as a "Creative dialogue between Pagan, Unitarian, Christian & other religions."

37. The "Circle Annual Report: Samhain 1988-Samhain 1989" reports that "In late summer, [Selena Fox] accepted CUUPS' invitation to speak at the General Assembly of the Unitarian Universalists being held in June 1990 in Milwaukee."

38. *Pagan Nuus* (5.1, Beltane 1991:2) reports that ". . . the total number of CUUPS chapters and potential chapters known to the Continental Office [is now] over 75." It also mentions "CUUPS' new sister organization, the British Unitarian Neo-Pagan Network (UNPN)" (ibid.) This last is under the sponsorship of Rev. Peter Roberts, a Unitarian minister in Lancaster.

39. Curiously, Mexican-American psychiatrist David Arredondo, with family connections in Matamoros, denies in a private conversation that the Matamoros killings were anything other than drug-crime warfare—claiming the idea of cult-oriented human sacrifice to be a pure media invention. Cf. Fawn Vrazo, "Residents shaken by ritual murders," *The Miami Herald*, Sunday, May 14, 1989:2.

40. John Dorschner, "Speak of the Devil: Psychotherapy Discovers Satan," *Tropic*, November 5, 1989:13. However, during his LSE seminar talk, "Satanism in the Contemporary West" (April 25, 1990), Gordon Melton claims these are cases of traumatized women (usually through preteen incest) that parallel the UFO abduction reportings. "In each case, the counsellors have become believers themselves."

41. "Five years ago, there were thought to be some 60,000 witches in Britain: today the number is estimated by some witches to have grown to 80,000. Prediction, the monthly magazine for astrology and the occult, has a circulation of 32,000. And Chris Bray, who ten years ago started the Sorcerer's Apprentice, now Britain's largest occult suppliers, deals with hundreds of orders each week and has some 20,000 regular clients on his books" (ibid.) In *The Occult Census: 1989—Statistical Analyses & Results* (Leeds: The Sorcerer's Apprentice

Press) p. 3, Bray claims that "at the present day we have a conservative estimated population of over 250,000 Witches/Pagans throughout the U.K. and many more hundreds of thousands of people with a serious interest in Astrology, Alternative Healing Techniques and Psychic Powers."

42. Shan (1988:40) identifies the Burning Times as "The christian persecutions of the 17th and 18th centuries when millions of people, mostly women, but not all, were tortured and killed. Probably only a few were real WITCHES but the terrorism of the Church forced the CRAFT underground. The isolation of very small groups that resulted led to the loss of much knowledge, so that by this century only fragments survived." On the other hand, D. Terry Boughner ("Gays & Witches," *Out Front*, October 21, 1988:15) states that "Estimates of numbers done to death by various horrible means range from several hundred thousand to a million, with an accurate figure probably somewhere in between." But Chris Bray, in his 'The Occult Census' circular, refers to "the Witchcraft Mania of the 15th & 16th Centuries during which an estimated 13 million innocent people were horribly murdered in Europe."

43. E.g., "Pagans see 'Satan', in the sense generally used, as a Christian paradox": Tenet No. 9 of " 'And it harm none'—a Pagan Manifesto" published by the Paganlink Network. Shan (1988:56) identifies Satan simply as a "Christian god form." Starhawk during her Alternatives lecture (4.6.90) called Satanism "a Christian heresy." K. S. (*Pagan Spirit Alliance Newsletter* 34, Summer 1989:9), says, "I prefer to refer to Satanism as another Christian denomination, just a splinter of all the Christian teachings." However, in the same issue (p. 12), M. A. cautions, "We should be very careful not to malign the Satanists. They have the same rights under the constitution as everyone else. . . . To complain about the lies and misinformation being spread about Pagans only to turn around and do the same thing to the Satanist as the Fundies have been doing to us, is hypocrisy plain and simple."

44. *The Occult Census: 1989—Statistical Analyses & Results* (Leeds: The Sorcerer's Apprentice Press).

45. Titled "The Occult Census" and sponsored by The Sorcerer's Apprentice, The Crescent, Hyde Park Corner, Leeds LS6 2NW. A photocopy of this leaflet is on file with the Centre for New Religions, King's College London.

46. On the other hand, Luhrmann's analysis should be compared to a statement appearing in *Pagan News* (Sept./Oct. 1990:10) by the Pagan Federation: "The Federation is Pagan first and foremost and does not seek to represent those who work outside that area in the more general field of the 'The Occult'. That is not to say or suggest that Ritual Magicians, Cabbalists, Chaos magicians and suchlike are no less worthy but simply that many of them come from non-pagan traditions and therefore fall outside our scope." The PF feels that Paganism includes the Craft, i.e., "It is quite possible and acceptable to be a pagan without being a witch . . . However, it is not possible to be a witch without being a pagan . . ." See further, Luhrmann (1989), especially pp. 32–38 and following.

47. Advertising brochure entitled "The Occult Census" and sponsored by The Sorcerer's Apprentice, The Crescent, Hyde Park Corner, Leeds LS6 2NW. A photocopy of this leaflet is on file with the Centre for New Religions, King's College London. This brochure also contains the statement that The Sorcerer's Apprentice has a "25,000 strong mailing file."

# Chapter 4

# New Age and Neo-paganism: Similarities, Contrasts, and Relationships

Similarities between New Age and Neo-paganism include eco-humanism or some variant, the belief in the intrinsic divinity of the individual, epistemological individualism, and exploratory use of theonymic metaphors not traditionally associated with the Judeo-Christian mainstream. Stewardship of the earth as a top priority associates both phenomena with the 'Green Movement' as their primary political expression.[1] On the individual level, the focus is invariably on personal growth, and here both developments converge with the aims and techniques found within the Human Potential Movement. Both New Age and Neo-paganism are structured along lines of religious consumerism, which is characteristic of the HPM, and both have a marked tendency toward spiritualization that has also become an increasing feature of the Growth Movement (Wallis, 1985). In all three areas, individual exegesis is the norm, and active proselytization is not practiced.[2] Where the creedless, non-doctrinaire attitude is encroached upon by a charismatic or authoritarian leader, we have instead groups (e.g., possibly DLM, TM, Rajneesh, *est*), which may be classified on the margins of the broad spectrum of New Age/Neo-pagan/HPM denoted by a diffuse belief-system, individualism, and boundary indeterminacy. The authoritarian marginal groups consist of followers rather than clients (see Beckford, 1985a; cf. Bird, 1978, Nock, 1933). Although perhaps to a lesser extent, New Age shares with Neo-paganism its reluctance to over-institutionalize. For the bottom line, therefore, we can say that New Age approximates more to a 'cult' than to a 'sect' (see Chapter 8 in this volume).

145

## The female metaphor

Foremost among the emerging symbols for the godhead is that of the Goddess. This is a stronger development within Neo-paganism (particularly Wicca) than within New Age and yet even Neo-paganism does not center exclusively on 'thealogy'.[3] Both movements, however, do recognize a need for a spiritual idiom in feminine terms. In Neo-paganism this is translated more readily into telluric, natural, and/or cosmic identity. With New Age, the female metaphor is more exclusively located with the neglected inner self of both women and men—an approach that is also part of the broader Neo-pagan consideration. This is not to imply that New Age does not recognize a supernatural reality. If anything, this recognition is more evident in New Age than it is in Neo-paganism, since the latter tends to approach the supernatural more as symbolic of psychological archetypes and latent powers within the human psyche. Moreover, in New Age the inclination is toward a hierarchical understanding of the supernatural as opposed to what might be termed the 'democratic' structuring of the supernatural with Neo-paganism. Nevertheless, a fundamentally animistic belief orientation pervades both movements.

Another difference between the New Age and Neo-paganism lies in divergent approaches to the 'otherworld'. New Age is perhaps more passive in the sense that it relies on revelation through meditation, communication from discarnate spirits, post-mortem experience, and memory from previous incarnations. Neo-paganism, on the other hand, takes a more active engagement with the otherworld through trance and 'flight of the soul' concepts. The Neo-pagan endeavors to experience the supernatural directly. However, with the growing study and use of shamanic techniques within the HPM and New Age movement, there is through shamanism perhaps the major convergence between Neo-paganism and the New Age phenomena.

## Materialism-spiritualism

Whereas both New Age and Neo-paganism share a stress on techniques that have the double focus of developing one's relationship with the universe as well as the achievement of commonplace goals, New Age tends to de-emphasize the material while emphasizing the spiritual. In Melton's terms, Swedenborg's championship of "the primacy of the invisible world" is the "scientific" lynchpin of the New Age movement (Basil, 1988:37). In Neo-paganism, the emphasis between materialism and spiritualism is perhaps more balanced, and, if there is an inclination, it would be toward the former. In general, in place of New Age's stress on the 'White Light', Neo-paganism—especially Wicca—incorporates the interplay between light and dark. Both movements, however, emphasize the nonrational. And both movements share the 'manipulationist' goal of realizing "the good things of the world . . . particularly long life, health, happiness and a sense of superiority or even triumph" (Wilson, 1970b:141), although this this-worldly goal-orientation is generally more evident in or exclusive to Neo-paganism.

This last point, however, is not always conceded—even within Neo-paganism. For instance, in a *Pagan Nuus* article entitled "Contemporary Pagan Spirituality and the New Age Movement" (Litha/Lammas 1988:1), Linda Pinti and Lesley Phillips contend that although the charges of narcissism concerning New Age are "an overly simplistic assessment" they retain nonetheless "a kernel of truth."

> In contrast, contemporary Paganism as a movement is decidedly community oriented, and manifests a deep concern for our relationship with all of nature.

In other words, the CUUPS newsletter editors raise the issue of self-indulgence and excessive focus on personal growth with which both New Age and the HPM have been charged by countless others and deny these very contentions for the ecologically minded and community-conscious Neo-pagan movement itself.

## Ritual

In another area, with Neo-paganism there is more stress on ceremony. New Age meetings often consist of lectures with only the slightest inclusion of ritual if at all. However, even Neo-paganism can indulge in ritualistic behavior that does not include specialists, paraphernalia, or even special time or space apart from a sensitized recognition of the here-and-now. Both movements share the type of 'individualistic ritual' characterized by prayer, meditation, inner visualization, etc. For both movements, in contrast to mainstream Christianity for instance, prayer would tend to be affirmative rather than petitionary.

## Reincarnation

Belief in reincarnation is one that is prevalent in both movements. The idea behind rebirth, however, tends to diverge between the groups. In New Age, reincarnation is part of the spiritual development of the individual psyche leading toward its ultimate apotheosis and/or re-mergence with the Godhead from which it came. Reincarnation is intimately interconnected with the very *raison d'être* of life and the divine plan of the Ultimate. Reincarnation for the Neo-pagan, by contrast, appears to put less stress on the notion of karma—the working out of past debts and mistakes. Instead, it is more simply part of the great eternal round of nature: birth-death-rebirth. There is perhaps—though by no means exclusively—more of an understanding of what Crowley (1989:56f, 154f.) calls metempsychosis, in which it is the life-force that reappears successively in different life-forms—both human and nonhuman. Crowley associates metempsychosis with the concept of immanent divinity. Nevertheless, within Neo-paganism and Wicca there is a strong presence of belief in reincarnation in which the personality itself continues and has some kind of accessibility to memory. Crowley links reincarnation with the transcendent concept of divinity.

## Ephemerality

As 'general' rather than 'specific' social movements, both New Age and Neo-paganism are largely composed of short-lived groups. These become vehicles for what Toffler (1970 [Wagner, 1983:162]) considers the norm of modern society: close, affectionate but relatively ephemeral relationships. There are exceptions to this within both movements (e.g., the Arcane School of Alice Bailey; the witches' covens in which entry is gained by initiation) but these tend to be exceptions of degree rather than kind. Nevertheless, collectivities within both New Age and Neo-paganism tend to produce a hierarchical status of spiritual development in terms of both "In-Group/Out-Group" and "Intra-Group" status (Wagner, 1983:136).

## Movement members' perception of mutual identity

The overlap of both Neo-paganism and New Age is best seen through comments made by leaders and others within the respective movements.

Despite the 'airy-fairy' criticism by many Neo-pagans of the New Age—including Monica Sjoo's denunciation of "White Lighters" and the alleged patriarchal domination of spirit over matter, there are others within Neo-paganism who readily identify with the New Age aspiration and/or expectation. Vivianne Crowley, through her book *Wicca: the Old Religion in the New Age*, is one of these.

> The theme of the Aquarian Age seems to be that of finding the divine within humanity, not outside; in finding the priesthood within oneself and not in some all-powerful mediatory figure. Here I believe there is a need and place for a religious framework which through ritual and celebration can reveal to us the place of humanity in the cosmos . . . Wicca can serve the religious needs of many in the Aquarian Age. (1989:242)

For the 1989 Beltane issue of *The Wiccan* (92:5f.), Crowley interviewed pagan writer Murry Hope, author of numerous works including *Celtic Magic, Greek Magic, Egyptian Magic, The Psychology of Ritual,* and *Olympus—an Adventure in Self-Discovery.* Under the pseudonym Athene Williams, Hope formerly wrote a regular column for *Prediction* magazine and, along with Tony Neate, founded a group called the Atlanteans, which now runs the Runnings Park conference center. However, in 1975, Hope's occult sympathies diverged from the predominant Christian framework to which the majority of the Atlanteans ascribed, and she left this association. Nevertheless, her pagan outlook remains within what might be termed a New Age interpretation, although she rejects such restricting magical and religious systems as the qabalah that assume an anthropocentric view of the universe. Instead, she contends that paganism and the nature religions preserve a broader perspective.

> "What," she asks, "says more for Paganism than Rupert Sheldrake's concept of morphic resonance?" This she sees as another way of expressing the Pagan belief that we are all part of the whole; that we are all part of one organism, and that the human, animal, plant and mineral kingdoms are all part of Gaia.

In other words, Hope finds contemporary scientific speculation "echoing earlier pagan thought." Like Crowley, she believes that "Paganism and the magical systems are highly relevant to the Aquarian era."

## Mike Howard

Another Neo-pagan spokesperson is Mike Howard, editor of a popular "Pagan Journal of the Old Religion" in Britain called *The Caul-*

*dron*. Howard frequently refers to the end of the Piscean Age. In his understanding, the New Age will be one in which "humanity rediscovers the Old Gods" (*TC* 53, Summer 1989:3). Moreover, in appraising the 1990s, Howard feels that

> an ecologically based religious movement could arise in the next few years. If not overtly pagan it would at least be Nature orientated and Gaia centred. In addition, . . . The Nineties are destined to be the decade when the feminine principle returns. (*TC* 55, Winter 1990:1)

Howard has noted that the "Aquarian impulse of the 'sixties' was one obvious influence on the direction neo-paganism was to take . . ." (*TC* 51, Winter 1988:3).

> As pagans we all (hopefully) recognize the requirements for an influx of feminine energy to balance our patriarchal society. With the coming of the Aquarian Age it is predicted, optimistically, that the male and female energies will eventually be balanced. (Ibid., p. 4)

This New Age harmony is to manifest in the area of ecology, the understanding of the sacredness of life and the reverence for Mother Earth that Howard argues is vital if the human race is to survive.

> In this respect it is possible that neo-paganism has the potential to become the future foundation for an ecologically based spiritual belief system in the Aquarian Age even though it is doubtful that the esoteric aspects of the faith could ever have a mass appeal. (*TC* 52, Spring 1989:2)

In Howard's understanding the New Age and Neo-pagan movements are further linked through the antagonism each elicits from the Christian fundamentalists. In his words, "the fundies have a bigoted inability to distinguish their Christian heresy of Satanism from neo-paganism and Wicca. Indeed, in the States New Age groups, the Theosophical Society and the Lucis Trust are all regarded as Satanic front organizations by dedicated fundies" (*TC* 55, p. 7). He foresees that

> If the 1990s are, as spiritual pundits predict, due to see the beginning of a mystical renaissance then we can be just as sure that the cause of religious fundamentalism will also increase as the 'old age' ideas clash with New Age ideals. (*TC* 52, Spring 1989:8)

Nevertheless, Howard can also lampoon what he designates "New Age vandalism." This includes "the indiscriminate seeding of psychically charged crystals at British sacred places by white American 'shamans' '' as well as native British New Agers who allegedly destroyed the St. Agnes labyrinth on the Isle of Scilly in a unilateral effort to transform a neglected place into a center for people to reconnect with natural forces (*TC* 54, Autumn 1989:3; 55 Winter 1990:6).

## Marion Green

Within the British Neo-pagan world, which includes not only Wicca but also Hermeticism, Druidry, Asatru, and Neo-Shamanism and overlaps with ritual magic, Marion Green is an established figure. She tends to speak in terms of "our Western Mystery Tradition." But along with Vivianne Crowley and Mike Howard, Green too entertains the New Age idiom as a compatible frame of reference for, in this case, "the Grail Mysteries which lie at the heart of our Western Tradition . . . [—] the Quest for the Grail, that mysterious something which will heal the Wasteland [that] has entered everyones' life in the shape of the awareness of the impending Green Revolution.''

> We can no longer be 'pagans' paying lip service to the Earth Mother whilst throwing away her generous gifts, misusing her bounty, ignoring her ever louder cries for help and relief. We must begin to lead the 'Green Revolution', not necessarily through poli[ti]cal means, but by trying to live in a Green Way. (*Quest* 80, December 1989:11)

This includes learning to recycle, using secondhand items rather than simply replacing them with new things, and changing our life-styles to redress the world's ecological balance even though the net contribution be minuscule. Along with these efforts, Green stresses the magical dimension which speaks directly to the Gods and Goddesses, the Great Ones, the Earth Mother or the Sky Lord or the Creative Principle. In this area, Green asks not only for the performance of magical acts but also the setting down "ways of ritual, magical work, healing and so on which will form the foundation of the ways occultism is carried into the Aquarian Age . . . [for] those who will certainly come after us.''

> We are the first generation living at the cusp of Great Zodiac Signs who have the information, gathered from all over the world, of what is going on, and so are in a better position to judge and weigh up what can safely be discarded from our occult knowledge and set it aside, whilst preserving all those arts, skills, psychic and mental training methods, the symbolism,

the mythologies, so potent on the inner levels and vital to a magical new age. (Ibid., p. 13)

Drawing on "our Celtic, Norse, Greek, Egyptian and Megalithic inheritance," Green argues that "We can journey simply, in the country of the mind, safely in our own homes, and rebuild the framework of the magical past in a new configuration for the Age to Come. Each one of us should take on this Never-ending Quest" (p. 14).

For the British magical tradition, in the early 1980s Marion Green helped establish "Green Circles" throughout the country. These are locally formed groups that meet once or more a month to study the Western Mysteries Tradition and perhaps to perform various forms of collective meditation, pathworking, visualization, or magical ceremonies.[4] Green also offers a QUEST correspondence course called "Magic For The Aquarian Age," which she describes as "a practical basic course with a text book and study papers, and a cassette of exercises, which are all sent out as a package." Being geared to allow the student to progress at his or her own rate, it provides the novice with a structure with which to approach the most important arts and techniques of the field. In the West Country, Green usually leads in addition a variety of one- or two-day courses as part of The Invisible College. Typical program titles include "Aquarian Magic—New Arts for a New Age," "Celtic Myth and Magic," "Village Witchcraft," "Practical Divination with Tarot/Runes/Trees," "Practical Ritual," "Being a Priest/Priestess—the Philosophy of Paganism," "Introduction to Dowsing," "The Grail Quest Today," and "Exploring Inner Worlds" (looking into ASCs [sic], astral travel, past life recall, meditation, path working, etc.) (*Quest* 80, December 1989:18).

Since 1970, Marion Green has been the editor of *Quest*—a quarterly magazine about Western ritual magic, witchcraft, divination, practical occultism, and pagan philosophy. It is one of Britain's longest running in the field and contains various articles, reports and announcements by Green, Diana Demdike, W. E. Butler, Scryer, and other known and not-so-well-known figures within the tradition. *Quest* plays a significant role in the networking characteristic of the Neo-pagan and New Age movements. As Green explains,

> There are a large number of pagan, occult, magical and New Age magazines, mostly produced, like QUEST by a few dedicated souls in their spare time. These are generally sold only by subscription or are to be found in a few bookshops so they rely on the Exchange Announcement

pages in other similar journals to spread the word of their existance. [*Sic*] QUEST usually produces, every other year, the QUEST List of Exoteric Sources, but owing to having no settled base for the last couple of years, this hasn't been possible, so in order to assist other mags. which have kindly mentioned QUEST in their lists, here are some of the many good small, occasional publications whose details arrived before our 1st May deadline. (*Quest* 78, June 1989:31)

Mike Howard in *The Cauldron* (53, Summer 1989:10) expresses the same sentiment: "TC has always had a policy of supporting new magazines since our first issue back in 1976 and supports the free exchange advertising system started in 1967 so that alternative magazines who could not afford advertising could be promoted and a free flow of information can circulate throughout the pagan movement."

As a 'pagan' proponent of New Age ideas, Marion Green is skeptical, however, of such HPM therapies as Scientology and *est* which "insist on perpetual re-examination of traumatic events so that the pain recedes." She argues that such an approach may instead simply cause the negative effects to sink deeper into the psyche where they lie dormant and ready to re-emerge at a later time.

We must watch the flow, become aware not only of the tragic and diverse effects which are going on around us, but also learn the lessons, look out for the root causes, seek to understand the will of the Mighty Ones, as they tidy up this planet to prepare it for the New Age. (*Quest* 78, June 1989:8)

Green recognizes that "Before there can be any kind of growth there has to be a breakdown of the previous state."

What appears to me to be happening is that as we are now in the dying decades of the Age of Pisces the great changes which will herald the New Age are pushing before them a wave of destructive energy. (Ibid., p. 5)

As these natural changes are inevitable, the Neo-pagan occultist is seen to be in the stronger position since "We, who have passed through the gates of initiation, into a lodge or coven or any other magical fraternity, know that death is awaiting us at any moment, in any place."

In general, Green advises to live one's magical life in secret but "to be known in our communities as good people, caring and sympathetic." However, in her own life, she has had to deal with all kinds of people from the media since about 1964, TV, film crews, newspapers, freelance journalists, writers, researchers, honest seekers trying to do a good job, and out and out perverts who tried to winkle their way into magic to discover the dark side for themselves. When we were able to explain what good works we do the radio producer always had to have an opposite view from uninformed church men whom we never met, to discuss points of view, or from the One Tame Mentally Disturbed Ex-Satanist Lady used in ALL exposees of magic! EARTH MAGIC tried to explain magic to the TV audience a few years ago, but the BBC crew were forbidden ever to make a film which showed the occult in a good light ever again! Recently local radio stations have been banned from discussing witchcraft and divination, and series on these subjects have been cancelled. (*Quest* 78, June 1989:30)

House of the Goddess's Shan, who maintains a similar high public profile, makes the same complaint—one that is indeed commonly heard within Neo-pagan circles. It is perhaps part of the same media/public image that accrues to Neo-paganism that leads Donald Reeves to disassociate himself and the Alternatives program at St. James, Piccadilly, so carefully from any connection with witchcraft or things pagan.[5] New Age has its own problems with media coverage and presentation, but New Age does not operate from a position already belabored by centuries of association with 'evil' or 'black magic'.

### Zachary Cox

Consequently, the overlap or cross-identity is more often one that is perceived by Neo-pagans with New Agers rather than by New Agers with Neo-pagans.[6] For instance, Zachary Cox, occasional contributor to Marion Green's *Quest* and editor of the *Aquarian Arrow* describes the readership of his magazine as "our own minority sub-culture—we pagans, magicians, occultists, witches, pantheists, New-Agers, speculative thinkers" (*Aquarian Arrow* 30, n.d., p. 3—the "Winter" issue of 1989/90). The perception of the pagan quest within a New Age framework and terminology shows a growing momentum within the contemporary Neo-pagan movement. Cox is alarmed over the "fundamentalist wing of the 'Green' movement" and recognizes the sociological need for an ethical-spiritual consensus.

Christianity wavers, in agonizing transition, Humanism lacks a transcendent dimension. We cannot meet fanaticism on its own level, or we lose all; yet we desperately need a vision of the human context which is above mere theologies, which begs no questions and which distinguishes mythic truth from factual truth, which can perform the same social functions which the Roman Church once performed, but on a higher arc, at a more abstract level. Just as the medieval Church stood outside of political form, so the new consensus must transcend religious form. (*Aquarian Arrow* 30:4)

Cox believes that "floating around in the mix of well-meaning naivete, self-deception, honest effort, egotism, self-indulgence and plain daftness which makes up the New Age fringe-culture, there exists the seeds for such a synthesis."

Elsewhere, Cox refers to "the wider plenum of pagans, occultists and New Age thinkers" whose planned conferences and conventions have frequently "been wrecked" by "patriarchal monotheist fundamentalists of *all* labels."[7] He sees "the Rushdie affair" especially as "of the greatest spiritual relevance to the Matter of Britain"—one which "should be of pressing concern to all those involved in the New Age and Aquarian fields of endeavour" (*Aquarian Arrow* 29:2). In an article entitled "Of Cults and Cultures" by Al Ewigkeit (presumably Cox), the idea of a new "religion"—as opposed to a new "cult" with its pejorative connotations—is further pursued:

The vast field of new growth—the proliferation of forms and teachings loosely collected under the aegis of 'Aquarian' or 'New Age'—is like a compost-heap in high summer—everything flourishes; some of it is ephemeral, some worthless, some perhaps downright bad; but here also is where the new forms are bred that shall become vehicles for a deeper and wider comprehension of the human experience—the meta-religion of the future. (Ibid., pp. 20f.)

To this "Grail Quest," Aquarians are seen as offering two essential contributions: (1) the Goddess archetype of the new grass-roots Paganism ("preciously valuable, a vital necessity") and (2) "a meta-religious restatement of the whole field, a description of the context of the Human Experience which can marry up the Humanist ethic with a wider [i.e., cosmic] vision."

## Beyond Britain

These references to a New Age/Neo-pagan consensus or at least the perception/presentation of pagan spirituality within a New Age termi-

nology are to be found beyond the confines of Great Britain as well.
For instance, in The Netherlands, although witches deny that they are
an outgrowth of the New Age movement—being instead a development
of the pre-Christian fertility religions—they base their beliefs on the
powers of the macrocosmos and positive thought. Their adoption of the
concept involving self-development allows an updating of an 'ancient'
religious system in conformity with the contemporary HPM and New
Age movement.[8]

The overlap of the occult and the New Age movement is also prominent in the United States. The move by Selena Fox away from a primarily Wiccan profile toward a religious orientation of nature mysticism
allows in particular a more direct pagan convergence with the ecological concerns of planetary healing that are becoming characteristic of the
New Age in general. Moreover, Fox's co-facilitating of public interfaith
worship services that blend Neo-pagan with Native American/Sufi/New
Age spirituality expresses the ecumenical potential that is increasingly
becoming recognized within the American scene between Neo-paganism and New Ageism. Her 1989 School for Priestesses held in July at
Circle Sanctuary and focusing on "Goddesscraft" was attended by
women who "came from all over the United States and England and
represented a variety of traditions—Wiccan, Hermetic, Native American, Mystical Christian, Hindu and New Age" ("Circle Annual Report:
Samhain 1988–Samhain 1989").

For its Summer 1990 issue (no. 37), the *Pagan Spirit Alliance Newsletter* Circle of Sharing topic was the question, 'What do you see as the
general similarities and differences between the New Age Movement
and Paganism?' About half the responses (twelve) felt that the two
movements are largely if not completely dissimilar. One person felt that
any similarities are merely superficial. Two respondents considered
New Age and Neo-paganism both similar and different; another person
claimed the two movements to be "complimentary." Editor Dennis
Carpenter does not "perceive clear-cut boundaries between the Neo-
Pagan Movement and the New Age Movement." Selena Fox finds the
two to be overlapping: "The New Age movement and contemporary
Paganism are both part of humankind's search for greater understanding of consciousness and healing solutions to individual and planetary
problems." Washington's North River Sanctuary assessed Paganism as
one of "many manifestations of the New Age"—a sentiment echoed
by one person among the eleven who thought New Age and Neo-paganism to be more similar than different. This same person felt that paganism is "helped" by New Age—a thought expressed as well by one of
the respondents who denied similarities between the two movements.

Among the similarities that PSA respondents see between the two movements, there are concern for the earth and environment, recognition of divine light dwelling in everyone, efforts for world peace and a better world, tolerance for other spiritual paths, perception of male and female aspects of the godhead, belief in reincarnation, the study of ancient psychic sciences (e.g., astrology, numerology, tarot, runes), study of mysticism and metaphysics, recognition of a spiritual/astral world, the notion of the interconnection of all, the use of dreams and interpretation, use of crystals, a shift toward organic foods and health, herbs and natural healing, use of shamanism and Native American spirituality, freedom of choice, respect for all life, a stress on the pre-industrial "biocultural traditions," freedom from established forms of worship, the notion that "we make our own reality," the valuing of intuition, interest in the occult, and the realization that both movements have the same enemy. Wiccan magic is recognized as similar to New Age visualization. Goals are frequently seen as being the same with only the names and terms being different. Both movements stress that the purpose of life is spiritual realization, and Dennis Carpenter claims that both "represent aspects of much broader changes in human consciousness which have been taking place since the 1960's." One respondent (M. A.) says, "If we Pagans are New Age, the similarities between us and other New Age religions are everything and the differences nothing . . . These difference are New Age strengths." E.: New Age "can be credited with having introduced many of us to Paganism by removing the stigma of evil and Devil worship from such benign Nature-based religions as Wicca." She adds that both Wicca and Zen are to be seen as aspects of the New Age movement.

Among the perceived differences, however, the PSA respondents tend to see paganism as more specialized, more true, more of a religion and less of a fad. Forms of celebration are also seen as different, and M. E. feels that paganism is "more boundary oriented in that either you are a Pagan or you aren't, but the New Ager can be a part of any religion and still be a New Ager." Among the adjectives applied by Neo-pagans to New Age are those of "goofy," "phoney" (spirituality), "looney," "repugnant," "obnoxious," etc. It is considered more expensive, more superficial (its roots being less deep), commercial, consumerist, fraudulent, spiritual marketing schemes, a Yuppie phenomenon, gameplaying for shock value, mostly Christian, more generalized, undisciplined, insensitive, ungrounded and seeking the quick fix, the instant answer. T. P. feels that whatever similarities do exist between the movements "are almost entirely due to intentional borrowing of terminology by promot-

ers and advertisers of 'New Age' services, or scams, and products.''
New Age is also perceived as including a greater sense of elitism—with
a generally lower level of commitment than with paganism, with a different "atmosphere" or aura, less emphasis on the personal and the
natural, with "guru chasing," UFO cults, reliance on a World Teacher
to come, with greater dilettantism, and as "not part of the night and
Moon.'' One respondent feels that New Age, unlike paganism, does not
insist on attunement of oneself with "the manifestation of Spirit in
Nature.''

## The gay community

Within both the United States and the United Kingdom, alternative
religious expressions are being increasingly seen as vehicles for those
outside the traditional faith systems of the mainstream.[9] Wicca in particular offers refuge for feminist activists and lesbians—viz. both Dianic and Shamanic branches. A Neo-pagan semi-organizational gathering for homosexual men in America is known as the Radical Fairie
movement (founded in 1979).[10] Both as well as other Neo-pagan individuals and/or groups identify frequently with the New Age movement.

> New Age religious groups offer more to gays than an 'all things are possi-
> ble' philosophy, and even more than simple acceptance of homosexuality
> as natural and God-given. For the most part, New Age groups encourage
> people to be out of the closet because that's consistent with recognizing
> homosexuality as an integral part of the whole person, and it's necessary
> to freely express all aspects of oneself in order to achieve the spiritual goal
> of wholeness, of authenticity. (*The Advocate*, 17 February 1987:29)

While traditional clerics refer to homosexuality as a 'sin', metaphysical clerics within the New Age umbrella tend to dispense with the concept of sin altogether. The usual New Age perspective emphasizes
instead notions of ignorance or error over those of moral transgression—an outlook more compatible for those following a deviant
lifestyle to that of the social norm.[11] Within the AIDS community, the
emphasis tends more toward healing efforts, which is a New Age prob-
lem-solving preoccupation rather than a Neo-pagan stress on creativity.[12] Nevertheless, as author Judy Grahn contends, the natural Neo-
pagan orientation of gay people is reflected in "the roles gays have
played in native cultures around the world . . . as visionaries, the religious leaders, the shamans and prophets for their people.'' In *Another*

*Mother Tongue* (1984), Grahn suggests that "throughout history and in diverse cultures, gay people have repeatedly been the caretakers of the spirit in their native societies" (quoted by McDonald in *The Advocate*, 17 February 1987:30).

## Feminism and metaphors of light and dark

Be this as it may, another perception is presented by Carol Eggleton in a letter to the *Wood and Water* magazine (issue 2.29, Autumn Equinox 1989:23) who complains that "it is so hard for anything other than safe, heterosexual and white writers to get recognition especially in the Occult/New Age scene"—contrary to what one might expect "in view of past and present persecution of any pagan religion." In other words, not all Neo-pagan outlook on the New Age movement constitutes a positive endorsement. Margot Adler (1986:207f.), for instance, contrasts Neo-paganism and New Age by the role of women in the respective movements:

Outside of Neo-Paganism in general, and Witchcraft in particular, the 'Aquarian Age' new religions have not been particularly comfortable with the idea of women as strong, independent, powerful, self-identified persons.

In fact, "Witchcraft is one of the few 'new age' religions where women can participate on an equal footing with men."

As already stated, Shan of London's House of the Goddess considers the New Age phenomena "too airy fairy." The strongest Neo-pagan condemnation of the New Age concept, however, comes from Monica Sjoo, who claims that in California where so much of the movement originates, it is also known as the "White Lighters."[13]

Sjoo is particularly critical of the "split-off between light and dark," which she finds characteristic of the "patriarchal religious thinking" constituting Christianity, Judaism, and Zarathrustrianism. In the Leeds-based *Pagan News* (March 1989:4), a "monthly newspaper of Magick and the Occult," Tanith Livingstone likewise complains of the

dualistic division into good and evil, or light and dark. Such categories are at best arbitrary, at worst the greatest stumbling block to achieving any real change in consciousness.

Livingstone cites the advertising leaflet for the "Harmonic Convergence" in which she counted more than a dozen uses of the word
"light" but not one of the word "dark." She recognizes a Neo-pagan/
New Age overlap in that both movements harbor the regressive concept
of some ideal Celtic, Egyptian, or Atlantean Golden Age ruled by a
protecting paternal god or maternal goddess. Though in the New Age
understanding the protecting parent is often replaced by extraterrestrials
or returning Atlantean Adepts with an advanced civilization, in either
case

> This imaginary perfect New Age is the false grail castle of Klingsor, made
> of candy-floss. It conceals the wasteland without transforming it. The New
> Age vision in many ways apes the heaven of Christian sects such as Jeho-
> vah's Witnesses—all is sweetness and light, the lions don't bite and the
> thorns don't scratch. (Ibid., p. 5)

The missing vital point in Livingstone's view is the incomprehension
that much learning comes from the darkness and a world with challenges. "We need pain to grow."
   Sjoo develops this light-dark metaphor even further and couples it
with a feminist, anti-patriarchal rhetoric.

> Patriarchy is anti-evolutionary and is set upon turning the Earth into the
> Wasteland or into a nuclear furnace . . . and considering the obsession with
> 'Light', at any cost it seems, one might be forgiven for thinking that New
> Agers would welcome even a radiated Earth. (*Wood and Water* 2.28, Sum-
> mer 1989:5)

Sjoo questions the New Age concern with self-healing and healing the
earth because it assumes that "the human (male?) mind is the self-
aware consciousness of the Earth and that without it She is passive,
unaware, dormant." For Sjoo, "Our original Mother is the Black Goddess of Africa, the womb and cradle of humanity in the mists of time."

> The patriarchal godfather is in contrast always distant, an impossible ab-
> straction that is not within us or in Nature. 'He' is—as Sir George Treve-
> lyan, an upper class New Age guru, says—a 'Divine architect' that 'de-
> signs' the world and somehow 'gives life' to Creation and the Earth, that
> is seen as female and, according to their logic, therefore 'passive'. She is
> in no way recognized as being a self-creating, autonomous and self-regu-
> lating ancient all-powerful Mother being. (Ibid., p. 4)

Sjoo prefers the pagan metaphor, which pictures the world as being born rather than made.[14]

## The cost differential

In her article "Some Thoughts about the New Age Movement" (a digest of an unpublished manuscript entitled "New Age or Armageddon?"), Sjoo also raises the contentious issue of money and costs of New Age therapies and workshops. Adler (1986:420) underscores this point when she quotes, "The difference between Pagan and 'new age' is one decimal point."

> In other words, a two-day workshop in meditation by a 'new age' practitioner might cost $300, while the same course given by a Pagan might cost $30. [However,] While Pagan workshops still cost only a fraction of similar 'new age' seminars, there's no telling what could happen if, Goddess forbid, Paganism became really popular.

For the time being, though, the cost differential between Neo-pagan and New Age workshops and programs remains a distinguishing feature. And though, in all fairness, in discussing its £180 cost for its "Experience Week," the Findhorn Foundation states in its *Guest Programme* brochure (e.g., November-May 1989/1990:19),

> Whilst attempting to meet our needs, we do not want to exclude those on a low income. A bursary fund is available and we encourage those who can give more to contribute to it in order that others may come who cannot pay the full amount . . .[15]

there remains a pagan concern over "the extravagant cost of many New Age events." *Pagan Nuus* (2.2:1) editors Pinti and Phillips remark,

> This same concern was recently brought home to us in a premarital counseling session with a low-income couple. When questioned about their religious identities, one of them asked quite earnestly if there was such a thing as "New Age for poor people." (Litha/Lammas 1988)

In a related sense, Edwin Schur, in his *The Awareness Trap: Self-Absorption Instead of Social Change* (1976), considers that the "awareness movement" only addresses the problems of the white middle class

affluent but diverts the poor "from advancing their real collective interests."

## Neo-paganism as part of New Age

Pinti and Phillips also point out Starhawk's criticism of New Age's
"we create our own reality" as perhaps partially true but capable of
producing a "blame the victim" syndrome as well as a rationalized
neglect of social-justice issues. They further mention the self-indulgence and excess personal growth focus of New Age that can exclude
community life. "In contrast," they argue, "contemporary Paganism
as a movement is decidedly community oriented, and manifests a deep
concern for our relationship with all of nature."

> We believe that Unitarian Universalist Paganism can play a significant role
> in helping provide a safe and objective forum in which to examine New
> Age concepts with openness as well as skepticism. As a sort of spiritual
> consumer advocate, it can help to critique and expose that which is fraudu-
> lent and fundamentalist in New Age thought, and at the same time provide
> a prophetic voice in support of those New Age ideas which truly promote
> spiritual and social evolution. (Ibid.)

Nevertheless, Adler (1986:304) reports that, apart from the Church
of All Worlds, "only half the other Neo-Pagans I interviewed thought
in such sweeping terms [as a New Age] total transformation of Western
society." Whereas this 'transformation' is the *sine qua non* of New Age
identity, an almost millennial expectation of quantum change is not
integral to Neo-paganism, and therein lies the chief difference between
the two movements. Though some pagans strive toward global transformation and others expect it imminently, Neo-paganism per se does not
define itself in these terms.

Consequently, the perception of an overlap with Neo-paganism by
New Agers is one that is encountered much less frequently than the use
of the New Age metaphor by Neo-pagans. This perception, if it does
occur, is also hampered by negative associations that have accrued to
paganism and that New Age seeks to avoid.[16] All the same, New Agers
do express the role of paganism within the New Age vision—even inadvertently as when David Spangler, in an attempt at "Defining the New
Age," states that

Often the New Age is seen as the pursuit of pagan religions, interest in Eastern philosophies or in the occult, or involvement with channeling, crystals, reincarnation, and other psychic phenomena. (*The New Age Catalogue*, New York: Doubleday, 1988:*xi*)

Spangler's thrust is that New Age takes many forms including such ostensibly non-religious ones (or ones at least not involved with the paranormal) such as efforts toward ecological restoration, new understandings of education, citizen diplomacy missions, decentralist empowerment politics, social change, or holistic thought.

Nevertheless, the pagan association with New Age persists—especially in the mass-media coverage. Even when the term 'pagan' or 'neo-pagan' is not explicitly used, the description that "New Age thought . . . directly or indirectly rejects the Judeo-Christian concept of a single, omnipotent God . . . [to] follow the view of many Eastern religions that there is a unity in the universe, of which all things, including God and humans, are equal parts," and, consequently, that "people themselves are deities" (Lindsay, 1986:7), the basic outlook of Neo-paganism is suggested. On one level, New Age is understood as a focus on psychological self-help and 'human potential' groups; on another, as a surge of interest in new metaphysical religions, mediums, the occult, reincarnation, psychic healing, satanism, "spirit guides," and other aspects of supernatural beliefs.

In his "New Age: Statement of Basic Principles," William Bloom includes "an instinctive knowing and experience of the sacredness and interconnectedness of all existence," "a new planetary culture [which] seeks to redress the contemporary imbalance between male and female, humanity and nature, and materialism and spirituality," and the attempt "to work with the best of the old and with the best of the new." These are each implicitly Neo-pagan concepts, although the term '[neo-] pagan' itself is avoided. And in the New Age journal, *The Eye of Gaza* (n.d., p. 5), Mary Scarlett refers to the three aspects of the Goddess as "the Mother, the Daughter and Absolute Deity." In fact, during the Unitarian Universalist General Assembly held in Little Rock, Arkansas, in 1987, Matthew Fox, sponsored by the UU Christian Fellowship, felt that the re-emergence of the Goddess as an image of the divine in Western religion was among the most important movements of our time.

Intrinsic to Mother Goddess power is the realization that everyone is an artist, that this creative power of divinity flows through all of us, we are all here to co-create the web, the web of existence, to reweave that web. (*Pagan Nuus* 1.3, Mabon/Samhain 1987:4)

Fox speaks of the anti-earth bias of Western civilization and the projection of the label "pagan" onto others as part of the concomitant genocide emanating from our repressed wilderness, sensuality, earthiness and ruralness. Speaking as a Dominican priest, he feels that

> the Biblical tradition does bring something very important to paganism, and that is the urgency of the prophets for justice, because paganism can fall into a mere cyclic repetition of rituals, and that the quest for justice is about changing the times as well as accepting the times. (Ibid.)

## Animism and shamanism

The strongest areas of overlap between Neo-paganism and New Age lie in the Earth Religions, Native American Spirituality, and Shamanism.[17] To a lesser extent, the doctrine of reincarnation in the West (which is "prominent in the belief systems of such groups as Theosophists, Anthroposophists, certain Spiritualist groups and many of the neo-Pagan sects": Bush, 1987:8) provides, as already noted, another link.[18] An underlying element behind New Age teachings/practices concerning Earth Religions/Native American Practices/Shamanism is the animistic perception that sees all things as imbued with an inherent vitality. Adler (1986:24f.) cites animism (along with pantheism and polytheism) as among "the most important ideas that underlie the Pagan resurgence," while Patricia Cannon Johnson (*ORE* 37:8) notes pagan animism "in the New Age recognition of devas and nature spirits."

Courses or workshops in shamanism, earth consciousness, and native symbolisms appear regularly among the programs of Alternatives, the Wrekin Trust, the Findhorn Foundation, and similar venues in the United States. For instance, Alternatives' William Bloom and Sabrina Dearborn gave a week-long course at Findhorn in August 1990 entitled "Devas, Fairies and Angels: A Practical Approach." In Findhorn's *Guest Program: April-December 1990*, Dearborn is described as bringing "a shamanistic approach to her workshops" (p. 25).[19] Within St. James' Alternatives program itself, lectures have included David Loxley on Druidism (March 13, 1989), Marko Pogacnik on ley lines and earth healing (April 10, 1989), Katie Marks on the usefulness of the shaman's tools (May 15, 1989), Inti Cesar Malasquez on the legendary shamans of Peru (July 3, 1989), Sun Bear on "Earth Medicine" (September 1, 1989, with a two-day workshop following), Leo Rutherford's workshop on the North American Indians' Medicine Wheel (October 7, 1989—Rutherford being described as "Britain's best known . . . exponent of the native American tradition [who] has studied and worked with many North American shamans"), and Helena Norberg-Hodge on Tibetan Buddhism in Ladakh (March 19, 1990).

Among the stronger convergences between New Age and Neo-paganism in Britain, we find the efforts of Spiral Publications and its editor Vee Van Dam.[20] Typical sentiment is expressed in an article on the "The 1990's" (*Door* 6, 1990:52f.), in which Dam describes the desire to be close both to nature and to spirit and the changes which advanced technology allows on this score—"that to me illustrates the true power of the New Age." She speaks in terms of both "evolutionary" and "initiatory change" as well as "the planetary initiation which is presently unfolding and . . . will first culminate in the year 2001." As part of the "Aquarian Age unfoldment," Dam explains in *Spiral* 5 (Samhain 1988:4) the launching of a new magazine, *Starcraft: Aquarian Shamanism*, which

> will deal with one specific issue with regard to Starcraft as a Shamanic Path, including all those different perspectives which Starcraft is apt to address, particularly with regard to working with Devas.

*Starcraft*'s logo, accordingly, refers to "Star-Magick, Starcraft, Deva Channellings, Psychic Skills, Natural Magick, Higher Consciousness, Trance States, Inner Focus, Spiritual Vision" as well as Nature and Spirit.

In the United States, the interface between New Age and Native American spirituality is even stronger than it is in Britain. In the "Spirituality Survey" produced by the *Body, Mind & Spirit* magazine (June 1989:83), 22 percent of the respondents had within the past year participated in Native American New Age teachings or practices. This was the same figure as admitted participation in New Age/Eastern religious events.[21] The Native American presentation occupies a prominent part of the "Spirituality" section in *The New Age Catalogue* (1988), which also covers Alice Bailey, Edgar Cayce, *A Course in Miracles*, Ram Dass, Hindu/Indian schools of thought, the Kabbalah, Sufism, Taoist/Buddhist contemplation, Zen, American and British Spiritualism, and Earth Religions. Native American figures profiled include Sun Bear, Black Elk (Oglala Sioux), and Carlos Castaneda/Don Juan (Yaqui), and the section also discusses the Peyote Religion.[22] Shamanic subjects are frequent features in the *Body, Mind & Spirit* magazine itself,[23] while

*The Whole Again Resource Guide* (1986/87 edition) included sections on Native Peoples (Traditional and Tribal Council Voices—ninety-seven American entries, thirty-one Canadian, one Australian and two British: *Natural Peoples' News* [an "International Native peoples' advocate tabloid"] and *Survival International Review* [an "Indigenous people international journal"]), Nature Religions (Wicca, Pagan, Hermetic, Magick), New Age (A Synthesis of Body, Mind, and Spirit), and Paths of Devotion (Truths from Many Movements). For the U.S. shamanic/native American tradition itself, two leading periodicals are *Shaman's Drum* and *Wildfire*. The former is "A Journal of Experiential Shamanism," which is "part of an informal network of people who practice and teach shamanism." The latter, in part a vehicle for Sun Bear, is a publication of the Bear Tribe Medicine Society dedicated "to supporting a public vision of harmony on the earth."

Both native shamanism along with its contemporary urban adaptations and the North American and other native traditions offer a venue by which the New Age can approach paganism and yet bypass the historical stigma associated with both the word 'pagan' and the Wicca/witchcraft that occupies so much of the Neo-paganism expression. In this light, Jane Alexander (1989:20) can proclaim that "while much of Occult teaching has a direct bearing on New Age philosophy it's fair to say that the overwhelming majority of New Agers would consider themselves neither magicians or witches." The Earth Religions, too, offer a means for an overlap of interest both through the emerging concept of Gaia consciousness (James Lovelock, etc.) and ecological restoration and again without the uneasy connotations that paganism on its own often retains. A more direct pagan link of this last, however, is reflected in "The International Sacred Sites Festival" which was celebrated in conjunction with the Harmonic Convergence of August 16–17 1987.

Sacred Sites include Mystery Schools (Centers of Knowledge), World Centers (Axis of the Universe), Sacred Mountains (Abodes of the Gods), Holy Waters (Sources of Life), Emergence Places (Sipapus: Wombs of Origination), Places of Enlightenment, Temples of Healing, Halls of Records (presently hidden from the world, but soon to re-emerge: Atlantis, Shambala, and Paititi). (*EroSpirit* 2.6, June 1987:4)

Jim Berenholtz proceeds to identify "sacred sites" in the Americas, Europe, the Middle East and Asia, Africa, the South Pacific, and Oceania. For Europe, such sites as Delphi, Mt. Olympus, the standing stones of Callanish and Iona, the Hill of Tara in Ireland, and the Tor of Glastonbury are mentioned. Berenholtz views these loci as "acupuncture points" that channel healing energies. It is through such locations—already recognized and actively used in one way or another by Neo-pagans—that a confluence of New Age and Neo-paganism is likely to find a physical and sociological expression.[24]

## New Age criticism of Neo-paganism

Apart from the general bias against paganism due to the West's biblical heritage and Witchcraft's negative and/or satanic associations, the chief criticism by New Agers against Neo-paganism is the materialistic orientation of the latter. New Agers tend to see Neo-pagans as "too this-worldly" and without a proper spiritual perspective. Indeed, as proponents of each movement accuse the other of narcissism, excessive ego-centrism, and overconcern with worldly preoccupations, a fundamental distinction between Neo-paganism and New Age relates to their respective reality evaluations and goal objectives. The former refers to the New Age attempt, following its Eastern heritage concerning *mâyâ* or the concept that all is illusion, to deny the reality of death, pain, etc. Reality is to be found on a spiritual level behind the apparent changes of the physical. This attitude to the pagan, however, constitutes a sort of whitewashing. Suffering is real, death is real—although the spiritual is *also* real.

This difference is in part reflected in the concept of the circle used by both the ceremonial magician and the Neo-pagan witch. For the former, the ritual circle is conceived of as a device by which to protect the magician from that which he invokes—classically a demon. Although a witch's circle derives from the magician's, its purpose is rather one of protecting from external intrusion or disturbance, particularly from the mundane. The Wiccan circle is an attempt to create what Mircea Eliade termed "sacred space and sacred time" or a land ruled by "the timeless truths of the myths and dreams of the human psyche" (Crowley, 1989:87). In New Age, however, the idea of a ceremonial circle is absent. William Bloom, in his Wren Café talk on "Devas, Angels and Fairies" (March 15, 1990), underscored this approach by denying any "need" for the ceremonial circle. When asked, he denied that there are negative spirits.[25] This worldview of the mental-spiritual as the sole reality—one composed only of goodness and light—is part of the Swedenborgian/New Thought and Eastern monistic heritages of the New

Age. The pagan inheritance is more dualistic in this sense, even though its dualism is essentially one of mind (spirit) and matter rather than one of good versus evil.

The virtual *soma sema* concept of New Age is a product of what to date has remained only an incipient metaphor of distinction but represents a divergent religious attitude that can be traced back to the *Rigveda* of India. This relates to the 'purpose' of the human condition. For the New Age, this purpose is more and more to be seen as something 'vertical'. The vocabulary is structured hierarchically into "higher realms," "higher selves," etc., and the goal is a "return to the source," Teilhard's "Omega Point of Convergence," the SFF's "to be one with God again," etc. By contrast, the emerging Neo-pagan view is not one in which everything comes from one divine Mind in which the human condition represents a 'fall from grace' but instead one that views life and humanity as part of the perpetual ascent and natural evolution of matter. The Neo-pagan view is more 'horizontal' than that of the New Age—being expressed in terms of the great round of life-death-rebirth. However, in the end, the 'horizontal' classification is inadequate, and Neo-paganism's chief metaphor is that of the "spiral dance"—one that includes both the eternal round and open-ended movement.

## The cultural meaning-system shift

In his analysis of America's religious tradition, Wuthnow (1976) posits a traditional-to-modern range of cultural meaning-systems in which both New Age and Neo-paganism may be seen as conforming essentially to a current shift within this range toward experimentation. For the United States, the *theistic* mode and individualism have been central; in the United Kingdom, theism alone seems to have prevailed over anything similar to "rugged American individualism." In the theistic orientation, God is identified as the agent who governs life; for the other, the individual himself is seen as in charge of his own destiny. *Individualism* recognizes no predetermined path. It is a form of consciousness in which the person occupies the position of authority. Willpower is accepted as the most basic virtue, but hard work, determination, thrift, and honesty are also stressed, while laziness, drunkenness, deceit, and such similar vices are to be avoided. The impetus is toward material success (seen as a sign of one's intrinsic worth) rather than social or religious experimentation or reform.

Theism, on the other hand, which lies at the core of every major American religious faith, is especially to be seen in the Puritan/Calvinistic legacy, which remains widespread in beliefs concerning (1) the negative image of man, which depends upon salvation through the redemption of Christ, (2) other-worldlyism, i.e., only God's miraculous intervention can solve today's problems, and (3) the literal truth of the Bible. Both New Age and Neo-paganism may be seen largely as reactions against this legacy, and with regard to social experimentation, theism's emphasis on God's governing power and man's weakness is seen as an especial deterrent. Nevertheless, "The individualistic mode of consciousness also appears [along with the predominant theistic] to have reinforced the degree of uniformity that was observed in value and in standards of conduct" (Wuthnow, 1976:105). In other words, there is a limit even within individualism beyond which one's independence cannot go. Individualism also tends to blame individuals for their own misfortune. Together, Wuthnow designates a meaning system that is comprised by a combination of both theistic and individualistic modes of thinking as *traditional*.

In contrast to the theistic, individualistic and traditional meaning systems, Wuthnow posits both the *social-scientific* and the *mystical*—both of which circumnavigate salient features characterizing New Age and Neo-pagan approaches. The combination of the two is called the *modern*. A blending of either the theistic or the individualistic with either the social-scientific or mystical is considered *transitional*. Like the individualistic, the modern social-scientific world view stresses the role of man rather than God in human affairs. It differs, however, in that social forces rather than individuals are emphasized as the governing forces. These forces are seen as family background, social status, income, the environing society, the political system, etc. In other words, "An individual does not simply choose his own goals, he is socialized into them" (Wuthnow, 1976:4). It is the primacy not of the personal will but of the social environment which is accentuated, and society itself becomes the image of transcendence (over the here-and-now of ordinary life). Despite the many different social scientific theories promulgated, however, the predominant view of social organization which this mode conveys is 'libertarian'—promoting diversity more than conformity, deviance more than strict obedience to authority, and change and reform more than static order.

. . . social scientists from Comte to Spencer to Durkheim to Parsons have tended to adopt at least an evolutionary view of social and cultural history and others have adopted an even more radical, apocalyptic view of social change. (Wuthnow, 1976:120)

Within the social-scientific perspective, "Diversity is not suspect as a possible flaw of character but is simply due to different environmental influences" (p. 121). Ironically, this perspective "commands a greater degree of 'individuality' in personal behavior than the traditional individualistic mode does." Rather than characters, souls or psyches, the 'self' has become the central concept: the self being neither immutable nor internally consistent but more capable of nonconventional experimentation. This is in part the rationale behind the Human Potential Movement.

By contrast, at the core of the mystical meaning system is the assumption that peak experiences are as important as the cognitive understandings in the other three meaning systems are for the meaning of life. This is to say that the mystical mode constitutes a non-cognitive belief system, an intuitive approach, "a mode that emphasizes intense ecstatic experience as the primary way of constructing meaning out of reality" (Wuthnow, 1976:123). In giving access to the meaning of life and the forces that govern life, intuition operates through the mystic and ecstatic experience. It allows a perception of a larger whole of which one is an integral part and thereby either resolves or 'transvalues' questions about ultimate worth, about evil, about suffering. In Wuthnow's understanding, the ecstatic, personal experience appeals especially to those for whom cognitive belief systems have become too numerous, that is, to those who are culturally and socially relative. Through such experiences, order is able to be projected upon an otherwise incoherent reality. In the mystical mode, "reality itself cannot be known or described directly but only approached asymptotically through the use of analogy" (pp. 125f.).

For the mystic, the agent governing reality is "his own mind-set—the mental framework through which one filters events and symbolizes them to himself" (Wuthnow, 1976:126). But mysticism is a different kind of individualism. The key thrust for the individualist is the exertion of "will power within a matrix of fixed laws," but the mystic denies or de-emphasizes such laws. He operates instead "within a matrix of sensory and symbolic conditions that determine his ability to construct reality" (p. 126). These conditions are both self- and socially imposed. But in constructing a 'theodicy' that copes with the problem of suffering, the mystical meaning system "tends more simply to devalue or transvalue the reality of suffering than to attempt a formal explanation for its existence'' (p. 128). The social implications of such a solution are ambiguous—leading to social and political apathy or even to antinomianism or anarchy. The frequent charges of narcissism against both New Age and Neo-paganism fit these implications. Following Troeltsch, however, Wuthnow sees that the mystical mode does indeed produce a desire for major social change despite an often inherent impotency toward all social problems. Nevertheless, the mystic mode contrasts with the desire of theism and individualism for strict obedience to institutional authority and status systems. And as Wuthnow points out, the example set by the American Transcendentalists leaves inconclusive whether the mystic meaning system—as found, for example, in the HPM—leads only to antinomian retreatism or to active involvement in efforts to reform or transform society itself.

> In general, the mystical meaning system seems to produce experimentation in life styles rather than conventionality, a quest for a diversity of nonconventional experiences rather than uniform patterns of conduct. (Wuthnow, 1976:132)

In this mode, ''Each person must create from his own experience that which is to have the most meaning for his own unique ends'' (ibid.).

> The mystical meaning system, in sum, appears to contrast sharply with the theistic and the individualistic modes of consciousness in that it contains predominantly libertarian strains with respect both to personal life styles and to larger social experiments rather than values stressing conformity to authority and to strict moral standards. (Wuthnow, 1976:133)

The mystical mode is in part a variant of the individualistic rather than the social—stressing free choice and individual responsibility. In other respects, however, it is like the social-scientific mode both in encouraging social and religious experimentation or reform and in a 'holistic' image of transcendence (for the social-scientific, society itself). But whereas this last advocates specific social programs and activities, the mystical tends to retreat from such involvements. Together, however, the mystical and social-scientific modes as described by Wuthnow incorporate what I have elsewhere designated the occult, spiritual, and social 'camps' or dimensions of the New Age movement.

Despite the suggestion that people gradually become more traditional as they grow older, it seems doubtful that young people will become as 'traditional' in their meaning systems as previous generations. The inference is that, according to Wuthnow (1976:164), ''a historical shift in meaning systems is taking place . . ."—one that clearly conforms to human potential and libertarian ideas and attitudes that are bedrock to both the New Age and Neo-pagan movements.[26] This orientation in either movement is variously composed of mystical or social-scientific mind-sets or a combination of the two. Nevertheless, Wuthnow finds that in contrast to the mystics, the social-scientific and modern types are more likely to come from a liberal background, and he concludes that "This difference suggests . . . even though the social-scientific types and the mystical types both now hold many of the same kinds of values and attitudes, the process by which they have come to their present positions is somewhat different" (Wuthnow, 1976:170).

## The New Age arena and the New Age/Neo-pagan imbalance

From the broader sociological perspective, and apart from specific theological attitudes as well as its meaning-system components, the 'New Age' terminology is an umbrella formula. Through it, many divergent religious or psycho-religious systems and traditions seek to capture the public imagination. Its phraseology is inclusive rather than exclusive. Among the various expressions that are vying for a place within the New Age movement—if not for the very vanguard of the movement itself—are the schools of Eastern mysticism, the Spiritualist-Psychic/ Theosophical-Occult, the Human Potential Movement, and the Neo-pagan spectrum. By its very nature, 'New Age' is a term of convergence—one that is more than the sum of its parts, or at least is not to be equated with any of its parts alone. Because it employs for the most part an idiom that is more neutral or more traditionally neutral, any identity by its constituencies with the New Age occurs locally and within the movement rather than by spokespersons speaking on behalf of the New Age as a whole. In other words, the identification of the New Age/Neo-pagan overlap is not readily a mutual process. It is for this reason that we find more Neo-pagan leaders and adherents using a New Age vocabulary and framework than we will find at present New Age leaders and adherents using Neo-pagan designations and symbols.

## Notes

1. During a gathering held at Hampshire College in Amherst, Massachusetts, in July 1987 to give form to the American Green movement, Charlene

Spretnak (author of *Lost Goddesses of Ancient Greece*) recognized the principle values of the Green Movement as "ecological wisdom, grassroots democracy, personal and social responsibility, nonviolence, decentralization, community-based economics, post-patriarchal values, respect for diversity, global responsibility, and a future-looking focus" (*Pagan Nuus* 1.3, Mabon/Samhain 1987:3).

2. For Neo-paganism, this situation is expressed by Charlene Suggs, then editor of *Circle Network News* (11.2, Summer 1989:3), who states, "To me, the amazing and satisfying thing about the spread of Earth-centered spirituality is that no one is converted to be a Pagan, but rather, Pagan is the word for the kind of person they naturally are. Over and over, I have heard people say 'I was always this way. I didn't know there was a name for it. I feel like I've come home'."

3. 'Thealogy' is a term frequently found in feminist and related writings denoting a theology focused on the Goddess.

4. During the twenty-second Quest Annual Conference held in London at the Art Workers Guild (March 11, 1989), it was estimated that between 450 and 550 people were actively involved in the Green Circles in Britain. Most groups were small—some with a core group of four; others, seven or eight. Green Circles were also cited for Hong Kong, Italy, Norway, Denmark, Belgium, and the Netherlands (two groups with forty to fifty members in total)—with some about to be formed in America and perhaps also in Australia. The Green Circle report stated, however, that with no central organization, many groups had lost contact with each other.The need and plan for a central register was mentioned. A magazine, the *Green Circular*, also functions as part of the Green Circles networking process.

5. An attitude expressed on November 20, 1989 during a discussion among Eileen Barker, William Bloom, and myself.

6. The overlap is also one that is increasingly being recognized by social scientists of religion (e.g., Barker, 1989).

7. In this particular case, Cox is concerned with the Reachout Trust—"a registered charity engaged in sectarian persecution and mischief-making, using the tools of calumny, innuendo and downright lies" (*Aquarian Arrow* 30:20f.).

8. "A consequence of the *New Age*-movement? Witches deny it. They are not 'new'; they reach back to the pre-Christian fertility religions. Nevertheless, they guide themselves primarily by 'Cosmic Forces' and the 'power of Positive Thought'. Through their 'self-directedness' or 'self-empowerment', witches have adopted a modern terminology" (Jasper Enklaar, "De evolutie van een natuurreligie: Hedendaagse hekserij," *NRC Handelsblad*, December 8, 1989:16—author's translation).

9. This statement might apply to The Netherlands as well, but I have no data for this.

10. Between 1979 and 1987, there had been more than 100 "Spiritual Conferences for Radical Fairies" around the country. These tend to be spontaneous expressions, often anarchistic and providing free-spirited communion. "Fairie

rituals are typically pagan in essence, honoring earth, fire, air and water, nature spirits and the seven goddesses" (Sharon McDonald, "Gays & Spirit," *The Advocate*, February 17, 1987:32).

11. Don Lattin ("AIDS and the Healing Spirit: Crisis Spawns a Search for New Theology," *San Francisco Chronicle*, February 27, 1989:A-1) reports that "thousands of gays . . . in the age of AIDS . . . are finding God in their own community, in their own experience, flocking to gay-oriented churches, synagogues and up-beat New Age congregations where words like 'sin' and 'judgment' rarely pass a preacher's lips." In fact, "Since the advent of the AIDS crisis, New Age religions have thrived in gay communities" (Elizabeth Fernandez, "A Spiritual Quest," *San Francisco Examiner* June 8, 1989:A-12).

12. This distinction was suggested by Robert Fritz ("founder and developer of DMA and Technologies for Creating") during a controversial St. James address on February 5, 1990 called "Fallacies of the New Age." Although described in the Alternatives Winter Programme 1989/1990 brochure as "one of the most creative and original thinkers in the New Age movement," Fritz suggested that in the United States he is more known as a "New Age critic." In the distinction between healing and creating, Fritz argues that "the intensity of the motivation stems from the problem focus." This means that the action designed to reduce the intensity of the problem is itself undermined as the problem is diminished. Creation, on the other hand, is not contingent upon need, belief, or the circular problem/problem-solving action dependency.

13. Apart from Sjoo, I have not come across this term for the New Age elsewhere. The term is possibly pejorative in that Sjoo perceives New Age as anti-materialistic (hence, light orientation) and anti-darkness (i.e., pro-white). However, there are undoubtedly some New Agers who would subscribe to this view and designation.

14. On another level, the Neo-pagan distancing from New Age is reflected in a humorous *Talking Stick* (Issue 2, Samhain 1990:37) checklist of indicators by which "pagan and magick groups" might identify and eliminate their increasing "infiltration" by New Agers: "(1) an unhealthy interest in dolphins; (2) a tendency to use words like *empowerment, transpersonal* and *awareness*; (3) an interest in attending expensive seminars, where they can really *relate* to others and *explore* their inner selves; (4) a reluctance to go into pubs; (5) a really gooey smile; (6) a curious habit of chatting to and *channelling with* anything vaguely resembling plantlife, and referring to it as a *deva* acquaintance; (7) a penchant for wearing organic, homegrown footwear, and anything ethnic or with a right-on badge attached to it; (8) the males of the species can often be seen sporting an unsightly growth of facial hair (as opposed to the Wiccan tradition where it is the females who display this characteristic); (9) an irritating tendency to invade your personal space with their *healing hands*, whenever the mention of a headache or similar ailment come to light; (10) corduroy trousers; and (11) a preoccupation with Karma, particularly when going through a bad patch (often referred to as an *intense inner journey of self discovery*)." The

article concludes with a warning to watch out for these symptoms and avoid these people. "They are dangerously boring."

15. In Findhorn's *Guest Programme: April-December 1990*:31, in which the Experience Week cost is listed as £180–240, the brochure explains: "Our guests come from different economic backgrounds and many parts of the world. To allow for this, we have decided to use a sliding scale for most of our programme costs. By offering a price range, we are trusting that you will be able to enrol at the cost most appropriate for you and that the Foundation will also meet its needs: a win/win situation." Bursaries are also available for Wrekin Trust activities ("We particularly welcome applications from students in full time education") and Alternatives ("The one-day workshops cost £25 and the two-day workshops cost £50. Some bursaries are available.")

16. The idea of this one-way distinction between New Age and Neo-paganism was reinforced to me by William Bloom in a private conversation following his "Devas, Angels and Fairies" talk at the Wren Café on March 15, 1990, when he expressed an uninformed attitude of modern-day witchcraft that reflected the more stereotyped mass media image, i.e., as something highly negative if not outright evil. Even when pressed to admit that witches are not nasty, bad people, he felt obliged to add, "But some groups are." Nevertheless, it must be added that during a subsequent conversation (March 19, 1990), Bloom retracted my earlier impression of his words and also stressed that "some of his best friends are witches or pagans."

17. The Pagan Federation of Britain recognizes Wicca along with Druidry, Asatru, and Neo-Shamanism as spearheading "the re-emergence of Nature religion." Nevertheless, "We keep up links with the native Pagan religions of Japan, Nigeria, North America, and anywhere else that wants to join in" (*The Wiccan* 91, February 1989:2).

18. A further area of study shared by both some Neo-pagans and some New Agers is the focus on the Cabala (Cabbala, Kabalah, Qabala, etc.), the esoteric tradition of Hebrew culture. Cabalistic studies are more prominent among ceremonial magicians than they are among Neo-pagans per se—the latter more often seeking metaphors and insight within indigenous European and other traditions (e.g., Celtic, Greek, Egyptian, even Paleolithic). Indeed, many Neo-pagans would question the assertion that the Cabala truly represents "the spiritual root of the Western tradition"—an issue that lies beyond the immediate subject of this book. It is enough, however, to note the presence of cabalism within the New Age 'consumer market': e.g., Philip S. Berg's *Kabbalah for the Layman* (1981), advertised in *The New Age Catalogue* (1988:121), or Z'ev Ben Shimon Halevi's five-weekend course on "The Way of the Kabbalah" at Regent's College in London as part of the Wrekin Trust program. See further, William Blank, "Torah and Tantra: Jewish Spirituality and the New Age," *Body, Mind & Spirit*, June 1989:58ff.,84.

19. Related to Findhorn Foundation is Newbold House, a residential community "dedicated to spiritual and personal wholeness and its relationship with the

Earth," which includes a two week training program, "The Gentle Warrior," combining "the meditation practise of 'just sitting', T'ai Chi Chuan, and the American Indian sweatlodge": Findhorn's *Guest Programme: April-December 1990*:29.

20. Spiral Publications, 8 King Street, Glastonbury, Somerset BA6 9JY.

21. The other results were: 47 percent attending a spiritual seminar or workshop, 47 percent visiting a psychic or medium, 35 percent visiting an astrologer, numerologist, or palm reader, 29 percent participating in a spirit channeling session, 23 percent visiting a psychic healer, 17 percent—Western Mysticism, 11 percent—Shamanism, 7 percent—Goddess worship, and 5 percent—Paganism.

22. The convergence between the New Age as a 'maturation of the 1960s counterculture' and the induced trance quest characteristic of Native American religion might also be seen in the advertising circulars for Quintessence (BCM Quintessence, London WC1N 3XX), which offers several smoking and/or tea mixtures of "legal psychotropic botanicals as used by native tribal shamans" under the rubrics of "Altered States of Consciousness Using Shamanic Roots, Herbs & Barks" or "Discover Shamanic States of Consciousness with Legal Highs." Quintessence as well as several other groups marketing similar products were represented by stands at the 1989 Prediction Festival held at the Battersea Town Hall in London (March 10, 11, and 12).

23. E.g., articles on Sun Bear (5.1, June 1986), "Shamanic Rescue of a Lost American in Sumatra" (7.3, May-June 1988), "The Healing Rituals of the Shamans of Ecuador" (7.4, July-August 1988), "An Interview with Lynn Andrews on Shamanism" (7.5, September-October 1988), "Meeting Don Juan" (8.1, January-February 1989), etc. In 1989, Lynn Andrews, author of *The Medicine Woman Series*, *Windhorse Woman* and *Teachings Around The Sacred Wheel*) offered "Shamanic Initiation Weekends" in Seattle (September 16/17), Atlanta (September 30/October 1), New York (November 4/5), Chicago (November 11/12), and San Diego (December 2/3).

24. A further reciprocal influence exists between the New Age/Neo-pagan movements and such cinematic productions as the 1987 *Powaqqatsi* (directed by Godfrey Reggio) and Kevin Costner's 1991 Academy Award winning *Dances with Wolves*. Films like these help to expand interest in Native American spirituality to which both New Age and Neo-paganism claim an affinity. Though a romanticized presentation of Third World toil, lifestyle, and religious practice largely in Asia, Africa, and South America, which uses a stunning musical score written by Philip Glass, the title of *Powaqqatsi* is a Hopi noun that refers to "an entity, a way of life that consumes the life forces of other beings in order to further its own life."

25. In a private conversation (March 19, 1990), William Bloom did in fact admit the existence of negative spirits but said he thought such an admission during his earlier talk "would have confused the issue."

26. Controlling age only, Wuthnow determines that modern types are about

seventy times more likely to experiment than traditional types. Controlling both age and cognitive sophistication, modern types are sixty times more likely than traditional types to be experimenters; mystical types, forty times more likely; social-scientific, thirty times more likely. Moreover, educational results are also consistent with the idea of a gradual shift in cultural meaning systems. Wuthnow found, for instance, that two-thirds of the modern type are college graduates, whereas only one-sixth of the traditional types have graduated. The comparable figures for both the social-scientific and the mystical are 50 percent each; for theistic and individualistic types, 25 percent each. In addition, nearly 50 percent of the modern type have atended graduate school, but only 6 percent of the traditionalists have. Other findings include that, apart from the traditional category, all others have an even distribution of males and females, and non-whites are more traditional (theist) than are whites.

## Chapter 5

# Survey Profiles of Particular New Age and Neo-pagan Groups

A questionnaire device has been used to develop a profile on both New Agers (using Alternatives, St. James' Church, Piccadilly, as a venue [SJA]) and Neo-pagans (attending either the House of the Goddess, South Clapham [HOG], or the Pagan Moon festivals held in the Students' Union Building of the University of London [PM]). I have attempted to formulate an idea of an individual's profession, income, family life, background, religion, sexual orientation, and self-perception. I have also picked three currently contentious issues in order to glean an understanding of the person's possible religio-political stance, i.e., their feelings on nuclear energy, abortion, and AIDS. In addition, I have endeavored to find out what the individual knows about NRMs in general; whether he/she would classify particular NRMs as New Age, Neo-pagan, or neither; and what his/her familiarity with, judgment of, and involvement with the New Age and/or Neo-pagan movements are and how the person's life may have been changed by these. Apart from a few profiles of specific leaders, I have looked for trends rather than specific delineations but have nevertheless tried to take note of the diversities of opinion and individualism. My chief objective is to develop an outlook on the collective participation in a particular New Age and Neo-pagan group and the salient differences—if any—that may identify and distinguish them. For purposes of comparison in an attempt to accent the possibility of various trends, I have put the general range of questions to three different control groups.[1] The remainder of this chapter focuses on the results of my surveys as well as those conducted by the Sorcerer's Apprentice in Leeds [SAOC], U.K., and by *Body, Mind, and Spirit* [BMS] and Margot Adler's 1985 questionnaire (Adler, 1986:443–65) in the United States.

On March 22, 1990, before a Pagan-At-Home in the House of the Goddess, I handed out a questionnaire to 20 visitors. Seventeen forms were returned to me. Shan's husband John did not attend the Pagan-At-Home but returned a completed form to me the following day. A middle-aged black woman took a questionnaire and other information on HOG that she had inquired about earlier to Shan but did not stay for the ceremony itself. This particular evening had a preponderance of men to women (only four of the latter including Shan but not the woman who left). Apart from one black male, all were white. The mean age for the women present was 29.25; for the men, 35.75.[2] The youngest female was 22; the eldest, 40. The youngest male was 24; the eldest, 60.

Another sampling was conducted with the Pagan Moon (PM) held at ULU on April 24, 1990. From this occasion, I received 24 completed questionnaires, while an additional return was posted to me via the House of the Goddess: 14 female, average age 36.85, youngest 18, eldest 76; 10 male, mean age 37.2, youngest 20, eldest 56; one 29-year-old gender-unspecified individual. For the PM group as a whole, 40 percent were between the ages of 18 and 29; 36 percent between 30 and 49—or 60 percent 18–34 and 16 percent 35–49—with 24 percent over 50.

Finally, for a New Age sample, I distributed 121 questionnaires on April 2, 1990 during the Alternatives gathering at St. James, Piccadilly, in London (SJA). The occasion was a lecture given by Page Bryant, an American who has studied and worked with various Native American traditions, on "The Wisdom of the Starwalkers." Fifty completed forms were returned to me that evening (2 were rejected), those filled in by William Bloom and Sabrina Dearborn (two directors of Alternatives) were to be collected later, and an additional number estimated by Bloom at seven were returned subsequently.[3]

Altogether, for SJA, I have calculated essentially a 45 percent return. This compares with a return of 85.7 percent for HOG (March 22, 1990), approximately 90 percent for PM (April 4, 1990), and, among my control groups, 53.2 percent for LL (March 27–April 4, 1990), approximately 60 percent for ECR (September–October 1989), and 100 percent for WCL (August 1989). For the SJA profile, 21 percent were between the ages of 18 and 29 and 69 percent between 30 and 49 (or 40 percent between 18 and 34 and 50 percent between 35 and 49), and 10 percent over 50, while 71 percent of the respondents were female.

However, for a wider profile on both the Neo-pagan and New Age movements, helpful insights are also to be gained through Adler (1986), the SAOC, and the BMS. Nevertheless, it should be kept in mind that due to differences in the sizes of the various groups, one person carries a 2 percent weight for St. James' Alternatives (SJA), 6 percent for the House of the Goddess (HOG), 4 percent for the Pagan Moon (PM), 2 percent for the London Lighthouse (LL), 2 percent for the East Coast Reunion (ECR), and 9 percent for the West Coast Lawyers (WCL).

## Adler's 1985 Questionnaire

Margot Adler's 1985 questionnaire provides inceptive insight into the contemporary pagan profile. She was particularly interested in the changes that had occurred in the Pagan community over the previous seven years, what were perceived as the most important issues facing the Neo-pagan and Wiccan communities, and what were one's feelings over using the word 'Witch', but she also asked questions relating to attitudes on drugs and to how one came to choose their present religious path. Regarding the attitude toward mind-altering substances, "Fifty-six respondents said, 'never, never, ever, ever use drugs' " (Adler, 1986:451f.). Adler had been particularly interested in this question because of the growing role of shamanism. She could add that "A majority of the people in the British traditions of Wicca also said, 'Don't use!' " Nevertheless, 76 percent of her sample felt that this decision was a matter of personal choice because these substances were "occasionally very valuable." And "Thirteen people [from a total of 195] supported the use of 'sacred substances' as a 'powerful tool', as long as they were used in sacred contexts." The legal problems were emphasized by many, and extreme caution was generally advocated.

As for the individual's path to Paganism, Adler (1986:445) found that 18.5 percent had arrived through feminism, 15.9 percent through reading books,[4] 13.8 percent through an interest in science fiction or fantasy, 8.2 percent through an interest in ecology or nature, 5.6 percent through the SCA (Society for Creative Anachronism), and 5.1 percent through religious/philosophical seekership.

Other findings included the self-perceived position of individual Neo-pagans: "fairly public" (29.2 percent), "middle-of-the-road" (29.7 percent) and "very secretive" (20.0 percent) (Adler, 1986:449). In the United States, Adler considers there to be "at least 50,000 to 100,000 active self-identified Pagans or members of Wicca." She notes the growing dominance of Wicca in the Neo-pagan community as opposed to other types of paganism more than a decade ago. She also finds an increasing interest in "shamanic and tribal paths" with at least "three different strains of Shamanic Wicca as traditions." Most importantly, Adler (1986:456) has found that respondents consider that "festivals and networks have become more important than established groups as an entry point into the Pagan community." There is moreover an increasing ecumenism and working "with other religious and 'new age' groups" as well as more communication and networking between Neo-pagan groups. "More newsletters (about one hundred). More legal Pagan organizations. More sanctuaries. More access. More gatherings."

### Rejection of Satanism

By far the most important aspect about Neo-paganism that participants wished to communicate to the public at large was the non-Satanic quality of the religion. Thirty-nine percent of Adler's returns stressed the ordinariness of Neo-pagans.[5] This is also the upshot of the SAOC. Chris Bray, extrapolating from the overall results, concludes that

> The OCCULT CENSUS has produced factual evidence that genuine occultists: (1) do not worship the Devil, (2) are not involved per-se in evil practices, (3) are not criminals, (4) are not sex fiends, (5) do not sanction child abuse, (6) do not sacrifice animals, (7) are not anti-Christian or non-religious, (8) are not idolatrous, (9) are not illiterate, (10) are responsible, thinking members of society, (11) really care what happens to our planet and the people on it, (12) are independent & self reliant and attempt to help others, [and] (13) are not part of a conspiracy to undermine society.[6]

J. M. Williams, in a review of the Occult Census (*Aquarian Arrow* 29, p. 32), comes to a similar conclusion: "Although as a sample of occultists, the self selected group is bound to be different from the total occult population in some respects (if only in their willingness to put pen to paper), the results fulfil at least one objective—that of dispelling the idea that all occultism is dangerous and antisocial."

### Use of the words 'witch' and 'pagan'

In Adler's survey, she found that 96.4 percent of her respondents considered themselves "Pagans." Only seven people objected to the word. Though the respective definitions varied widely, "most agreed that Pagans were members of pantheistic, tribal, shamanistic nature religions, and that modern Neo-Paganism embodied a respect for the earth and nature's laws and a conception of deity as immanent'' (Adler, 1986:459). In addition, ''About two-thirds of those who answered the questionnaire considered themselves Witches'' (Adler, 1986:460). Reasons given for using this word ranged from: honoring those who died during the Inquisition; it is a word of power; it is especially appealing to women; it suggests unconventionality; and it has an association with traditional natural healing. Those opposed to the word did so largely on the grounds of the negative public conceptions of what the term signifies. Many preferred the words ''pagan,'' ''wiccan,'' or ''shaman'' to that of ''witch.'' The *Pagan Spirit Alliance* Issue 25 (Spring 1987) was devoted likewise to the question of using the word ''Witch'' to describe one's beliefs and practices. Those who objected to its use represented 37 percent of the respondents; 60.5 percent were in favor.[7]

## The Sorcerer's Apprentice Occult Census of 1989

The SAOC provides further profiles on the British occultist. Regarding residence, 45 percent were homeowners, 53 percent tenants, and 2 percent travelers. Forty-eight percent drive an automobile. Sixty percent play a musical instrument (guitar 29 percent, piano/organ 16 percent, drum 8 percent, and trumpet 7 percent). Asked when the participant first became interested in occultism, 67 percent were 17 years old or less, 22 percent 18–25, 6 percent 26–35, 3 percent 36–45, and 2 percent 46–60. Over three-quarters of the respondents believed in reincarnation, with 2.3 being the average previous life experiences. Thirteen percent had been prejudiced against in employment because of their beliefs; 25 percent had been ostracized socially. Nevertheless, 71 percent felt that occultism had helped them in their social lives.

### Working of magic

Though 43 percent of the Satanists admitted to working magic for an evil purpose, only 14 percent of the occultists had—with the average number of times 3.3. Twenty-two percent of the occultists had known other people who had worked ''black magic''—3.5 being the average number of people known. On the other hand, 73 percent of the occultists had worked magic for a good purpose—approximately 35.5 times. And 66 percent had known an average of 18 other people who had worked positive magic. When asked specifically if magic had been worked by them for the benefit of others, 66 percent said yes—and for approximately 28 times. Another 64 percent knew of others (average 14) who had done the same. Nevertheless, 43 percent believed that the occult could be harmful to society, but a resounding 94 percent felt it to be beneficial in this sense.[8] And 41 percent had experienced more than 20 occult/psychic/paranormal/unexplained happenings.

## *Animals*

Sixty-four percent (26 percent of the Satanists) admitted to keeping a pet (cats 55 percent; dogs 35 percent), and 99 percent ("the largest percentage polled to any question") denied ever killing an animal or bird in the pursuit of magic. Asked if they had evidence of anyone killing an animal or bird in the pursuit of magic would they report them, 60 percent said yes, while 70 percent of the Satanists said yes.[9]

## *Diet and medicine*

Fifty-eight percent of the respondents were whole-food or diet conscious. Thirty-three were vegetarians; 4 percent vegans; and 63 percent meat-eaters. Regarding vegetarians, 36 percent identified as witches, 32 percent as pagans, and 7 percent as Satanists. For illness, only 4 percent would resort solely to orthodox medicine, and only 5 percent would use solely alternative medicine, while 12 percent would use self-help alternative medicine, and 79 percent would employ a mixture of self-help and orthodox medicine.

## *Newspapers, television, politics*

Of the SAOC sample, 56 percent were regular readers of newspapers. *The Guardian* polled highest with 20 percent as the most likely to be read followed by *The Independent* (16 percent), "local dailies" (10 percent), the *Times* and *The Daily Mirror* (each 8 percent).[10] Sixty-six percent of the sample regularly watched television, with Channel 4 polling 46 percent of the votes as favorite channel, BBC1 (23 percent), BBC2 (16 percent), and ITV (15 percent). A resounding 94 percent of the respondents affirmed an interest in "the plight of our ecology," 4 percent said they were not interested, and 2 percent were uncertain. As far as associations that might further this interest, 49 percent were members of Greenpeace, 14 percent Friends of the Earth, 8 percent

World Wildlife Fund, 6 percent Sacred Trees Trust, and 6 percent National Trust. In order of preference, the political party of choice by the respondents would be (1) Green, (2) Liberal, (3) Democrat, (4) Labour, (5) S.D.P., (6) Marxist, (7) Communist, (8) Conservative, (9) Trotskyite, and (10) Anarchist. Fifty-nine percent felt that politics could effect social change. Thirty-three percent believed that politics did not have the ability to succeed in social change; 15 percent were undecided on this issue. Although 39 percent of those polled revealed an interest or concern in politics, only 6 percent admitted that they were an active participant in politics—the lowest of any activity with sports being only marginally higher.[11]

Among the respondents, while 4 percent did not know, 24 percent were in favor of the perpetuation of compulsory religious education in the national school curriculum, and 72 percent were against. However, if the curriculum were to include "balanced reviews of a wide cross section of beliefs including pagan/psychic/alternative beliefs," 85 percent were then in favor (in this case, 13 percent were still against, and 2 percent did not know). The SAOC also discovered that 85 percent of those polled believed that the Christian church was chiefly responsible for the misinformed image of the occult. Another 82 percent put the blame on the newspapers, 68 percent on other written media and magazines, 66 percent on "Dennis Wheatley type exhibitionists," 57 percent on television and radio broadcasts, 43 percent on other orthodox religions, and 34 percent on successive governments.

## Perception of public and self-image

The SAOC asked each respondent to list three things he/she felt non-occultists get most upset over regarding occultism, three "untruths" erroneously associated with occultism/witchcraft, and three improvements that might take place within "the occult scene." The SAOC report listed "the media's image of devil-worshippers and black magic" (which polled 27 percent) as the "most upsetting misunderstanding." This was followed by "fear of death and the unknown" (22 percent), "the idea that occultism involves blood sacrifice," and "the idea that occultism involves sexual perversion" (19 percent each). Fourteen percent chose "the idea that all occultism is evil."[12] The fallacies thought to be associated with occultism are similar: "it's all devil worship & Satanism" (57 percent), "it's an excuse for sexual perversion" (31 percent), "they sacrifice animals and humans" (29 percent), "they concern themselves with evil/evil things" (20 percent), and "they abuse children as part of their ceremonies" (17 percent). The consensus on improvements ranked as "more good publicity/press coverage" (25 percent), "clearer teachings and more openness" (22 percent), "recognition of paganism as a religion," and "the spread of truth" (14 percent each).

## Social advantage and occult interest

To the question pertaining to the "social advantages of involvement in occultism," 26 percent consider that it gives community spirit among like-minded people, 20 percent argue that it makes one aware of other people's feelings, 16 percent feel it bestows more social confidence, and 12 percent find that it provides a source of trustworthy friends. To glean the individual interests of British occultists, each respondent was asked to distinguish among sixteen areas in terms of (1) no interest, (2) curious interest, (3) serious interest, and (4) committed belief. Table 5.1 gives a percentage breakdown of occult interests. The indication is that 46 percent of the occultists surveyed identify as pagans, 42 percent as Witches,[13] while the predominant interests are healing, ritual, divination, spells[14] and mindpower—with lesser but substantial interest in herbalism, psychology, and astrology. Apart from Satanism, there is relatively little concern with theosophy, spiritism, chaoism, hypnotism and cabalah.

## The BMS Spirituality Survey of 1989

The SAOC figures are also of interest when compared with those for the readership of *Body, Mind, & Spirit*. In the magazine's "Spirituality Survey" (June 1989),[15] only 7 percent admitted participation during the past year in Goddess worship—a figure that compares markedly with the 46/47 percent of British occultists identifying as Witches or Pagans.[16] Another point of contrast would be the joint 77 percent in the SAOC who expressed a curious or serious interest or committed belief in astrology, whereas only 35 percent in the *BMS* survey had visited an astrologer, numerologist, or palm reader in the last year. On the other hand, American New Agers revealed a 47 percent participation in a spiritual workshop or seminar, including visiting a psychic or medium, while Britain's occultists expressed a similar interest or belief in Spiritism, i.e., 43 percent.[17] *Body, Mind, and Spirit* asked specifically about "psychic" healing, and 23 percent of their respondents had been to a

**TABLE 5.1: Occult Interest**

|            | *No Interest* | *Curious Interest* | *Serious Interest* | *Committed Belief* |
|------------|---------------|--------------------|--------------------|--------------------|
| Astrology  | 23 | 26 | 26 | 25 |
| Chaos Magic| 56 | 24 | 12 | 8 |
| Divination | 25 | 15 | 25 | 35 |
| Healing    | 22 | 17 | 24 | 37 |
| Herbalism  | 27 | 19 | 25 | 29 |
| Mindpower  | 25 | 14 | 28 | 33 |
| Paganism   | 21 | 12 | 21 | 46 |
| Psychology | 29 | 16 | 30 | 25 |
| Cabalah    | 39 | 19 | 23 | 19 |
| Ritual     | 28 | 14 | 23 | 35 |
| Theosophy  | 64 | 19 | 11 | 6 |
| Satanism   | 75 | 15 | 6 | 4 |
| Spells     | 32 | 13 | 21 | 34 |
| Spiritism  | 57 | 18 | 13 | 12 |
| Witchcraft | 16 | 16 | 12 | 42 |

psychic healer in the previous year. The SAOC, however, asked only about healing in general, and its results do not compare meaningfully with those of the *BMS* survey.

## *Religion, gender, age, education, and profession*

The New Age spirituality survey nevertheless furnishes a profile of its respondents that at the same time is different in the focus of its concern from the questions put to the Neo-pagan community by Adler, the SAOC, or myself. Figures for religion in which raised, however, were roughly similar: Protestant (52 percent), Catholic (27 percent), Jewish (3 percent) and none (11 percent) (see below, Table 5.4). Seventy-three percent of the random sample were female; 20 percent male. The age breakdown was 18–34 (23 percent), 35–49 (42 percent), and over 50 (35 percent).[18] For education, the *BMS* survey found that 18 percent had attended high school, 45 percent some college, 18 percent had earned a bachelor's degree, and 12 percent an advanced degree. Regarding occupation, 25 percent were Professional/Technician, 19 percent Retired/Unemployed, 13 percent Clerical, 12 percent Service, 11 percent Managerial, and 6 percent Sales.

Asked which religion the *BMS* readership considered themselves now, 17 percent answered Protestant, 11 percent Catholic, 2 percent

Jewish, 15 percent New Age, 10 percent other, and 35 percent none. Whereas less than half thought of themselves as religious, the vast majority (94 percent) considered themselves "spiritual." Though 64 percent felt that "organized religion is outmoded in this day and age," a full 92 percent believed in life after death, while 81 percent accepted belief in reincarnation.[19] This last compares to the SAOC's "more than 75 percent" who believed in rebirth.

## Occult experiences and beliefs

Other *BMS* findings include 78 percent who had had psychic/intuitive experiences, 77 percent who had known who was on the phone before picking up the receiver, 75 percent who had known something would happen before it occurred, 72 percent who had experienced *déja vu*, 59 percent who had had a dream that foretold a future event, 47 percent who had had an out-of-body experience, 47 percent who had contacted a deceased friend or relative, 34 percent who had experienced a ghost or spirit entity, and 26 percent who had had a near-death experience. Fifty-nine percent felt that New Age teachings or practices had altered their religious beliefs. Fifty-eight percent felt that their concept of God was not the same as the concept of God in the Bible. Eighty-three percent denied that there is only one "true" religion or path. Nearly three-quarters of the respondents felt that New Age thought had altered their life in general. This was usually described as an openness to other belief systems as well as a new appreciation that we all share the planet. Finally, 74 percent were "optimistic about the future of planet earth," but most expressed the sentiment that this depends on improving relationships between ourselves and humanity and the planet itself.

## Social Composition of Selected London-based New Age and Neo-pagan Groups

### Profession

By profession, the various groups break down into the percentages listed in Table 5.2. Note that the PM figures include only those forms returned to me on this occasion; attenders to HOG on March 22, 1990, though also present for the Pagan Moon celebration, did not complete questionnaire forms a second time. The additional response I received in the mail indicated the person (38M) to be unemployed.

**TABLE 5.2: Membership of Selected Groups by Profession**

| | House of the Goddess | Pagan Moon | Saint James Alternative | London Light House | East Coast Reunion | West Coast Lawyers |
|---|---|---|---|---|---|---|
| Computer, programming, technology | 6% | 4% | 11% | 1% | — | — |
| Journalism, writing, publishing, etc. | 24% | 8% | 5% | 7% | — | — |
| Research science | — | — | 2% | 2% | 2% | — |
| Nursing | — | — | — | 17% | — | — |
| Engineering | — | — | — | — | 4% | — |
| Civil service/ social work | 12% | 20% | 4% | 11% | — | — |
| Management & administration | — | 12% | 9% | 18% | 20% | — |
| Teaching, crafts, etc. | 24% | — | 17% | 1% | 18% | — |
| Artists, musicians, photographers, etc. | 18% | 12% | 7% | 2% | — | 9% |
| Students | — | 14% | 11% | 4% | 4% | — |
| Lawyers | — | — | 2% | 1% | 4% | 91% |
| Physicians and dentistry | — | — | — | 2% | 2% | — |
| Finance, accounting, investment | — | — | — | 6% | 6% | — |
| Secretarial work | — | 14% | 9% | 5% | 6% | — |
| Therapy, psychoanalysis | — | 10% | 12% | 2% | 2% | — |
| Tradesmenship | — | — | — | 5% | — | — |
| Unemployed | 6% | 4% | 11% | 4% | — | — |
| Housewives | — | 4% | — | — | 10% | — |
| Self-employed | 6% | — | — | — | — | — |
| Other | — | — | 4% | 12% | 8% | — |
| No answer | — | 4% | 4% | 5% | 6% | — |

By contrast to my figures (Table 5.2), Adler (1986:446f.) found computer programmers/systems analysts/software developers the highest single profession represented among her sample. Together with technical writers and scientists, this amounted to 16 percent (according to Adler, but 14 percent is more accurate). The SAOC does not give figures or percentages for occupation but states "Occultists are more likely to follow careers in Journalism/Writing; Nursing or Engineering; Computer Operator/Programming; Civil Service; Horticulture; Management or to become Self-Employed" (p. 14). The highest-ranking profession among the HOG participants on March 22, 1990, were teachers—though this includes Shan ("Clan Mother—Organiser, Teacher, Counsellor, Writer"), Shan's husband John ("Self-employed craftsman and sometime Open University Tutor"), and Shan's assistant Barry ("Craftsman/Teacher")—which would comprise 23.5 percent versus Adler's 7 percent for a combined Teacher/Craftsperson category. In general, the professional background of the pagan groups as well as the Alternatives respondents cuts across middle-class mainstream society with an absence of blue-collar workers and for SJA in particular a noticeable presence of people whose professional work relates them directly to the HPM, teaching, and the field of New Age techniques.

## HOG—income, origins, and family background

Most HOGers (8) indicated an income between £5–10,000, two below this amount, one in the £10–15,000 range, three between £15 and 20,000, and one over these figures.[20] The greatest number (6) indicated that they had been raised in London. Two were from Scotland, two from Wales, one from Cornwall, one from Devon, and one came from New Zealand. The remaining four hailed from Newcastle-upon-Tyne, Northampton, Nottingham and Huntingdon.[21] Eight considered the financial status of their families as "lower-middle"; five "upper-middle," and two "poor."[22] Only two respondents affirmed that their parents had divorced during their childhood.[23]

### Education

Regarding education, there were no respondents in any of the groups who indicated having had less than a secondary education. There was also on the questionnaire an option for "further education." The response ranged from 62 percent (LL) to 68 percent (PM). Finally, a question was included concerning "qualifications" (GCSEs, GCEs, etc.) These may be broken down to "O" levels, GCSEs, etc., with an average 41 percent (SJA) to 48 percent (PM); "A" levels, 18 percent (HOG) to 29 percent (LL); B.A., B.Sc., etc., 28 percent (PM) to 41 percent (HOG and SJA); M.A., M.Sc., etc., 2 percent (LL) to 17 percent (SJA); and Ph.D.: 4 percent (SJA), 6 percent (HOG), 8 percent (PM), and none for LL. In general the figures show no marked difference in educational levels among the four groups.

## *SJA—income and family background; marital status compared with that of other groups*

For the SJA profile, the income breakdown was as follows: 21 percent below £5,000, 23 percent £5–10,000, 35 percent £10–15,000, 12.5 percent £15–20,000 and 4 percent above £20,000 while another 4 percent did not answer this question. Fifteen percent described their family's financial status during childhood as poor, 49 percent as lower-middle, 34 percent as upper-middle, and only one person (2 percent) claimed to be from a wealthy family.[24] A higher than usual number of respondents in the other groups indicated that, during childhood, their parents had divorced (27 percent).[25] Of a potential 100 percent possibility (that is, respondents were asked to give multiple answers if applicable), the comparative figures for (1) single status, (2) married, (3) unmarried partnership relationship, (4) divorced, and (5) widowed for the other groups are listed in Table 5.3:[26]

## Group Comparisons on the Basis of Religion and Perceptions of God

Table 5.4 shows percentages for the various groups indicating religion in which raised. I have included national breakdowns for both the United States and the United Kingdom as well.[27]

**TABLE 5.3: Marital Status**

|   | *HOG* | *PM* | *SAOC* | *LL* | *ECR* | *WCL* | *SJA* |
|---|---|---|---|---|---|---|---|
| 1 | 53% | 28% | 50% | 67% | 6% | 27% | 56% |
| 2 | 24% | 32% | 37% | 12% | 69% | 36% | 19% |
| 3 | 18% | 20% | 13% | 19% | 0% | 36% | 12.5% |
| 4 | 18% | 12% | 11% | 5% | 18% | 9% | 17% |
| 5 | 0% | 8% | — | 0% | 2% | 0% | 0% |

**TABLE 5.4: Religion in Which Raised**

|  | Prot. | RC | Jewish | Other | None |
|---|---|---|---|---|---|
| USA 1957[28] | 62.2% | 25.7% | 3.2% | 1.3% | 2.7% |
| USA 1971[29] | 65% | 26% | 3% | 4% | 2% |
| Melton[30] | 42.7%[31] | 25.8% | 6.2% | 15.2% | 10.1% |
| Adler 1985[32] | 60.8%[33] | 23.5% | 5.4% | 1.8% | 8.4% |
| HOG[34] | 55.9% | 23.5% | — | 11.8% | 8.8% |
| PM[35] | 62 | 14% | 8% | — | 16% |
| SJA | 61%[36] | 14% | 12.5% | 6%[37] | 6% |
| BMS | 52% | 27% | 3% | — | 11% |
| ECR | 44% | 20% | 31% | — | 2% |
| WCL | — | 64% | 18% | 6%[38] | 6% |
| LL | 64% | 19% | — | 2%[39] | 7% |
| UK[40] | 46.3% | 18.7% | 0.5% | 7.5% | 27% |

The most notable aspect of the three focal groups is the comparatively high presence of former Jews in Alternatives. In fact, both Malcolm Stern and William Bloom, co-directors of SJA, come from Jewish backgrounds. There is also a moderately high presence of people who were raised Jewish for the Pagan Moon celebration of April 7, 1990, though none for the House of the Goddess gathering of March 22, 1990. The *Social Trend* figures for the United Kingdom are given for comparative purposes only. They represent percentages of the British population who currently identify as Protestant, Catholic, etc., whereas the other figures in Table 5.4 represent the percentage *origins* of each group by religion. In general, the four British groups correspond with each other though a higher than average percentage of PMers had no religious background and a higher than average percentage of HOGers had a non-mainstream religious background.

Because of the greater diversity of contemporary religious beliefs, it is more difficult to classify present religious beliefs in tabular form. For example, when asked what were their religious preferences now, HOG respondents answered: not certain (2), Wicca or Craft (4), Gardnerian (1), Wicca/New Age (1), Natural (1), Pagan (2), mildly Pagan (1), feminist Pagan (1), occultist (1), Spiritual (1), Freedom (1), and none (1). Among the Pagan Moon of 7 April 1990, the range included: Pagan (8), Wicca (5), Pagan/Wicca (2—including Vivianne Crowley), Shamanic Craft (1), Shaman (1), Jewish Pagan (1), non-Roman Catholic (1), non-Islamic Sufi (1), Bahai (1), Seeker (1), and None (2). One person (76F former Anglican) did not respond to this question.

## SJA

Current religious preference for the SJA respondents revealed the greatest diversity. Twenty-three percent claimed no present religious identity—cf. 35 percent for BMS, 6 percent for HOG, 8 percent for PM, 50 percent for LL, 22 percent for ECR, and 91 percent for WCL.[41] Only 8 percent of the SJA respondents identified their current identity as "New Age." Another 16 percent ranged between Buddhist, neo-Christian Buddhist, Hindu, and Vedic, 10 percent described their religious preference as "spiritual," and another 8 percent used the terms "Pagan" (3) or "Goddess religion" (1). The Christian element is only to be identified within the following: neo-Christian Buddhist (42F), open-minded Christian (35M), Quaker (37F), and "a mixture of many: Christian/Spiritualist/Buddhist, etc." (40F)—representing 8 percent of the total. And apart from the unspecified "Orthodox," the only semi-Jewish response was listed as "Hindu/Jewish" (30F). Two people spoke of "The God (force) within (me)." Other responses include none-Taoism, none-nature, religious (nonspecific), open, eclectic, my own path, own inner guidance, no religious dogma, alternative, any, and all pathways.

### Pagan and control groups

For comparative purposes, HOG breaks down to 35 percent witch-craft, 29 percent pagan, etc.; PM: 28 percent pagan, 20 percent Wicca, 12 percent Pagan/Wicca plus one Shamanic Craft, one shaman, etc. and two replied "none"; SAOC: 46 percent pagans, 42 percent witches—with "curious, serious or committed belief" in the former 79 percent and in the latter 84 percent; Adler (1986): 96.4 percent pagans, 67 percent witches. The control groups are as follows: for LL, 50 percent none, 14 percent Protestant, 12 percent Asian religions, and 5 percent Roman Catholic, plus one Islam, one "universal," one "world," one "pagan," and one "spiritual"; for ECR, 31 percent Protestant, 27 percent Jewish, 22 percent none, 16 percent Roman Catholic, plus one "Roman Catholic/universal" and one "combination of many"; for WCL, 91 percent none plus one "on hold."

### Belief in God

Perhaps the widest show of individuality is to be found among the answers to the question concerning belief in God. Among the HOG

respondents, no one selected the option "Don't know."[42] The others
were [1] A real personality, [2] A fiction, [3] An impersonal force, and
[4] Other. Multiple answers were encouraged, and three people selected
the first,[43] one person the second,[44] and four the third.[45] For the last
option, the answers ranged from "The infinity," "An indivisible matrix
of energy of which we are a part," "What you make it," "Big! Small!
In between!" "The one in between all the above," and "Probably a
whole hierarchy of beings."[46]

The percentage responses for belief in God were (1) a real personality: SJA 6 percent, HOG 18 percent, PM 8 percent, LL 7 percent, ECR
22 percent, WCL 0 percent; (2) a fiction: SJA 0 percent, HOG 6 percent,
PM 4 percent, LL 24 percent, ECR 4 percent, WCL 27 percent; (3) an
impersonal force: SJA 33 percent, HOG 24 percent, PM 36 percent, LL
24 percent, ECR 31 percent, WCL 9 percent; (4) don't know: SJA 12.5
percent, HOG 0 percent, PM 4 percent, LL 26 percent, ECR 16 percent,
WCL 45 percent; and (5) other: SJA 52 percent, HOG 41 percent, PM
48 percent, LL 17 percent, ECR 31 percent, WCL 18 percent. The results indicate that the secular San Francisco Bay Area lawyers and London Lighthouse secularists rank highest in holding the idea that God is
a fiction. Only one person in both HOG and PM thought the same; none
held this view among the Alternatives respondents; and two people
among the conservative ECR. However, both the ECR and HOG are
out-of-step with the rest with a higher consideration of God as a real
personality. Apart from WCL, between one-quarter to one-third of
those in each group would hold that God is an impersonal force. There
is little uncertainty on this question among the pagan groups. The
American West Coast lawyers ranked highest in not knowing what God
is; Alternatives falls between the pagans and the British secularists
(London Lighthouse) on this front. The New Agers and the Neo-pagans,
however, reveal a much greater degree of individuality in their conception of the Godhead.[47]

## Comparison of Group Members' Self-Perception

To delineate the aggregate self-perceptions of the various groups, respondents were asked to select from a list of various indications. For
instance, among HOG, there were six indications of Religious, six Political, five Social activist, ten Fun-loving, seven Serious, and eight Romantic.[48] For a comparison among group profiles, the collective percentage responses, when asked to indicate how the individual would

describe himself/herself, were the following: as religious (SJA 37.5, HOG 35, PM 48, LL 12), political (SJA 19, HOG 35, PM 48, LL 12), social activist (SJA 17, HOG 29, PM 40, LL 38), fun-loving (SJA 65, HOG 59, PM 72, LL 76), serious (SJA 67, HOG 41, PM 60, LL 60), romantic (SJA 54, HOG 47, PM 68, LL 60), and/or other (SJA 37.5, HOG 41, PM 40, LL 29). Extrapolating from the resulting figures, it would appear that the general religiosity of the New Age Alternatives, House of the Goddess, and the Pagan Moon gathering (representing a broader spectrum of the pagan community) are comparable. The London Lighthouse, the only non-religious group, correspondingly reveals a markedly less degree of religiosity. On the other hand, both the political and social activist involvements of the St. James respondents are noticeably less than the pagan and secular groups. The remaining categories indicate no noteworthy distinctions.[49]

### Sexual orientation

Finally, respondents were asked to indicate their sexual orientation. Percentage respondents indicate the following: heterosexual: HOG 65, PM 70, SJA 74, LL 26, ECR 94, WCL 82; homosexual: HOG 18, PM 4, SJA 8, LL 61, ECR 2, WCL 18; bisexual: HOG 6, PM 16, SJA 6, LL 6, ECR 4; and celibate: PM 2, SJA 11, LL 5. One HOG respondent wrote in "sexual," while Shan replied with "shamanic." Among the Pagan Mooners, there was one no answer and one person (32F—the mother of twins) listed herself as "non-classified." The high homosexual profile of the London Lighthouse reflects its origins as a response by the gay community to the AIDS crisis. We find, on the other hand, among the Neo-pagan and New Age groups a relatively similar percentage of heterosexual lifestyles versus the homosexual/bisexual. The most noteworthy point is the higher than average degree of celibacy among the Alternative New Agers.

## Attitudes Toward Crucial Contemporary Issues

There are several urgent issues in contemporary society that have been widely debated. In order to understand where New Agers and Neo-pagans stand on these questions, I have asked about attitudes toward nuclear energy, abortion, and AIDS—putting the same questions to the control groups as well.

## Nuclear energy

On the nuclear energy question, the options were (1) it is too dangerous to be a feasible source of energy, (2) it is the most viable energy
source for our future needs, (3) the lesser of two evils,[50] (4) acceptable
with proper supervision and waste disposal, (5) don't know,[51] and (6)
other—being asked to specify.[52] Only *one* answer was requested. Considering that nuclear energy is too dangerous to be a feasible source of
energy, the liberal/radical WCL group ranked high with an 82 percent
affirmation; the conservative ECR, low with only 14 percent.[53] SJA
scored 60 percent on this response, PM 64 percent, LL 62 percent, and
HOG less than the others with 38 percent. Nuclear energy was acceptable with proper supervision and waste disposal to 10 percent of the
PM, 18 percent of both LL and WCL, 24 percent of SJA, 26 percent of
HOG, and 57 percent of ECR.

## Abortion

The abortion question asked for multiple answers among (1) generally in favor, (2) in favor ONLY under specific circumstances, (3) the
choice is the woman's alone, (4) against in ALL circumstances, and (5)
against in SOME circumstances. Half of all the groups sampled (52
percent of the aggregate) feel that the choice on abortion is the woman's
alone.[54] The pagan groups rank on the low end of the scale when asked
if they are generally in favor of abortion (HOG 12, PM 20 percent); the
American groups rank highest (ECR 53, WCL 64 percent); and both
Alternatives (37.5 percent) and the secular London Lighthouse (36 percent) fall between the two extremes. However, both SJA (21 percent)
and PM (20 percent) are inclined more than the others (HOG 6, LL
7, ECR 6, WCL 0 percent) to sanction abortion only under specific
circumstances; the same percentage of the PM group are against abortion in some circumstances (cf. HOG 6, LL 2, ECR 8, and 0 percent for
SJA and WCL).[55]

## The AIDS issue

When asked to check one answer among the following: AIDS is (1)
God's punishment, (2) A natural calamity, (3) Engineered by the CIA,[56]
(4) Don't know, and (5) Other, among HOGers, 3.5 indicated the second (one replaced the word "calamity" with "event"); 1.5 responded
to the third possibility with an additional 1.5 adding the proviso "possi-

bly''; and 4 took the forth option.[57] The AIDS question also reveals a variance among the various groups. Less than half (46 percent) of the SJA identified the disease as a natural calamity, while 19 percent did not know, and 23 percent thought it something other. For HOG, the natural calamity response was even lower—only 21 percent. For PM, on the other hand, natural calamity was the answer given by slightly more than half the respondents (52 percent), only here was also the only response I received indicating that the disease was God's punishment (55M). For the WCL, all but one (no answer) called AIDS a natural disaster (91 percent).[58]

### Familiarity with and Attitudes toward New Age

Regarding familiarity with the New Age movement, 14 HOGers said they were; 3 said they were not. Thirteen thought it was "generally positive," 1 (John) classified it as "generally negative," 1 thought it to be both, and 2 (including Shan) avoided the answer. While 2 did not know enough to say and 5 thought it too broad a concept to say, 2.5 considered New Age "The religion of the future"; 1.5, "A religion of the future." While John thought New Age both "Nonsense" and "Well-meaning but still nonsense," Shan selected the second of these options with the addition: "not realistic."[59] The four write-in answers were: "Change" (43M), "A tendency" (35M), "Evolving relationship with the supernatural" (60M), and "Something trendy for rich people with a concience" [sic] (31F).

Comparative figures for the PM (April 7, 1990) were 19 being familiar with New Age (i.e., 76 percent versus HOG's 77.8 percent); 4 were not familiar; and 2 did not answer the question. Seventeen people or two-thirds of the PM respondents considered New Age generally positive; 4 did not; and 4 did not answer. The HOG response to the New Age being generally positive was 72.2 percent. Among the PMers, 4 considered New Age "a religion of the future," 3 thought it "well-meaning but still nonsense," 8 thought it "too broad" a concept to say, 5 avoided the question, while 5 checked the "other" category: "seriously and dangerously flawed" (32F), "a natural change in ideas" (25M), "a 'religion'?" (33M), "a philosophy" (Vivianne Crowley), and "a general tendicial [sic] attempt to improve the way people treat themselves & the rest of the universe and make them more aware of the spiritual" (38M).

Although 75 percent of the SJA respondents admitted to being familiar with the New Age movement, there was actually greater familiarity of the same among the pagan community: PM (76 percent) and HOG (82 percent). However, whereas 85 percent of the Alternative respondents affirmed New Age as generally positive,[60] only 68 percent of the PMers[61] and 79 percent of those from HOG did the same.[62] For the LL, 29 percent were and 67 percent were not familiar with New Age (1 n.a.; 1 not sure); and 43 percent thought it generally positive, 10 percent negative, one person both, and 43 percent did not answer the question. For ECR, 22 percent were familiar, while 18 percent thought it positive and 16 percent chose negative.[63] Among WCL, 45 percent were both familiar and thought New Age generally positive.[64]

Asked to describe New Age as (1) the religion of the future, (2) a religion of the future, (3) nonsense, (4) well-meaning but still nonsense, (5) too broad a concept to say, (6) insignificant, (7) never heard of it, (8) do not know enough to say, and (9) other, the fifth (SJA 39, HOG 29, PM 32, WCL 27 percent), eighth (LL 33, ECR 24, WCL 45 percent) and ninth (SJA 29,[65] HOG 24, PM 20, WCL 18 percent) options drew the highest responses with no answers comprising 20 percent of PM and 59 percent for ECR. Not one person in any of the groups examined thought New Age as insignificant, yet only one-quarter of both the SJA and HOG respondents considered New Age as a or the religion of the future. This last reduced to 16 percent and 17 percent among PM and LL, respectively. The two American control groups expressed the least feeling that New Age would be part of the future, but these results might also need to be balanced against the earlier dates of the American surveys. The SJA and the two London-based pagan groups—with the former leading—all substantially recognized the inherent broadness in the concept of the New Age itself. Only the conservative American East Coast group and the secular London Lighthouse possessed claimants who had never heard of the ''New Age.'' All three secular groups frequently felt they did not know enough about the New Age to make any prediction about its future viability.

## Familiarity with and Attitudes toward Neo-paganism

### Pagan responses

Only one person in this HOG survey claimed not to know anything about Neo-paganism (25M). There were eleven identifications of it as a nature-based religion and nine as Goddess worship.[66] Under the option of "Other," three people specified that "It's what you make it" (43M), it "needn't be a religion" (30M),[67] or "It seems to attune the cycles of nature" (25M).

Among the PM responses to familiarity with Neo-paganism, two did not answer the question, and twenty-three (92 percent) said they were familiar, and all these considered it at least generally positive. On this last, of the seventeen HOG responses, three skipped the question, twelve answered "positive" with another person adding "mostly," and one person answered "both" positive and negative. In aggregate, 79.4 percent of the HOG respondents affirmed the positiveness of Neo-paganism. For the PM, 22 (88 percent vs. HOG 64.7 percent) think of Neo-paganism as "a nature-based religion"; 11 (44 percent vs. HOG 52.9 percent) described it as "Goddess worship." One person also checked that it is "harmless." There were two "other" descriptions: "it is powerful" (32F) and "above [i.e., nature-based and Goddess worship], but still a corruption of older, more effective teachings" (26M).

## SJA and control groups

Familiarity with Neo-paganism among SJA was 52 percent no to 42 percent yes, and it was described as generally positive by 40 percent, negative by 6 percent, while 52 percent did not answer the question. Familiar and positive were the respective assessments of both HOG (88 percent and 79 percent) and PM (92 percent and 92 percent). In LL, 24 percent were and 67 percent were not familiar with Neo-paganism; while 24 percent thought it positive, 11 percent negative, one person thought neither, another said both, a third did not know, and 60 percent avoided the question. The ECR expressed only a 7 percent familiarity and 84 percent non-familiarity—with one person answering "yes & no." No one thought it positive; 20 percent considered it negative. Among the WCL, no one was familiar with Neo-paganism, although 2 people (18 percent) thought it generally positive; 3 or 27 percent did not know; and 5 or 45 percent did not answer.

## Comparison of group descriptions of Neo-paganism

Respondents were also asked which best fits his or her description of Neo-paganism: (1) it is dangerous devil worship, something Satanic, (2) it is nature-based religion, (3) it is Goddess worship, (4) it is harmless, (5) it is something degenerate, (6) don't know anything about it, and

(7) other. Since multiple answers were allowed, each percentage represents a figure against a possible 100 percent affirmation. See Table 5.5.

The table shows that the pagan groups make the strongest identification of Neo-paganism with nature-based religion primarily and as God-
dess-worship secondly. As mentioned above, HOG's additional three
responses were: "it's what you make it," "needn't be a religion," and
"it seems to attune the cycles of nature." The three secular groups
show the greatest ignorance about Neo-paganism, while one quarter of
the SJA respondents also "don't know anything about it." Nevertheless, from a New Age Alternatives perspective, Neo-paganism is predominantly seen as a nature-based religion. Few people of any group
saw Neo-paganism as dangerous or degenerate, but few likewise affirmed that it was harmless. The SJAer who thought of Neo-paganism
as degenerate (33F) added "maybe not in all forms." Another (40F)
said, "Am suspicious of paganism—(linked with black magic)," while
a third (27F) proclaimed that it is "to [sic] broad a subject to make any
comment on." The two additional comments made by LL include "all
first five categories + where religion meets nostalgia" (31M) and "creative and co-creative base." The one comment made by an ECR respondent (50F Catholic [practicing]) was "emphasis is too ego-cen-
tric."

## Perception and Knowledge of NRMs

To develop an understanding of 'insiders' and 'outsiders' perception
of alternative religious possibilities, I also asked each group how they
would describe the post-1970 new religious movements in general.[68]
Multiple answers were allowed, and the choices given were (1) coercive,
totalitarian groups using deceptive and 'brainwashing' techniques, (2)
open groups stressing self-realization and development, (3) irrelevant

**TABLE 5.5: Description of Neo-Paganism**

|       | 1   | 2   | 3   | 4   | 5   | 6   | 7   | n.a. |
|-------|-----|-----|-----|-----|-----|-----|-----|------|
| SJA   | 0%  | 40% | 17% | 6%  | 2%  | 25% | 4%  | 19%  |
| HOG   | 6%  | 66% | 54% | 6%  | 6%  | 6%  | 18% | 0%   |
| PM    | 0%  | 88% | 44% | 4%  | 0%  | 0 % | 8%  | 4%   |
| LL    | 5%  | 21% | 6%  | 0%  | 0%  | 50% | 5%  | 14%  |
| ECR   | 8%  | 4%  | 0%  | 2%  | 2%  | 45% | 2%  | 33%  |
| WCL   | 0%  | 18% | 9%  | 0%  | 9%  | 64% | 0%  | 0%   |

'hogwash', (4) don't know anything about them, and (5) other. The results indicated that the highest consideration (18 percent) of NRMs as nonsense was held by WCL, 7 percent in the LL, and 4 percent of the ECR. Half of the LL responses knew nothing about them, slightly less than one-third for the ECR, and roughly one-fifth for the SJA and WCL each.

As might be expected, the perception of NRMs as self-development groups was prominently higher among New Age Alternatives respondents (62.5 percent versus 38 percent PM, 36 percent WCL, and 24 percent for LL and ECR). Correspondingly, their perception of the same as autocratic, mind-controlling endeavors was the lowest (10 percent versus 21 percent LL, 24 percent PM, 35 percent ECR and 36 percent WCL). None among them or the Pagan Moon people thought of the NRMs as irrelevant nonsense, and few in the control groups thought the same. Interestingly, the highest degree of paranoia vis-à-vis the NRMs is expressed by the American groups, while the London pagans and those associated with the London Lighthouse express a more moderate view between the Americans and those from St. James. One-fourth of the respondents from both LL and ECR considered NRMs open and positive; one-third of the San Francisco Bay Area lawyers and of the Greater London pagans thought the same. However, expressions of knowledge about the NRMs was highest among the PMers, whereas the SJA ranks lower than the WCL. Greatest unfamiliarity was revealed by LL.[69]

To gauge the NRM question, I also asked respondents to identify from a list of various groups, personalities, and/or events which were New Age and which Neo-pagan.[70] Some people expressed their uncertainty with a question mark. Since the list of NRMs was expanded for the later samplings, some groups were not included on the ECR questionnaire.[71]

With few exceptions, there appeared to be little understanding of, or familiarity with, NRMs by participants in any of the groups investigated. The highest 'correct' score—and indeed the highest of any score—is the 60/65 percent identification of Wicca as Neo-pagan by the Neo-pagan groups themselves (PM/HOG). On the other hand, though there was recognition of such New Age phenomena as the Aquarian Conspiracy (27 percent), Harmonic Convergence (29 percent), and Transcendental Meditation (35 percent) by a significant number of Alternatives respondents, there was often the same if not greater recognition of these as New Age by the pagan community as well (PM/HOG: 28/47, 24/35, and 36/18 percent). Nevertheless, Alternatives did express a higher than usual understanding of Wicca as Neo-pagan (29 percent)—indicating some reciprocal knowledge between the two communities. As for TM, it received the highest recognition of any NRM by the two secular control groups. Twenty percent of the ECR even correctly labeled it New Age. Nevertheless, ECR also relatively highly assessed the Unification Church as "New Age" (16 percent)—presumably because its theological position often speaks in terms of a new age. Ananda Marga, Brahma Kumaris, COG, Scientology, ISK-CON, Nichiren Shoshu Buddhism, and the UC are not New Age but were all the same identified as such—or sometimes as Neo-pagan—by individuals across the study groups questioned. The case of Carlos Castaneda is interesting. He was perceived by SJA as New Age, by HOG as Neo-pagan, and by the other three groups as equally New Age and Neo-pagan.

The question concerning perception of the post-1970 NRMs in general was not included in the HOG survey, but the PM responses to this question revealed several split answers. In total, 9 indicated their perception of them as "open groups stressing self-realization," while 5.5 checked "coercive/totalitarian groups using deceptive/brainwashing techniques" (one of these last also indicated that he "did not know anything about them"). Two people did not answer, and there were 7 individual answers: "any of the above, depending on the moment" (32F), "all of the above—they vary" (26M), "there are too many groups for one answer" (37F), "some good some bad very variable" (20M), as well as: "an aspect manifesting (finally!) of the Aquarian Age" (32F), "I don't know what you mean by the 'post 1970 NRMs' rather what that includes" (46F), while one person (32F) only checked the Other category without giving an explanation.

When asked to identify which NRMs were New Age, which Neo-pagan, and which neither (i.e., to leave blank), every entry from a list of twenty-five apart from Wicca was labeled New Age by at least one person of the HOG group. Three people identified as New Age the Aetherius Society; three selected est/The Forum; two, Insight/MSIA; one, 3HO; two, Subud; two, Temple ov Psychick Youth (TOPY); one, Naropa Tibetan Buddhism; and three, TM.[72] The high scorers as New Age were the Aquarian Conspiracy (8), the Harmonic Convergence (6), and Rajneeshism (5). While Shan considered both est and Scientology as "Satanic," John marked both entries "New Age" with the following statements for the former:

Probably quite evil; seems to work by demolishing the candidate's self-esteem, then convincing him or her—when they are in a very vulnerable and uncritical state; that the only way to rebuild their self-esteem is to accept The Teaching. This sort of thing radically offends all the criteria of my own Pagan value-system.

The Brahma Kumaris, Subud, TOPY and Naropa were identified by HOGers once as Neo-pagan, and, while Melton (1986b) includes Carlos Castaneda as an independent New Age teacher or personality, 6 people in this survey consider him Neo-pagan. There were 11 respondents who identified Wicca as Neo-pagan.[73] Among the PM of April 7, 1990 responses, 15 (60 percent vs. HOG 64.7 percent) indicated Wicca as Neo-pagan; 1 marked New Age, and 1 marked New Age/Pagan. This last was also given for the Harmonic Convergence, which otherwise was identified as New Age 6 times.

## Effects of Participation

### *HOG (and PM) responses*

The last questions on this questionnaire dealt with the individual's involvement with a New Age and/or Neo-pagan group or center and how his or her life might have been changed accordingly. Two people of the HOG group[74] admitted to involvements with both movements, but one claimed "these are informal matters" and used the word "interesting" to describe the effective changes in his life. The elder had been involved in Positive Living for eighteen months, Fountain for one year, and the Atlanteans for nine months among the New Age groups; and with HOG for six months. The reasons given for the New Age involvement were "Nice people & it's entertaining"; for HOG—his third time, "Interesting people and activities," but "Who knows?" the changes effected. A twenty-five-year-old male left the Neo-pagan question blank but listed Green Circle as a three-month New Age involvement.[75] His life had been changed by

> Becoming more aware of internal processes within oneself. Being able to examine my reactions to different people and situations on different levels. Becoming aware of radical [*sic*] different modes of thinking and feeling and different philosophies. Meeting people who have a radical [*sic*] different approach to life.[76]

Eight HOGers mentioned only their Neo-pagan involvement (seven list HOG) with no New Age connections. One (31F) attends "about 20 times a year'' ''because it's a good night out and different,'' and it has made her ''more centred.'' Another (24M) attends ''every two weeks'' ''to learn about myself and others and to relax and meet people.'' A Pagan/Wiccan (33M) for seven years before meeting others has attended HOG twice a month for two years ''to meet socially/to work'' and has been ''enriched; strengthened; exciting [*sic*]'' An opera student (22F) has been ''Involved with [an] active group in Cardiff for 3 years,'' and describes having

> Been involved in Nature worship since very young [but] only within the last three years actually developed an acknowledgment that I was a pagan witch and began to be in control of my psyche and my perceptions, etc.

Barry (30M), who has been involved with HOG for three years because he ''enjoys it and meets friends'' describes his consequent changes as:

> Loss of feelings of isolation -> greater confidence in both life in general and my practice. Eventually gave up my career as a result of this contact and now make (or attempt to make) a living by building drums which I sell mainly in the Pagan community.

John (40M), who had been Pagan/Wiccan four years before making contact with others and who has attended HOG permanently for two years and four months, writes the following concerning how his life has been changed as a result:

> The precise details are unimportant. The vital datum is that when I first became aware of the Craft (it was in a bookshop); I burst out laughing with *recognition*; this is mine; this is for me; I have come home. This feeling of recognition and coming home is, in my experience, what all witches and pagans report (although it is important to remember that, although this is a common factor throughout, the variety of individual experiences is infinite.) When I moved to London in 1987, I got in touch with House of the Goddess, via a small ad in ''City Limits,'' because I wanted to meet people of my own cut and stripe, with whom I could socialise happily, without feeling the need to be cautious or inhibited about mentioning my values and beliefs.
>     Over the intervening years, I became increasingly involved in the affairs of House of the Goddess, and developed a strong friendship (tested through some powerful ups and downs) with Shan, the Priestess and moving spirit. Eventually; and to our mutual surprise; we handfasted, at the Summer Solstice of 1989. I always felt the Craft was my home; I never

expected it to be as good as this. How has my life been changed? I am a man who has come home.[77]

Shan (40F), on the other hand, who had been a Pagan/Wiccan ten years before making contact with others, founded HOG five years ago. She explains:

> I have found scope to be a leader in a woman centred community that deeply values my work as a woman. I have found great joy in helping others come to real power in their lives. I have been healed of man hating! I have acceptance as an intelligent mystic without becoming marginalised. I was desperately lonely and now I am loved. Craft serves freedom right now; when it ceases to do so I'll drop it. Hope I don't have to.[78]

## SJA responses

Asked about involvement with a New Age group or center, ten SJA responses listed St. James' Alternatives program, while another three mentioned St. James along with Findhorn; one with Monkton Wyld (Malcolm Stern);[79] and one with New Connexions. Length of involvement ranged from three months (2) and 7 months (1) to one year (4), 15 months (1), and two years (2).[80] Attendance is usually once per week or twice per month,[81] and the reasons for and effects of attendance varying accordingly:

> 35F: "Enjoy lectures and debates"; "Pleasure in meeting people and sharing ideas, but recognise a fair amount of 'airy-fairy nonsense' in the movements. No greatly significant changes—I'm still afraid to die!"

> 36F: "I enjoy it and feel refreshed and energised usually"; "I have looked at myself in different ways since involvement in new age culture."

> 25M: "I like the ideas"; "I find I can handle my life more easily around the *logic* of the New Age Movement."

> 40F: "I like them—feel good there"; "I feel relaxed."

> 46F: "My main contact with like-minded people"; "Makes me feel good to know others who I can empathise and connect with. I feel I belong, after being alien for years."

> 62F who has "become more open, self aware on the roads of healing, spiritual development and alternative medicine."

> 42F whose involvement has "help[ed] me find certain answers to questions I have always wanted to ask."

40 + F who has been "made calmer."

32M who claims as a result "I am more optimistic about life and the world."

Two people have attended Enlightenment Intensives over a four-year period: 43M—reason: "Enlightenment"; how changed: "Considerably"; and 24F—reason: "I have found enlightenment (a glimpse)"; changes: "It has changed my attitude toward life completely." One man (37) has practiced Transcendental Meditation daily for nineteen years because "I love it. It has transformed my life." A woman respondent (33) had formerly been with the Emin [Foundation] for ten years. This was "good in some ways, in others manipulative, destructive and a waste of time—good introduction to spiritual concepts and values." Among other people from Alternatives expressing New Age involvements, their reasons and consequences are the following:

50M: St. Marks Community—2 years; every day—we lived together "cos we loved it." It has "help[ed] me to see my light within and come awake from a 45 years sleep and become the real me!!!"

33F: Spiritual healing programs/massage courses for two years one time per week because it "gives a focus and spreads a new way of being which is lighter." Effect: "lighter."

42F: White Eagle Lodge four years two times per week because "I grow and make friends and sing and heal." "My life is happier. I feel more sure that it has meaning and purpose. I am able to be myself more naturally."

60F: Oak Dragon Project, which has involved attending camps to or three times per year for the last four years. She re-lists Oak Dragon under the Neo-pagan question claiming that "there is a Neo-Pagan element in it." The reasons for attendance listed are: "Rich meeting of intuitive, intellectuals, it's from all walks of life." Changes: "Making me far more open and confident in my own responses. I have found my 'voice'. Also feel more at ease in the natural world, which I find is at present teaching me more than religious institutions. It gives me authority as a *WOMAN*!"

46F: The Forum (*est*) and Loving Relationship Training. Ten year involvement "whenever I feel the need to learn more." Reason: "To learn and explore;" effect: "I have broken away from much of my negative conditioning. I explore and challenge my mind. I have gained deeper levels of communication and friendship. I have gained a wider awareness of 'other than self'."

Two respondents from St. James admitted involvement with a Neo-pagan group or center. One (32M) "occasionally" attends the Eagle

Wing Centre for Contemporary Shamanism. He used the word "radically" to describe how his life had been changed. The other (35M) has had "occasional contact with Wicca" and finds it "interesting; seems relevant with emphasis on earth, feminine principle." Beside an involvement with TM (fourteen years), he also attends about eight times per year the Fellowship of Inner Light (five years). His reason: "Meeting interesting, loving people, self-exploration, gaining knowledge." And through TM, he has "made friends, gained self-knowledge, techniques for rest and relaxation."

Six respondents gave descriptions of how their lives have been changed without specifying a New Age or Neo-pagan involvement.[82] One (31M) says simply: "Too soon to tell." Another (27F) mentions "A new philosophy for life which stresses each person[al] value uniting body, mind and spirit." One man (35) admits that "Although not a member of any group, the New Age has helped me understand more about myself and other people and the forces at work around us." Another person (41F) feels that "New Age reading, material, talks, workshops have given hope, I have renewed my faith in God/the Universe, regained my power and positive outlook towards our planet and its kingdoms." A woman (28) feels that New Age has "totally" changed her life through "A belief that nothing is coincidental, as we sow, so we shall reap." And lastly, a woman (36) claims that "My life *has not* been changed through my involvement by any of the above-mentioned groups, although perhaps the beginning was through TM. But I have recognized in Sai Baba a very powerful MASTER—who is **transforming me from the inside**."[83]

This last captures a common theme uniting most responses from my SJA survey—namely, the internalization of the religious/spiritual experience. This was echoed in respondents' description of God (e.g., "God and Goddess within me," "a force within and without," "within us," etc.) In general, however, and in conclusion, my studies confirm the knowledge of their respective movements by the participants within them. They also indicate the generally mutual familiarity between Neo-pagan and New Age, though this is found not to be a strictly reciprocal understanding. Moreover, there appears to be a general lack of knowledge by the public at large concerning NRMs and New Age and Neo-paganism in particular.

## Addendum

For profiles of New Age leaders, David Spangler (age forty-five) is a teacher/writer by profession with further education and an annual in-

come above £20,000 ($32,000). He describes his family during child-
hood as of upper-middle financial status. He is married, heterosexual,
with three children (ages: seven, four, and one). Raised ''Christian'' but
listed no religious preference now. He describes himself as religious,
political, fun-loving, and romantic. He feels nuclear energy is acceptable with proper supervision, the choice on abortion is the woman's
alone, and AIDS is a natural calamity. He has not known anyone with
AIDS and checked ''don't know'' for his belief concerning God. New
Age is generally positive but is too broad a concept to describe. He is
familiar with Neo-paganism, sees it as generally positive and as a nature-based religion. The post-1970 NRMs he would describe as open
groups stressing self-realization and development. The only specific
NRM he identified was Wicca (as Neo-pagan). At the time, he had been
teaching at the Chinook Learning Center for the past twelve years.

Malcolm Stern (40), co-director of Alternatives, answers the same as
David Spangler except his income is between £5–10,000 ($8–16,000),
he received a secondary education along with O and A levels, has two
children (aged eight and two at the time), was raised Jewish but considers himself Buddhist now, and describes himself as social-activist, fun-
loving, serious, and romantic. He feels nuclear energy is too dangerous,
is generally in favor of abortion, and considers AIDS a natural calamity.
He has known one or more people with AIDS or HIV infection. God is
''the energy of the universe.'' New Age is *the* religion of the future. He
identifies as New Age Ananda Marga, Aquarian Conspiracy, Brahma
Kumaris, Harmonic Convergence, Naropa Buddhism, and TM. He identifies as Neo-pagan the Aetherius Society, Carlos Castaneda, Rajneeshism, and Wicca. His ten-year New Age involvement is with St. James'
Church and Monkton Wyld.

William Bloom (42), co-director of Alternatives, is a writer/educator
with a Ph.D. and an income between £15–20,000 ($24–32,000). He
was raised in London in a family of upper-middle financial status. He
is married and has a son from a former marriage, who was fifteen years
old at the time. Religion in which raised: Agnostic/Humanist; religion
now: New Age. Bloom describes himself as political, social activist,
fun-loving, and serious. He feels that nuclear energy is ''Probably ok
in long term; more R & D needed . . . stop it now''; that abortion is the
woman's choice alone; that AIDS is a ''Symptom of mass human
karma''; and that God is a real possibility ''But so big I can't quite
grasp his/her extent.'' New Age is generally positive and both ''The
religion of the future'' and ''Too broad a concept to say.'' His familiarity with Neo-paganism causes him to see it as generally positive and a

nature-based religion. NRMs in general are "open groups stressing self-realization and development." The Aquarian Conspiracy, Brahma Kumaris, *est*, Castaneda, Harmonic Convergence, MSIA, and Rajneeshism are judged New Age; Wicca as Neo-pagan. Bloom has been associated with Alternatives and Findhorn for fifteen years for "Money/Vocation" reasons but adds that involvement has "Accelerated my transformation, my understanding of the divine and my understanding of community—local and cosmic—and my responsibilities."

Sabrina Dearborn (35), co-director of Alternatives, is a psychic counselor and spiritual healer with further education and an income between £5–10,000 ($8–16,000) who hails from Boston, Massachusetts, and a lower-middle financial status. She was raised in "Christian/Metaphysics" and is "New Age" now. She describes herself as fun-loving, serious, and spiritual. Nuclear energy is too dangerous, abortion is the woman's choice, AIDS is a natural calamity (both she and Bloom know people with AIDS/HIV infection), and "God" has been amended to "God/des" [*sic*] but no answer was checked. New Age: positive and the religion of the future; Neo-paganism: positive nature-based religion and Goddess worship. NRMs: open, etc.; New Age: Aquarian Conspiracy, *est*, Castaneda, HC, and MSIA; Neo-pagan: Wicca. Dearborn's New Age involvement has been with Alternatives for two years—attending once or twice per week, six times per month. She is also "involved with a loose knit network of people exploring 'pagan' ceremonies" and has "had contact with Pagans since I was 14 years old." Her New Age/Neo-pagan involvements have made her "feel more loved and . . . more loving. I am more interested in positive social/political reform and community. I have a deep sense of self and more confidence in my ability to work with and teach others. Life has purpose and meaning. I have a personal relationship with the Divine."

## Notes

1. LL = the London Lighthouse ("a centre for people facing the challenge of AIDS"); ECR = a collective fiftieth birthday celebration for an American East Coast high school reunion held at the Parsippany Hilton in New Jersey on the weekend of September 22–23, 1989 (questionnaire forms were placed on an information-and-registration table along with stamped return envelopes); WCL = a group of eleven people (ten lawyers plus one non-lawyer husband) from the San Francisco Bay Area vacationing in the south of France. For LL, seventy-nine forms were distributed (randomly to visitors/staff/residents) and forty-two returned. Twenty questionnaires were collected during the evening of

March 27, 1990, another ten on March 29, 1990, a further ten by April 3, 1990. A final two—one sent by post—were collected from the Lighthouse reception desk on April 5, 1990.

2. I have not included myself in these figures.

3. On the 23rd of April, I returned to St. James for the additional forms, but approximately five minutes before I arrived the Alternatives' cash box was stolen from a side room to the church along with the remainder of the completed questionnaires, which had been kept in a carton container along with the money box. The count of seven is based on Bloom's guess. Moreover, the completed forms of William Bloom and his wife Sabrina Dearborn were not returned to me until the 27th of June. Consequently, the results from Bloom and Dearborn's questionnaires have not been included in the general statistical analysis of the SJA returns.

4. "Books mentioned included *The Spiral Dance* (7), *Drawing Down the Moon* (6), *When God Was a Woman* (2), *Positive Magic, The White Goddess, Womanspirit Rising, The Complete Art of Witchcraft, Holy Book of Woman's Mysteries, Witchcraft the Old Religion*."

5. This figure is uncertain, and there could be a misprint in the text. Adler (1986:453) states for this answer "more than half the responses (76)." But, if as she says earlier, she received 195 returns, this assessment is not correct.

6. The Occult Census 1989: The First Ever Statistical Analyses of the Population, Involvements, Interests and Opinions of Occultists in the United Kingdom (Leeds, Yorkshire: The Sorcerer's Apprentice Press), p. 37.

7. The total response was 38, of which 23 were in favor and 14 were opposed. One person for the use of the word *witch* said "yes, but carefully and mostly privately." Another said "yes, but guardedly." Of those against, one person specified her opposition only to using the word in public. Two had specified "personal reasons," and another denied that, as a polytheistic sorcerer, the word was applicable to him. One respondent was neutral over the word's use.

8. When asked how occultism might benefit society, 19 percent of those polled thought that occultism develops a sense of spirituality. Another 14 percent felt that it accelerates evolution of the planet and species. This was matched by those who see occultism developing in others a respect for the ecology of the planet. Eleven percent perceive balance and harmony as a result; 10 percent argue that it makes people more positive and fulfilled.

9. "Only 1 Satanist had ever killed an animal or bird in the pursuit of magick" (*The Occult Census: 1989*:26).

10. The others: *Daily Mail & The Sun* (7 percent each), *Today* (6 percent), *The Observer & Daily Express* (4 percent each), and *Sunday Sport* (2 percent).

11. The ranking of active participation in "mundane or other interests" is as follows: (1) reading for pleasure—48 percent, (2) creative arts—32 percent, (3) travel, (4) health foods, (5) ecology and music tied, (6) cinema and cooking/cuisine tied, (7) community/charity work—16 percent, (8) sport, and (9) politics. For the interests expressed in various aspects of the occult itself, see the end of this section.

12. To the question "who objects to your interest in the occult?" the answers ranked as follows: mother (19 percent), clergy (16 percent), father (15 percent), brothers and/or sisters (11 percent), friends (10 percent), workmates (9 percent), other (9 percent), spouse (5 percent), and doctor (3 percent).

13. The SAOC report says (p. 18) that "to most occultists Paganism signifies the more religious aspect of Witchcraft and Witchcraft is considered to embody both the religious and the magickal [*sic*] or shamanistic aspects of this ancient fertility cult."

14. Serious interest and/or committed belief in "spells" is represented in aggregate by only 55 percent of the sample—a figure that is largely balanced by another segment of the occultist population that has either no interest or only a curious interest in the same. For the SAOC, "This leads us to believe that 32 percent of occultists find in Occultism a solely religious framework for their lives" (p. 18).

15. These and the following "figures are based upon a random sampling of 600 questionnaires drawn from a total pool of 4,000 responses." See also Chapter 4.

16. The results diverge even more widely if one considers the *BMS* survey figures of last-year participation by New Agers in Shamanism (11 percent), Goddess Worship (7 percent), or Paganism (5 percent) and the curious or serious interest or committed belief in Witchcraft (84 percent) or Paganism (79 percent) by British occultists.

17. By contrast, Adler (1986:445) found only five people out of 195 (or 2.6 percent) who had had psychic experiences that in this case led them into Neo-paganism.

18. In the SAOC, the comparable figures are: 18–29 (48.1 percent) with 18- and 19-year-olds comprising only 4.5 percent, 30–49 (39.74 percent) and over 50 (12.16 percent). The HOG figures for March 22,1990 are: 18–34 (64.7 percent) and 35–49 (23.5 percent)—or 18–29 (23.5 percent), 30–49 (58.2 percent)—and over 50 (5.9 percent).

19. In 1969, 73 percent in the United States were expected to affirm belief in life after death (Gallup Opinion Index, February 1969). To the question whether religion was thought to be losing its influence in the United States, in 1957, 14 percent considered that it was; in 1962, 31 percent; in 1965, 45 percent; in 1967, 57 percent; in 1968, 67 percent; and in 1970, 75 percent (Gallup, Report No. 70, pp. 45, 47). In 1970, whereas only 14 percent believed religion was increasing its influence (7 percent thought there was no difference and 4 percent had no opinion), a Gallup poll published in January 1975 indicated that 31 percent now believed that religion was increasing its influence (Rosten, 1975:545).

20. One said his income varies. There was one who did not mark this question. For the PM of April 7, 1990, there were 7 indications of income between £5–10,000, another 6 between £10–15,000, 2 between £15–20,000, 3 over £20,000, 6 below £5,000, and 1 n.a.

21. PM (April 7, 1990): 13 from London, 4 from England (Bristol, Manchester, Poole, Surrey), 2 from Wales, 3 from the United States (New York, Los Angeles and St. Louis), 1 from Sydney, 1 from Rome, and 1 n.a.

22. No one checked "wealthy," and two did not answer the question. PM: 5.5 poor, 11.5 lower middle, 5 upper middle, 2 wealthy, and 1 n.a.

23. PM: four divorced parents and one whose parents had separated.

24. Fifteen (31 percent) SJA respondents were raised in London another 33 percent were from elsewhere in England (one person only specified the United Kingdom); one from Wales; and one from Jersey. There were also two Europeans (Amsterdam, and near Copenhagen), four Africans (one Egyptian, one South African, and two from Zimbabwe), one New Zealander, three Canadians, and four Americans. There was one n.a. to this question.

25. Comparative figures for divorced parents during childhood are PM (16 percent), HOG (12 percent), LL (12 percent), ECR (10 percent), and WCL (9 percent).

26. Respondents had an aggregate of sixteen children (one grandchild): three below the age of 5, two between 6 and 12, one teenager, eight between 20 and 29, and two over 30. Comparisons for children would be SJA (nine parents or 19 percent of the total; sixteen children), HOG (two or 12 percent; five), PM (eleven or 44 percent; twenty-one + ten grandchildren), SAOC (62 percent), LL (four or 10 percent; sixteen), ECR (forty-five or 92 percent; approximately twenty children + seven grandchildren), WCL (six or 55 percent; four).

Regarding present marital status for HOG, there were three indications of "divorced"; nine of "single"; four "married"; and three "unmarried partnership relationships." Shan's spouse John indicated "married" to this question, while Shan wrote in "handfasted"—the Wiccan form of marriage. Though their union presumably does not have legal sanction, I have included it under the "married" category rather than as an "unmarried partnership relationship."

27. The U.K. percentages are rough estimates for comparative purposes based on Tables A.19 (p. 21) and 11.6 (p. 166) in Tom Griffin (ed.), *Social Trends* 20 (London: Her Majesty's Stationery Office, 1990). I have employed the 1987 and 1990 figures—the original source being the *United Kingdom Christian Handbook 1989/90*, MARC Europe. Nevertheless, I suspect that my own LL figures might correspond more accurately to the national averages concerning religious background, and, if so, there would be a general conformity with the composition of the three London-based religious groups in this study: HOG, PM, and SJA.

28. Rosten (1975:334). Religion not reported: 0.9 percent.

29. Gallup, Report No. 70.

30. Adler (1986:44).

31. I.e., Protestant and Sectarian. Adler (ibid.) reports that Gordon Melton had found the religious background of the Pagan community "mirrored the national average very closely."

32. Adler (1986:44).

33. Adler's actual figures are: Anglican 9.0 percent, Other Protestant 39.2 percent, Mixed (Catholic and Protestant/Anglican) 7.8 percent, Unitarian 3.0 percent, and New Thought 1.8 percent.

34. Religion in which raised broke down to four Church of England, four Roman Catholic, one "Christian," one "vaguely Christian," one "Christian rebel," one Methodist, one "je ne sais pas," one "none," and one person (John) checked both Church of England and Welsh Congregational, while another answered both COE and "none." Shan, on the other hand, had a more eclectic answer: Rousseau/Apache/Stoicism.

35. The specific breakdown of PM responses for religion in which raised comprised 13.5 or 54 percent Church of England, 3.5 or 14 percent Roman Catholic, 2 or 8 percent Jewish, 1 Protestant, 1 Baptist and 4 or 16 percent none. In this case there is more divergence with the Melton, Adler, and HOG figures, though a parallel is still discernible when Jewish is taken as Other.

36. Church of England, Church of Wales, Southern Baptist, Methodist, Presbyterian, etc.

37. One humanist (62F0, one Eastern Orthodox (28M), and one "Orthodox" [*sic*].

38. Mormon.

39. Islam.

40. These estimates are computed from the 1987 figures (Table 11.6, p. 166) and the 1990 estimates (Table A.19, p. 21) in Tom Griffin (ed.), *Social Trends* 20 (London: Her Majesty's Stationery Office, 1990).

41. The one non-lawyer husband in this group (34M and former Mormon) described his current religious preference as "on hold."

42. Two people did not answer the question.

43. John added: "Please note that Jehovah is only one particular manifestation of the God."

44. This was Shan who also selected the first and third options and, under "Other," wrote in "Goddess." By contrast, Vivianne Crowley when answering this question simply checked the option "an impersonal force."

45. There were three additional answers that might be included here: "a force," "an immanent force" and "the life force."

46. The PM responses on April 7, 1990 to the question about God were as follows: real personality (2), fiction (1), impersonal force (9), don't know (1), and n.a (1). Among the specifications for "other," I received the following answers: "which god?" (33M), "non-specified" (32F), "the universe itself" (20M), "everything" (32F), "within" (18F), "all those and more" (55M), "can't answer this. why don't you ask about the Goddess?" (37F), "within yourself" (18F—also checked "a real personality"), "a bad term for a good state of mind" (26M), "a good state of mind taken to extremes by narrow minded people" (25F), "a matter of opinion/perception" (32F), and "a general tendicial [*sic*] attempt to improve the way people treat themselves & the rest of the universe and make them more aware of the spiritual" (38M).

47. Among SJA, the answers ranged from the great spirit within and without, a sense of Good [*sic*] within everyone, within everything, inner wisdom, [an impersonal force] and within us all, a force within and without, God & Goddess in me, part of oneself, within us, my life force within, a personal force, an energy, the overriding energy (love), life force/energy, [an impersonal force] manifest/unmanifest, the energy of the universe, is everyone, everything and everyone, all of these and more beside, everything—all of us—life, [an impersonal force]—not sure, a loving mystery so far, my friend, husband of the Goddess, and "what a question."

LL's answers for the other category were: overrated—pretty irrelevant to our day to day survival—female (sometimes) (20F),an energetic force permeating everything (53F), all around/orgone energy (31M), none of the above (35M), all (42M), and the other category checked but unspecified (38M).

WCL's additional responses were "collective unconscious and creator of life" (39F) and Other checked but unspecified (41F). For ECR, God is "unknowable" (50F Jewish), "a higher power" (50F none), "almighty heavenly being—true force for a good life hereafter" (51F Methodist), "part of me" (49F combination of many), "certainly a possibility!" (49F Protestant), "a personal spiritual friend & comforter which through faith in Him all things are possible" (50F Methodist), [a real personality "and"] (50F Christian), "love, a force, personal & universal" (46F RC/Universal), "symbol of hope & peace" (48F Jewish), "a necessary explanatory concept" (49M Jewish), "if anything, a sort of universal consciousness" (50M Jewish culturally), "superconsciousness" (50M Protestant but mainly for form [weddings, funerals, etc.]), "a fatal dream" (51M none), "an extension of self" (25F none), and "developed to scare people to the church" (17M agnostic).

48. Shan indicated all six descriptions and added "sexy" and "charismatic." John also checked all six and wrote in: "All of the above and at different times; non-specific variance." Other write-ins were "active" + F (24F), "I am" (43M), "wide open" + all 6 (30M), "unfinished" + FSeRo (35M) and "spiritual" + F (32M). Two people avoided the question altogether (24M, 60M), and the individual breakdowns of the remainder are as follows: F (25M), Ro (32M, 54M),Se (25M), FRo (31F), RePSe (33M), RePSoF (22F), and all six (32M).

PM (7.4.90): Religious (7), Political (11.5), Social Activist (10), Fun-loving (18), Serious (15), and Romantic (17). Write-ins: "philosophical" +FSeRo (25M), "misanthropic, artistic, animal lover" +PFSeRo (22M), "weird" + all 6 (32F), use of the sign for infinity +RePSoFRo (55M), "loner" +ReRo (20M), "lazy" (33M), "yes—I am sure there are others" +ReFSeRo (46F), "bizarre" +FSeRo (25F), "iconoclastic" +ReFSeRo (26M), and "fairly spiritual" +PFSeRo (32F). Vivianne Crowley profiled herself as ReSeRo.

49. Eight (17 percent) people in the SJA described themselves as "spiritual"; two, as "seekers." Other responses: "intellectual + analytical" (30F), "dancer, cat lover, poet" (42F), "definitely other" (28M), "independent/femi-

nist'' (40F), ''incurable idealist!'' (35F), ''reflective, helpful, understanding'' (22M), ''questioning'' (40 + F), ''spiritual life' '' (24F), ''spiritual, artistic'' (27F), ''spiritually joyous'' (33F), ''fun-loving + serious, romantic + hard-headed'' (60F), ''??????'' (43F), ''pisshead'' (31M), ''I'm all of those'' (27F), ''a human becoming!'' (36F), ''waking up—beginning to live'' (39F), and ''childlike, spontaneous, free'' (46F). For the PM, the other responses were: ''iconoclastic'' (26M), ''bizarre'' (25F), ''misanthropic, artistic, animal-lover'' (22M), ''loner'' (20M), ''weird'' (32F), ''fairly spiritual'' (32F), ''philosophical'' (25M), ''lazy'' (33M), [use of the infinity sign] (55M), and ''yes—I am sure there are others'' (46F).

50. Percentage responses: HOG and WCL none, PM 4, SJA 2, LL 4, ECR 4.

51. Percentage responses: HOG 12, PM 8, SJA 6, LL 10, ECR 10, WCL none.

52. Under the option of ''other (please specify),'' in HOG (24 percent) one expressed ''No interest''; another said simply, ''It exists''; a third said ''dangerous'' but asked ''if safe power will evolve out of it''; and Barry, Shan's ''right-arm'' assistant, wrote in that ''It can't be disinvented.'' The SAOC in its questionnaire form also asked, ''Do you condone the use of nuclear energy?''—but the results of this particular question were not included in *The Occult Census: Statistical Analyses & Results* booklet. Instead, 78 percent of its respondents opposed ''the use of nuclear arms''; 20 percent were in favor. Asked if one thought there could ever be a good reason for war, 38 percent answered ''possibly yes,'' 4 percent ''emphatically yes,'' and 58 percent replied ''no.'' For the PM (12 percent), responses included ''Necessary—at least until clean fusion available (assume you are refering [*sic*] to state of the art fission power)'' (26M); ''I am sure we have much to learn about it'' (46F); and ''stop it'' (29?). Two people chose this answer for SJA and one person from LL—specifiying ''Social control.''

53. An equal number thought nuclear energy to be the most viable energy source for our future needs. Other percentage responses for the second option were PM 2, SJA 1, LL 2, and none for both HOG and WCL.

54. The group breakdowns are as follows: SJA 50 percent, HOG 59 percent, PM 60 percent, LL 57 percent, ECR 43 percent, WCL 45 percent.

55. The percentage of the women who admitted to having had an abortion in the groups is as follows: SJA (26 percent), HOG (25 percent), PM (36 percent), LL (26 percent), ECR (16 percent) and WCL (43 percent)—once again with the Pagan Moon gathering along with the San Francisco secular group being out-of-line with—and perhaps significantly higher than—the others. There were none in PM and WCL who were against abortion in all circumstances; 2 percent each in SJA, LL, and ECR; 6 percent in HOG.

56. SJA 6, HOG 17, PM 12, LL 6, ECR 6, WCL 0 percent.

57. Specifying the last option, one person considered it ''Another sex/death lesson from no one'' (30M); one wrote: ''Possibly emerged from homosexual activity'' (60M); another thought it ''Part of nature's gift/act of God(dess)''

(54M); and one called it an "Immune disfunction of society" (32M). Two respondents indicated that it was engineered artificially—John adding "not necessarily by the CIA." By contrast the April 7, 1990 PM answers to the AIDS questions were as follows: natural calamity (13), CIA (3—1 with the proviso of "probably"), 3 did not know, 1 n.a., and one person (55M former Catholic) considered AIDS as "God's punishment." Four people checked the Other category: "a disease" (32F), "a disease & a challenge" (46F), "a very clever microbe adopting [*sic*] to its circumstances" (37F), and "an unpleasant disease of unknown origin" (26M). Eight respondents knew of someone with AIDS or HIV infection; 16 did not—one "not to my knowledge" and one (VC) "d/k!"

58. The same number affirmed that they knew someone with AIDS/HIV infection. Comparable figures are SJA (31 percent), PM (32 percent), ECR (35 percent), HOG (41 percent), and LL (93 percent). The other percentage comparisons include as a natural disaster: SJA 46, HOG 21, PM 52, LL 65, WCL 91 percent; and don't know: SJA 19, HOG 26, PM 12, LL 14, ECR 4 percent, and WCL none. For the "other" category, write-in responses for SJA (23 percent) include: "as we sow, so shall we reap ???" (46F), "a symptom of man's dis-ease" (39F), "a spiritual challenge" (28F), "it is here with us to awaken us" (41F), "a disease" (43F), "fact of life" (33F), "a shame" (27F), "an opportunity" (32M), "we all chose it to become closer" (22M), "symptomatic of what's being done to earth" (29F), "nature's population control" (25F), "not very nice" (28M), and "a way of preventing a dreadful disease we need to find" (40F).

Other responses for the LL (12 percent) along with current religious preference (RP): "a syndrome" (30M; RP:?), "a dimension of the problem of pain" (28M; RP: none), "unjudgementally Acquired Immune Deficiency Syndrome" (20F; RP: "no energy to spare for such matters"), "vague notions of karma/ destiny" (31M; RP: agnostic), and "a symptom of the general malaise affecting the earth mostly due to our attempts at 'conquering' nature but also possibly due to cosmic influences" (53F; RP: "spiritual path through dance/ T'ai chi/ minimal living, etc.").

Other responses along with RP for ECR (14 percent): "how isolated we've become" (46F; RP: Roman Catholic/Universal), "not 'natural' but due to man's habits like sharing needles, etc." (49F; RP: none [agnostic]), "a preventable calamity!" (49F; RP: Protestant), "a warning to the human race of waste" (49F; PR:"combination of many"), "a viral illness and its consequences" (49M; RP: Jewish), "a disease" (48F; RP: Jewish), and "simply a disease" (50M; RP: Methodist).

59. Shan and John's attitude toward the New Age was made even stronger to me the following day during a discussion that lasted most of the night. They were both adamant in not wanting to have anything to do with the movement or be associated in any way. John's answer on the questionnaire expresses a common theme underlying their mutual rejection: "My basic feeling about New Age groups is that they are, at their best, both learned and well-meaning; but

they are too 'nice'. They tend to fail to acknowledge basic human aggression as a valid force. To fail to honour something so basic and powerful is neither safe nor intelligent.'' Shan feels that the movement has nothing of value and nothing to offer one either now or in the future. She throws out the notion of 'newness' (Aleister Crowley spoke of the ''New Age'' at the turn of the century) as well as the idea that any imminent changes are likely to happen. When I suggested that the New Age metaphor might be thought as an infant not yet able to survive on its own but one in need of nourishment and guidance, John's response was that the ''baby should be strangled in the crib.''

60. Four did not answer, one person said ''both'' positive and negative, and a 25F pagan described it as ''negative.''

61. Sixteen percent said ''negative,'' and the same number did not answer.

62. HOG: negative (9 percent), no answer (12 percent).

63. Specifically, there were eleven admissions of New Age familiarity out of a total of forty-nine completed questionnaires; thirty-seven people were not familiar. From the total response, there were nine people who thought New Age generally positive; eight who assessed it generally negative. These figures may be compared with the Gallup Organization's data release from its more recent Gallup Mirror of America poll (''Americans look askance at the 'New Age','' *San Francisco Chronicle*, August 6, 1990). Twenty-nine percent of Americans have heard of the New Age movement (cf. ECR's 22 percent). Of these, 18 percent view it favorably, but 49 percent do not. The article adds, ''Unfavorable opinions are particularly strong among Protestants, evangelicals and those who attend church regularly. In fact, about one-third of those who have heard of the New Age movement say it is a threat to traditional religions, a sentiment that jumps to 50 percent among 'born-again' Christians and is generally higher among more religious Protestants.''

The same poll determined that nationally 11 percent of the American population believe in channeling, 2 percent have participated in it, 3 percent have used rock crystal for healing purposes, and 1 percent have resorted to pyramid use for its purported healing powers.

64. These figures may be compared with the Chronicle Poll conducted by Mark Baldassare & Associates, March 16–19, 1990, of San Francisco Bay Area residents of whom only 20 percent expressed a favorable view of the New Age movement; 28 percent, an unfavorable attitude; and 52 percent were undecided. This poll was a telephone survey of 600 Bay Area adults and has a margin error of 4 percent. See Don Lattin, '' 'New Age' Mysticism Strong in Bay Area,'' *San Francisco Chronicle*, April 24, 1990.

Other findings from this survey include 44 percent of Bay Area adults who believe in the personal God ''written about in the Bible, who watches over us and answers our prayers''; another 44 percent who envision the divine as an impersonal ''spiritual force that is alive in the universe and connects all living beings''; and 57 percent who agree with the statement that ''Nature, or Mother Earth, has its own kind of wisdom, a planetary consciousness of its own'' (32 percent said no; 11 percent did not know). Belief in contact with the supernatural: 38 percent yes, 52 percent no, 10 percent don't know; contact with a self-transcending powerful spiritual force: 27 percent yes, 73 percent no; belief in reincarnation: 24 percent yes, 63 percent no, 13 percent don't know (Gallup national averages are 23 percent, 67 percent, and 10 percent respectively); belief in astrology: 24 percent yes, 70 percent no, 6 percent d.k. (Gallup: 12 percent, 80 percent, 8 percent); meditation or yoga practice: never 54 percent, daily 19 percent, once per week 16 percent, less frequently 11 percent; use of an HPM technique (e.g., *est*, Lifespring, Scientology, etc.): 92 percent no, 8 percent yes; consultation with a psychic, channeler, shaman, or trance medium: 92 percent no, 8 percent yes; and belief that meditation practices and psychological therapies assist self-transformation, increase in consciousness and human potential realization: 62 percent yes, 29 percent no, 9 percent d.k.

65. "Positive" (20M), "gentle people into person[al] growth and spiritualism" (50M), "individual spiritual responsibility making changes in life style to serve the planet" (32M), "an orientation rather than a religion" (36F), "the essence of now" (46F), "creating a better world" (32M), "a way of living" (30F), "too much emphasis on light" (25F), "a vision which brings a new set of values for now and the future" (33F), "another mind-set" (28M), "a positive, spiritual and caring way of living and developing" (62F), "optimistic" (40F), and "new way of life" (53F).

66. John checked both these options as well as "It is harmless" but with special emphasis on Neo-paganism as both "dangerous devil worship, something Satanic" ("Yes; we work with real demons; helping people to deal with their own worst fears") and "degenerate" ("in terms of conventional morality, most definitely; we love parties, and lots of booze and dope").

67. Barry.

68. This question had not been included on the sampler put to HOG.

69. Perhaps a greater insight into this question might be gained by respondents' comments. The PMers reveal the most accurate insight (see text above). One SJA response was "I don't know which ones you are referring to—is it the ones on t.v., or what?" (40F), but in general, SJA comments correspond to those of PM: "depends on the group/motives, etc." (30F), "varies according to the group" (36F), "some good, some bad" (35F), and "cannot generalise" (32M), while one (28M) simply wrote in "religions," and another (36F) considered NRMs both coercive/totalitarian and open but added the following comment: "However, in other parts of the world there is a growing threat to the New Age thinking which comes from blind fundamentalism and I believe the New Age thinking is heading for a violent clash with fundamentalism (Christian and particularly Moslem)."

The four LL comments reveal a more varied spectrum: "various!" (28M "pagan of sorts" involved with Communes Network, etc.), "some I would describe as positive; some, like born-again Christianity, as repressive and retrogressive" (36M none), "people searching for meaning/significance" (31M agnostic), "moneyspinners—George Orwell's '1984' lives on; a hierarchy's bid for Power, Power, Power" (20F "no energy for . . .") The two WCL indications for "other" were not specified. One ECR respondent (49F none [agnostic]) wrote for the NRMs: "a search for meaning & group belonging."

70. This question more than any other elicited feelings of anxiety and guilt among respondents in all the groups examined. Many people had not heard of any of these groups—or very few at best. I often had to assure them that there were no 'right' answers, that I was simply endeavoring to find out what they did or did not know. One comment added on to his form from the LL (34M) expresses a typical reaction: "I hope this is of some use, I felt unable to answer the questions. The more it went on, it became far too in depth for me to make any sense of it, sorry! I think it was a bit frustrating as I wasn't sure what you were trying to get at and what you wanted from me."

71. This question itself was not included in the WCL questionnaire.

72. For TM, one person marked "neither but New Age possibly." The same person listed Scientology, Tibetan Buddhism, and the UC as "neither."

73. One person in addition did check the Wicca entry without indicating into which movement they would place it. John added to his form: "N.B. Wicca is far from the only form of Witch craft." This last was made more clear the following evening when Shan insisted on the distinction between her tradition of "Shamanic Craft" (with its awareness/sensitivity to psychological development) and Wicca (with its emphasis on formalized ritual). Upon closer analysis, this last was essentially "Alexandrian Wicca" since "Gardnerians, Hereditaries and Traditionalists will work with us." Dianics were considered a special case. Nevertheless, the more usual use of the terms 'Craft' and 'Wicca' is interchangeable—e.g., ". . . the religion Wicca, also known as the Craft" (Adler, 1986:10).

74. Both claimed to have been a Pagan or Wiccan thirty years before making contact with others—one aged forty-three; the other sixty.

75. Reason: "You meet other people who have similar interests."

76. Four people of the PM respondents did not answer the last series of questions. Four indicated a New Age involvement—one (46F) through "healing and therapy"; another (38M) expressed a four-year involvement with Rainbow Circle Camps (twice yearly, reason: "natural surroundings/be with like-minded people/avoid unnecessary social constraints"); the others identified Wicca as New Age: 42M (four-year involvement; twice-weekly attendance); 76F (thirty-six-year involvement whose life has been changed "completely" as a consequence); and 34F (i.e., Vivianne Crowley who has a seventeen year involvement, who lives "at the Centre" and because "it benefits me & others"). VC had been a pagan or Witch four years before making contact with others. The changes incurred to her life as a consequence include: "Purposeful; fulfilled; caring for others; at peace; intellectually satisfied—philosophical framework; a sense of place in the cosmos."

77. This theme of 'coming home', of the joy of recognition the Pagan/Wic-

can experiences when he/she first discovers the identity of self-held beliefs and the fact that others share these same beliefs, is a common one found throughout contemporary Neo-pagan literature (e.g., Adler, 1986; **PSA** 22; etc.)

78. Nine PM respondents indicated a Neo-pagan involvement: 33M (a Morris dancer, but the others aren't pagans, 10 years, once per week if possible, why not? [so I can get pissed!]; it must have been a long time . . . ; more satisfying [don't forget my organic garden]), 20M (Pagan Federation for 3 months through postal contact because of a lack of personal contacts; the first postal contacts took 1 month; changes: I realised what I had been all my life, that there were others like me and a way of structuring my beliefs and methods. Now trying to get involved. I'm a lot happier, stronger and self-confident. I like people now), 56M (HOG for 3 years—attending once per month "for contact with like minded people"; 9 years before contact with others; changes: more at ease and relaxed, my attitude to others much improved, able to help people healing wise), 32F (Wiccan coven since 4 years, 2 times average per month because "it is my path . . . & has been since childhood; 15–20 years before contact with others; "I'm much more centered, happy, at ease with myself and my body, and my direction in life is much cleaner and solider"), 55M (30 years, an Elder; 10 years before contact with others), 25F (Green Circle for two months; made contact first; "much more aware of life. More responsible, but still have fun"), 23F (HOG and Suzanne's P.A.H. for 6 months 4 times/month; 4 years before contact; a much healthier emphasis on the self—"Do what ye will but harm none"), 32F (Pagan Pathfinders since 1.5 years once/week because "good training in techniques, friendly group, information about events"; "I have become part of a stronger social network") and 38M (HOG about 3 years about once every two or three months to "be with like-minded people/ give meaning to my life/positive attitude"; about 2 months before making contact; changes [presumably both HOG and Rainbow Circle Camp]: "Gives meaning to my life because it helps me to see myself as part of nature. Helps me to accept myself and other people, and become wiser. A religion with responsibility but without guilt—a welcome alternative to Christianity, and to other religions which over-emphasize asceticism").

Eight PM respondents indicated no New Age or Neo-pagan group but mentioned the time involved before they made contact with others as well as the changes effected: 32F (some months/one year but still making contacts; still to decide), 61F (some years; more aware of people!), 18F (very short time—$^2$/$_3$ times; self-realisation), 37F (about 2 years—that is, all my life, but it hadn't got a title until 2 years ago; I have become more spiritual and more in tune with stresses and strains in my body), 18F (about 1.5 years; my contact with other pagans is rarely through groups—more through friends and co-incidence, and I work mostly on my own, through choice, but am interested in starting a covern [sic] with friends), 57M ($^5$/$_6$ years; exciting), 26M (1–2 years—I was about twelve!; it hasn't, through the above—although a pagan group I am an "associate member" of gave me the background necessary to establish my own system), and 25F (they caused it; I've started learning).

79. Alternatives' director Stern lists his New Age involvement as ten years.

80. One woman (29) lists a five-year plus involvement with St. James/Findhorn (where she has lived) and describes life changes as "self-empowering, inspiring, supportive like-minded people." The woman (30) who has been involved with St. James (5 years) and New Connexions (1.5 years) did so "initially to learn more" but "now mostly social." Changes involve "meeting more like-minded people."

81. Other variants: once per month (3), three times per month, twice per week (53F—why: "To meet with 'like' people"; changes: "It has given me a new awareness of life"), and "Whenever there's something interesting" (36F—why: "Personal interest/development").

82. A seventh simply asks, "What about astrology? healing? the Green Movement?"

83. Several LL respondents also admitted to involvements with a New Age or Neo-pagan group. One man (38) had been involved with the Lucis Trust for twenty years—attending twice per month—but did not feel his life had changed accordingly. Another (36) was involved with Neo-paganism through "romantic literature" but said, "I am a loner." A 63-year-old Canadian priest has "floated through many [New Age and Neo-pagan groups] for various lengths of time." One woman (53) is not involved with a particular or regular group but, for three and a half years now has done circle dance at weekend, summer camps and "our own group." She practices minimal and "green" life-style and visits St. James, Turning Points, etc., occasionally. These have "Given me a new sense of direction; made me aware of broader aspects of spirituality; made me more aware of "rational" forces; brought me to realize how rewarding cooperation in groups can be and how we need each other for support."

Another LL respondent (28M) has lived during the last four years in two different Communes Network communities and is also involved with a co-counseling group. He reasons that "This is part of the revolution, creating our own structures, gaining control of our lives." He claims that "It has given me much greater control over my life; my housing, my work, my diet. . . . It has put me much more in touch with my feelings. It has created for me a lasting network of warm, exciting, intelligent, challenging, supportive friends."

Another (31M) has lived for two and a half years in an Edward Carpenter Community communal house that stresses "gay community, ruralism and holistics." He says that "my involvement has tended towards the therapy/co-councelling [*sic*] and artistic ends and away from holistics. I feel my life has been utterly changed. Although I am still very lost, there is so much more purpose and direction and meaning to my life simply from understanding more about what makes me and others tick. Also a belief that humans are essentially good, no great (!) and that we can get back to that essential us."

Finally, a woman (20) has been a pagan or Wiccan for "years [but] I still don't make contacts." She has "Become more realistic I suppose. Learnt that sexism & racism & heterosexism is EVERYWHERE and that Pop-goddess (popular Goddess type worship) is very WHITE and can be oppressive to women. . . ."

*Chapter 6*

# New Age and Neo-paganism as Practiced and Observed

## Methodology

In the collection of information for this dissertation, I have relied in part on participation/observation in as many New Age and Neo-pagan functions as possible since the fall of 1988—including attendance at such events as the Prediction Festival, the Quest Annual Conference, the Mind, Body & Spirit Festival, etc. I have concentrated on both London's House of the Goddess (as a Neo-pagan venue) and St. James' Alternatives program of Monday evening lectures (as the most accessible and general New Age forum).[1] Admission to most New Age events as a participant/observer is almost fully without problem. Difficulty is only more likely to arise when it is a question of attending sessions of individual groups or NRMs within the New Age spectrum of identity. For instance, during the opening morning session of the Arcane School Conference (June 17–18, 1989), I was asked to leave the meditation in "Weavers in the Light" and "Bridge to the Future" when it was learned that I was not a 'formal' Arcane School student. No explanation was given.[2]

There is comparatively a greater difficulty involved in participation/observation at Neo-pagan events. The Green Circle groups first founded by Marion Green serve as introductory occasions for individuals wanting to know more about magic, occultism, and paganism. Since I have subscribed to the magazine *Quest*, I am therefore eligible to attend the Quest Conference held annually in March. The House of the Goddess also serves as means for pagans, witches, and occultists to make initial contact with the area. A beginning problem for anyone interested in this

223

field of religious development, however, is that of initial contact. Both the New Age and Neo-pagan movements operate through word of mouth and extensive networking links.

I first learned of the New Age concept through an *International Herald Tribune* article about J. Z. Knight/Ramtha entitled " 'New Age' Invades American Way of Life: Corporations study Uses of the Occult; Critics Fear Efforts at Mind Control" by Robert Lindsey (October 3, 1986). Although I was aware of witches' covens and (Neo-)paganism in general, initial contact with any of these was a much more difficult matter and had to wait until I came across a quasi- (but adequate) address of the U.S.A.-based Church of Circle Wicca in Melton (1986b). I was thereby able to join both Circle, Inc. and the Pagan Spirit Alliance and through the 1987 edition of the *Circle Guide to Pagan Resources* secured addresses for the London-based Green Circle, *Quest List of Esoteric Sources* and *The Q Directory* (published by the Neopantheist Society), while the Fall/Winter 1987 copy of *Circle Network News* supplied me with the address of Mike Howard's *The Cauldron*. This last led to further subscriptions to *Door: Pagan/Occult Directory* published in Glastonbury and to *The Wiccan* (through which I subsequently became a member of the Pagan Federation). In *Door* or *Spiral's "Directory of Occult Resources"* I learned of The London Web, which "Connects all folk interested in the God/dess, Witchcraft, Paganism, Shamanism, Women's Mysteries, the Occult, Druidism, Divination, etc., Local groups, teachers and networks in and around London." I phoned the listed phone number, and a prerecorded message gave information about The Magical Teahouse, which at the time was open from Wednesday through Sunday from 4 P.M. to 11 P.M.[3] I went and met "Clan Mother and High Priestess" Shan and became involved with the House of the Goddess.

Acceptance into Neo-pagan and/or Wiccan functions for me has been gained in part through my own earlier involvement with a San Francisco coven in the late 1960s, an animistic-pantheistic belief-system and my ability to participate in idolatrous worship through a conviction that it constitutes a cathartic submission of self. On the other hand, in contrast to New Age events, direct note taking during pagan ceremonies is not only not conducive to the concentration and group involvement that is required, it is also forbidden,[4] and I have had to rely on recall and the making of notes at the conclusion of meetings or gatherings. Certainly the use of recording devices would be inappropriate, whereas I have employed these at St. James openly and without problem. On one occasion, during a pagan chant recording session I was asked to leave the

House of the Goddess by Shan when, due to my unfamiliarity with the words, I had to consult the manual and appeared "to be an observer and not a participator."[5]

In general, I have had few difficulties in attending either Alternatives or HOG. In both places—though particularly the latter due to a greater sense of intimacy and the smaller numbers present—I have found a welcoming, friendly atmosphere and have made many acquaintances and perhaps even a few friends. I wish now to precede with a description of the Pagan Moon ceremony held at the Students Union Building of the University of London, Mallet Street, on the night of the full moon, 10 March 1990.

## The Pagan Moon of March 10, 1990

As part of the preparatory introduction, Shan explained to the thirty-four people in total who remained for the ceremony scheduled for 7 P.M. but not begun until more than an half hour later that "In the circle you can do no wrong."[6] The ceremony functioned as the culmination to the day's events (the rooms had been hired from 2:30 to 10:30), which included a "Talk/Workshop with Shan (Clan Mother, House of the Goddess)" at 3:00 and the "Lost People of Ravensbourne," shamanic drummers, at 5:30.[7] The advertising leaflet for the Pagan Moon celebrations (and for HOG and Shan's availability as counselor, ritualist, and instructor) states: "Everyone welcome. Bring drums, pipes and your dreams!"

In the introductory explanation, Shan continued, "Once the circle is cast, none may leave it." But she added that this is not an inflexible rule,[8] although people who do leave can disrupt the energy concentration for the others. This rule does not apply, however, to children under thirteen (one present) and animals. In fact, during the ceremony, one adult (male, late teens or early twenties) did leave the room.

Shan proceeded to ask the consent of the circle to trust her planning[9]—explaining further that the ceremony consisted of seven stages that were nevertheless flexible as well. She was reluctant to "lay these out" completely in order "to save the mystery."[10] Before the actual casting of the circle, a passing-of-the-bowl rite took place so that the celebrants could be purified. This consisted of each person "casting off their negatives" into a bowl of water mixed with salt taken from the western altar and then handed to the next person on their right (i.e., widdershins or counterclockwise) while declaring, "May you be free from anxiety and fear.'' The casting meant that the individual verbally declared whatever was bothering her or him at the time or in the immediate past—e.g., illness, aches, unemployment, loneliness, etc. Because of the number of people present, two circles were formed for this part of the ritual, and two bowls were employed. Under ideal conditions,[11] after everyone had shed their negatives, the bowls would be emptied into a river or a stream.[12] On this occasion, the ''negatives'' were discarded in the w.c. across the hall. The two bowls were refilled with fresh water and replaced on the altar in the western side of the room.[13] Anyone who had to use the toilet facilities was asked now to do so before the casting of the circle itself. Perhaps upward of ten people took advantage of this opportunity.

Shan now bade us to walk briskly in a circular counterclockwise fashion. Eventually, during a second stage, the pace was slowed to a slow walk. A third stage consisted of the slowest movement possible—with the heel of the forward foot touching the ground as the heel of the back foot simultaneously lifted off the ground. The slowest walking alone occupied a period of ten to fifteen minutes.

One large circle was re-formed. Shan had selected four men to invoke the elements.[14] I was asked and chose to call forth fire, the ruler of the south. Shan's husband, John, invoked water in the west; Barry, a self-styled Buddhist Pagan and regular figure at HOG and the Pagan-at-Home evenings, asked for the presence of earth in the north. I did not know the fourth person by whom this part of the ceremony began with the invocation of air in the east. Shan had explained that it did not matter what we said, i.e., we did not have to employ any standard text, but she asked that since I had selected fire I make the invocation correspondingly dramatic and passionate. I identified fire as the power of vitality, warmth, and light and bid this 'guardian' to come to our circle—bringing therewith enlightenment. As each invocator spoke, the others gathered behind him and faced the named direction. During my invocation to the element of fire, the group collectively snapped their fingers.[15]

The next stage consisted of the re-formation of one large circle with everyone at first holding the hands of the persons next to them. We began with the following chant:

> We are the old people;
> We are a new people;
> We are the same people
> Stronger than before.

This was eventually superseded by other chants including:

> We are the flow,
> And we are the ebb.
> We are the weaver,
> And we are the web.

And:

> Isis, Astarte, Diana, Hecate, Demeter, Kali, Inanna.

As the various chants built up in momentum and overlapped, they were accompanied by drumming and screaming. Two circles erupted spontaneously: a stationary circle on the outside whose constituents clapped hands to the general rhythm of the drums, and an inner moving circle contained by the outer. This singing section of the ceremony lasted a full forty-five minutes if not longer.[16] It culminated when Shan proclaimed, ''The power is raised!''[17]

At this point everyone seated themselves randomly, and drums were used to create a trance-like atmosphere so that ''each could call out their vision.'' Four silver bowls filled with water (two of these were the same that had been employed during the opening purification) were taken from the western altar and passed around the group. Each person said aloud how they 'saw' the moon reflected in the bowl's water.[18] Next the candle tapers were taken from fire's altar in the south, passed around to each person present, and each was lit by a flame taken from the altar and also passed around. This was the 'wishing' part of the ceremony in which the elements of fire and water are combined. The individual made a wish—usually aloud though some were scarcely audible—and then extinguished the taper in one of the four bowls of water that were also circulating still. Wishes ranged from world peace to the finding of a lover.

The bread and wine were now circulated and consumed. A bowl of Aqua Libra was also included for those who preferred a non-alcoholic beverage. The general procedure is to thank the Goddess aloud for something before imbibing. This 'feasting' was accompanied by more drumming but on a more low-keyed level.[19]

Finally, each of the original invokers was asked to thank their respective elemental guardians for their presence and bid them to depart. The candle on each altar was extinguished in turn. One large circle was again formed for the closing kissing rite. This consisted of a one-by-one kissing the cheeks and lips of the person to the individual's right along with the words:

> Merry meet.
> Merry part.
> And merry meet again.

Shan concluded with a final proclamation: "The circle is open but unbroken!" The ceremony disbanded around approximately 10:00—having lasted nearly two and one-half hours.[20]

## HOG's Pagan-At-Homes

This Pagan Moon celebration conforms to the general format followed for the biweekly Pagan-At-Homes held at the House of the Goddess on alternate Thursday evenings.[21] The number of those attending these last usually varies between eighteen to slightly over thirty. They are preceded and followed by casual social chat sessions that occur in Shan's apartment.

The temple is a freestanding structure that is reached from behind Shan's flat. Within the temple, candles for each of the four altars to the elements as well as one in the cauldron, which is suspended overhead in the middle of the circle, have already been lit when the participants take their positions.[22] They seat themselves in a circle while Shan drums and chants softly—being joined in this musical introduction by a few others with drums of their own and others who clap hands to the general rhythm. When the mood is set and the music grows fainter and finally silent, Shan then welcomes everyone to the House of the Goddess, especially those who are there for the first time. She makes various announcements (other people may join in here as well if they have a particular product to sell, a need that someone else might be able to fulfill or an event they want others to know about). For these occasions, however, "someone puts something in the pot."[23] Instead of the casting off of unpleasantness into salt and water as occurs with the Pagan Moons and the celebrations of the Wiccan festivals themselves, everyone on these occasions mentions "something dark" and "something light" that has occurred in their lives during the past week or two. This part of the ceremony is also known as the "Darklight Circle" and the "gossip circle." Shan stresses that if one does not wish to say anything, "a squeak will do." Metaphorically, each person's comments (or noises) are "put in the pot." In practice, several of the regulars will talk at length about the various problems and changes that have been occurring in their lives.

Another difference with the Pagan-At-Home apart from the absence of the wishing/moon-reflecting bowls is the inclusion of a 'game or exercise' section presided over by a mistress or master of ceremonies previously selected by Shan. On one occasion, Barry had each of us select the name of a deity from a bowl and then find the person who had the deity name that complemented one's own. For instance, I picked "Frey" and had to ask my way around until I located the person who had the name that obviously matched—in this case, "Freya." On another occasion, Jennifer led the group through different breathing exercises while each person was seated in a yogic position. Another format is to be led through various touching exercises with one or more partners while the 'receiver' keeps his or her eyes closed.

The singing/chanting and drumming is little different than that for the Pagan Moons, but the spiral dance here is the focal point.[24] Everyone takes the hand of the persons next to them, and the circle begins to rotate. Shan will break the circle at some point and lead the rest into an inner circle. Eventually, she will then take those still joined by hand beneath the arms of two people further down the human chain. The culmination is inevitably one large group of people tightly pressed together. This position may be held for fifteen minutes or longer while various individuals moan or scream or continue to sing and/or chant. Eventually, everyone falls silent, and only the heavy breathing of the group is heard.

The Pagan-At-Home concludes with the passing of two bowls of wine—one red and one white—around the circle. The inauguration of this part of the rite is usually undertaken by a couple (e.g., husband and wife, two lovers, etc.) who sprinkle a bit of the wine ("to the Goddess") with their fingers from the bowl they are holding either in the direction of the four altars or toward the circle's center while making an invocatory statement. The "Merry meet—merry part—merry meet again" kissing ritual terminates the formal side of the gathering.

On March 22, 1990, for the Pagan-At-Home that followed the first Pagan Moon, those who had assembled decided to have a 'discussion' circle rather than the usual 'doing' circle. Shan requested input from the others on how the Pagan Moons and Pagan-At-Homes should be maintained and yet contrasted from each other in the future. The consensus argued for the maintenance of the Pagan-At-Homes that Shan first began in January 1986. The greater intimacy over the larger and more public Pagan Moon gathering emerged as a key element in the affection most expressed for the Pagan-At-Home. On this occasion, following the opening Darklight Circle but before the discussion, everyone stood to greet the elements.

Shan instructed the participants to face air-east and raise their arms over their heads and then imagine themselves as trees waving about in the breeze and "feeling their own space." Facing fire-south, we were asked to rub our pelvic regions vigorously—several growling or screaming—and then shake the energy out of our hands toward the altar. Facing water-west, we scooped up imaginary water from the floor with our hands and gently poured it over ourselves from above our heads. This was done three times. Earth, on the other hand, is labor, so facing north we tugged on invisible ropes using arms and shoulders. Finally, facing the circle's center, we were asked to form with our hands or minds the image of something or someone with love or desire but then to let the image dissolve in recognition that though it/he/she may be with us for a long time, it is not ours forever.

The result of the 'talking' circle on this occasion was the decision to continue the Pagan-At-Homes but to vary them between 'discussion' and 'doing' circles. The remainder of this evening's format followed the usual procedure: chanting/dancing with a moving circle inside a stationary one, the wine/thanking celebration, and the kissing conclusion rite. As Shan was leaving the room, she called over her shoulder, "Would the last person to leave the temple blow out the candles?"

## St. James' Alternatives

One major distinction between Neo-pagan/Wiccan events and New Age gatherings is the greater ceremony involved with the former. By some pagan standards, House of the Goddess rituals are largely informal—e.g. if compared to British Druidism, Alexandrian Wicca (Crowley, 1989), the Sabaean Religious Order, and the Church of the Eternal Source (Adler, 1986) among others. But although someone like Serena Roney-Dougal employed the formalized casting of a circle and invocation of the four directional elements for a vision quest exercise she conducted during a workshop given on January 21, 1990, in general, New Age meetings contain minimal amounts of ritual.[25]

An Alternatives evening at St. James, Piccadilly, for example, begins with three brief rituals "to support us throughout the week." In the first, three volunteers from the audience come forward to light three candles—a blue candle for truth, a pink one for love, and a white candle for "the quality of the speaker's choice."[26] Next the participants are enjoined to observe a few minutes of silence as "an opportunity to bring ourselves present and focus on the evening." By a show of hands, a vote determines whether the meditative silence should be of two, five, or ten minutes duration. On every occasion that I have attended, it has always been five minutes.[27] It is always stressed that those who do not wish to meditate need not do so but should instead simply enjoy the quietness of the surroundings. Finally, each person is requested to turn to someone he or she has not come with, introduce themselves, and chat together for a few minutes. Again, it is stressed that people need not do this if they do not wish to. After these opening rites, announcements are made and the evening's speaker is introduced.

After the talk and a question-and-answer session, the chairs in the front of the church before the main altar are removed and most people form into a circle holding hands to sing and/or dance. This singing takes the usual form of a three-part round or cannon led by either Malcolm Stern or Sabrina Dearborn, two of Alternatives' directors. Food is supplied for the evening by the Wren Café. There is first a thirty-second meditation by those at the head of the queue while holding hands 'to stem the stampede'. The conclusion of the evening is therefore a casual one of eating and conversing—with several people usually continuing a discussion with the meeting's speaker. The formal section lasts about two hours—beginning at 7:00. The church must be emptied by 10:15. The entrance fee is £3 ($4.80) for employed people; £1 = 50 ($2.40) for the unemployed.[28]

## Greater ritual use in Neo-paganism

The slightly different emphases between New Age's focus on self-development and Neo-paganism's on self-empowerment may account for the greater use of ritual and myth by the latter. In a sermon given by Carolyn Owen-Toyle,[29] "Paganism or Neo-Paganism" is described as "a diverse and decentralized religious movement" in which its adherents "share a goal of living in harmony with nature and view humanity's sophisticated 'advancement' and separation from nature as the prime sources of alienation." Owen-Toyle explains that ritual is central to pagan worship and "is looked on as a way to eliminate alienation" and restore a feeling for and harmony with nature. Its purpose is "to change a person's mind," and though this might be seen as the same goal in New Age, here the predominant technique among the multitude that is available, the *primus inter pares*, is meditation. But for Neo-paganism this altered state of consciousness is sought through the working of magical-religious ritual, which, through the close physical contact that is often involved, produces, as Durkheim indicated, an auxiliary functional effect of group integration. In the Neo-pagan rites and use of myth, a collective energy is sought that is itself believed to have transforming power.

## Notes

1. "Alternatives of St. James's is dedicated to New Age thinking: ideas which provide creative and spiritual alternatives to currently accepted Western thought. Our purpose is to provide a friendly atmosphere in which to taste the best of New Age ideas. We are dedicated to the freedom of each individual to choose her or his own path of personal and spiritual growth" (e.g., "Alternatives: Spring Programme 1990").

2. The conference was held in the Regency Room of the Charing Cross Hotel in London. I was, however, allowed to attend the lectures, general discussion, and group meditation held that afternoon and again the following day celebrated as World Invocation Day.

3. 33 Oldridge Road, Clapham South, London SW12 8PN; tel. 01-673 6370.

4. This was pointed out to me when I asked Shan to read the first draft of this chapter. She writes: "We may not have witnesses. Only participants. 'Be here now'." She told me that this applies equally to recording devices and that anyone found to be employing such would be expelled from the circle. However, after the circle has been 'opened', it is fully possible to make notes, and Shan herself would be willing to assist anyone for purposes of both recall and accuracy.

5. My own lack of singing talent or ability to carry a tune may have been a contributing factor to the "something is not right, and I think it is you" declaration made to me by Shan at the time. Shan's later statement upon reading this section says: "Because you seemed to be silent and that made others self-conscious. Quality of sound, knowledge of words irrelevant. Chanting is not singing."

6. On other occasions, Shan has explained that the words *should, must* and the expression *I can't* are forbidden ones within a coven or a circle. Moreover, Craft worship is non-congregational. It is participatory instead. "As soon as one enters the circle, one is a priest or priestess."

7. Concession stands on craftwork, books, magical supplies, rune and tarot readings, and contacts were run by Atlantis Bookshop, Akashic/The Something Else Shop, Wyrdstone Workings, DragonProducts, Genesta, Dusty Miller, and

Berkana. "More than eighty people" attended for this, the first Pagan Moon celebration.

8. Shan adds in her later memo: "for non witches."

9. Shan refers to this by formally asking the assembled company for their permission as the "scrupulousness of consent." She promises not to do anything embarrassing or to compromise anyone's beliefs.

10. The seven stages are (1) Planning, (2) Purification, (3) Casting Circle, (4) Raising Energy, (5) Working, (6) Communion and (7) Opening Circle.

11. Or, according to Shan, "country conditions."

12. During the midwinter solstice ceremony at HOG (December 20, 1989), the contents of the bowl were thrown out the temple's door into the rain with the verbal command, "Be gone!" Shan explained upon reading this that the midwinter disposal was an impromptu solution due to the inclement weather. Use of a toilet is the normal procedure "in the city."

13. Each directional element possessed an altar. Incense was burned on the altar of air in the east; the candle tapers used later in the ceremony were kept on fire's altar in the south; wine was in the west; bread kept on earth's altar in the north.

14. She notes upon reading this account that this "was total innovation to have men cast circle. Normally done by women."

15. Or so I thought. Shan tells me that what I heard was the clapping of hands—"quite spontaneously without prompting."

16. Shan corrects: "20 minutes I think—that's subjectively a very long time." However, I might add here that although I had counted the number of participants as 34, Shan had been under the impression that the number present was closer to 50 because "I am used to feeling the numbers with which I am working." This was certainly incorrect.

17. Shan adds: "I say this when those present have made it obvious so it is not my decision." Moreover, it was just before this proclamation that the one person, who had not been participating in either the inner moving circle nor clapping hands in the outer stationary one, had left the room.

18. Presumably and ideally this rite would take place outdoors beneath the light of the full moon, and participants would actually see the moon's reflection. (Upon reading this footnote, Shan writes: "Beautiful idea but we did not dream so well.")

19. When it became necessary to add an extra bowl of wine for the communion part of the ceremony, the water in one of the moon-bowls was poured out through the window.

20. Shan corrects this assessment: "Ritual always lasts much longer or shorter than it seems—we go 'beyond the bounds of time'. This one actually 7.30 P.M.–9.30 P.M."

21. Shan states after reading this sentence: "To me they're very different. PAH [is] not so formal."

22. Each person has made a £1 = 50 ($2.40) donation before entering the temple.

23. In Shan's words: "Each must put something in the pot for something to happen to all."

24. Shan points out that the "Spiral Dance [is] often done in full ritual as well."

25. This is not to say that Neo-pagan festival gatherings cannot be non-structural and non-ceremonial as well. For instance, I observed the Hallowe'en night of October 31, 1989 on Glastonbury Tor in Somerset. The crowd—about 50–60 near midnight—was with few exceptions young people in their teens and early twenties. Many had brought sleeping bags. There was use of alcohol and some "recreational drugs." Several people had brought along fireworks of various kinds. The site was frigidly cold with almost unremitting winds, and several attempts were made to establish a fire within the Tor itself in one corner. It was not until later that a successful fire was created in a metal container that was placed outside and downwind from the Tor. Various forays for wood and kindling occupied part of the night's duration—different parties of youth volunteering to descend the hill at different times. The fireside quasi-ritualistic conversation that occupied much of the night could be termed a kind of hippie/esoteric talk—virtually abstract to an outsider but nevertheless exhibiting a continuity of accord that apparently allowed its duration. By morning, most had succumbed to the cold and had departed. About nine people, however, had brought the festival's observation through. What I found most interesting on this occasion was the lack of organization or planning. In fact, it was essentially a spontaneous affair that was structured simply by the reputed sacredness of the site and the fact that this was one of the chief Celtic pagan/Wiccan commemorations.

26. On January 29, 1990, for example, Dina Glauberman chose "hope"; on February 5, 1990, Robert Fritz picked "creating"; on February 12, 1990, Sir George Trevelyan selected "vision"; on February 19,1990, Alix Pirani chose "healing vitality"; and on March 19, 1990, Helena Norberg-Hodge asked for "wisdom."

27. The one exception, "to be creative" (in line with the speaker's choice of quality for the evening), a compromise was effected between those wishing only two minutes and those for five, and on February 5, 1990 the silent period lasted only four and a half minutes. Even as late as September–October 1994, while admitting beforehand that the winning vote was *always* for five minutes, the evening's announcer still felt obliged to honor the ritual of the vote itself.

28. A more ritualized Alternatives event is the celebration of Wesak, the full moon of May and the Buddha's birthday, which William Bloom refers to as the highlight of the New Age year of festivals. Though this last point might be contested within New Age collectively and is more reflective of Bloom's Alice Bailey background, the occasion of 9 May 1990 provided the most ceremonial gathering I have witnessed for any strictly New Age assemblage. The Church of St. James was filled with '700 candles' along the altar, altar railing, the pew aisles, and the upper balcony that overlooks the church on three sides.

The evening began with an introduction and explanation made by Bloom. We were asked to find the seventh chakra and group-soul above our heads. The ceremony was primarily one of collective (or "working/service") meditation that followed the lighting of the candles, a "heart collection" ("becoming aware of the group's oneness and alignment"), an opening chant of *om padme hun* led by Malcolm Stern, a narration of the Wesak legend, its interpretation by a female dancer, and a chanting of *namo amida bu su.*

The "working meditation" itself was led by Bloom. It consisted of our "centering as individuals," "linking in light," ten minutes of "consciousness healing"—sending love throughout the world/anywhere in the world that the individual felt necessary, a return to the group, then a ten minute meditation on the crown chakra using "concentration and focus" in order to "touch the highest source on behalf of all we have touched so that love can flow through us" before "letting the energy come down through us and flow out completely" during a one-to-three minutes of *om* chanting. The purpose of this exercise was "to channel/invoke a blessing."

A communion of water, an interval of "joyous singing" and an exchange of "peace"-hugging between individuals concluded the one-hour forty-five-minute celebration.

29. *Pagan Nuus* 3.3 (Candlemas/Ostara 1990:6). Owen-Toyle is co-minister of the First Unitarian Church of San Diego, California, and the 1990 President of the Unitarian Universalist Ministers' Association.

# Chapter 7

# Church-Sect Typologies

In his evaluation of the effect on the sociology of religion by the proliferation of research into the new religious movement, Thomas Robbins (1988a:27) mentions that there has been "the tendency to restrict the scope of inquiry to certain controversial groups such as The Unification Church, Hare Krishna or Scientology, which emerged in the late 1960s or 1970s and have been involved in controversies over 'brainwashing'." Citing Beckford (1985b), Robbins notes that "New Age" currents and "Neo-pagan" and occult groups "have not received abundant sociological treatment." In beginning an attempt to remedy this lacuna, it must be stressed nonetheless that 'New Age' is frequently employed as an umbrella term covering numerous Hindu, Buddhist, Sikh, Islamic, Theosophical-Occult, Spiritualist-Psychic, and New Thought Metaphysics groups. Judging by their self-identity "with the New Age Movement through their literature or by their regular attendance and participation in 'New Age' events," Melton (1986b) includes such new religious movements that indeed have received strong sociological investigation as Transcendental Meditation (Maharishi Mehesh Yogi), Rajneesh Foundation International[1] (Bhagwan Rajneesh), 3HO (Yogi Bhajan), Divine Light Mission[2] (Guru Maharaj Ji), Arica Institute (Oscar Ichazo), and est[3] (Werner Erhard), among others. In this light, the "scholarly *cohort*" may not be quite as tight and polemic as Robbins contends.

To move beyond the more narrow focus on controversial NRMs, greater sociological research in New Age/Neo-pagan groupings is now desirable. A useful tool in any investigation in this direction might be the church/sect/cult typologies developed through the efforts of Troeltsch, Niebuhr, Yinger, Bryan Wilson, Charles Glock, Rodney Stark, Robert Bellah, Frederick Bird, Thomas Robbins, Dick Anthony,

237

and Roy Wallis. If no clear-cut typology emerges without flaws of conceptual ambiguity and substantive inconsistency, we have nonetheless practical concepts—particularly those developed by Wilson, Bird, Robbins, Anthony, and Wallis—which help to locate the place and range of the New Age Movement.

## Troeltsch's church-sect-mysticism typology

In general, the church-sect distinction among sociologists is first attributed to Max Weber in *The Protestant Ethic and the Spirit of Capitalism*. N. J. Demerath (*JSSR* 6.1:82), however, contends that

> Far from originating with Weber, the dichotomy had been near the heart of Catholic theology for some time before, and Troeltsch [1931:431–35] cites it in scholarly usage as early as 1875.[4]

Nevertheless, regardless of whoever originated the church-sect dichotomy, it is clear that it was Troeltsch who developed its earliest substantial elaboration. For him (1931:338), both the church and the sect—though essentially different from each other—constituted legitimate Christian organizations. If the former stood closer to the Pauline Christ while the latter to the man Jesus (Eister, 1973:376), the sect was all the same not to be regarded as an embryonic church-type but as an independent sociological form of Christian expression.

In his *Die Soziallehren der christlichen Kirchen und Gruppen* (Troeltsch, 1931) written between 1908 and 1911, Ernst Troeltsch developed under the influence of Max Weber's church-sect dichotomy a church-sect-mysticism typology that further examines the historical role of Christian church culture as a sociological (rather than theological) phenomenon—here with the "church" representing the institutional mediator between Christian sacramental redemption and the social-political order. In Troeltsch's understanding, the "church" legitimates Christian eschatological theology with the social and cultural norms of the people-at-large. By contrast, the socially marginal "sects" polarize the inherent tensions between religion and society by repudiating cultural norms as impediments to the full actualization of a Christian ethical life for their adherents. For Troeltsch, however, a more-or-less compromising third form of social Christianity is understood by "mysticism" in which the "religious individual" synthesizes the conflicting drives of society and religion within himself and thereby diminishes the depersonalizing tendencies of capitalism. Through the mystical tradition, the church itself may be thought to be re-legitimatized in its role as social-political legitimator since mysticism "leaps over or complements traditions, cults and institutions" that may be associated with either church or sect (Troeltsch, 1910:4).[5] Troeltsch (1931:729–46) sees both "philadelphianism—the formation of groups round spiritual directors and deeply experienced leaders"—and organizations—"formed on the family pattern . . . by people who lived the community life"—as organizational types inspired by mysticism (see Nelson, 1969:155).

> Mysticism is depicted in terms of a growing individualism, in which there is little desire for organized fellowship and in which emphasis is placed on the importance of freedom for the interchange of ideas. The isolated individual becomes paramount. . . . [In] contrast to other forms of religious group the emergent organization has neither the concrete sanctity of the church-type institution nor the radicalism of the sect. . . . Gradually, thinks Troeltsch, 'the third type has come to predominate. This means, then, that all that is left is voluntary association with like-minded people, which is equally remote from Church and Sect'. (Hill, 1973:55f.)

Hill (1973:56), in turn, makes the pertinent observation that "The original concept of 'mysticism' has been converted by subsequent writers into the category of the 'cult' . . ." Nevertheless, he argues that Troeltsch overlooked the denominational stage in the emergence of the mystical cult from the church-sect dialectic. Instead, it is Niebuhr who perceived the less extremely individualistic but still fluid and pragmatic organization labeled the denomination—charged by "a lack of dogmatic orthodoxy."

Despite its limitations and confinement to the Christian tradition per se, Troeltsch's *Social Teachings* provides an initial classificatory framework for understanding religious organizations as socially mainstream, marginal, or personal orientations with various consequences for the embracing community. The church-type, in Troeltsch's understanding, seeks to establish itself as a powerful organization—endeavoring ultimately to attain influence over as much of humanity as possible. To this goal, the church is forced to compromise its means for its ends—for example, diluting a strict moral code in order to draw the maximum number of adherents into its fold. But unlike the church, the sects and mystics have little if any interest in either the salvation of society or the securing of control and authority. A characteristic sectarian response to the world and its fate is one of indifference. For the mystic, on the other hand, instead of concentrating on the Christian sectarian goal of living according to the ethics of Jesus, the foremost aim becomes one of union with God. In other words, the mystic exhibits an even greater detachment than the sect member's indifference to the world.

In general, Troeltsch's typology has been criticized for a lack of generality (it is not universally or even widely applicable), analytical clarity (it is not highly formalized or systematically interrelated) and formal theory (it cannot be used as a basic building block) (Johnson, 1971:125). Swatos (1977:201f.) refers to the "Troeltschian syndrome," that is, "the confusion of Troeltsch's theological project with Weber's sociology." Nevertheless, Swatos feels that "church-sect is a valuable and useful theoretical orientation and that as a research tool it has enabled a tremendous amount of data to be organized and reported to the sociologist of religion and the general public as well."

## Niebuhr's sect-to-church

It is H. Richard Niebuhr who has come to be considered as Troeltsch's successor. Like Troeltsch, he is, as a Christian churchman, primarily interested in the Christian phenomenon. Nevertheless, Niebuhr's classical work, *Social Sources of Denominationalism* (1929), developed Troeltsch's " 'typology' from a sociologically sterile to an analytically fruitful formulation" even though its application was largely restricted to American Protestant organizations (Eister, 1973:390). According to Allan W. Eister (1973:400), Niebuhr's enduring contribution is the emphasis he made on the principle "that all forms of religious organization are profoundly and inescapably affected by the social and cultural contexts in which they exist."

But where Troeltsch considered church and sect as independent sociological forms, Niebuhr emphasized the developmental connection between the two—finally seeing the sect as the predecessor or undeveloped expression of the church-type. The unfortunate consequences of this for sociology has led to a frequent confusion between the sect-to-church hypothesis and the church-sect typology. Nevertheless, Niebuhr's main concern was to locate the social sources of division: one in which "Denominationalism . . . represents the accommodation of Christianity to the caste-system of human society," that is, to "the castes of national, racial and economic groups" (1929:6). This accommodation in Niebuhr's view signified a failure by Christian religious organization:

Christian ethics will not permit a world-fleeing asceticism which seeks purity at the cost of service. At the end, if not at the beginning, of every effort to incorporate Christianity there is, therefore, a compromise. (1929:5)

Though Niebuhr rarely distinguishes "denomination" from "church" (unless in reference to the Church of Christ), I feel that his value-laden and negative notion of "compromise" as applied to churches or denominations and even to sects in certain situations entails a bias that is incommensurate with the objective and detached demands of social science.

Social scientists are interested not in evaluating the *quality* of the sect as a Christian agency in the world but look rather to its characteristic attitudes, social control mechanisms, and capacity to endure as a type of social group having certain ascribed 'ideal-type' traits. (Eister, 1973:373).

Despite the contextual refinements of Troeltsch's typology, Niebuhr's conceptual framework remains provincial (that is, Christian) and frequently vague—conceptually drifting between his structural division thesis and his sect-to-church developmental thesis. This lack of standardization and precise definitions along with Niebuhr's lack of value neutrality has called forth the need for a greater conceptualization that is both clear and consistent and useful in the analytic study of non-Christian sects and movements as well.[6]

## Becker's ecclesia, denomination, sect, and cult classification

A further attempt in this direction occurred in 1932 with Howard Becker's four-part typology presented in *Systematic Sociology on the Basis of the Beziehungslehre and Gebildungslehre of Leopold von Wiese*. Becker's adaptation of von Wiese's classification of religious organizations comprises the ecclesia, denomination, sect and cult (Becker, 1932:621–28). Consequently, it was Becker who systematized the contributions of Weber, Troeltsch, and Niebuhr into a typology containing several subtypes and concurrently translated the category of mysticism into that of "cult." In his discussion of Becker, Hill (1973:61) notes that "The shrine and the cult . . . both represent extremes of religious individualism in which the personal encounter with the transcendental is of prime importance." Hill (64) also sees that

"Becker's typology, with important modifications, represents the earliest and most frequently used systematic attempt to provide abstract conceptual models for the analysis of the whole range of Christian organisations."

However, similar to Niebuhr, Becker promotes as of primary interest the very social characteristics or relationships that Troeltsch considered secondary. Becker's church or ecclesia faces the same conflict between propagation of transcendental principles and effective operation as a system of human relationships. Becker's essentially Niebuhrian concept of compromise is no less value laden. The church is seen to be typified by its compulsory character; the sect, by its elective principle.

For Becker (1932:626), the denomination is a distinguishable unit, a coalescence of "sects in an advanced stage of development and adjustment to each other and the secular world." It is really an advanced state of the sect without its original intensity. In other words, Becker has located a developmental stage along the continuum of Niebuhr's sect-to-church hypothesis. But along with this refinement of polar typology between church and sect, Becker adds a fourth type in the form of the cult—once again a further differentiation of the sect. The cult is in reality, according to Becker, an extreme form of the sect—one which emphasizes the private and personal and even mystical dimensions. As we follow Becker's continuum from cult to sect to denomination to ecclesia, we move from the personal through the socio-ethical to the abstract.[7]

One main difficulty with Becker's typology is its foundation on "abstract collectivities" or ideal realities rather than on ideal-types or constructs.[8] An "abstract collectivity" is unable to be closely connected with any actual group of human beings,[9] and despite McKinney's defense (1966:24) that "extraction" involves comparisons from central tendencies as opposed to comparisons of "ideal limits," Swatos (1976:135) points out the analytical confusion that occurred before this *post facto* explanation was made. For Johnson (1963:541), "Becker's typology . . . is unsystematic, discursively developed and obviously limited to a few historical circumstances."

## Yinger's typological modifications

Also building upon Troeltsch's pioneering work and again without the Weberian distinction between ideal types[10] and verifiable "mixtures" of data, J. Milton Yinger, in his desire to replace, extend, or refine an insufficient church-sect dichotomy and adequately describe the full range of data, has further developed the typology of religious models—progressing from a typology of four subtypes in 1946, to one of six subtypes with three subdivisions of sect in 1957, and, finally, to one of six main subtypes with a further subdivision into two species of universal churches and three of sects in 1970.

> On the basis of two criteria—the degree of inclusiveness of the members of a society and the degree of the function of social interaction as contrasted with the function of personal need—a six-step classification can be described that may prove useful. (Yinger, 1957:142f.)

Yinger's seminal contribution concerning the sixfold classification and the criteria upon which it is based is to be found in his *Religion, Society, and the Individual*, published in 1957.[11] This work was superseded in 1970 by his *The Scientific Study of Religion*, where he further refines the measurement of social interaction as determined by

> The extent to which the group accepts or rejects the secular values and structures of society

[and]

> The extent to which, as an organization, it integrates a number of units into one structure, develops professional staffs, and creates a bureaucracy. (1970:257)

On these bases, Yinger considers there to be the universal church, the ecclesia, the denomination or class church, the established sect, the (transient) sect, and the cult. In this context, however, Hill (1973:90) states that ''There comes a point when the proliferation of sub-types in a general typology begins to blunt the heuristic potential of ideal types.''

Nevertheless, Yinger (1970:257) appears to qualify his typology from the beginning with the disclaimer that ''The universal church does not readily fit into a typology of religious organizations because it tends to include all types.'' In its institutionalized forms, the universal church is to be seen in the Roman Catholic Church of the thirteenth century, the smaller compass of Calvinism, or various instances of Islam. It is not, by contrast, a successfully functioning institution of the pluralistic society. For Yinger, because of the complexity to be found even with the homogeneous society in which the universal church does effectively operate, the institution itself "tends to be characterized by a complex ecclesiastical structure." This last, however, does not apply to the distinction that Yinger names the universal diffused church, namely, the Durkheimian "single moral community" of the isolated, often preliterate, and tribal society in which religious beliefs and practices infuse the communal life without apparent or even existent tangible religious organizations separate from the social system itself.

For Yinger, both the universal institutionalized church and the universal diffused church are similar in their societal scope but distinct in their organizational structure. In modern societies at least, the institutional and diffused forms of the universal church are not to be found but serve instead as classificatory poles between which the actual differentiated religious systems appear. Consequently, the degrees of complexity of religious structures range between those in which both (1) religious units are integrated as well as (2) religious professionals and (3) bureaucratic structures are present to those in which none of these are to be found—with bureaucratic structure the first to disappear, followed by the absence of religious professionals as one approaches the least complex forms.

It is the ecclesia that, as a non-elective institution, most closely approximates the institutionalized universal church. Yinger's examples include the established national churches such as the state churches of Scandinavia, the Church of England, or the pre-1915 Russian Orthodox Church. The distinguishing factor between the ecclesia and the universal institutionalized church, however, is the less successful ability of the former to incorporate sectarian tendencies. For Yinger, a modified form of the ecclesia (a diffused variety as opposed to the typical institutional Christian ecclesia) applies to those Eastern countries in which Hinduism or Buddhism predominate.

Like the largely conservative ecclesia, the denomination is usually conventional and respectable. It often represents, as with most 'mainstream' Protestant bodies in Western societies, an accommodation to respectability and secular powers. For Yinger, the denomination (or class church) would still be subsumed within Troeltsch's conception of the church rather than the sect. But unlike the relative intolerance to other groups on the part of both the ecclesia and the sect, the denomination is more accepting. This openness extends from one tolerating other religious groups to one in which admission of members is determined by the individual himself on a voluntary basis. But again as with the ecclesia, Yinger sees the denomination ranging between institutional and diffused levels of integration.

Between the denomination and the less tolerant sect, Yinger places the established sect as a more permanent movement that is more inclusive and structured and less alienated than the sect itself. In general, the established sect exhibits a greater accommodation to the secular world. Possible examples might consist of Quakerism, Mormonism, and American Judaism. Here again, depending on greater or lesser organizational complexity, Yinger distinguishes between the established sect proper and the established lay sect. The latter more strongly resists tendencies toward professional leadership and bureaucratic structural development.

In delineating the established sect, Yinger describes as well the sect itself. For this last, he follows essentially the understanding expressed by Troeltsch of the sect as a conflict organization, usually ephemeral, and preferring isolation in its rejection of the compromises made by the church. In the sect-to-church focus inaugurated by Niebuhr, however, Yinger explains the transformational motives by which a sect becomes either an established sect or a denomination. He sees the protest movement as either the individual-regeneration sect with a primary emphasis on reducing individual anxiety and sin, or the ethical-protest sect whose chief concern while confronting an evil society is with the need for social justice and reform. The former tends over time to develop into a denomination; the latter, into an established sect or a withdrawn, isolated community.

> We may say . . . that a sect will become a denomination instead of an established sect if the protest it represents can readily be absorbed into the dominant religious stream without a serious challenge to the secular social structure and without the necessity for a reorganization of the religious pattern. (Yinger, 1970:272)

Yinger gives Christian Science as an example of a sect that has become a denomination, while the Mennonites as an outgrowth of the Anabaptists he would not even after three centuries consider an established sect.

Beside the distinction between the sects whose original concerns are either individual or social, Yinger considers the sect organizationally as either a sect movement (having greater complexity) or a charismatic sect (usually an earlier, more simplified form).

> It is more complicated than that, however, for the extent of early structuring may be a critical variable that influences the likelihood that a sect will become established. Ephemeral groups, lacking any structure, come and go. Their contemporaries may be aware of them, but they disappear from

history. Those groups that come together into a movement, with at least a
minimum level of organization, are probably no more influential over their
individual members, but they play a more important role in society.
(Yinger, 1970:274)

But Yinger also subdivides the sect according to "three possible responses to an undesired situation." These are analytic types to which
existing organizations conform at best as approximations. Developing
a classificatory scheme that sees sects as participation oriented, power
oriented, or value oriented[12]—correlating respectively to the individual
mystic, prophet, or ascetic as understood by Weber—Yinger describes
a sectarian typology of acceptance sects, aggressive sects, and avoidance sects. He is careful to maintain, however, that although all three
responses are likely to co-exist in any given movement, one is more
likely to predominate over the others.

The examples suggested for the acceptance sect include the Japanese
Seichô no Ie, the Oxford Group Movement, the League for Spiritual
Discovery, and (early) Christian Science. In general, society and its
normative values are not rejected by these sects, but an innovative
means bordering on the mystical or esoteric is employed toward the
attainment of movement goals. By contrast, the aggressive sect repudi-
ates the sect's position within society (rather than society itself) and
thereby endeavors through reform and self-assertive if not defiant behavior to better place itself in the social milieu. It comprises a quasi-
optimistic though religious response—even when this takes on political
protest or certain militant overtones—to both poverty and impotence.
Though the "pure type of aggressive sect" is most apt to appear within
societies undergoing strong revolutionary tension, the examples of this
type include many Christian sects in Africa (e.g., the Congolese Église
de Jésus-Christ sur la Terre par le Prophète Simon Kimbangu), the Anabaptists, the Levellers, Münsterites, the American Ghost Dance movements of the 1870s and 1890s, the Salvation Army (though modified by
strong individualistic acceptance tendencies), and the Jehovah's Witnesses (modified by inclinations toward ascetic withdrawal). This last,
however, shades closer to the avoidance sect, for which Yinger gives
the following explanation:

> If one cannot accept society . . . or have hope of reforming it, . . . one can
> devalue the significance of this life, project his hopes into the supernatural
> world, and meanwhile reduce his problems by forming into a communion
> of like-minded fellows. This is a common sectarian protest in the "devel-

oped'' world, where aggressive protests are more likely to be secular than religious in nature. (Yinger, 1970:277)

Yinger gives as examples of the avoidance sect the early Quakers, the Hutterites, the Amana Community, various 'communist' communities in the Christian world, and the Pentecostals. These last, however, seek less the isolated community of withdrawal as they do trances, visions, and glossalia: their avoidance techniques comprise temporary escapes from this world into another. In other words, their responses are ''more symbolic than physical.''

Lastly, Yinger (1970:280) considers the cult as a group ''at the farthest extreme from the universal church'': ''It is usually small, short-lived, local, and built around a charismatic leader.'' Nevertheless, Yinger allows that as a sect may become established, so too might a cult become permanent—and relatively large.[13] In early stages, however, the cult is usually a new and syncretistic movement that is characteristically small in size, unstructured, dominated by a charismatic leader, and in search of the mystical experience. ''They are similar to sects, but represent a sharper break, in religious terms, from the prevailing tradition of society'' (p. 279). In other words, and this is the key distinguishing factor, the cult is a product of not only social alienation but especially an alienation from the traditional religious system. Nevertheless, in general, Yinger tends to re-merge the cult with the sect—with the latter being distinguished only by a greater degree of organization and self-consciousness. His concept of the cult as representing a sharper break from the dominant religious tradition of a society in which it originates is similar to that of Becker and Geoffrey Nelson as well as Stark and Bainbridge.

In refining this elaborate classification of religious groups, Yinger has played an influential and significant role in the further development of the church-sect typology employed by sociologists of religion. This typology remains, however, essentially the church-sect dichotomy first elucidated by Weber and Troeltsch. In his discussion of cults becoming permanent cults, sects becoming established, or sects evolving into denominations, Yinger appears to be close to employing a Niebhurian sect-to-church hypothesis. But, differing from Niebuhr's analysis, a religious group is seen as able to move in either direction along Yinger's classificatory axis. For instance, when referring to the denomination—which is characterized, ''whether out of necessity or out of conviction, by norms of tolerance''—Yinger points out the relative intolerance of both the church/ecclesia and the sect when compared to the more

middle-range denomination so that "An ecclesia that [readily participates in intergroup activities] no longer sees itself in inclusive terms; it
too has become a denomination" (Yinger, 1970:265). This, for Yinger,
characterizes what has largely become the case with the Roman Catholic Church in the United States. In fact, Yinger goes even further in his
(admittedly exaggerated) suggestion that "the civil religion is now the
church and most traditional religious bodies in the United States are
now sects.

> In the case of Roman Catholicism, this sectarian quality is compounded of
> three elements: 1) alienation from many of the values of the secular world;
> 2) some continuing opposition to norms of pluralism, tolerance, and the
> separation of church and state; . . . 3) some continuing protest against the
> lack of brotherhood, charity, and universalism in the economic and politi-
> cal orders. This last should remind us that the Catholic Church has always
> contained a sectarian quality obscured by an inflexible use of any typol-
> ogy. (Yinger, 1970:271)

Yinger points out that in countries where Roman Catholicism includes
the vast majority of the population, the Church conforms to the ecclesia
type, but where it competes as one of several churches, it is instead a
denomination.

Perhaps the strongest criticism that might be leveled against Yinger
is his use of abstract models rather than development of a taxonomy
from empirical evidence. But he choses his analytical approach inten-
tionally so that his resultant typology might have "greater usefulness
in crosscultural and crosstemporal comparisons" (1970:275). He also
argues that both procedures—namely, illustrating each ideal type with
organizations that approximate them, or searching for typological similarities and differences among particular organizations—eventually
"should arrive at the same place."

It is obvious that as new religious movements both New Age and
Neo-paganism conform more to the sect-cult end of the scale than to
the area comprising the church-ecclesia. Before proceeding to examine
exactly where if anywhere these religious movements and their various
manifestations fit the typology or, rather, the various understandings of
the sect and cult subdivisions proposed by different sociologists, it is
first advisable to continue further with clarifying the sect and cult forms
of religious organization themselves, their placement within the church-
sect typology or some alternative model, and finally the perennial question among sociologists concerning the very utility of the church-sect
typology itself.

## Berger's sectarian typology

Peter Berger (1954:478) has developed a sectarian typology consisting of three broad movements: enthusiastic, prophetic, and gnostic.[14] The first, centering on "an experience to be lived," breaks down into four subtypes: the Revivalist and Pentecostal—stressing the need to "save" the world; and the Pietist and Holiness groups, which seek to avoid the world. The prophetic movement with its "message to be proclaimed" consists of world-warners, the Chiliastics (e.g., the Adventist groups); and the world-conquerors, the Legalistics (e.g., Jehovah's Witnesses). The gnostic movement comprises the Oriental (e.g., Buddhist groups), New Thought (Berger cites the Rosicrucians as an example), and Spiritist. In Berger's understanding (1954:479), "In the gnostic type there is always indifference to the world."[15]

## The cult concept

Berger (1954:471) acknowledges Troeltsch's third category of mysticism (in addition to the church and sect) but devalues it as "not quite so individualistic and free-flowing as liberal science of religion assumed." Robertson (1970b:115), on the other hand, can so completely overlook Troeltsch's third category that he proclaims "Troeltsch's initial typology was, strictly speaking, not a typology at all, but rather a dichotomous classification of religious collectivities in terms of their empirical characteristics."[16] Mysticism he dismisses as "unproductive of collective continuity" (Robertson, 1970b:143n16).

Nevertheless, Michael Hill (1973:80) links the "cult" with Troeltsch's third sociological type: "The concept of cult, taken from Troeltsch's "mysticism" by Becker and refined by Yinger, has had a precarious status in most discussions of Christian organization." Yet, J. B. Snook (1974:192) perceives that Troeltsch designated this area expressly because "much modern religious experience would be expressed only in very loosely institutionalized form" (see Troeltsch, 1931:381).

In W. R. Garrett's words (1975:205),

While the concept of mysticism has mainly experienced wholehearted neglect at the hands of sociological investigators, it nonetheless represents a profoundly potent, if not essential, tool in the stock of analytical constructs available to researchers engaged in religious analysis. (See also Wallis, 1974:301).

This is particularly true in the contemporary religious resurgence that involves "experiential forms of spiritual expression from occultism to non-Western religions to fundamentalist revivalism." There is, correspondingly, all the more need in "the scientific study of religion" for the notion of mysticism. In fact, as Garrett (1975:208) points out, even to Weber "the asceticism-mysticism dichotomy—far more fundamentally than church and sect—came to represent the basic action orientations typically appropriated by historic individuals in their response toward the world."

Garrett cites Parsons (1949:674f. [1954:205f.; see 1965:*xxxiiif.*]), Aron (1970:271f.) and Nisbet (1966:261–63) in linking Weber's concept of charisma with Simmel's "piety" and Durkheim's "the sacred" as well as Troeltsch's mysticism, the "effervescent numinal experience"—or what Troeltsch subsequently referred to as "radical religious individualism." In Troeltsch's 'typology', the attainment of grace is reflected objectively in the church, subjectively in the sect, but differentiated from the perception by both of God as transcendent; mysticism centers on the experience of God or the supernatural as immanent (Troeltsch, 1910:2–5).

As Gustafson (1975:225) discerns, to Weber and Troeltsch, "mysticism has no particular sociologically distinctive organization, although it does have distinctive social consequences." Because mysticism possesses no social organization per se, it has been largely ignored in Anglo-American sociology of religion, which has preferentially focused on the study of religious organization. Nevertheless, Troeltsch clearly understood mysticism to represent an "analytically discernible sociological type," and, consequently, Garrett (1975:221)—especially in line with our focus on New Age and Neo-pagan phenomena—pertinently observes that

> Revivalist conversion, the thrust of Transcende[nt]alism toward participation in the Over-soul, and even more recent ecstatic flights into supernaturalism and the occult, all these phenomena might very well be comprehended more proficiently when scrutinized in the light of Troeltsch's mysticism construct.

There is consequently little justification for deleting "the third type from Troeltsch's tripartite typology."

Though this last may be true, in the expanded typologies of the church-sect continuum, the sect and cult are often closely associated—especially in their overlap in terms of deviance or protest (cf. Campbell, 1972:119f.). Consequently, Martin Marty (1960:126, 129f.) argues that, in addition to Protestantism and Roman Catholicism, sects and cults together constitute a "third force" in Christianity within America—with sects being essentially negatively oriented and attempting to isolate adherents from mainstream value systems; whereas cults are positively oriented and usually gathered about charismatic leaders or clans. Marty sees the cult as providing surrogates in a depersonalized society. Instead of sectarian sacrifice, the cult offers substance through esoteric and mystical approaches. If the cult does require some withdrawal and isolation, it is in order to offer "more in the middle of the world"—not less.

## Campbell's concept of the cultic milieu

Campbell (1972:120) traces the development of the concept of the cult from Troeltsch, Becker, Mann, Marty, Martin, Yinger, Jackson and Jobling, and Nelson in contrast with a tendency to use the term merely as a referent for "any religious or quasi-religious collectivity which is loosely organized, ephemeral and espouses a deviant system of belief and practice." In consequence, there have arisen two views about the nature of cults: "mystical," that is, in line with Troeltsch's original formulation of mysticism, groups that conform to characteristics of mystical religion; and "deviant," that is, a view held by Lofland, Stark, and Taylor Buckner that recognizes the essential feature as a product of the group's deviant or heterodox position vis-à-vis the "dominant societal culture." See further, Wallis (1976:11–18).

Sociology of religion tends to compare the cult with the sect. The former is described as individualistic, loosely structured, making few demands on members, tolerant of other organizations and beliefs, and it is not exclusivist. The sect is contrasted on all these points, and it furthermore does not have as rapidly changing a membership or the same degree of ephemerality. But Campbell contests the Glock and Stark position that cults necessarily either succeed quickly and become sects or disappear as quickly in the face of societal opposition or absence of a charismatic figure. In short, he argues that cults must be viewed as phenomena that simply do not conform with the present theories of sectarianism. Chiefly, sects are "clearly circumscribed entities

with specifically formulated belief systems and organizational structures which have a tendency to persist over time'' but are instead
sharply contrasted to cults with their ''undefined boundaries, fluctuating
belief systems, rudimentary organizational structures'' and their continual process of formation and collapse (Campbell, 1972:121).

In reference to Colin Campbell, Hill (1973:81) concludes that ''The
whole problem of defining a religious organization by its *lack* of organization might be solved by referring to a *cultic milieu.*'' On the individual level, there is in the cult formation and dissolution a high turnover
of membership, but the overall pool of membership itself represents a
constant, largely stable feature of society. It is this more permanent
''cultural underground of society'' that Campbell (1972:122) calls ''the
cultic milieu.'' He explains it as including ''all deviant belief-systems
and their associated practices'' as well as ''unorthodox science, alien
and heretical religion, deviant medicine, . . . the collectivities, institutions, individuals and media of communication associated with these
beliefs.'' Despite his tendency toward over-generalization, Campbell
claims that

> Substantively it includes the worlds of the occult and the magical, of spiri-
> tualism and psychic phenomena, of mysticism and new thought, of alien
> intelligences and lost civilizations, of faith healing and nature cure.

This cultic milieu, Campbell (1972:127) argues, despite its apparent
diversity and heterogeneous collection of traditions and practices, is
nevertheless ''a single entity''—one that is the more viable focus of
sociological inquiry rather than the individual cult itself. In fact, ''the
organizational form most typical of the cultic milieu is not the cult but
the 'society of seekers'.''

The unity of the cultic milieu in Campbell's understanding rests on
the deviance of all the individual cultural components within the milieu
in contrast to ''the dominant cultural orthodoxies.'' These last are unspecified by Campbell but would presumably include such things as
orthodox science, mainstream religion, and allopathic medicine. As a
result, for the cultic milieu, not only is there a common cause in defending individual freedoms relating to beliefs and practices, there is also an
overriding attitude of mutual sympathy and support. The underground
tradition tends then ''to be ecumenical, super-ecclesiastical, syncretistic
and tolerant in outlook'' (Campbell, 1972:123). The cultic milieu is
fostered by syncretization, the communication media, consumer selectivity and experimentation as well as by the common ideology of seek-

ership. Campbell, however, is not clear when he attempts to fuse the deviant aspect of the cultic milieu with mysticism ("its most prominent part"), and his analysis is definitely wrong when applied to Neo-paganism and Wicca, which, in fact, do not depreciate the role of ritual and ceremony.[17]

In Campbell's analysis, mysticism is the dominant religious component of the cultic milieu, but it is not the only one: "The other forms of 'deviant religion' which are well represented are the pre-Christian pagan traditions of magic, witchcraft, sun worship and the like" (Campbell, 1972:125). The mystical tradition, on the other hand, Campbell would find in the religions of Hinduism and Buddhism, their influences in the West, and particularly their beliefs in reincarnation and the prohibition on the taking of animal life—"almost the hallmarks by which the cultic religious groups identify themselves." Nevertheless, considering the basic beliefs that Campbell ascribes to the mystical position—namely, the religious ideal as a state of unity with the divine that is potentially attainable by everyone, the underlying unity of all consciousness and life, etc.—we find a position that is equally held by Neo-pagans themselves. Campbell's explanation for this fusion of ideas is simply the "syncretization" that is among the chief characteristics of the cultic milieu itself. I find this clarification unsatisfactory because it is inorganic and does not elucidate what would unify the disparate elements of a conjectured cultic milieu or at least provide it with an identifiable sense of integration.

Despite some of the shortcomings in Campbell's concept of the cultic milieu, he has nonetheless offered a sociological perspective by which analysis of new religious movements may be approached. He delineates the various kinds of institutions that belong to and emerge from the occult underground tradition, and he perceives how the decline of the influence of the Christian churches in the advent of increased secularization has been to the advantage of "cultic culture."

> Thus the principal bulwark against heresy and superstition has greatly diminished and the many pre-Christian varieties of religious belief and practice are free, for the first time in many centuries, to spread throughout society. In addition, the relativism and tolerance of cultural pluralism which, it is claimed, are concomitants of secularization, have greatly assisted the increased acceptability of these 'heretical' beliefs. (Campbell, 1972:131)[18]

Moreover, despite the conflict between traditional orthodox belief and the emerging scientific worldview, it is less obvious that religion in all its forms should likewise be so threatened. "The potential for conflict would, in fact, appear to be greater for religions which emphasize a personal, and transcendental conception of God than those which hold to an impersonal, non-intervening and immanent notion of the divine" (Campbell, 1972:132).[19]

Campbell (1972:135) sees the possibility that secularization may be creating "the circumstances for the emergence, not of a secular scientific society, but of a society centered on a blend of mysticism, magic and pseudo-science." In other words, secularization may actually encourage the growth of the cultic milieu. Nevertheless, this cultic milieu is defined primarily in terms of its deviant status (e.g., unorthodox medicine, pseudo-science, exotic forms of worship, non-traditional religious ideas, etc.), although the ideology of seekership and its manifesting institutions play an identifying and uniting role along with "two important elements within the milieu [which] are the religious tradition of mysticism and the personal service practices of healing and divination" (Campbell, 1972:135). But if it is the heterodoxy implicit and explicit within the cultic milieu that primarily defines it vis-à-vis the mainstream societal culture and yet, in discussing the diminishment of orthodoxy in the face of secularization Campbell (1972:131) can questionably say "What has been traditionally treated as categorically deviant and subject to secular sanctions as well as ecclesiastical wrath is gradually becoming *merely variant*" (italics mine), the author appears to pull the rug out from beneath the very sociological concept he is proposing.

Despite Campbell's contention that the cultic milieu is "much broader, deeper and historically based," it is popularly known as "*the* underground." But because of their doctrinal precariousness, lack of recognized authority, and casual commitment, cults in Campbell's as well as Wallis's understanding are fragile institutions perpetually threatened with re-absorption into the amorphous occult underground. One solution to this cultic problem of institutional fragility has been and remains the development of a cohesive sectarian collectivity. Another, however, might be the radicalization of the entire pagan-mystical subculture itself. In other words, the New Age Movement could be an attempt to incorporate as much as possible of the cultic milieu itself as a comprehensive cult in place of merely keeping it the source of individual cult collectivities.

## Nelson's cult typology

Among the more refined typologies of cult phenomena is that developed by Geoffrey Nelson (e.g., 1968, 1969). Moreover, his is one of few attempts to synthesize the mystical *and* deviant aspects of the cult expression into a single sociological conception. In Nelson's understanding, cults may be structured either hierarchically or democratically; they can be distinguished from "mystical groups"; and they may be syncretistic. Essentially, however, they are either *charismatic* (gathering around a mystic or psychic, i.e., a charismatic personality) or *spontaneous* (an informal gathering of like-minded people), and in all cases cults begin as *local cults*. If they develop organizational structure, these groups become *permanent local cults*. If the cult expands (i.e., branches) or links with other, similar groups, it may develop a centralized organization. Charismatic cults then become *unitary centralized cults*; spontaneous cults grow into *federal centralized cults*. If, however, there emerges "a diffused collectivity composed of isolated individuals and/or local groups united only in holding common basic beliefs [having], no formal organisation"—even if some of the associated groups are highly organized, we have what Nelson (1968:359) calls a *cult movement* (e.g., the Spiritualistic movement in Britain).[20]

Nelson accepts the primary cult criteria enunciated by Rodney Stark that the cult is a collectivity that makes a fundamental break with the religious tradition of its hosting culture. Utilizing Benton Johnson's and Max Weber's concepts of the emissary/ethical and exemplary prophets (respectively, the agent of a personal God who makes ethical demands and the religious figure who *shows* men how to live in accord with an impersonal godhead), Nelson (1969:159f) argues that the religious development from exemplary prophecy (e.g., the cult) does not fit the same sect-church typological continuum.

> The concepts of church and sect reflect the dichotomy of attitudes to the world that exists in all ethical monotheisms. . . . This dichotomy does not exist in Eastern religions based on exemplary prophecy. . . . The world may indeed be viewed as illusory, but it is not judged to be either good or evil in the ethical sense, only in the instrumental sense.

In other words, "The Sect-Church continuum basically measures movement from a pole of rejection of the social order to one of acceptance, whereas the Cult-New Religion continuum . . . may be used to measure the growth from dissident cult to dominant belief system" (Nelson, 1968:359).

Although there are some difficulties with Nelson's analysis (e.g., the implication that sects do not produce new religions), he has delineated a concise manner in which to view the cult per se. His secondary criteria for cult identity include the fact that cults are composed of "individuals who have had or seek mystical, psychic or ecstatic experience" and that they are chiefly preoccupied with problems of individuals rather than the wider concerns of society. On the whole, Nelson follows the church-sect-mysticism tripolar concept first formulated by Troeltsch in preference to its later developments by Niebuhr, Becker, and Yinger into a unilinear continuum.

Moreover, Nelson doubts the validity of Colin Campbell's single cultic milieu, but in constructing a classificatory system of NRMs according to their emphatic acceptance-toleration-complete rejection of the main props of Western culture, namely, Christianity, scientific materialism, and economic materialism, Nelson erroneously considers there to be only nine possible types instead of the actual eighteen (1987:73). Rejection of Christianity but acceptance of both scientific and economic materialism is understood only in terms of rationalism, atheism, or Marxism. He apparently does not consider Neo-paganism under this combination. New Age, on the other hand, is questionably allocated to a position among the rejecters of all three major elements in the Western tradition.

In his later work, Nelson (1987) examines the functions of NRMs using Robbins and Anthony's 1978 theoretical classification of these as socially integrative, socially disintegrative, socio-culturally transformative, or socially insignificant (Robbins and Anthony, 1978)—pointing out that Robbins and Anthony's integrative thesis involving the socialization process that NRMs are said to promote "has never been tested." As for the disintegrative theory, Nelson dismisses this as the Durkheimian/structural-functional assumption that "a specific *religion* has a monopoly of control over the beliefs and values upon which the system is based . . ." Instead, there simply

appears to be a relationship between the rise of new religious movements and the disintegration of pre-existing systems. (Nelson, 1987:176)

## Stark and Bainbridge's typology of cults

In Charles Glock and Rodney Stark's *Religion and Society in Tension* (1965), the area of organizational resolutions to various types of subjective deprivations that individuals or groups experience relative to others in a society is analyzed. The authors perceive five types of deprivation. The responses to the economic, social, and organismic types are religious if these are sought as compensations, but the responses are generally secular when they constitute attempts to overcome the original sense of deprivation. Social deprivation, arising from uneven valuations of individuals or groups by a society, has the church as its logical religious response; for the economically deprived, it is the sect. The religious organizational resolution for organismic deprivation (perceptions of objective or subjective disability whether mental or physical) Glock and Stark explain as the healing movement. If healing is the exclusive concern of a religious movement, it is apt to be "cult-like."

People who suffer ethical ("basically philosophical") deprivation have definite values but ones in conflict with the prevailing norms. Those experiencing psychic deprivation are without a meaningful system of values by which to interpret and organize their lives. Both forms yield both religious and secular resolutions. Ethical deprivation finds its counter expression usually through short-lived movements, fads, or reform (rather than revolutionary) movements. The typical religious solution to psychic deprivation, however, is the cult. These responses are generally extreme, and, if economic factors play a contributory deprivational role, a possible outcome is the radical political movement. For Glock and Stark, the entire occult milieu consists of people suffering psychic deprivations (e.g., Theosophy, Vedanta, the I AM movement, the Flying Saucer groups). Their prognosis for each cult itself is that either it succeeds and establishes the dominant social norm, or it dies.

The Glock and Stark conception of the cult is an alternate to that developed subsequently by Roy Wallis. For Glock and Stark, the cult is understood as a religious movement whose basic source is different from the primary religion of the culture in which it develops.[21] Stark has continued with William Bainbridge to develop yet another inclusive typology for religious movements, which must be considered along with its various strengths and weaknesses as a possible tool to be further utilized in the investigation and analysis of the New Age Movement and Neo-paganism.

Without distinguishing between the church-sect typology and the sect-to-church hypothesis, Stark and Bainbridge (1985:67) attest that "Fifty years have now passed since H. Richard Niebuhr first made it evident that a church-sect theory was desirable and likely to be possible." Stark and Bainbridge's point of departure is Benton Johnson's postulated continuum representing the degree to which a religious group rejects its surrounding sociocultural environment, but they prefer the more two-way notion of *tension* to that of rejection since not only might a sect or cult reject society, they might also *be* rejected *by* society. In this, they are close to Wallis's axis of respectability-deviation, but they go further in differentiating tension under "three integrated but conceptually distinguishable and measurable aspects of subcultural deviance":

> *difference* from the standards set by the majority or by powerful members of society, *antagonism* between the sect and society manifested in mutual rejection, and *separation* in social relations leading to the relative encapsulation of the sect. [Nevertheless,] These are not to be considered as three different axes of tension or as three dimensions of sectarianism. . . . they may be considered separately for purposes of measurement . . . (Stark and Bainbridge, 1985:66)

The key warrant for their theoretical concept as they see it is that tension can be measured. They blame use of Weber's ideal-type and sociology's "multidimensional typological schemes that produce primarily unorderable mixed types" as the chief impediments preventing empirical testing heretofore.[22]

In their attack on Weber, Stark and Bainbridge (1985:20; 1979:122) appear to be confusing *definition* with the *ideal-type* itself. They admit that comparison with the ideal in physics is direct and unambiguous—thus permitting measurement, but, without specifying how, they claim that "Weber's types prevent comparison and measurement, despite his claim that 'they are indispensable for this purpose'." In their search for an underlying unidimensional axis of variation (of the type found in Johnson's continuum of tension), these authors stress the need for the use of attributes over that of correlates for the establishment of useful definitions.

Following Johnson (1963:544), who sees that

> religions enforcing norms on their adherents that are sharply distinct from norms common in secular quarters should be classed as relatively sectarian, [whereas] bodies permitting their members to participate freely in all phases of secular life should probably . . . be classified as churches,

Stark and Bainbridge (1985:23) identify the *religious institution* with the stable sector of the social structure, the low tension end of Johnson's axis, that is, as "a cluster of roles, norms, values, and activities associated with the performance of key social functions." By contrast, the *religious movement* exists in high(er) tension with its sociocultural environment, that is, "religious movements are social movements that wish to cause or prevent change in a system of beliefs, values, symbols, and practices concerned with providing supernaturally based compensators."[23] A religious movement moving in the direction of less tension with its environment is a "church movement." One that moves in an opposite direction toward the high tension pole of the axis is a "sect movement."

In adding "some complexity to Johnson's elegant parsimony," Stark and Bainbridge (1985:25) differentiate between the sect, which is a schismatic movement, and the cult, which is not. Both are religious movements as opposed to religious institutions, but "sects have a prior tie with another religious organization," whereas cults, being non-schismatic, are products of either cultural innovation or cultural importation. They have no "prior tie with another established religious body in the society in question" but, representing an independent religious tradition, are something new—arriving by either "mutation or migration."

Stark and Bainbridge (1985:26) maintain that ". . . a theory of sect formation simply will not serve as a theory of cult formation, [although] a theory to explain sect formation can . . . be applied to cults to explain their schismatic tendencies."[24] This seems to be begging the point, and it is perhaps worth noticing that in applauding the return to sociology of the use of Weberian-Wilsonian ideal-types of *verstehen,* John Wilson (*JSSR* 13.3, 1974:371), reviewing Wilson (1973), denigrates the "functionalism and the survey analysis of Charles Glock and his cohorts." Nevertheless, Stark and Bainbridge do provide a potentially useful understanding of cult organization.

The most diffuse and least organized form of cult Stark and Bainbridge term the *audience cult.* These are least apt to constitute religious movements according to Stark and Bainbridge's definition since they deal in vague and weak compensators of modest value (e.g., mild vicarious thrill, social entertainment, etc.) They have virtually no aspects of formal organization—with membership being primarily a consumer activity through "magazines, books, newspapers, radio and television." Though members might gather to hear a lecture, in general they do not congregate physically and there is little if any recruitment.

The *client cult* is seen as more organized than the audience cult, though here too, in offering valued and specific compensators, these are magic—as opposed to religious—movements: ". . . their main business is selling compensators rather than rewards, and the compensators are relatively specific and not embodied in a total system of ultimate meaning" (Stark and Bainbridge, 1979:127). They tend to revolve about some human potential technique, some astrological service, or any other kind of specific occult product claiming to offer a restricted return. The central relationship is essentially one between consultant and client, there is little organization of adherents, and there is a general absence of attempt to solidify clients into a social movement.

"*Cult movements* are full-fledged religious organizations that attempt to satisfy all the religious needs of converts" (Stark and Bainbridge, 1985:29). They offer a much larger package of compensators including the most general type characteristic of ecclesiastical and sectarian movements.

> Nevertheless, cult movements differ considerably in the degree to which they attempt to mobilize their members and to usher in the 'New Age'. Many cult movements are very weak organizations. They are essentially study groups that gather regularly to hear discussions of the new revelations or latest spirit messages gained by the leader. Little more than modest financial support, attendance at group functions, and assent to the truth of the cult doctrines is asked of members. Frequently, the group observes no moral prohibitions more restrictive than those of the general society. (Ibid.)

Other cult movements, however, conform more to conventional sects with higher levels of commitment and greater degrees of tension with the external world. Tension increases in turn as participation of adherents becomes more total.

At the very least, Stark and Bainbridge have in their *The Future of Religion* (1985) provided some applicable tools and concepts for the study of sects and cults as new religious movements and for that of the New Age Movement and Neo-paganism in particular. Their inquiry not only explores cult formation and organization, but also sectarian/cultic development in the United States, Canada, and Europe. They have furthermore devoted chapters to two particular movements: Scientology and Transcendental Meditation. There are doubtless difficulties with some of their conceptualizations and model applications, and we must investigate these more thoroughly as we seek to evaluate them in our analysis of New Age and contemporary paganism.

### Eister's cult typology of cultural crisis response

Allan Eister (1972) departs from Glock and Stark's definition of the cult and sees cult movements as a response to cultural crises. He delineates a range of cultic responses: (1) syncretistic and innovative, perhaps ethical, but not esoteric—e.g., Baha'i, (2) combining conventional religious elements with essentially non-religious ideas and practices—e.g., New Thought, (3) esoteric—e.g., Theosophy, (4) seeking non-social objectives such as "self-awareness," "self realization," wisdom, insight, and the like—e.g., Vedanta, ISKCON, Subud, Soto Zen, Human Potential Movement, Transcendental Meditation, etc., and (5) apocalyptic, but differing from well-known Christian sects—e.g., The Process (Eister, 1972:328).

Eister acknowledges that the cult represents a more vague and unsatisfactory concept than the sect, but whereas the sect is usually oriented toward the restoration of a past tradition or toward an "otherworldly" future, the cult tends to look toward the present and future. The cult is more "open" than "closed," is without defined criteria of membership, and is less tightly controlled by rank-and-file members. Nevertheless, Eister's classification of cults (more correctly, cult responses) lacks the parsimony and clarity to be found in Nelson's typology and cult-new religion continuum. Moreover, R. Laurence Moore (1986) raises a serious contention to Eister's main thesis that cult movements are essentially "responses to culture crises." Moore argues that America has always been pluralistic and that "sectarianism" is a normal American phenomenon. In fact, "It is impossible to locate a period in American history when so-called small sects were not growing at a faster clip than denominations then viewed as large and stable" (Moore, 1986:x).

## Wilson's fourfold subtypology of sects

When we turn to elucidations concerning the subtypes of sects, then it is foremost to Bryan Wilson that we must look—particularly his examination of the relationship between the circumstances of sect origins and the various types of sectarian response. An early taxonomy proposed by Wilson (1959) comprises four delineations "within the context of Christianity": conversionist sects, adventist or revolutionist sects, introversionist or pietist sects, and gnostic sects. But, "by incorporating [the subtype of Gnostic sect] into his schema, Wilson has obliterated the cult as a separate category" (Hill, 1973:80). Nevertheless, this fourfold typology is held to be consistent with Yinger's understanding that the established sect is a product of an original sectarian perception concerning an evil nature as part of society, while the denominationalizing sect develops instead from the sectarian attitude, which seeks to reduce individual anxiety or guilt (cf. Yinger, 1957:151f.).

For Wilson, a sect is typically a voluntary association in which membership "is by proof to sect authorities of some claim to personal merit." Other characteristics include an emphasis on exclusivity and personal perfection; use of expulsion for those guilty of doctrinal or ethical deviance; the priesthood of all believers, which automatically entails a high level of lay participation; and a fundamental hostility or indifference to the environing society or state. Wilson's more general characterization of the sect differs from that of Becker and Yinger in considering "subjectivism, informality, the expression of fervor, and poverty . . . characteristics [which] appear to belong to certain subtypes only" (Wilson, 1959:4).

By contrast, the denomination is seen as "formally a voluntary association [but one which] accepts adherents without imposition of traditional prerequisites of entry, and which employs purely formalized procedures of admission" (ibid.). The emphasis is placed on educating the younger generations rather than seeking converts through evangelism. And in being characterized by latitude and toleration, the use of expulsion becomes not an available recourse in general. Moreover, the denomination's doctrinal ideology and self-conception are either ambiguous or de-emphasized. Other features include a professional ministry, formal services, and restricted lay participation. More important, however, is the non-combative attitude vis-à-vis the prevailing culture, secular society, or state—the standards and values of which are accepted. Unlike the sect, the cult does not require intense individual commitment.

As we have seen in Wilson's fourfold "sub-typology" of sects, Becker's concept of the cult has been eliminated and in general subsumed under the category of the gnostic sect. This last, unlike the indifference to the world of Berger's gnostic type, is seen as emphasizing some body of esoteric teaching and/or 'wishful mysticism' to achieve not a rejection of the world's goals but rather their attainment. These include material well-being, worldly success, health, self-realization, and happiness. Within the framework of Protestant Christianity in which Wilson delineates his typology, for the gnostic, "conventional Christian eschatology is replaced by a more optimistic and esoteric eschatology; Christ is a wayshower, an exemplar of truth, rather than a saviour" (Wilson, 1959:6). The charismatic leader is often a central feature of these movements, and a psycho-cosmological or mystical doctrine frequently replaces more standard and secular scientific explanation. The examples suggested for the gnostic sect include Christian Science, New Thought movements, Koreshanity, and the Order of the Cross.[25]

Unlike the gnostic, however, the other sectarian subtypes as first seen by Wilson tend to reject the world or its values. For the introversionist sectarian, worldly goals are replaced with more exalted and pietistic or internal values. The conversionist seeks to alter the world through altering/converting people to his or her evangelical—usually orthodox fundamental or pentecostal—view.[26] The revolutionist or adventist, by contrast, expects the world to alter (imminently) on its own through divine intervention; his response instead is one of preparing for the new dispensation.[27] While Jehovah's Witnesses and the Christadelphians are suggested as examples of the adventist sect, the Quakers, the Amana Community, and some Holiness movements are seen as introversionist sects. For the conversionist sect, the examples given are the Salvation Army and the Pentecostal sects.

In examining the circumstances of sect emergence, the internal structure of sect organization, the degree of separateness from the world, the coherence of sect values, and group commitments and relationships, Wilson finds differing tendencies among his four sect-types, i.e., (1) Gnostic, (2) Introversionist, (3) Conversionist, and (4) Adventist (see Table 7.1). In general, Wilson sees the gnostic and introversionist sects maintaining a belief in the gradual unfolding of truth or grace; the conversionist as evangelizing the truth; the adventist, making the truth difficult to obtain. An emphasis on an elect is to be found among gnostic and introversionist sects. The gnostic sectarian's commitment is to the leader or ideology; the introversionist's, to the fellowship along with moral commitment; the adventist's, to the movement's specific doctrine and morality and hence to the brethren themselves; while the conversionist remains the least sharply exclusive. Wilson sees the fellowship value as particularly strong for both the introversionist and adventist, while the conversionist sects only partially conform to the *Gemeinschaft*. In the gnostic movement, on the other hand, the fraternal concept is alien, and inter-devotee relationships are secondary. As the *Gesellschaft*, the gnostic's commitment is first to the ideology and leadership.

In this investigation of Christian sects, Wilson is particularly interested in the progress of the sectarian movement to a denomination. He concludes that

> sects with a general democratic ethic, which stress simple affirmation of intense subjective experience as a criterion of admission, which stand in

**TABLE 7.1: Differences Among Wilson's Four Primary Sect Types**

|  | 1 | 2 | 3 | 4 |
|---|---|---|---|---|
| Spontaneous development[28] | yes | — | yes | — |
| Schismatic | — | — | — | yes |
| Organizational revival | — | — | yes | — |
| Maladjusted communities[29] | — | yes | yes | yes |
| Maladjusted individuals | yes | — | — | — |
| Persisting deprivation | — | yes | — | yes |
| Clandestine response[30] | — | yes | yes | — |
| Migration | — | yes | — | — |
| Ministry development | — | — | yes | — |
| Resistance[31] | — | yes | — | yes |
| Unimportance of worship | yes | — | — | — |
| Central board allegiance | Christian Science | — | — | Jehovah's Witnesses |
| Isolation: | — | — | — | — |
| communistic | — | yes | — | — |
| organization | — | yes | — | — |
| linguistic social | yes | yes | yes | yes |
| Insulation: | — | — | — | — |
| distinctive dress | — | yes | — | — |
| group endogamy | yes[32] | yes | —[33] | yes |
| Evangelism | no | no | yes[34] | yes[35] |
| 2nd generation recruitment | difficult | yes | variable | yes |

the orthodox fundamentalist tradition, which emphasize evangelism and use revivalist techniques, and which seek to accommodate groups dislocated by rapid social change are particularly subject to denominationalizing tendencies. (Wilson, 1959:14)

These tendencies are intensified if any type of pastoral order is involved in the sect's organization; likewise, if the members are ineffectively separated from the world. Wilson has in mind with this last the proselytizing efforts by conversionists and their consequent exposure to the world with its dangers of alienation for the evangelizing agent. Consequently, it becomes clear that the conversionist sect is the most likely candidate for transformation into a denomination. By contrast, the adventist and introversionist sects appear "to be best protected from this development." On the other hand,

> The Gnostic sect is in some ways less clearly protected, but its distinctive ideology performs in some measure the functions which social insulating mechanisms perform for other types. (Wilson, 1959:15)

## Martin's concept of the denomination

Between Wilson's fourfold typology of religious sects in 1959 and his expansion of the same to a classification of seven subtypes in 1963 (cf. Wilson, 1969a), David A. Martin published his examination of the denomination in the *British Journal of Sociology* 13.1 (1962). As had Wilson in his earlier work, Martin restricts his inquiry to within the Christian tradition—with the denominations *prima inter pares* being Methodism, Congregationalism, and the General Baptists. Although referring to the "sociological impulses of Christianity," Martin appears at times to be veering close to a Niebuhrian value-laden position.[36] He rejects usage of the term "cult":

> Church, denomination and sect embody tensions and goals directly implicit in Christianity but the cult is Christian only marginally, partially and incidentally. . . . Indeed, the rise of the cult is concomitant with the rise of forces making for dechristianization: the interdependent phenomena of impersonality, diminished fellowship and 'egocentricity' which characterize it are indicative of its sub-Christian status. (Martin, 1962:4)[37]

Nevertheless, Martin does succeed in delineating various salient features of the denomination:

> The denomination does not claim that its institutional borders constitute the one ark of salvation. . . . Its attitude to organization and to cultic forms tends to be pragmatic and instrumental, while its sacramental conceptions are subjective . . . related to a fundamental individualism. In the field of eschatology its conceptions are traditional and in the field of moral theory its conception of the relation of faith to works is dynamic but balanced. (Martin, 1962:11)

In many respects, Martin's understanding of the denomination is similar to Wilson's and, save for its restriction to analysis within the Christian tradition, to Yinger's—except that the latter recognizes the denomination as a stage along the church-sect continuum, while Martin stresses the distinction of the denomination from both the church and the sect. Martin, for instance, sees the attitude of both the sect and the church to those outside its membership as "'damned''; the denomination by contrast takes a "relatively tolerant" outlook toward outsiders. It is not in possession of unique truth or authority and, consequently, is "more responsive to the climate of contemporary opinion" than either the sect or the church. Moreover, its essence is to be found in a "unity of experience" rather than one of organization.

One of the key features in Martin's understanding of the denomination is that it is a "sociological type *sui generis.*" He does not view denominations as transformed sects but, as with Methodism and Congregationalism, as never having been sects. They are independently originating "spiritual brotherhoods or clubs" whose underlying principle of organization is a priesthood of all believers. Though the sect also professes this last, it differs from the "delegated democracy of the denomination" either through a total lack of organization due to an attitude that views a separated ministry as superfluous or perverse or through a quasi-military type of organization.

> Whereas the denomination is characterized by moderation the sect is either communist or anarchist, revolutionary or quietist, nudist or uniformed, ascetic or licentious, completely sacramental or non-sacramental, worshipping in a wild communal rant or, like the Seekers, in utter silence. (Martin, 1962:7)

Though Martin often sounds more like a Christian theologian than a detached social scientist, he sees the denomination as standing in contrast to "sectarian organizational extremism" and closer to the church in retention of at least the formal trappings of structure and titles. For instance, "The separated ministry is retained, but *basically* as a matter of propriety and convenience" (Martin, 1962:7 [italics mine]).

However, Martin's denomination is presented as closer to the church and farthest from the sect in the area of eschatology. The typical sectarian attitude is described as one either of passive waiting or of active preparation and engagement for the millennium—with a corresponding refusal to attempt any amelioration of present conditions. But unlike the sect whose members are largely alienated or rejected from society as a whole, the denomination has a vested interest in the present social order. It retains the traditional eschatology of heaven and hell. "This single fact places a sociological gulf between denomination and sect"—disallowing the possibility that the traditional or true denomination could have ever once been sectarian (Martin, 1962:9).

Almost inadvertently Martin appears to delineate a kind of subtypology of the sect as well. Whereas the church is presented as necessitated by its inclusive sociological character to be compromising or accommodating, the sect takes an opposite approach of either licentious antinomianism (characteristic of the pantheistic sect) or of ascetic, "even suicidal" perfectionism (the dualistic sect). But due to its fundamental individualism, the denomination manages to avoid all three positions. Being particularly characteristic as a social phenomenon occurring in the United States or the British Commonwealth, the denomination, which is typically lower middle class, belongs to the culturally and economically individualistic society.

A polarity between individualism and collectivism is allowed alongside one between conservation and change. "The church, the denomination and the sect each stand in a specific relation to these twin polarities" (Martin, 1962:11f.). In general the church is collectivist; the denomination, individualistic. "The sect either drives the individualism of the denomination to the anarchist extreme or it drives the collectivism of the church to the communist extreme" (ibid.). With the other polarity, the church tends toward conservation; the sect, toward either revolutionary change or "quietism and pacifism." But "The denomination, which is at home in an individualistic society, tends to be for or against change according as to whether the change promotes or threatens individual values" (ibid.). Nevertheless, Benton Johnson (1971:125), for instance, while recognizing the contribution made by Martin to the Niebuhr-Becker legacy and the subsequent work of Wilson, feels that "the simplistic adding" of the denomination as a type has "generally been carried on without reference to guiding criteria that might give the efforts conceptual unity and coherence."

Wilson (1969a:362f.), moreover, takes exception to Martin's viewing of sects as simply eschatologically adventist and either revolutionary or disillusionedly quietist. "Sects are not easily marshalled into a few dichotomies."

> The Brethren, Quakers and Christadelphians are neither communist nor anarchist; the different Darbyist groups, Jehovah's Witnesses, Church of God in British Isles and Overseas, the holiness movements do not worship in a wild rant nor in total silence; the Assemblies of God are neither ascetic nor licentious. But who would deny that these are sects?

For Wilson, Martin's theological or doctrinal analysis restricts comparative study by ignoring "the ways in which separate elements combine together," overlooks the organizational and dynamic aspects relating to possible transformation, and "runs the risk of stigmatizing the sect and characterizing it in terms which are essentially normative."

## Wilson's sevenfold subtypology of sects

Perhaps Martin was at least a goad to Wilson that inspired him to broaden his original fourfold classification of sects into a more comprehensive typology having application to sectarian analysis in non-Christian and non-Western situations as well. Using a central criterion of the sect's response to the world, Wilson renames the gnostic sect manipulationist and adds three new types: the thaumaturgical, the reformist, and the utopian sects.

> Any typology of sects must point up . . . that sects pass through processes of change. . . . All organizations are prone to suffer an attentuation [sic] in commitment to their original values . . . The sect manifests this tendency most particularly in its response to the world. Indeed, the structures, duties and official doctrine are much more resistant to change. But the attitude towards the outside world . . . constitutes the major issue of debate between the sect and the wider society . . . (Wilson, 1969a:372)

Although sects as ideological movements stress the maintenance and/ or propagation of their doctrinal positions, Wilson (1969a:361) argues that "If the sociology of religion is to move forward, we must create categories which allow us to study comparatively the social functions and development of religious movements." His sevenfold typology, being based on sectarian response to the world, is a deliberate attempt "to shun categories dictated too specifically by characteristics of a particular theological tradition" (ibid.). Wilson's typology remains versatile in that it recognizes "the ideological character of sects" without de-emphasizing sect members' ways of life, "which also necessarily affect the manner in which they accept, reject, neglect or attempt to transcend, to improve or to transvaluate the opportunities which worldly society may offer" (Wilson, 1969a:364).

Of the new types added to his sub-classification, Wilson's delineation of the utopian sect (he himself stating that it is "perhaps the most complex type") is the least satisfactory, being sketched primarily by comparisons: more radical than the reformist sect, less violent (at least potentially) than the revolutionary sect, more socially constructive than the conversionist sect, and withdrawing into perfectionist communal living as part of an original vision rather than the defensive vicinal segregation typical of the introversionist sect. Candidates for consideration here include the Tolstoyan communities, the Oneida Community, the Brüderhof, and possibly certain sections of the Christian Socialists.

The reformist sect for Wilson (1969a:369) answers the need in a "dynamic analytic approach to religious movements" for "a category corresponding to those groups which, though sectarian in more than one respect, have affected transformations in their early response towards the outside world," i.e., from an original revolutionary attitude to a later introverted one. The history of the Quakers is cited as a typical example. The reformist sect is characterized by "a very strong sense of identity [and] studies the world in order to involve itself in it by good deeds." Though remaining in some sense apart from the world, it is no longer hostile or indifferent to society but seeks through a modified association to serve as a critical role model.

The thaumaturgical sect differs little from the manipulationist sect in many ways apart from a more personal and less universalist response to the world. Its primary characteristic is to seek the personal experience of the supernatural. Their interest is not in gnosis per se but in communication with spiritual powers and the dead for predictive and miraculous purposes. In seeing their principal representatives embodied in the likes of the Spiritualist Church and the Progressive Spiritualist Church, Wilson cites the seance as the most typical activity. As chiefly an audience rather than a fellowship, one interested more in the public demonstration than communion with the godhead or a savior, Wilson sees the activity of the thaumaturgist bordering more on the magical than the religious.

Though both the New Age Movement and Neo-paganism possess various attributes that have affinities with characteristics belonging to one or more or several of Wilson's typology of sects, both conform—at least superficially—to features typical of the thaumaturgical and manipulationist sects. Both essentially accept the goals of the outside world. Although the manipulationists "frequently proclaim a more spiritualized and ethereal version of the cultural ends of global society," the important point is that the ends themselves are not rejected (Wilson, 1969a:367). The manipulationist sects

> offer special techniques and verbal modes of assurance which justify the pursuit and attainment of cultural goals. These movements are thus of the type sometimes called 'cults' . . . positively oriented towards the outside world.

Despite the similarities between the manipulationist and thaumaturgical sects, the former along with the introversionist sect are unlikely to emerge in an underdeveloped country. Instead, the kind of indigenous sects that flourish in what one might call the mission territories are either the thaumaturgical or the revolutionary (adventist), although conversionist orientations emerge as secondary responses—all together, those positions that "place far greater emphasis on the autonomous operation of the supernatural than do the others" (Wilson, 1973:28).

Since one of our preoccupations in any examination into the New Age Movement and Neo-paganism will entail determining the extent into which either or both movements conform chiefly to Wilson's manipulationist or thaumaturgical sects, it is helpful to mention at this point the various features he discusses concerning these two types. Although Wilson refers to the thaumaturgical sect as one of two possibilities likely in the pre-literate society as an original response, it does not automatically follow that the same type of sect cannot or does not emerge within those societies characterized by relatively advanced stages of cultural development. Wilson sees the thaumaturgical and revolutionary sects as primitive and simple responses that permit considerable elements of fantasy.

> Both clearly existed in the history of Christianity; although the thaumaturgical response has given rise to fewer sectarian organizations as such, it has existed within the Christian tradition in cult movements of one kind or another, or as residual paganism. (Wilson, 1969a:380)

Wilson points out that the healing sects are often quasi-developments from the Christian thaumaturgical tradition itself. Nevertheless,

Thaumaturgical practice characterizes primitive religion and magic, and when societies reach the degree of complexity where religious deviation becomes possible, thaumaturgy becomes an almost inevitable part of it. (Wilson, 1969a:376)

By contrast, the universalist feature of the manipulationist sect is a cultural variable that is found only among the culturally more complex stages of social development. Since "A manipulationist sect can come into being only when metaphysical thought has extended into the religious and philosophical traditions of a society" (Wilson, 1969a:374), its appearance seems to be dependent, at least in part, on a breaking of traditional religious functionaries' educational, intellectual, and religious monopolies.

Sects of this type tend to succeed among semi-intellectuals who have some knowledge of scientific or philosophical reasoning and imitate it up to a point. . . . These sects comprise more 'educated' people; they are unlikely to originate from the working classes. They tend to offer visions of prestige and power, as well as the short cuts for achieving them. They attract groups who have some ambition in this direction. The special means offered by the sects to attain these goals are defined in terms of verbal techniques and metaphysical theories. They use a language which attracts confidence and creates assurance, . . . Well-being in this world, perceived in terms of health, wealth, comfort and social status, constitutes the practical sanction for these sects' teaching. The achievement-oriented society offers its rewards through extremely competitive processes. In response, these sects offer new methods which allow an escape from tensions and the achievement of cultural goals, especially for those who are sensitive to social status, and struggle to attain it. Sects of this type were particularly significant during the nineteenth and twentieth centuries in industrial societies. (Ibid.)

Are these New Age? On the basis of the New Age data examined in Chapter 2, the answer would seem to be 'yes'—at least partially. But we must await a more definitive answer to this question after finishing our examination of the other typologies.

## The "church-sect obituary"

Meanwhile, the very church-sect typology, into which Wilson's sub-classification of sects fits, has itself been called into question and its utility in sociological research doubted. In 1971, James E. Dittes (381) referred to the "strong four-part obituary for church-sect" published four years earlier by N. J. Demerath, Allan W. Eister, Erich Goode, and Paul Gustafson.

In actuality, Gustafson does not reject the church-sect typology per se but points out that if an original typology is inadequate, there is either the tendency to develop another typology or to create subtypes to cover the inadequacies. Referring to the Niebuhr-Becker-Yinger tradition, Gustafson (1967:67) states that "The increasing numbers of units and sub-units does demonstrate that there is dissatisfaction with the basic typology." He proposes returning to the two ideological dimensions on which Troeltsch's church-sect typology rests: the universalistic-particularistic concept of membership in which the Christian church aims to be a universal phenomena and yet places emphasis upon the particularistic salvation of individuals, and the objective-subjective means of grace in which this last is obtained either through the mediating church itself or through a God-person relationship. On this basis, Gustafson develops a fourfold typology whose subdivisions he does not name apart from the universalistic-objective (UO), the universalistic-subjective (US), the particularistic-subjective (PS), and the particularistic-objective (PO) designations. Gustafson finds the UO dominating in the West until the emergence of US groups with the Reformation and the subsequent development of the PS category. The PO "has not readily been found."

If Gustafson, however, attempts to salvage the church-sect formulation by returning to Troeltsch over Niebuhr, Goode (1967a:77) is much less hopeful.

As it stands today, it is a hodge-podge of definition and empirical correlates and empirical noncorrelates. It has no power to explain or elucidate. Unless it undergoes a radical revision which is universally accepted by researchers and theorists in the field, church-sect must be seen as a dead concept, obsolete, sterile, and archaic.

Along with this we have Demerath's verdict (1967a:83f.) that "the church-sect framework could stand replacement, and almost any alternative may be preferable so long as it is *not* theologically rooted or religious in its primary intent," whereas Eister (1967:85)

would argue not only that the conceptualization is unreliable, but that excessive, and insufficiently critical, reliance upon [the church-sect 'dimension'] may well have blocked more vigorous and impressive development of a sociology of religious phenomena. It is at least questionable whether the distinctions drawn between church and sect in typological terms have led to important new insights or to knowledge which would not have been gotten otherwise.

Eister is particularly opposed to the legacy that, post-Niebuhr, presents "the notion of church-sect as poles of a continuum rather than simply as discrete categories" (Swatos, 1976:134)[38] as well as empirical research founded upon a faulty conceptualization. Nevertheless, Eister (1967:89) does reserve the possible utility of such "concepts of church, sect, cult or other 'types' of religious organization taken separately and developed on a basis of broad acquaintance with actual religious movements and organizations."

Wilson (1973:12), too, is opposed to typologizing according to "theological conceptions of religious protest," and feels that " 'the sect', if we continue so to call such movements, is no longer to be understood by direct contrast with 'the church'." In fact, Wilson argues, the sect as a self-distinguishing protest movement may be a reaction against not necessarily church organization but rather the state or the secular institutions of society or even particular groups or institutions within the society. Moreover, Wilson (1973:13) finds the post-Troeltschean classifications of religious bodies or movements by the degree of their institutionalization to be "a clearly inadequate procedure for movements that have arisen outside the boundaries of established Christianity."

## Johnson's justification model of church, sect, etc., identity

Benton Johnson (1963:540) points out that Troeltsch's definitions of church and sect, being derived in the main from an historical examination of pre-nineteenth century Christian Europe, naturally forced him to assume "that a Christian society would have a legally established, politically protected religious monopoly" such as the Roman Catholic, Anglican, Lutheran, and Orthodox communions. "Within this historical context it was almost inevitable that alternative religious expressions would have the character of protest movements." Johnson (1971:126), stressing the need for "the use of analytical properties [that lead] toward universality and away from the parochialism of typologies based on descriptions of historical cases," finds inadequacies with most sociologists within the Troeltsch-Niebuhr tradition—including people like

Peter Berger and Milton Yinger who have in fact attempted approaches based on analytical properties. For instance, Howard Becker's typology is seen as too limited and unsystematic; Yinger's, as unclear, contradictory, and based often on extraneous characteristics; Berger's, as operationally difficult and conflicting with prevailing usage.

For Johnson (1963:542), since "the major theoretical aim of sociology . . . is to elucidate a variety of particular problems by means of a limited number of concepts and principles of general applicability," the continual development of new types or subtypes (e.g., Troeltsch's concept of the "Free Church" for representing Calvinism) to cover various mixed cases, new or otherwise, is simply an unsatisfactory solution. Moreover, the newer typologies, he feels, have rarely if at all specified all the elements actually employed. Consequently, in reformulating the church-sect typology, Johnson (e.g., 1957:90) turns to a single variable comprising a liturgical-ethical orientation to justification, that is, "Our interest . . . will be specifically in that regularly undertaken set of behaviors which out of all other permissible behaviors enjoys a primacy in the affirming of religious status." This is what Johnson terms the *process of justification.*

The problem with Johnson's typology is that it is expressly relevant to Christian institutions rather than to a broad spectrum of religious movements transculturally.[39] Johnson more or less concedes that the church-sect distinction is really applicable only to groups within the Judeo-Christian-Islamic tradition. On the other hand, by employing an ethical-liturgical axis against which to measure the means of justification and determine a religious group as either a church that accepts the social environment in which it exists or a sect that rejects the same,[40] and by locating the environment(s) and/or the specified group(s), Johnson has presented a device that is "well adapted to comparative analyses." Since his real interest is to investigate contemporary American society as "one of the few industrial nations of the world that has not undergone a marked decline in popular religious interest since the beginning of industrial development" and "as the second major historical example since the beginning of the Christian era of a culture that has an essentially comprehensive and integrative religious system" (1963:545), Johnson delineates an interesting and informative picture in which most American religious bodies are basically churchly (e.g., Methodists, Presbyterians, Congregationalists, Episcopalians, Lutherans, Baptists, Disciples of Christ, the Evangelical-United Brethren, and Reformed and Conservative Judaism) while those that are closer to the sectarian end of the continuum are the Orthodox Jewish community and the Roman Catholic Church. Sectarian in a limited sense only and certainly less so than the Roman Catholics would be the Mormons, the Seventh Day Adventists, the more militant non-revivalist fundamentalists (e.g., Orthodox Presbyterians, Christian Reformed), and Bryan Wilson's conversionist sects (the holiness and pentecostal movements).

In a later work, Johnson examines Wilson's "informally" and "unsystematically" presented theory of sect development and judges it nevertheless better than Niebuhr's theory, which is simply "wrong." Johnson recognizes the two basic variables in Wilson's theory as the character of the environment and the character of the sect itself, but he points out that "The world may compromise the sect, but some sects are able to compromise the world by making an impact on it" (Johnson, 1971:129). This two-way process is seen as allowing a more fruitful and accurate understanding of sect development vis-à-vis the social environment—by-passing Wilson's more limited preoccupation with how a sect merely keeps itself protected from the world rather than become a possibly dynamic factor of influence upon its world.

In the same work, Johnson also investigates the denomination—"a religious organization that accepts the rules governing all voluntary associations in modern western society" (1971:133). He is here looking again specifically into American society and argues that any institutional body is considered sectarian on the basis of its attitude toward the "rules of the American Way of Life." If a religious body changes its position from one of opposition to acceptance of the rules, the process may be labeled compromise or secularization since the organization has yielded to external pressure and relinquished theologically legitimated practices. The denomination itself remains to some degree sectarian in that it neither dominates or accepts the environment in which it exists. Consequently, Wilson's theory of sect development on strategies adopted for purposes of relating to the external society may, according to Johnson, become applicable to denominational strategy as well.

Nevertheless, William Swatos (1976:139) sees a fundamental lack of integration in Johnson's model. Although his

> theoretical scheme manages to comprehend the basic property of the 'internal' religion component of religio-social integration, [it] fails to provide adequate theoretical grounding for the integration of this property into any theory of the larger social system within which it may be located.

Swatos wonders whether this deficiency does not result from an acceptance of Troeltsch as the inaugurator of church-sect theory rather than

Weber—with a corresponding lack of methodological consideration of the ideal type. This last is explained by Eister (1973:369) in contrast to the quantitative model of multivariable equations describing functional interrelationships. The ideal-type presents a totally different "principle of explanation" or, rather, understanding—one that works on a basis of "logico-meaningful relationships" of subjective intentions of "typical actors" in "typical situations." The ideal-type seeks to present an "empathetic inside look" into plausible connections between ends and means. In Weber's words, the ideal-type is an "analytical construct"— one not expected to be found in reality but nonetheless useful as a basis for comparison and measurement. Stark and Bainbridge (1979:122), however, deny this contention in stressing that it is attributes and not correlates that are mandatory in a definition. These authors support Johnson's solution for defining the church-sect axis and develop their own theory for religious movements from it. We shall return to their conceptualization shortly.

## Robertson's typology based on legitimacy and membership

Meanwhile, another reformulation of the church-sect typology has been undertaken by Roland Robertson (1970b:123) on "the bases of religious legitimacy as perceived by the effective leaders of the organization and . . . the operative principle of membership." For Robertson, the church-sect typology is applicable in social contexts rather than cultural ones, that is, relevant for the study of social-relational aspects of religious collectivities but not their doctrinal ones. He understands there to be either religious movements (aiming to effect some form of social change) or religious organizations (existing for the benefit of its members) or, even, at any given point of development, an organized religious movement. In this schema, there emerge the uniquely legitimate types of church and sect; the pluralistically legitimate types of denomination and institutionalized sect—with the church and denomination based on an inclusive membership principle; the sect and institutionalized sect, on an exclusive one. These are, however, restricted to the religious organizations or organized collectivities, that is, those that "manifest a system of institutionalized roles and procedures regulating man's religiosity" (ibid.).

As Robertson explains, this typology is rooted in the Troeltschian tradition since its point of departure is the religious basis of the relationship between the organization and its environment. In pointing out alternate approaches founded on a much wider variety of characteristics, Robertson (ibid.) states that

> Yinger's inclusion of the criterion of contribution to the integration of society is one end of an alternative-extreme in this matter, which extends at the other to Johnson's argument that it is the purely *internal* doctrinal characteristics of a religious collectivity which should furnish the basis of typological explication.

Robertson feels that his typology steers a middle course between the societo-centric position of Yinger and the religio-centric one of Johnson. Nevertheless, Swatos (1976:141) argues that because Robertson's model is itself Troeltschian, it is also religio-centric. It does not allow a clear focus on the mutual interdependence of the religious organization and the socio-cultural environment. Moreover, like Troeltsch, Robertson still does not emancipate himself from working almost exclusively within the Judeo-Christian tradition.[41]

## Swatos's fivefold church-sect-denomination model

All the same, Swatos feels that Robertson has accomplished "a tremendous service" through the construction of his model. In his own endeavors toward development of an integrated church-sect theory, Swatos (1977:201), who feels that "church-sect is a valuable and useful theoretical orientation and . . . research tool," uses Robertson as a point of departure. As do Robertson, Gustafson, and Wallis, Swatos employs two dimensions upon which to formulate his model. One of these, using a concept developed by Peter Berger and Thomas Luckmann, is called the "social organization for universe-maintenance." Robertson (1970a:101f.) identifies this dimension as the rigid or flexible monopolistic-competitive tendency. Swatos's other factor is Johnson's acceptance/rejection of the social environment. These produce five types, which Swatos tentatively names as church, entrenched sect, established sect, dynamic sect, and denomination. For him, this typology combines the original Weberian distinction of church and sect with the "accumulated achievements and failures" of sociology since Weber.

In his discussion of the cult, Swatos (1981:18f.) rejects distinguishing typologically between sects and cults on the basis of schismatic or spontaneous-foreign origins (e.g., Stark and Bainbridge) because this understanding "becomes theoretically inefficient when it is put to any use beyond that of origins." Swatos also appears critical of Wallis's inclusion of the cult in the church-sect continuum, arguing that cults are not necessarily religious organizations but simply collectivities centered on a charismatic figure (either real or legendary) whose honor or followed prescriptions are believed by followers to improve their lives. It is only when a cult begins to make "formal religious claims" that "it begins to move into the category of formal religious organizations and can then be treated in a church-sect framework" (Swatos, 1981:20). In addition, Swatos points out the relativity involved in terms of both position and value judgment with such concepts as "deviance" and "conventionality." Cf. Wallis (1975a).

Nevertheless, Swatos finds value in Stark and Bainbridge's subtypology of cults with the exception that he would consider "cult movements" as actually being sects—only audience and client cults, by lacking coherent organization and specific religiosity and thereby not falling within the church-sect framework, would really be "cults." Also excluded from the framework is the religious order that instead operates "within the established framework of a church." Swatos (1981:21f.) sees the distinction between the cult and the religious order in that

> cults are collective mystic responses to both the world and the central problem of meaning, whereas orders are ascetic responses to these same categories of experience.

In the contemporary rise of cults, Swatos (1981:24) sees "a corresponding decline in religious orders."

Nevertheless, Swatos's two-dimensional model of religious collectivities is more or less an alternative to Wallis's model, which is based on Robertson's unique or pluralistic legitimacy dimension, on the one hand, and, on the other, the environment's perception of the specific group in terms of a respectability-deviance criterion. Swatos (1976:142) feels that his and Wallis's models diverge chiefly because the latter "does not specify the social conditions under which the various organizational forms are or are not likely to develop," and because Wallis through "his grounding in the Bryan Wilson—Geoffrey Nelson tradition which is essentially non-Weberian as far as church-sect theory is concerned [is led] to think of 'sect' as something given or fixed, rather than something defined in the research process." Before, however, taking a deeper look into Wallis's understanding of "ideological collectivities'' and in particular the cult, it is perhaps more advantageous at this point to return first to Wilson.

## A further look at Wilson's sectarian typology

In his introduction to *Patterns of Sectarianism* (1967:4), Wilson too, like Swatos, points out the danger of erroneous sociological thinking that the reification of concepts is capable of producing. Wilson clearly states that a judicious typological use may facilitate sociological explanation, but these "must always be of use in application to empirical data. Typologies are not explanations in themselves . . . ''—concluding that "Only as types are usable to explain processes are they really justified."[42] He has provided the most extensive research not only on sects themselves but on their retention of sectarian characteristics as well. Wilson has, however, eliminated the category of the cult through use of the Gnostic sect subtype. Marty, on the other hand, maintains that sects have negative orientations toward the values of the surrounding society while cults are positively oriented, and that both together constitute a residual "third force." For Jackson and Jobling, in the mystic-religious cult, esoteric practices are utilized to maximize the votary's religious experience. By contrast, the world-affirming cult uses its esoteric practice to develop success, prestige, and power in the world for its adherents. Of Wilson's three new subtypes subsequently added to his typology, the thaumaturgical corresponds to mystic-religious responses, while the reformist is like a denomination yet retains a sectarian structure.

In this important area, Hill (1973) examines Martin's conclusions concerning the non-sectarian characteristics of denominations—even in their early history—in which they are certainly not Niebuhr's "mature sects." In fact, the denomination is opposed to both church and sect not only in that there is no institutional monopoly of salvation but also in its maintaining a fairly tolerant position. Basically the denomination is *reformist* and neither conservative (church) nor revolutionary/indifferent (sect).

Wilson explains that sectarian organization is inevitably limited by theological commitment, which in one form or another promotes the sects' separation from the world. Nevertheless, the sect is not an "interest association" but rather a movement if not an organization that seeks to maintain faith and procure salvational blessings for its members in this world or the next.

These particular characteristics—the ultimate voluntaryism of sect alle-
giance; the distinctiveness and apartness from the wider society, and especially from its religious organisation; the inappropriateness of rational criteria to its operations; and the interim nature of the sect's conception of its
mission—all affect the type of organisation which sects evolve. (Wilson,
1967:10)

Wilson is at pains to indicate that Troeltsch developed his concept of
the sect largely from knowledge based on adventist movements. Niebuhr, on the other hand, turned to the conversionist movements of nineteenth-century evangelical American Protestantism. Though these undoubtedly constitute sects—and sects in the understanding of popular
usage; Wilson through his expanded typification has endeavored to produce a more comprehensive presentation of the full range of sectarian
organization—one that redefines the sect in terms of "separate minority
religious movements" (cf. Wilson, 1973).

As a pattern of institutionalized procedures for regulation of the
movement's activities, sect organization, according to Wilson, must
minimally include agencies, persons, or procedural arrangements for
determining meeting places and agendas, for controlling others (such
as calling and presiding over meetings), for acceptance of new members, for the socialization of new members, for evaluating members
both new and old in terms of worthiness or transgression, for maintenance of belief and practice, for regulation of the sect's dealings with
external authorities, and for administrative and instrumental decision
making. The circumstances of origin is another factor, along with response to the world, that is a determinant of sect organization. Sects
may arise through the efforts of a charismatic figure, through schism,
through spontaneous group experience, through revitalization attempts
within more traditional movements, or through non-denominational revivalism. In each case, the circumstances of origin produce limiting
factors upon the form the sectarian expression may take.

Based on an empirical examination of twenty-one representational
American Protestant sects, Michael Welch (1977) put Wilson's typology to test. Welch employed a multidimensional scale with which to
graph sect similarity on the basis of sectarian retreatism from the secular world versus secular activism and the high or low level of organizational precariousness. The results showed that

while Wilson's (1969) typology may adequately represent the similarities
between sects of the introversionist, manipulationist, and thaumaturgical

types, it does not perform as well with sects of the revolutionary, conversionist, or reformist types. (Welch, 1977:134)[43]

Welch grants that the typology does appear to make some doctrinal distinctions but was disappointed with the lack of clarity within the organizational dimension. He would prefer not to lump doctrinal and organizational considerations together as the sectarian response to the world.

Specifically, Welch's findings indicate a high level of disparity (mutual non-proximity) within each matrix cluster representing the reformist, conversionist, and revolutionary sects. Moreover, there appears to be a second or separate cluster of conversionist sects (labeled Conversionist II). Welch wonders whether these "more extremely isolationist sects may represent a type of sect empirically and analytically distinct from that originally identified by Wilson" (ibid.). This speculation is reminiscent of Yinger (1970:276), who missed within Wilson's classification "any reference to sects that seek to alter the world by direct action, sects that shade off toward political and even military protest movements, a type well illustrated by the Levellers" (cf. Johnson, 1971:128).

Admittedly, those of us who find Wilson's typology attractive and helpful must nevertheless concede that its ambiguous presentation prevents ready discernment of inconsistencies and omissions. Moreover, "The formulation of a general theory incorporating causal explanations of cult movements appears to go far beyond the possibilities of ordering the complex body of available data" (Wilson, 1973:501f.). This situation allows several directions of departure. One route might consist of revamping the entire conceptualization involving subtypes of religious organizations—such as is seen in the work of Stark and Bainbridge; another would be to refine if not the entire typology à la Yinger then to continue further in the direction of Wilson as did Wallis and focus upon a specific area within the typology.[44] Wallis has chosen to concentrate on understanding the new religious movement.

## Wallis's departure using the social movement

While Wilson (1988:954) understands secularization as a largely contemporary "process by which religious thinking, practice and institutions lose significance, and become marginal to the operation of the social system," he argues that "many new movements are themselves

testimonies to secularisation,'' that is, ''in the West at least, they are
. . . very much the creations of a secularised society'' (1988:965). In
*Sectarianism: Analysis of Religious and Non-religious Sects* (1975a),
Roy Wallis presents an early foray into a continuous fascination with
the new sectarian movements. He considers that definitions of the ideological collectivity founded on doctrinal content are insufficient or irrelevant for the treatment of sociological problems. He distinguishes the
cult and the sect instead on the respective belief-system's perception of
access to truth or salvation in terms of legitimacy: pluralistic for the
cult; unique for the sect (cf. Wallis, 1975a:47). The cult and sect are,
however, not exclusively religious movements; they may also be on
occasion purely sectarian collectivities. Eister (1972:329) makes the
same point regarding the cult.

In 1979, Wallis expanded his investigation into the more comprehensive social movement with his *Salvation and Protest: Studies of Social
and Religious Movements*. In this diverse series of essays, Wallis explores various aspects of social movements—with religious movements
considered to be a possible sub-class. He defines social movements ''as
relatively sustained collective efforts to change, maintain, or restore
some feature(s) of society or of its members, which employ relatively
uninstitutionalised means to promote those ends,'' but the author is not
offering a theory of social movements. The way that they are defined
is not consequential for his enterprise (1979a:1). Seeking instead to
understand social phenomena as a combined outcome of both the interpretation of the world by human agents and their situation within it,
these essays attempt generalization and explanation based on a relatively close study of a few particular movements. In Wallis's opinion
(1979a:3), employing ''the (alleged) model of the natural sciences, with
abstract theories and a nomological-deductive mode of explanation''
has, in sociology at least, only produced results that ''have often been
unconvincing, uninteresting, or both, particularly in the field of social
and religious movements.''

Wallis stresses the need for some account of the actors' experiences
to be gained from the actors themselves, but this in turn raises the question of *reliance*: how much of the participants' accounts can be taken
''at face value''; how much is justificatory rather than explanatory?
According to Wallis, there is no general rule to be followed. Instead, the
problem is one of practical method and entails evaluating statements
made by participants and informants in consideration of their role in
the situation's structure, their biographical experience, their conception
of the audience, their proximity to the circumstances discussed, their

reliability and consistency, etc. In other words, the researcher must entertain such possibilities as "Do they have a position to defend?", ". . . an axe to grind?" ". . . something to hide or someone to impress?" "Did they see it happen?" or "Do they produce different accounts in different circumstances?" In his attempt to delineate a practical approach, Wallis's essays presented in this collection are based on the assumption that social events are constituted by human activity of a meaningful kind and in order to explain this activity, to understand it, the researcher must learn its language, interpret its symbols, and acquaint himself or herself with the reasons people have for engaging in it.

In a chapter devoted to examining "goal displacement" and "routinisation of charisma" in the National Festival of Light (NFOL), Wallis explores the concept of "relative deprivation" in a specific context. He is in particular opposed to the model that construes movement goals and ideology as objective "facts" against which changes in presentation and practice can be measured, one that sees a sequence of events or stages corresponding to initial movement mobilization through a charismatic leader and a subsequent institutionalizing shift to rational-legal forms of authority and administration. Instead, Wallis finds in the NFOL that movement goals may be formulated in the very process of recruitment rather than as *a priori* and clearly defined appeals to relatively deprived but potential adherents. Since the following of a social movement "engages in selective perception and interpretation of a movement and its goals," a movement's stated goal is rather a rhetorical device having flexible interpretations and applications. Moreover, Wallis also proposes that "charismatic and rational-legal orientations may be *immanent tensions* within a social movement, rather than *sequential phases*" (Wallis, 1979a:130f.).

Wallis (1979a:144) suggests that the researcher's perception of co-existent tensions as distinctively different stages may be the result of analyses conducted distantly from the "action." His criticism of the sequential model is that it "glosses vital processes." "Statements of 'movement goals' and strategy are first formulated *in interaction* with initial recruits."

Although Wallis explicitly declares his intention to focus closely upon one or a few movements, there remains the danger of forming explanations and generalizations from too limited a base. There is the inherent risk that the movements selected by Wallis (1979a) for study (e.g., the NFOL, Scientology, Christian Science, Children of God, Mrs. Keech's cult, the Aetherius Society, and the National Viewers' and Listeners' Association) may be broadly atypical. This is not a criticism per se, nor even a call for a definition of the 'typical' movement (though this might help), but rather an appeal for extending the exploratory base to allow for more comparison between groups and more supported generalization developed from them. Wallis (1984) and Wallis (1988) tend to meet the objections I express here.

## Wallis: The concepts of legitimacy and schism, and his fourfold typology

In his earlier works, Wallis (e.g., 1975a, 1975b) has sought to trace the overall sectarian development of movements that were originally non-exclusive cults: Christian Science, Scientology, the Aetherius Society, Unity, etc. In these efforts, Wallis construes a typology of religious collectivities into which we might place his later analyses of the NRM. But whereas in Wallis (1984) the determinative onus appears to rest with the group itself and *its* perception of or reaction to the outside world, in this more comprehensive typology (e.g., 1975b:90), one of two distinguishing factors is the social environment's external perception of the group: whether respectable or deviant. The other factor is the criterion of legitimacy: whether unique or pluralistic. Consequently, we arrive at the fourfold model shown in Table 7.2.

**TABLE 7.2: Wallis's Fourfold Typology**

|                            | Respectable | Deviant |
|----------------------------|-------------|---------|
| Uniquely legitimate        | Church      | Sect    |
| Pluralistically legitimate | Denomination | Cult   |

Deviance is a measure of divergence from the "normatively sanctioned forms of belief prevailing at any time." Legitimacy relates to "epistemological" individualism for the denomination and cult; to "epistemological" authoritarianism for the church and sect. In other words, with "no clear locus of final authority beyond the individual member," the denomination and cult remain doctrinally and structurally loose and tolerant. There is no authoritative source for judgments of heresy.[45]

In this understanding, since sects claim privileged access to truth and salvation, they possess some authoritative locus for legitimately accepted accusations of heresy. Although Benton Johnson and Milton Yinger indicated, as with the position of the Roman Catholic Church in the United States, that an organization may become a sect through external changes in the social environment itself, Wallis (1975b:93) considers sectarian emergence more simply "as schismatic movements from existing denominations; as a result of interdenominational crusades; or through a process of development from cults." Since his more immediate interest is with the arrogation of authority involved with transition from cult to sect, this more restricted presentation of sect development is not significant. He is here concerned with the former cult's abandonment of elements that tied it to the "cultic milieu" and its development (as a sect) of new doctrinal elements to further separate it from both the general occult field and its competitors.

A common theme found throughout the collection of essays in Wallis (1979a) is that of *legitimation*. Wallis sees the inability to attain a necessary level of legitimacy as the chief factor behind the failure of some movements to develop a stable institutional and recruitment base—namely, "Civil Assistance" and "GB75," two "citizens' action" movements of 1974. Without an established legitimacy, these movements were unable to adapt subsequently irrelevant aims to changing circumstances nor to establish new aims to replace outmoded ones. Moreover, with too broad a conceptualization of the problems faced, these movements could not appeal effectively to any particular constituency.

One method for the fragile ideological movement to develop a cohesive collectivity, however—one suggested by both Christian Science and Scientology—is to pursue a strategy of sectarianization. Through elaboration of a transcendental ideology, a more rigorously controlling central authority may become legitimated. Both the impersonalization and standardization of the central authority have the effect of weakening alternate sources of authority. Consequently, "the focusing of commitment upon the leader and central organisation, and engagement in conflict with the wider society and competing belief systems, tend to enhance the integration of the movement and more clearly define its ideological boundaries" (Wallis, 1979a:43).

Related to legitimacy is the propensity to schism, that is, the breaking away of one group of erstwhile supporters of a social or religious movement. Wallis cites this process as a prominent aspect in the dynamics of many such movements. Once again, however, he contends a basic trend in sociological research and theory—in this case, explaining schism in terms of motivations of those concerned or in the underlying social divisions themselves. Following Joseph Nyomarkay (1967), Wallis finds a more fruitful approach through discerning the *structural condi-*

*tions* that aid or counter schism. Rather than accepting the reductionist approaches of Richard Niebuhr, Christian Dawson, S. L. Greenslade, Mayer Zald and Roberta Ash, Robert Doherty, or Milton Yinger, Wallis (1979a:177) argues that "There seems . . . to be no reason to believe that we shall ever isolate any common underlying theme in these accounts of motivation or social differentiation beyond the belief that one party could no longer remain united with another, and that schismatic groups tend to be socially more homogeneous than the parent bodies from which they become divorced."

Instead of motivational theories that fail to explain several important aspects of schism or are simply inadequate as complete explanations, Wallis opts for a theory of differential propensity to schism. This theory is developed from Nyomarkay's distinguishing between movements in which authority and legitimation are derived either from charisma or from ideology. In so doing, Nyomarkay reorients the problem from one of why schisms occur to one of accounting for the differential propensity to schism of different movements as well as explaining why they occur in some movements at certain stages of development but not others. But Nyomarkay's point of departure is only seminal since ". . . it seems that the matter is not simply one of an analytical distinction between charisma and ideology" (Wallis, 1979a:181). Instead, the schismatic propensity is directly related to the perceived availability of sources of legitimation within a movement, that is, to the degree to which access to the means of legitimation can be secured by some range of movement members independent of the mediation of (other) power holders.

In discussing legitimacy, Wallis points out the different forms it may assume within any given movement. For instance, legitimacy may occur in the person and sayings of the leader or in some set of sacred writings or an oral tradition. It may also be available in various divisions of power positions within the movement's organizational structure. In some movements, personal revelations directly received by individual members are considered legitimate. Or, in other cases, legitimacy may be seen in the largely impersonal mandate of the headquarter's organization. Consequently, schism involves employing either *alternative* means of legitimation from those mobilized by the movement's power holders, or the *same* means in those situations in which access to them is widely distributed throughout the movement.

Building upon but also contrasting with both Zald and Ash's conception of *exclusive* and *inclusive* movements, and Nyomarkay's *totalitarian* and *non-totalitarian* movements, Wallis proposes his distinction between movements that are *uniquely legitimate* and those that are *pluralistically legitimate*. The former possess sharply defined doctrinal boundaries; the latter, by contrast, accept the validity of alternative paths and are therefore more tolerant of different factional groupings. These are, of course, Wallis's 1975 distinction between the sect- and cult-types of ideological collectivities.

By combining the means of legitimation as either singular or many with the availability to the means of legitimation by one, a few (i.e., an elite) or many, Wallis develops a more multifaceted schema for schismatic propensity:

Wallis gives the following examples of each cell:

Cell 1—the Nazi Party

Cell 2—the Marxist movements (if ideology is accepted as providing the only means of legitimation).

Cell 3—the spiritualist tradition (where contact with transcendental powers and beings is widely believed to be available to all members, and mediumistic possession thus provides a ready means of challenging established authority).

Cell 4—The CPSU under Stalin (who could legitimate his position by means of his claimed unique role as interpreter of the ideology, but also by his role as chief of the party bureaucracy and even head of state).

Cell 5—Theosophy (in which the charismatic authority of Helena Petrowna Blavatsky and William Q. Judge conflicted with the rational-legal authority of Henry Steele Olcott).

Cell 6—various bodies within the Pentecostal movement (since all born-again believers are capable of charismatic possession by the Holy Spirit, and therefore legitimate challenges to authority are widely available).

As Wallis understands, the propensity for schism increases directly with the availability of means of legitimating authority. The more bases

**TABLE 7.3: Schismatic Propensity According to Wallis**

| | *Means of Legitimation* | |
| --- | --- | --- |
| *Availability* | *Singular* | *Plural* |
| One | 1 | 4 |
| Few | 2 | 5 |
| Many | 3 | 6 |

of legitimacy there are, or the more widely available they are, the greater the possibility for schism to occur. This is seen as clearly compatible with the recognition that schism propensity varies inversely with centralization, that is, with the arrogation of power and authority to a small number of persons or institutional foci. When this arrogation is concentrated, there exists less available means of legitimacy to others with a corresponding decrease in the likelihood for successful schismatic attempts.

Following Weber and Bryan Wilson (1975), Wallis (1979a:186) acknowledges that a charismatic leader represents the strongest possibility for a break to occur within an existing institutional order, but nevertheless charisma, though fluid and not tied to visible and accepted institutional forms, is not the sole form of authority to which a new appeal may be made, and within a group experiencing various degrees of innovation, "traditional authority" may become the source for schismatic legitimation, whereas a movement that has become highly institutionalized might find the "rational-legal authority" providing a rival base for legitimation.

On the other hand and at the other end of the centralization-decentralization axis, that is, within groups that espouse some degree of direct access to the transcendent for others beside the leader, charisma becomes diffused and weakened. In such movements, divisions may be frequent, and groups may divide and re-coalesce rapidly, but schism itself rarely amounts to any deep changes in belief-system or application of the movement's tenets.

Unless as with Christian Science where the authority and legitimacy has been effectively centralized in a bureaucratic apparatus, new movements are inherently unstable and tend toward destabilization with the death of their charismatic leader. This tendency increases in those movements in which the charismatic leader has not unambiguously designated a successor or some form of alternative leadership.

With his model for schismatic propensity in mind, Wallis concludes that the source of fission propensity is to be found in the availability to means of legitimating a challenge to the prevailing leadership and claiming loyalty from some section of movement support. For groups within the Spiritualist tradition, legitimacy is open and available to the general body of believers; within such movements as the Christadelphians or the early Brethren, legitimation may be less broad and more limited to an informal elite. For these last, the informal personal influence and acknowledged leadership in local levels in the absence of any clearly centralized institutional authority may provide fissionable sources of legitimation. The same applies even more deeply to groups possessing a democratic or individualistic ideology which allows no privileged interpreters of the truth. These include not only spiritualist groups, but also those within the pentecostal traditions, Marxist parties, and Quakerism.

The situations of Christian Science, Dianetics, and other teacher-and-practitioner movements also allow a destabilizing prospect in that authorities locally institutionalized can become deployed against a centralized authority. Even within the centralized authority of a movement, competing factions may emerge as sources for schismatic rupture. Examples of this last are to be found in the conflict which developed between the charismatic Jeffreys as founder of Elim and the bureaucratic administration that had evolved (cf. Wilson, 1961); in the rivalry that ensued between Blavatsky and Olcott in Theosophy; or in the dispute between the Board and the Trustees of Christian Science that followed Mary Baker Eddy's death.

"Rather than structural conditions *constraining* actors independently of their motivation," Wallis (1979a:191) suggests "that in the case of schism these factors explicitly or implicitly enter into the motivation of actors to pursue a schismatic course of action." In other words, the probability that some followers might be induced successfully into disaffection depends on the degree to which a schismatic leader can justify and validate his actions. This last is dependent upon the perception of what means of legitimation are available—a correlation with the actual availability of such means.

In his *Salvation and Protest*, Roy Wallis has provided a discussion of various salient features to be discerned in the development and transitions of social and religious movements. Whether the various characteristics discussed by Wallis—especially his typological theory of schismatic propensity—are applicable to the New Age phenomena is an issue we shall explore subsequently. Nevertheless, as Wallis has stressed in this work, a key factor in judging the stability and changes within any grouping—including both the breakaway sect and the spontaneous new religious movement—is the source or sources of legitimacy with which the group operates.

## Robbins and Anthony's monistic-dualistic typology

Meanwhile, following upon Robert Bellah's conceptions of religious evolution and "civil religion" (1967, 1969), Dick Anthony and

Thomas Robbins (1982a) have seen the development of new religious movements as a response to the crisis and decline in American civil religion. According to Choquette (1985:46), these writers have developed "one of the most comprehensive views of new religions." They perceive two main types of response: (1) *dualistic* movements, which reaffirm elements of traditional moral absolutism in an exaggerated and strident manner, i.e., the authoritarian "civil religion sects" and (2) mystical and therapeutic *monistic* movements, which affirm relativistic and subjectivistic moral meaning systems. The former are seen to subdivide into traditional and youth-culture types; the latter, into ascetic and egoistic types. Robbins (*JSSR* 16.3, 1977:311), in his review of Glock and Bellah (1976), considers "Wuthnow's data [to] support the notion that "monistic" Eastern mysticism and "dualistic" neo-fundamentalism embody contrasting resolutions of the contemporary spiritual and moral crisis which appeal to different types of individuals."

The civil religion sects protest against the ambiguity, relativism, and permissiveness of modern culture and reaffirm a "theocentric ethical dualism." They also endeavor to reform the political process and its assumptions—generally in a conservative direction. These groups are usually either "neo-fundamentalist," such as the Jesus People, or "revisionistic syncretic"—e.g., the Unification Church. There are, however, other groups as well: the Children of God, the People's Temple, Synanon, etc. Characteristically, the effort of the dualistic movement is toward the reformation of the political community, often through relevant sectarian supernatural methods. Strong resistance to their efforts by the social environment at large may lead to the establishment of alternative communities intended as future American social models. These may become highly structured "total institutions" that are decisively segregated from the wider society.

The monistic groups, on the other hand, see the world in terms of *maya*, that is, as ultimately illusory or epiphenomenal. Beyond the impermanence and unreality of the material world, there is postulated to be a metaphysical unity transcending all polarities. The essentially ethically relativistic approach of these groups toward this "oneness" stresses inner spiritual awakening through exploration of intrapsychic consciousness. The means employed are either technical, that is, using standardized procedures of an instrumental kind (Transcendental Meditation, *est*, Scientology, even Krishna Consciousness) or charismatic, that is, through intense veneration of exemplary leaders regarded as possessors of advanced consciousness (e.g., Meher Baba, Guru Maharaj-Ji, Charles Manson). Alternately, enlightenment is described as one-level in such movements as Transcendental Meditation (TM), *est*, or Scientology where it is attained relatively rapidly or even immediately upon conversion; or two-level—Meher Baba, Yogi Bhajan, or Healthy-Happy-Holy Organization (3HO)—in which the sought-after quality of consciousness is more difficult and rarely attained. For Robbins (*JSSR* 16.3, 1977:312), "Eastern monism entails a world view not necessarily more 'scientific', but perhaps less conspicuously nonscientific . . . than anthropomorphic conceptions of a personal creator God."

Along with their concepts of monistic and dualistic meaning systems, Anthony and Robbins further consider such new religious forms as adaptive and marginal movements, charismatic and technical movements, and univocal versus multivocal cognitive styles. For Choquette (1985:47), these authors have developed "A unique typology that organizes the wide variety of groups in a useful way." They acknowledge that the term "cult," though frequently applied to deviant, marginal, or therapeutic religious groups, has "no precise consensual meaning." Their understanding of the "marginal movement" is one in which the convert tends to "drop out" of conventional structures and become isolated in self-sufficient, authoritarian communal institutions. By contrast, converts to the "adaptive movements" (e.g., Meher Baba, TM, and *est*) tend toward reintegration into conventional vocational, educational, and familial roles. Intermediate groups might contain encapsulated "core" members surrounded by noncommunal participants of "limited liability." Examples given include Scientology, the Divine Light Mission, Baba Muktananda followers, and various Tibetan and Zen Buddhist movements. (Cf. Robbins et al., 1975).

The chief theoretical models for the formation of new movements are seen by Robbins (1988b:103f.) as (1) the *psychopathological*, which views cults being created by "disturbed" persons and most likely to succeed during times of societal crisis when a predominant number of people experience the same difficulties, (2) the *entrepreneurial*, in which a founder fosters new meanings in order to propagate them and exchange them for substantial rewards, and (3) the *subcultural-evolutionary* which "views cults as expressions of *novel social systems* composed of intimately interacting persons." Robbins argues that these are really complementary models rather than mutually exclusive ones. The first two focus on "a single prophet-producer of new meanings, who ultimately exchanges them with followers." Moreover, the entrepreneurial is linked to the possibility of "cultic lineages" since the innovative cultural items are really new *combinations* of already existing cultural elements. While market precariousness fosters vulnerability

among world-affirming movements (Robbins notes in particular the decline in TM and DLM), charisma problems tend to be connected with
world-rejecting groups.

In evaluating new movements, Robbins (1988b:134) discusses various recent attempts to formulate typologies of NRMs as well as assimi-
late the cult concept to the church-sect framework. But he cautions that

> Typologizing 'new movements' presupposes that the boundaries of the
> entity being typologized are known; however, 'NRMs' denotes a rather
> ambiguous phenomenon . . .

Moreover, how really 'new' are the NRMs?

Returning to the Robbins-Anthony typology per se, the subdimen-
sions of "charismatic movements" and "technical movements" are
considered various types of the monistic meaning system. The former,
encountered through such figures as Meher Baba, Muktananda, and
Rajneesh, are those groups that comprise intense devotional relationship to exalted masters perceived as embodiments of some form of spiritual apotheosis. The technical movement, by contrast, focuses upon a
standard technique as the means toward spiritual realization. These include such repetitive practices as meditation, chanting, or "auditing"
(cf. Robbins, Anthony, and Richardson, 1978).

The one-level and two-level breakdowns of the monistic movement
are further described as literal-univocal and symbolicist-multivocal, respectively. Robbins and Anthony recognize the paradox, however, in
the evangelical revival, which expresses a multivocal and "enchanted"
supernatural content through a rationalized (i.e., literalistic, dogmatic,
and empirically interpretative) univocal form. Likewise, this duality applies to various human potential and quasi-mystical groups. Nevertheless, the authors (cf. Anthony, Ecker, and Wilber, 1987), proceeding
from an assumption that reductionism is to be avoided whereas the restoration of "spiritual enchantment" is to be encouraged, feel that the
above mentioned distinctions (e.g., univocal-multivocal, monistic-dualistic, and technical-charismatic) might constitute the basis for a critical
typology applying to contemporary religious movements.

## Wallis's rejection-accommodation-affirmation typology of NRMs

But Wallis (1984) has objections to Anthony and Robbins's analyses.
He points out for instance that ISKCON (Krishna Consciousness) con-

forms to traditional Hindu thought, i.e., that it is monistic, yet has designs in transforming the social and political order. New Vrindavana is conceived of as a model of the new world. Moreover, following Bird, not all Eastern-originated groups are monistic—e.g., Vedanta may take the form of ontological and ethical dualisms, and there are important distinctions among religions that develop from the different faiths of Buddhism, Hinduism, Taoism, and Islam. Wallis concludes that the real test of a typology rests with its utilitarian aspects—especially in its ability to identify the salient features of, in this case religious, phenomena on a theoretical basis that can tolerate critical appraisal.

In his *The Elementary Forms of the New Religious Life* published in 1984, Wallis presents a further typology constructed around the ways a new religious movement may orient itself to the social world in which it emerges. He conceives of a conceptual space bounded by three poles: rejection of the world, affirmation of the world, and accommodation to the world. The first denigrates the world and its traditional values. The examples given include ISKCON, the Children of God, the People's Temple, and the Manson Family. By contrast, TM, *est*, Scientology, and the Human Potential Movement affirm the normatively approved goals and values belonging to the world. The accommodating movements either mildly acquiesce or mildly disapprove of the ways of the world and remain indifferent to it as far as religious practice is concerned. Subud is closest to the accommodation point of the conceptual triangle; Neo-Pentecostalism ranks lower. The Jesus People, Meher Baba, and Divine Light Mission are understood as more mixed cases between the poles of rejection and affirmation; Nichiren Shoshu is a mixture of accommodating and affirming elements.

Wallis's schema is intended only for post-World War II new religious movements in the West. Though the accommodation groups would seem to be more compatible with a wider range of forms and ideologies, they are less characteristic of today's emerging movements. Usually they are pre-World War II and of little numerical significance such as the Aetherius Society, or, as in the case of Neo-Pentecostalism, they flourish as an ''adjunct to another movement.''

Wallis's conceptual triangle is similar to that of Yinger (1970:278) which, however, incorporating Wilson's terminology for sects, is more descriptive and historical. In this schema, the points are labeled aggressive or revolutionist, acceptance or gnostic, and avoidance or introversionist—with conversionist along the aggressive-acceptance continuum, pentecostal along the acceptance-avoidance, and adventist along that of the avoidance-aggressive. Wallis sees his world-affirming category corresponding to the acceptance or Wilson's gnostic classification. However, his world-rejecting type includes the avoidance or Wilson's introversionist type and the adventists but not the conversionists. Consequently, the aggressive-revolutionist does not correspond to Wallis's schema, which, moreover, finds nothing in Yinger to approach the world-accommodating type.

Wallis concedes that Wilson's study of religious sects is a broader one than is his own analysis of new religious movements, but he agrees with Wilson that a movement's response to the world is the crucial factor. For Wallis, the purpose of a conceptual scheme is one of identifying key elements and orientations that appear to exercise predominant influence over a movement's structure or orientation. For the "post-war West," he delineates the "three analytical types of orientation" of world-rejecting, world-affirming, and world-accommodating movements. In *The Elementary Forms*, Wallis's argument is that "each type of new religious movement has distinct social sources and constituencies" (p. 128). Part of this distinction stems from differing approaches to the issue of inclusiveness and exclusiveness,

> which in turn derives from the diffuseness or specificity of the salvational resources offered, and the conception of its soteriological uniqueness which any movement can convey. (Ibid.)

Although the New Age Movement and the New Age religions in general will be seen to conform to Wallis's world-affirming type, in many cases there are important world-rejecting features as well (e.g., millenarianism, inner elite corps, charismatic leader, etc.) and even, in some cases, elements of the world-accommodating movement. Therefore, it is advisable at this point to examine more closely the delineations of these definitive responses.

Larry D. Shinn (*JSSR* 24.3, 1985:329f), however, questions to what extent Wallis really does conceptualize three basic types of new religious movements (NRMs)—seeing instead that Wallis posits only the world-rejecting type against the world-affirming/world-accommodating ones.

> In sum, Wallis is not at all convincing in his argument that there are three basic typologies of NRMs, but instead seems to confirm that there are two basic types, one which is predominately religious and points to some kind of super-natural power ("God") and one which points to some kind of pervasive power which humans themselves can control.

Shinn has seen that Wallis actually describes dualisms of religion versus quasi-religion or religion versus magic.

Whatever the merits of this and additional criticisms made by Shinn in reviewing *The Elementary Forms*, it is certainly true that Wallis pays little attention to the contended world-accommodating type. Nevertheless, while admitting here a more "limited empirical prominence and theoretical interest," for him the world-accommodating new religion makes a distinction between the spiritual and the worldly in a manner, which is quite uncharacteristic of the other two types. It is not primarily a social matter but a provision for solace or stimulation of the personal interior life. For instance, in the Renewal Movement, which stresses a typical personalistic orientation in its beliefs and expectations, there is not a protest against the world or society but one against the prevailing religious institutions and their perceived loss of vitality. In the accommodating type, there is usually enthusiastic participation in a characteristically collective form of worship. For the individual, this revival of an explicitly religious commitment is a private reassertion rather than a public transformation.

The accommodating movement's unhappiness with the impersonality and instrumentalism of the prevailing social order is shared by the rejecting type, only here the perception is usually more intensely colored by the radical belief that the environing world is fundamentally evil so that the organized reaction becomes truly sectarian and correspondingly one of strong to extreme alienation. Although in the context of a Christian culture the world-rejecting movement appears more conventionally religious than would the average world-affirming type, it has provoked the greater antipathy and hostility through its isolation and insistence upon the severance of new recruits' familial and other previous ties. However, in their expectation of an imminent total transformation of the world, that is, the supernatural establishment of a heaven on earth, the world-rejecting movements share what has been cited as the central tenet of New Age belief.

For the world-rejector, the active response to a perception of a hopelessly corrupt world is millennial (e.g., the Children of God, Unification Church). This reaction may even take the form of a full or quasi-revolutionary behavior or at least preparation. The passive response to a world viewed as beyond reform is, on the other hand, typically one of introversion (such as Krishna Consciousness). This pursuit of salvation by gathering into tight communities of the elect bears certain resemblances to various New Age communal efforts (e.g., Findhorn, Perelandra, Steve Gaskin's The Farm), but these last are not withdrawn from a world perceived as "tainted" in order "to preserve and cultivate their own holiness." They conform more closely to Wilson's concept of the utopian sect rather than the introversionist. In contrast to New Age, the marginality of the world-rejection movements is such that there is an overt acceptance that their beliefs and values cannot be accepted within the prevailing social order. Out of this belief in possession of a revealed truth utterly at variance with the wider society, they tend to segregate from the world into highly cohesive units in which 'truth' and heresy are such by authoritarian definition rather than individual decision.

By contrast, the world-affirming movements are usually characterized by doctrinal laxity and tolerant voluntarianism. They tend to eschew the world-rejecting movement's subordination of the individual (his interest, will, and autonomy) in order to strengthen collective solidarity and eliminate disruptive dissent. Frequently, as in groups such as Scientology and Transcendental Meditation, there is little emphasis upon communal cohesiveness. Also, in accepting a more individualized, universalized, and secularized concept of the divine, the world-affirming movement will in fact tend to lack the features traditionally associated with religion. They are, in Wallis's terminology, "quasi-religious," but he also describes them *as* religious in that they offer access to supernatural, magical, and spiritual powers and capabilities. The source of unhappiness is approached as internal, within oneself, rather than as something in the social structure. Man is inherently perfectible. To this end, the individual movement, at home in a commodity-oriented market world, offers techniques, recipes, and knowledge to reduce the disparity between aspiration and actuality.

Referring to Wilson (1973), Wallis suggests that there are two fundamental responses to the demand for salvation from the perception of evil in the world today: the millennial transformation expected through major social upheaval, and the belief in some form of magical means by which to eliminate evil. Such responses are no less absent from advanced societies. In fact,

> The world-affirming movement is a modern version of the almost ubiquitous phenomenon of magic; the invocation, or manipulation, of occult forces or powers for personal ends. The ends may have changed somewhat from physical health, fertility and freedom from witchcraft, to psychological well-being, enhanced self-confidence and freedom from socially ingrained inhibitions, but the enterprise is essentially the same. (Wallis, 1984:122)

The main attribute of the world-affirming movement is the provision of techniques for self-exploration and self-cultivation within the social structure, which is "largely taken for granted." In the world-rejecting movement, this human potential is reserved to the leader or founder upon whom the inferior devotee is dependent for his or her own perfection. By contrast, the world-affirming collectivity engages in "the nonstop celebration of the self" in which liberation becomes "the mission of the post-Freudian therapies." Theirs is not so much the offer of alternatives to the "anonymity, impersonality, individualism and segmentalism of modern life" as it is the offer of salvation to those who have little or no quarrel with a world that is largely taken for granted. In this way, they tend to avoid the isolation and numerical insignificance that results from extreme rejection. Moreover, recruitment becomes inclusive and a more gradual process of socialization in contrast to the exclusiveness of the world-rejecting sect, which demands a sharp break from a morally corrupt world.

If we are to look for salient correspondences between Wallis's concept of the world-affirming NRM and the New Age phenomena, one prominent area is to be found in the high subjectivity of both to changes in consumer tastes. As Wallis (1984:91) states, "Susceptibility to fluctuations in the market may thus mean that particular world-affirming movements are relatively transient in character." In other words, though the leisure, consumer, non-durable commodity market typical of advanced capitalistic societies is likely to remain, the dictates of fad, fashion, and sensationalism along with exploitation by leaders and failures to deliver the long-term personal changes sought make world-affirming movements themselves collectivities of questionable duration. Nevertheless, the *type* itself is in "no danger of an early demise," and the same might apply to the New Age Movement as a whole— regardless of the varying fortunes of the particular groups that identify with it. Both individually and collectively, New Age groups must organize themselves as a "clientele of sovereign consumers" functioning in a free-market system. But one significant trend to be noticed in the development of several world-affirming movements over time is an increasing shift toward a spiritual direction (e.g., the Human Potential Movement, Dianetics-Scientology). The New Age Movement itself may be a product of this overall tendency within world-affirmation.

Nevertheless, there are some more immediate distinctions between New Age and the world-affirming type, which Wallis's survey does not make especially clear. One pertains to the distinction between the latter and its rejection of the dualism of the world-rejecting movements. This

dualism Wallis describes as "a concrete conception of the transcendental realm and the coming transformation of the earth in a physically
tangible millennium." This he denies for the world-affirming type in as
much as this last denies the materialist assumptions upon which the
dualistic view is predicated. Though this is certainly not true for the
Neo-pagan, it is also unlikely to be true for the New Ager even apart
from the more strictly pagan components of his make-up and despite
the idealistic philosophy that holds that "perfection results from realizing that everything is *already* perfect." How unphysically tangible the
"millennium" is expected to be is a question we must pursue through
our subsequent empirical investigations.

Again, Wallis's contention that world-affirming movements (he ex-
cepts Soka Gakkai) lay little stress on the idea of God or transcendental
entities and on the engagement of worship seems inapplicable to Neo-
paganism, to the pagan elements of New Age, and perhaps even to New
Age in general. This is another question that must be put to the empirical test. However, following Donald Stone (Glock and Bellah, 1976),
Wallis sees a world-affirming tendency to prefer "spiritual" to "religious" as well as to see religion itself more in terms of psychology.
Though this is certainly true within a section of New Age thinking,
such a simplified glossing may obscure important distinctions that are
yet to be discerned.

Larry Shinn has judged Wallis's 1984 book to be one of "conceptual
ambiguity and substantive inconsistency." In his review of the work he
contends that the descriptive generalizations that Wallis has made—
granting even that he is presenting a dualistic analysis of the NRM
rather than an intended tripartite one—do not withstand careful scrutiny. In particular, Shinn points out that though Wallis argues for the
formative influence on many world-affirming faiths from Hindu and
Buddhist idealist philosophy, the Hare Krishna or ISKCON movement
is both theistic and world-negating. Likewise, many missionary Zen-
inspired NRMs, though monistic or non-theistic, are also world-rejecting.

To his defense, Wallis (1984:73) also refers to middle-ground or
mixed types among the post-World War II new religious movements.
For instance, the Divine Light Mission and 3HO (Yogi Bhajan) as well
as followers of Meher Baba and large sections of the Jesus People combine elements of all three types, drawing on both conventional society
and the counterculture. In particular, with the decline of this last, many
of these movements provided a vehicle for the eventual reintegration of
former "drop-outs" into the social mainstream.[46] Subsequently, these

collectivities have either tended to disappear or transform into more conventional movements. Nevertheless, New Age itself appears to belong in large part to this mixed category or middle-ground. It contains elements of all three types. But if so, then the question arises as to what this classification really tells us.

Whatever its shortcomings, Wallis's analysis of the new religious movement on the basis of its response to the world provides us with an additional investigative tool with which to approach the study of New Age and Neo-paganism. In the very least, Wallis has delineated a typical feature of many world-affirming movements, namely, the emergence of a world-rejecting ethos among inner cadre members—particularly when the organization develops a world-transforming mission. In such cases there develops what Wallis terms a "hierarchy of sanctification." Greater "truth" becomes the exclusive property and varies proportionally with each stage of increased commitment. But along with this comes the exercise of totalitarian control—the typical feature of the world-rejecting movements; a variable feature of the world-affirming movements.

> Intimacy, community and intra-movement elite status have gained a higher priority than worldly achievement or self-realisation as originally envisaged. For [the more committed] as for the adherents of world-rejecting movements, the self and personal identity will become subordinated to the will and personality of the leader. (Wallis, 1984:124)

Consequently, many world-affirming NRMs develop an institution comprising an inner elite corps. In the words of Zald and Ash (1973:85), "A single MO [movement organization] may have attributes of both the inclusive and exclusive organization, even the inclusive movement must have some central cadre." Since world-rejection and exclusiveness are generally high correlates, when a world-transforming endeavor develops in a world-affirming movement—especially among an inner cadre—inclusivism may remain at lower levels, but an exclusivism becomes characteristic of the "higher" stages of advancement and commitment. The inner circle becomes correspondingly more akin to a world-rejecting organization and adopts a more sectarian position vis-à-vis society in general.

### Bird's devotee, discipleship, and apprenticeship movements

Frederick Bird (1978; 1979b) has distinguished various new religious movements by (1) the relationship of followers to masters, and (2) the relationship of the religious seekers to the sacred power they revere. On this basis, movements were classified according to a composition consisting of (a) devotees of a sacred lord or spiritual truth—e.g., Neo-Pentecostals, DLM, ISKCON, Nicheren Shoshu, Chinmoy, (b) disciples of a revered or holy discipline—e.g., Zendo and other Zen centers in the American West, Dharmadhatu, Integral Yoga, Shakti, Gurdjieff, or (c) apprentices skilled in unlocking the mysteries of a sacred, inner power—e.g., Silva Mind Control, est, TM, Scientology, Arica, and Subud.[47] Devotees seek to become one with Holy Being, i.e., either through their revered leader or Truth. "Disciples claim ultimately to seek a mystical, enlightened consciousness by following a prescribed discipline of meditation" (Bird, 1978:184)—not only momentarily "but in some abiding fashion. . . . They seek to realize an enstatic rather than ecstatic state of mind." Disciples usually consider themselves not as members of groups as they are students of a particular discipline. There are usually several initiation rites.

"Apprentices ultimately seek to realize greater power or well-being." They pursue "higher powers or spirits for immediate, often secularly defined, ends" (Bird, 1978:184f.). Leaders are not revered, and there are relatively stylized initiation rites. Ritualistically, the group in which one learns technique "is viewed simply as a class." By contrast, the group for the devotee becomes an important point of reference—devotion to the Holy Being includes devotion to a group of fellow devotees, generally exclusive, and meditation usually takes place within the group. There is usually only one initiation rite. For the disciple, on the other hand, group meetings are important chiefly "as the context for meditation and discipline." There is usually a series of initiation rites.

Bird (1978:185f.) notes that "The orientation of apprentices to their ritualized activities is the least religious of the three types." "Apprentices most closely resemble adherents of the New Thought movement: they share the same self-conscious concern for health and success," but they emphasize ritualized techniques and exercises over strengthening their power-to-will or by developing marketable characters. These new religious groups of apprentices are generally not "compensatory movements."

In summarizing this fresh approach to alternative religious movements, Bird (1978:187) stresses that the salient feature of NRM members is their seeking personal well-being—not through traditions (e.g., social conventions, religious groups, or systems of etiquette) or rational programs (e.g., ideology, a plan of action, or an ethic), but through "practicing some ritualized forms, which are not only authorized by a charismatic authority, but are felt to bestow a kind of secret, hidden charisma on practitioners themselves."

For Bird (1979b), one noteworthy factor in the new religious movement's appeal lies in its particular approach to the problem of "moral accountability." He argues that NRMs induce in their adherents feelings of moral non-accountability. This stems from a reduction of responsibility both to oneself and to others. This process is augmented by use of moral models that lessen the distinction between actual behavior and ethical expectation. Using his threefold typology (1978), the distinctive relationship between followers and revered leaders or various sources of sacred power is seen to furnish a definite means by which moral responsibility is mitigated. *Devotee* groups tend to relativize received moral expectations and attain moral "innocence" through re-identification with their sacred alter ego as their "real" self. *Disciple* groups stress detachment and an understanding of an ultimate reality in which moral standards are irrelevant. *Apprentice* groups aim toward personal autonomy, which includes the individual's moral self-evaluation. In the conversion of spiritual enlightenment into technical mastery, the apprentice seeks to maximize rewards in a guilt-free context.

While Roy Wallis (1984:69) claims that "the theory overgeneralizes a limited and particular feature into a universal explanation" and cites Moonies and Hare Krishnas as countervailing examples, James Beckford (1985a:73) finds favor with the overall schema for interrelating practical ethics and metaphysical doctrine within the change and moral conflict of modern Western society.

## Other classifications or taxonomies of NRMs

An alternate typology suggested by Hill (1973) is that developed by Joachim Wach. Despite its shortcomings, Hill finds value in Wach's consideration of two forms of religious protest: secession and the *ecclesiola in ecclesia* (representing protests within). The latter may take the form of the *collegium pietatis* in which the "meeting" is its typical sociological expression, the *fraternitas* with its more loosely based withdrawal, or the (religious) *order* with its more formal and segregated expression as well as insistence on permanent loyalty.

In another approach, the amorphous area of mysticism, cults, and new religions is understood by Anton Shupe (1981) as "fringe religions." He views these through a variety of five perspectives: (1) the criminological in which groups are perceived as a threat, (2) the philosophical, which looks to the internal consistency and validity of doctrinal beliefs, (3) the anthropological, which places groups within the range of cultural change and diffusion, (4) the social psychological, which examines their attitudinal-behavorial relationship, and (5) the social structural, which focuses on "fringe religious" groups in action along with their patterns of interaction. For Shupe, all these perspectives are important before we can more completely understand the particular group and the complex of new religions as a whole.

Richardson, van der Lans, and Derks (1986) suggest a "typology of disaffiliation modes" (see Chapter 1 in this volume). They delineate contributing factors that shape the likelihood and success ratio of disaffiliation: the communal or non-communal nature of the movement; and whether the movement conforms more to the cult-type (open and loosely defined) or to the "sect-like group" (doctrinal and cohesive). The authors suggest disaffiliation patterns for each organizational setting.

## Generic and quasi-historical classifications of NRMs

In another study of new religious movements, Coleman and Baum (1983), three areas are cited as growing most quickly: (1) Christian and Jewish neo-orthodoxy, (2) U.S. and European neo-Orientalism, and (3) the "human potential movements" (e.g., est) influenced by Eastern traditions. The authors focus on the second of these. The appeal of the East to youth in the West is attributed to factors of simplicity, freedom to explore the inner self, and the search for meaning beyond the material. Secondary considerations concern community, a holistic approach to the life-to-death cycle, and a slower pace to life. This volume contains a general theoretical article by Anthony, Robbins, and Schwartz, who counter the ideas often promulgated that these groups are simply narcissistic, pathological, or merely exotic consumer phenomena. The authors explain that the underlying attractions are not "rational-humanistic socio-religious values" but those "supernaturalistic and subjective values" emerging from Eastern and Western-orthodox beliefs. Employing a technique of Weberian analysis, they uncover the possibility of "scientific-technical rationality" coexisting with both "ethico-metaphysical" and "practical" rationalisms as viable outcomes for religious life in a "rationalized" social world. They call for a revitalization of religion through research.

Along with Robbins and Anthony, Stark and Bainbridge, Wilson, Wallis, and some of the other sociologists of religion who have provided us with analytical models and typologies, we encounter such generic classifications of new Western religious movements as those employed by Robert S. Ellwood, Jr. (Choquette, 1985:3–17) or J. Gordon Melton (Hinnells, 1984:455–74). Each of these is deficient in various respects but nevertheless suggestive of a more historio-organic approach.

Ellwood's classification consists of the following groups: (1) Theosophical, Rosicrucian, Gnostic (i.e., the Ancient Wisdom tradition); (2) New Thought; (3) Spiritualist/UFO; (4) Occult/Initiatory; (5) Neo-paganism and its allies; (6) Eastern Religions I: From India; (7) Eastern Religions II: From East Asia; (8) Eastern Religions III: From Islamic Countries; and (9) Christian Movements. Melton, on the other hand, suggests a breakdown into families of modern alternative Western religions: (1) the Latter-Day Saint Family; (2) the Communal Family; (3) the New Thought Metaphysical Family; (4) the Psychic/New Age Family; (5) the Magical Family; (6) the Eastern Family; and (7) the Middle Eastern Family.[48]

A classification is composed through an arbitrary selection of shared characteristics, but if it depends in whole or part on extraneous features, its utility may become seriously limited. For example, Melton's inclusion of the ''communal family'' entails an organizational feature that has no application or contrast in the other groups. In Melton (1986a), he cites only two instances—The Farm and the Church of Armageddon—which not only derive from radically different traditions but have little if anything in common apart from an isolative-communal practice. The same applies in his more comprehensive, earlier work in which he admits that ''An arbitrary classification has been adopted for purposes of presentation'' (Melton, 1978:31).[49]

> By their very nature, communes tend to be cut off from the world and do not group into subfamilies. A basic grouping could emerge along highly structured-loosely structured lines or religious-nonreligious lines. Neither is wholly satisfactory. (Melton, 1978:30)

Moreover, as a further illustration of the inadequacies of generic identities, the New Age Movement itself cuts across subgroups in both Ellwood's and Melton's classifications.

A more serious flaw in such quasi-historical taxonomies stems from the quasi-historical approach itself. This tends to confuse the developmental picture of how, where, or from whom a religious movement took its inspiration or origin. Nevertheless, both Ellwood and Melton help to locate and delineate various seminal traditions, and rather than suggest a category of such groups per se, it is perhaps sufficient and less constraining to recognize simply these central influences and the offshoots that have developed from them. Consequently, apart from the pagan/neo-pagan and Christian followings themselves, the American and/or Western metaphysical tradition takes its origins from the ideas of Anton Mesmer (1734–1815), Emanuel Swedenborg (1688–1772), Rosicrucianism, and Eastern mysticism.

Briefly, the *New Thought* religions, comprising Unity, Divine Science, Religious Science, and Christian Science—all but the last identifying with the New Age Movement—drew their original inspiration from mesmerism and, via the transcendentalism of New England, Eastern mysticism. Mesmer and Swedenborg's teachings together constitute the conceptual forces behind the birth of *Spiritualism*. This last has played and continues to play a key formative role in the development of various offshoots—e.g., the Urantia Foundation (considered New Age by Melton) and the UFO groups. Perhaps, however, the earliest psychic movement to emerge from Spiritualism—one that equally incorporated tenets of Eastern mysticism—has been *Theosophy*. This last in turn has given rise to Rudolph Steiner's Anthroposophy, Alice Bailey's Arcane School (both identified as NA, that is, New Age) and Guy Ballard's "I AM" Religious Activity—a possible offshoot of which is Mark Prophet's Church Universal and Triumphant (NA). And, finally, the paradigms of Spiritualism and Theosophy along with that of Rosicrucianism have produced various initiatory magical schools; the Gurdjieff traditions; and the quasi-psychotherapeutic *Human Potential Movement*, which includes Scientology, the Process Church of the Final Judgement, Synanon, and the Erhard Seminar Training (NA).

The above sketched overview is at best brief and highly simplified, but see Chapter 2 for a greater detail of the salient features of the various groups and the roles they have played vis-à-vis and within the emerging New Age Movement. Eastern mysticism, of course, continues to play a significant part in the metaphysical tradition as a whole as well as in the New Age Movement in particular.

There has been since the 1960s, however, a more direct transplanting of Indian and oriental groups from East to West. The Indian groups are generally Hindu or Hindu-Jain-Sikh or, even more broadly, Hindu, Jain, Sikh *and* Buddhist insofar as Buddhism is itself a development from Hinduism. The more prominent of the Hindu groups that identify with the New Age Movement are Maharishi Mehesh Yogi's Transcendental

Meditation, Bhagwan Rajneesh's Rajneesh Foundation International (strictly speaking, a Jain offshoot), Baba Ram Dass's Hanuman Foundation, Swami Muktananda's Siddha Yoga Dham of America, Da (Bubba) Free John's Johannine Daist Community, Pamahansa Yogananda's Self Realization Society, and even Ramakrishna and Vivekananda's Vedanta Society and Krishnamurti Jeddu's Krishnamurti Foundation as well as various Tantric yoga groups. The Sikh religion finds new religious movement expression in the West through Yogi Bhajan's Sikh Dharma (3HO) as well as groups that have arisen from the Sant Mat tradition (Guru Maharaj-Ji's Divine Light Mission, Kirpal Singh's Ruhani Satsang, and John-Roger Hinkins's Movement for Inner Spiritual Awareness). New Age Buddhist groups in the west are represented by both Zen Buddhism and Tibetan Buddhism (e.g., Trungpa Rinpoche's Naropa Institute). The Islamic tradition is represented by Pir Vilayat Khan's Sufi Order, Oscar Ichazo's Arica Institute, and Meher Baba's Friends of Meher Baba. All the above mentioned groups in this paragraph ''have identified themselves with the New Age Movement through their literature or by their regular attendance and participation in 'New Age' events'' (Melton, 1986b:120). Other leading Eastern groups appearing as new religious movements in the West include the International Society for Krishna Consciousness (Hare Krishna), Ananda Marga, followers of Sathya Sai Baba and Shri Aurobindu (all Hindu), the Nichiren Shoshu Academy (Soka Gakkai), and, from Islam, Subud (Indonesian Sufi), the ''Black Muslims'' (the World Community of Islam in the West), and Baha'ism.[50]

The pagan/neo-pagan tradition in the west, largely Melton's ''magical family,'' which he subdivides among ''ceremonial magic,'' ''witchcraft'' (or ''Neo-Paganism''), and ''Satanism,'' and Ellwood's ''Neo-Paganism'' and its allies (''ethnic/spiritistic Afro-American religions,'' ''revivalist Neo-Paganism'' including Wicca or Witchcraft, ''ceremonial magic,'' and ''Satanism''), has roots that extend in modern times from Rosicrucianism and, more particularly, Freemasonry but which are themselves developments of the Western esoteric-occult tradition perennially expressed through theosophy, theurgy, astrology, and alchemy and which itself dates primarily to the late Roman empire's schools of Neo-Platonism, Neo-Pythagoreanism, Alexandrian Hermeticism, and Stoicism. The metaphysical counterculture took more definitive form in the Renaissance through the Qabbalah, Hermeticism, and the works of Paracelsus. In the seventeenth century, Joannes Andreae brought Rosicrucianism into prominence. The following century saw the emergence of Illuminism and, within this tradition, Swedenborg.

Despite the common elements and themes underlying the Western metaphysical subculture, it nevertheless remains a heterogeneous and disparate association. For instance, in considering his Neo-Pagan category, Ellwood (Choquette, 1985:9) says that

> Satanism is included in this section for convenience, but it should not be confused with Neo-Paganism, Wicca, or magic. It has a quite different relationship to the dominant religious heritage of our culture, the Judeo-Christian, than do these other groups. The former do not see themselves as worshipping Satan, but simply as preferring a different and older pantheon altogether than the Judeo-Christian.

By contrast, "Satanism is a magical religion which has as its central dynamic the rejection of and attack upon Christianity" (Melton, 1984:465). Likewise, within this complex category, the Afro-American spiritistic religions of Voudon and Santeria have been placed. To date, these play a marginal (though perhaps increasing) role vis-à-vis the central stream of Neo-paganism and the more general understanding of New Age.

The central areas within this modern magical tradition are ceremonial magic groups and, especially for this study, witchcraft and (neo-)paganism. These last are identified by Melton but only linked by Ellwood. T. M. Luhrmann (1989:3), on the other hand, distinguishes the two in her presentation of modern magical practice. She sees four rough groupings—all descending from the nineteenth century Order of the Golden Dawn: the Western Mysteries, ad hoc ritual magic, witchcraft, and paganism. The Western Mysteries most directly continue the original practices and structures of the Golden Dawn or its offshoot established by Aleister Crowley, the Ordo Templi Orientalis. These may frequently be conservative and even Christian. The ad hoc ritual magicians draw their inspiration chiefly from the Golden Dawn but are more casually formed and spontaneously created as well as individualistic. Both groups, the Western Mysteries and the ad hoc, conform largely to Melton and Ellwood's "ceremonial magic" division.

Witchcraft (or the Craft) is recognized by Luhrmann (ibid.) as an invention by Gerald Gardner, a former initiate of Aleister Crowley's, which first occurred in the 1930s.

> Although witchcraft in its modern form bears some resemblance to the Western Mysteries, its ethos, symbolism and structure are quite distinctive.

"Rather it is a form of polytheistic nature religion based upon the worship of the Mother Goddess . . . more properly called Neo-Paganism . . ." (Melton, 1984:464). For Ellwood (Choquette, 1985:9),

Wicca or Witchcraft shares with the Neo-Pagans a sense of pre-Christian European spiritual affinity. But although mostly a modern reconstruction in fact, Wicca looks more to traditional folk religion than to the pagan great traditions for its roots.

For Luhrmann (loc. cit.),

Paganism . . . is a catch-all category to include rituals which are framed in terms of a non-Christian nature religion and are magical in intent, but are not confined to small initiated groups. These practices are, as it were, witchcraft's casual cousins. They share the same symbolism without the elaborate initiatory structure.

Compare to this Ellwood's revivalist Neo-Paganism (loc. cit.), which "consists of groups endeavoring to revive the pre-Christian religions of the Egyptians, Greeks, Celts, or Norsemen, or to construct pagan faiths broadly in their style." In summing up his discussion of the broader category of Neo-Paganism, Ellwood concludes that

virtually all extant American groups in this category stem from the 1960s generation; they were naturally congenial to the counterculture's interest in ecology, mystical experience, occult symbol systems, and feminism. Theirs has been a movement in considerable flux; most groups in this set have been ephemeral even by new religious movement standards. Nonetheless, as some have disappeared, others have formed: they clearly respond to some deep contemporary need. (Choquette, 1985:9–10)

The relationship between Neo-paganism and the New Age Movement, their contrasts and similarities, has been the specific focus of this book's investigation. To this end, the generic differentiations we have just discussed are necessary in pointing the way toward any more detailed examination into the history of these religious movements and how and why they were formulated. Nevertheless, historical description, as important as it is in delineating the identity and directions of social movements—religious, new religious, or sectarian—is not sufficient for a true sociological analysis. To this end, the church-sect typology along with its amendments, emendations, and alternate suggestions might comprise a principal tool by which to measure sociological position and change in understanding the Neo-pagan and New Age types of new religious movements. If in the end the very typology is found wanting and unhelpful, we must discard it, but this process in itself would nevertheless be of sociological value in coming to terms with at least one area of contemporary religious expression and organization. The typology is only a tool—one to be used if it seems applicable and until a better piece of equipment is developed. James Dittes (1971:382), in concluding an article on psychology's extrinsic-intrinsic distinction and sociology's church-sect typology and the judgments of obsolescence they have received, feels that "both typologies show considerable promise of surviving their obituaries. They must be doing something right, or at least something congenial to many social scientists." Be this as it may, we must now ask whether the church-sect typology is specifically applicable to the New Age and Neo-pagan movements.

## Notes

1. Barker (1989:201) refers to "Rajneeshism." The 'official' religion of Rajneeshism, however, was disbanded in September 1985 (Clarke, 1987:8). On December 28, 1988, Rajneesh accepted the Japanese Zen Buddhist Katzue Ishira's prophecy that he was the reincarnation of Gautama Buddha. After four days, Rajneesh then declared himself no longer to be an incarnation of Gautama but to be "Buddha in my own right." See *Hinduism Today* 11.3 (March 1989:16). He has since been known as Osho ("master"). Following his death on 19 January 1990, the day-to-day affairs of the Osho community have been administered by an "Inner Circle" or committee of twenty-one sannyasins. See E. Puttick, "The Rajneesh Movement: An Update," *Religion Today* 6.1 (n.d.:13f.). In a private conversation with me, Ms. Puttick explained that the administrative ashram in Poona, India, is now known as the Osho Commune International. The "inside" name used by members themselves for the movement is "sannyas"; the "outside" name, i.e., one imposed externally, is the "Rajneesh Movement."

2. Now known as Elan Vital—a name that was "adopted in the early 1980s" (Barker, 1989:177).

3. "The title 'est' is no longer formally used by Erhard, nor by his associates and the participants . . ." W. W. Young (Clarke, 1987:131) claims that from her perspective "The full title of the related groups which . . . make up this group is presently entitled 'The Centres Network' or 'The Society for Contextual Studies and Educational Seminars'." Young refers "for the sake of clarity" to the entire movement as "The Network." Barker (1989:170) states that "The Centres Network organises the Forum (which has now replaced *est*). . ."

4. Hill (1973) cites Weber as the first to note the dichotomy of church and

sect but recognizes that little detailed treatment of the contrast is actually articulated by Weber. Rather, his efforts largely amount to the sociological reformulation of a theological distinction. According to Hill (1973:51), whereas Weber conceived of movement of sectarian groups toward church-type organizations on the basis of "the routinization of charisma and on the emergence of a mass style of religion," Troeltsch envisioned a "dialectical resolution of the church-sect opposition and the development of a third type of religious organization in the form of mysticism."

5. P. M. Gustafson, "The Missing Member of Troeltsch's Trinity," *Sociological Analysis* 36.3 (1975:224f.): Ernst Troeltsch, "The Stoic-Christian Natural Law and the Modern Secular Natural Law," mimeo—forthcoming in *Troeltsch's Collected Papers*, edited by James Luther Adams.

6. Further "weaknesses of Niebuhr's analysis derive mainly from his paying relatively little attention to the *internal* dynamics of religious collectivities. . ." (Robertson, 1970b:118f.). He stresses, for instance, the *development* of disciplining procedures rather than their *effectiveness*. Other problems stem from classification rather than ideal-type analysis. Jehovah's Witnesses and Seventh Day Adventists, for instance, become churches or denominations because they have exceeded first-generation membership and have developed educational agencies despite their radical social divergence. Wilson (1982:97f), on the other hand, sees Niebuhr as having "over-generalized his observations," and he recognizes that Yinger's development of the concept of the established sect has "clearly disputed Niebuhr's generalizations."

7. Liston Pope (*Millhands and Preachers*, New Haven: Yale University Press, 1942) presents twenty-one indices by which movement from sect to church could be measured. "Pope's analysis . . . remains as the earliest and indeed one of the only attempts to isolate a complete range of factors that are precise enough to form the basis for a programme of quantitative research" (Hill, 1973:66f.). In other words, Pope "offered a number of empirical criteria on which the transformation of sects into churches might be measured."

8. In Fichter (1983), Stark and Bainbridge argue against the Weberian use of correlates to establish the ideal-types of church, sect, and cult. These authors prefer use of attributes and follow Benton Johnson's focus on degrees of tension between the collectivity and its host society. In the same volume, however, David Martin asserts the opposite and finds correlates legitimate means toward establishing constructs while rejecting the criterion of tension. His use of the Russian Orthodox Church in the Soviet Union and the Roman Catholic Church in Ireland as situations the Stark-Bainbridge typology cannot explain, however, may not be apropos examples elucidating conflicts between the American state and NRMs. See further, Martin (1983).

9. Greater abstractness as a "differentiating characteristic simply means that abstract collectivities cannot be perceived as totalities and that they are not so closely linked with the physical presence of a plurality of human beings" (von Wiese and Becker, 1932:561f.).

10. Nevertheless, as Hill (1973:71) observes: "The fact that Yinger prefaces his original discussion and punctuates his later versions with very helpful statements about the heuristic value of ideal-type concepts in general makes his work one of the clearest and most accessible approaches to the problem."

11. In an earlier work, *Religion in the Struggle for Power* (1946), Yinger first presented a four-part typology of Christian groups: universal church, ecclesia, established sect, and sect. With a vague analytic boundary of separation between them, "only a higher level of organization and of self-consciousness distinguishes a sect from a cult" (Hill, 1973:72).

12. Yinger uses here the classificatory schema for social movements in general developed by Ralph Turner and Lewis Killian (1957).

13. Cf. Geoffrey Nelson, "The Concept of Cult," *The Sociological Review* 16 (1968:351–62). For Nelson (p. 357), "all founded religions can be seen as having developed from cults."

14. Respectively, (1) Revivalist/Pentecostalist; Pietist/Holiness; (2) Chiliastic; Legalistic; and (3) Oriental; New Thought; Spiritist.

15. Hill (1973:93) sees the gnostic as at least one important source of new religious movements as well as revivals of more institutionalized ones.

16. Wilson (1969a:361) refers to "Troeltsch's dichotomy," and Swatos (1976:133) states that mysticism or Troeltsch's "*third* type of religious behavior . . . is now simply dropped from consideration by 'church-sect' theorists."

17. For Campbell (1972:124f.), the mystical religious response tends "to neglect the historical, ecclesiastical and ritual concerns of religion. It has no need for dogmas, sacraments, ministry or indeed any formal organization . . . Such a position leads . . . to a depreciation of history, ritual and organization . . ."

18. In private communication, Peter Clarke indicates this to be "a very weak and not convincing argument." Clarke states that "this freedom has been around for a long time now." However, surely any decline in ecclesiastical influence and rise in individual freedom is a cumulating process. Moreover, it is the growing *perception* of freedom and its corollary of actual expression that are emerging—in this century and more definitely in its latter half—as impetuses behind the networking that undergirds the New Age/Neo-pagan movements, the cultic milieu, and related 'heretical' orientations.

19. In answer to Peter Clarke's query on this point, conflict between science and the concept of a transcendent, personal God who 'intervenes' with this world and is known through revelation is inherently greater than with an immanent, impersonal deity that is identifiable with the world—including the scientific principles through which it operates. Another viewpoint on this issue is expressed in the examination of Alan Tobey's discussion of Yogi Bhajan (3HO) in which Robbins (Hadden, 1977:312) concludes that "Eastern monism entails a world view not necessarily more 'scientific', but perhaps less conspicuously nonscientific (I don't say 'unscientific') than anthropomorphic conceptions of a personal creator God."

20. Nelson (1987) reserves the term "sect" for those reform movements that usually originate within an existing church and may themselves evolve eventually into an independent church. For the cult, he considers there to be four ideal-types based on concentrated or diffused authority and either the "philadelphic" group centered on a religious leader or the "family-patterned" religious community. Accordingly, the possibilities comprise the spontaneous (diffused) cult, the charismatic (concentrated) cult, the autocratic (concentrated) community, and the democratic (diffused) community.

21. Cults are "religious movements which draw their inspiration from other than the primary religion of the culture, and which are not schismatic movements in the same sense as sects, whose concern is with preserving a purer form of the traditional faith" (Glock and Stark, 1965:244).

22. Martin (1983:41) counters Stark and Bainbridge's rejection of defining correlates in establishing a polarity. Since "restorations work by *creatively imagining* the past, not by reproducing it," Martin specifically denies the schismatic sect and innovative cult polarity. Schism itself is "notoriously innovative" (e.g., the Old Believers, or religious orders—"a sort of schism"—which "restore and innovate simultaneously"). In other words, schismatic origins need not automatically be "backward-looking" attempts at restoration. Martin (1983:39) also criticizes Stark and Bainbridge's use of a "foreignness" element by which to identify the cult since this "obscures the very different character of varied importations and removes the continuity of social character which so often survives the crossing of frontiers." Moreover, taking exception to Stark and Bainbridge's employment of a tension continuum by which sects and cults are distinguished from more institutionalized organizations, Martin (1983:41) argues that "the kinds of tension are, in fact, so varied that it is difficult to see how they can be placed along a continuum of *degrees* of tension." He denies that "a common sociological character" can be assumed between the Roman Catholic Church and the Jehovah's Witnesses simply because both may be in tension with the wider society as in the Soviet Union.

23. For Stark and Bainbridge (1985:8), religions are defined as "human organizations primarily engaged in providing general compensators based on supernatural assumptions." "A compensator is the belief that a reward will be obtained in the distant future or in some other context which cannot be immediately verified" (1985:6). As such, they range from specific compensators promising a specific, limited reward to general compensators consisting of promises of much greater and intangible scope—e.g., a happy afterlife, eternal life, etc.—which, moreover, generally serve as solutions to questions of ultimate meaning. Consequently, "Religions are social enterprises whose primary purpose is to create, maintain, and exchange supernaturally based general compensators" (1985:172). But in acknowledging religion as a unique source of maximum compensators that make it clear "that atheistic versions of Buddhist philosophy failed to attract any substantial mass following despite being sponsored by powerful and eloquent intellectuals," Stark and Bainbridge have nevertheless over-

looked the point that no Buddhist (lay or otherwise) hopes for anything other than to opt out of the life-death-rebirth cycle. There are several inherent deficiencies in Stark and Bainbridge's more limited definition of religion involving a supernatural assumption. Even so, as long as their usage of religion as something involving a supernatural referent is recognized as a restricted one, we can nevertheless proceed *pro tempore* within this contextual understanding. All the same, it is perhaps relevant to point out here some of Roy Wallis and Steve Bruce's criticisms of the Stark and Bainbridge theory of religion, which they nevertheless applaud as a noble attempt deserving the highest standards of critical praise. In their argument, Wallis and Bruce state: "Committed to uncovering hidden motives lying beneath public rhetoric, sociology has widely rejected the possibility that symbolic goals and values could *really* be what actors sought in such enterprises, and they have therefore denied the reality claimed by these actors and imputed to them motives derived from an analysis of the presumed latent functions of such beliefs and actions." While Wallis and Bruce themselves see the factors leading people to accept religious beliefs and goals as many and various, "Stark and Bainbridge have elevated one of these to the status of complete explanation, and in so doing they have trod the same path and fallen into the same quicksands as Freud, Marx and Durkheim did before them" (Wallis and Bruce, 1984:18f.).

24. In other words, "Cults are not the result of schism (although, once founded, cults become subject to schism)" (Stark and Bainbridge, 1985:36). But what are these new schismatic bodies if they are not cults?

25. In a later work, Wilson (1969a:368) includes Unitarians, Psychiana, Scientology, and Rosicrucianism as typical gnostic groups. Little stress is placed not only on the idea of a personal savior but on any emotional relationship with the godhead. There is little interest in eschatology. "They are interested in results in this world, and the hereafter seems to them simply an enhancement of present joys."

26. Cf. Wilson, 1969a:364f. For the conversionist, "man is entirely responsible for his actions." The stressed relationship between the individual and a personal savior is primarily an emotional one rather than one to be expressed in either symbolic or ritualistic terms. But Wilson claims that because man is corrupted and therefore the world is also corrupted without the revivalistic "conversion" of the men who constitute it, "This type of sect takes no interest in programmes of social problems and may even be actively hostile towards them." One wonders, however, about the Anti-Cult Movement (descendant of the American Moral Majority) which is composed largely of evangelical fundamentalists but nevertheless is reckoned among the leading political lobbies in the United States.

27. Unlike the conversionist's belief in the individual's moral and essential free will, the eschatological revolutionary or adventist adopts a deterministic outlook to explain the world—one in which the individual's fate is pre-determined.

28. Around a local charismatic leader.

29. Or occupational groups.

30. To persecution.

31. To organizational change.

32. If marriage is approved at all.

33. Usually expected.

34. But most vulnerable.

35. But best prepared.

36. E.g., "That we should have allowed ourselves to analyse in these dichotomous terms [of church and sect] seems to me to indicate the extent to which vulgar Marxism has penetrated the shape and style of our thinking," Martin, 1962:4.

37. Nevertheless, along with the idea that the cult represents a sharper break from the dominant religious tradition of the society in which it originates, Hill (1973) considers that Martin would include the cult's individualism among its "fundamental" criteria. Moreover, Martin indicates that, within the Christian tradition at least, in contrast to the sect, cults are more likely to use biblical sources in providing insight rather than legitimation.

38. In Eister's own words: "the frequent confusion of sect-to-church 'hypothesizing' with church-sect 'typologizing'." (1967:85)

39. In Johnson's own words, his analytical approach "is curiously restricted to western religions" (1971:126).

40. As with D. A. Martin, however, Johnson (1963:543n12) does not consider the cult to be part of the church-sect distinction. ". . . the cult's outlook can hardly be called historically Christian."

41. For Robertson's reply to these criticisms, see Robertson (1977:197–199). Swatos (1977:202f.) responds to Robertson's particular points.

42. Wilson proceeds to provide us with perhaps the most detailed understanding of the sect we have within sociological studies of religion. As Michael Welch (1977:125) puts it, "Wilson's (1961, 1967, 1969, 1971, and 1973) studies, in fact, remain the most important and comprehensive work done on religious sects . . ."

43. "Only the utopian type was excluded from the final analysis after it was found that virtually no *purely* utopian religious sects were represented in the coding sources at this time" (p. 127, n. 1).

44. As John Wilson (*JSSR* 13.3, 1974:366) understands it, however, Bryan Wilson has not continued within the Troeltschian-Niebuhrian tradition: "His solution has been to abandon the sect-denomination-church terminology altogether . . ."

45. "Hence in movements such as spiritualism, New Thought, and much of the flying saucer movement, heresy is a concept without clear application" (Wallis, 1975b:91).

46. Conversely, the early Process, for example, provided a situation by which those "who, although highly integrated into society, [could seek] means

of transcending or escaping the conventionality which this involved . . .'' (Wallis, 1984:122).

47. Cf. Bird's subsequent classification (Bird and Reimer, 1982:9f.) of Western devotional groups (e.g., the Charismatics, the Jesus groups, the Lubavitcher movement), the countercultural devotional groups (e.g., Nichiren Shoshu or Shinran Buddhists, Divine Light or Krishna Consciousness, or Sufi groups), and discipleship/apprenticeship groups (comprising *both* yoga groups, T'ai Chi groups, Vedanta meditation groups, Zen centers, etc., *and* movements such as *est*, Arica, Silva Mind Control, Psychosynthesis.)

48. Melton (1984:459) refers to ''eight 'families' of alternative religions'' in the United States and other Western countries but proceeds to name only seven. In his earlier classification of American religions, Melton (1978) suggests two Psychic and New Age Families: (I) including Swedenborgianism, Spiritualism, Theosophy, the Alice Bailey Movement, Liberal Catholicism, and the I AM Movement; and (II) including Rosicrucianism, other occult orders, drug-oriented groups, flying saucer groups, and unclassified New Age groups. Moreover, in *The Encyclopedia of American Religions*, Melton subdivides the Eastern and Middle Eastern Family into three families: Jews and Muslims; Hinduism, Sikhism and Jainism; and Buddhism, Shintoism, and Zoroastrianism. This last is particularly unsatisfactory. Additionally, Melton includes a tenth grouping of ''New Unaffiliated Religious Bodies,'' which includes Jesus People, Gay Religion, Mail-Order Denominations, Politically and Socially Oriented Bodies, Miscellaneous Churches, and Hawaiian Family Churches.

49. Moreover, in this work there is some ambiguity in Melton's description of the primary religious body, for though he identifies this in terms of churches, denominations, sects and cults, he otherwise tends to use the terms ''primary religious body'' and ''church'' interchangeably.

50. Melton (1978) includes Gurdjieff and the followings he has inspired under ''Islam and Related Groups.'' At the same time, as ''Unclassified New Age Groups,'' Melton places the Church of Scientology, the Process Church of the Final Judgement, ECKANKAR, the Movement for Inner Spiritual Awareness, the New Age Church of Truth, New Psychiana, the Arica Institute, Inc., etc. This particular category is especially misleading and confusing, for, although it includes the Association for Research and Enlightenment (Edgar Cayce), Melton also places here the Unification Church and Jim Jones's People's Temple Christian (Disciples) Church.

# Chapter 8

# Conclusions:
## Evaluating Church-Sect Theory, Its Modifications, and Replacements in Application to the New Age and Neo-pagan Movements

Benson and Dorsett (1972:139) refer to "the dated confines of church-sect theory," which prove inadequate in application to the complexity and variety of the contemporary religious scene. According to Beckford, (1987:391), the vocabulary of "church," "sect," and "cult" is largely a question of judgment—being measured against the orthodox mainstream. Moreover, Benson and Dorsett feel that overuse of the church-sect theory prevents fruitful and comparative employment of concepts from the formal organization field pertaining to social movements in general (see also Beckford, 1977). Meanwhile, Hill (1973:90), in a statement directed chiefly against Yinger and his expanding sect and church subdivisions of 1946, 1957, and 1970, states that "There comes a point when the proliferation of sub-types in a general typology begins to blunt the heuristic potential of ideal types."

Dissatisfaction with church-sect theory has become widespread in the sociological study of religion and of new religious movements in particular, and there have been several attempts to develop new conceptual schemes. Among the more promising of these—with especial focus on the NRM, we find Bryan Wilson's typology of sects; Wallis's classification of world-rejecting, world-affirming, and world-accommodating NRMs; Anthony's typology based on the categories of unilevel-multilevel, monistic-dualistic, and technical-charismatic bipolar dimensions;

315

and Bainbridge and Stark's understanding of audience cult, client cult, and cult movement.

Benson and Dorsett (1972) have likewise suggested a new "theory of religious organizations" based on a four-dimensional scheme comprising bureaucratization, professionalization (of the clerical role), integration, and secularization. Their classification allows for pinpointing the contradiction between the hierarchical authority of bureaucracy and the emphasis on collegial control in a professional structure. These sociologists suggest that professional structure is compatible with both integration and secularization (expansion of the domain of the religious organization) while bureaucratization is not. A chief handicap to Benson and Dorsett's schema is its unwieldy nature and its focus primarily upon the congregation-type denomination. Moreover, there is, as the authors admit, little supportive evidence for the contradictory effects of bureaucratization and professionalization on secularization and integration. Nevertheless, this conceptual scheme allows a means by which to approach the interplay between denominations (caught between bureaucratic and professional pressure) and communities (seeking integration and secularization).

## Change-oriented movements

Another attempt to locate NRM study within the broader research pertaining to social movements in general has been spearheaded by Gerlach and Hine (1970) who identify five "operationally significant" factors that they consider "the most effective analytical instruments for movement study we have discovered" (1968:38). By focusing on the "inner dynamics" of the movement itself, Gerlach (1971:816) recapitulates these factors as organization, recruitment, commitment, ideology, and opposition. Both Hine and Gerlach hesitate in labeling these as "necessary conditions" but argue that such "facilitating conditions" as deprivation, disorganization, and maladjustment are simply enabling and external factors that may have originally caused the genesis of the movement but are not explanatory in its subsequent appeal or spread.[1]

Gerlach and Hine have concentrated on "movements of revolutionary change," and their findings may not be strictly applicable to Neopaganism—at least in all cases. In their study of Pentecostalism as illustrative of the broader subject of "change-oriented movements," the authors emphasize "fervent and convincing recruitment"—an element that does not appear to be noticeably present in either New Age or Neo-paganism. Another factor that is questionable in the promotion of both movements is the "bridge-burning, power-generating act" of commitment. Nevertheless, it is within the domain of organization—specifically the reticulate, acephalous, and segmentary movement—that Gerlach and Hine provide an alternative analysis that is highly applicable to the New Age and Neo-pagan phenomena and yet is compatible with some elements of the church-sect typology.

## Cult conceptual problems

One contemporary reluctance toward utilization of the church-sect continuum as a tool of analysis stems from the multiple meanings that have accrued to the term "cult." In popular use, it is often employed interchangeably with "sect" and frequently carries an antisocial or pseudo-religious stigma.[2] But in contrast, a number of sociologists (among them Becker, Yinger, Nelson, and Stark and Bainbridge) produce an ambiguity by developing a conceptual demarcation based on deviance in which the cult becomes a group which makes a radical break with a dominant religious tradition while the sect is a schismatic movement developing within that tradition.[3] This leads Robbins and Anthony (1987:399) to ask whether the Unification Church, for instance, is a cult or a Christian sect.

Another sociological concept of the cult defines the collectivity by its absence of clear boundaries and its looseness and diffuseness of organization (Campbell, Eister, Richardson, Swatos, and Wallis). In this use, the cult lacks centralized leadership, clear organizational boundaries, and standardized doctrine and is presumed to be ephemeral.[4] Wallis (1976) claims that in order to survive, the cult must transform into a centralized authoritarian sect.[5] Otherwise, it will become re-absorbed into the general "cultic milieu."[6]

## Geoffrey Nelson

Nelson (1968, 1969) combines both the elements of ephemerality and deviance in his understanding of the cult. In this, he is close to the earlier position of Wallis (1975a, 1975b) who assimilated cult/sect analysis into the broader church-sect typology and approached the cult as deviant and pluralistically legitimate. The difficulty with this stance nevertheless remains the difficulty in objectively appraising what constitutes deviance or what Stark considers a "fundamental break" with the religious tradition of the host culture. Nelson has, however, moved the cult concept away from the sect-to-church unilinear continuum developed by Niebuhr, Becker, and Yinger and back to Troeltsch's church-sect-mysticism tripolar model. His typology of cults considers groups to be charismatic or spontaneous, local (permanent if an organizational structure is developed), or centralized (unitary if charismatic; federal if spontaneous). For the New Age and Neo-pagan movements, however, it is his concept of the "cult movement" that has greatest applicability, that is, a diffused collectivity of individuals and/or individual groups united by belief rather than formal organization (Nelson, 1968:359).

## Church-sect theory and the New Age and Neo-pagan movements

But while emphasizing the personal experience of the ecstatic, mystical or psychic as a second criterion for cult identity, Nelson does not appear to grasp the desire for social transformation that is often part of the New Age impetus and sometimes a part of Neo-paganism. Moreover, in his classificatory system of NRMs by their acceptance, tolerance, or complete rejection of Western culture's main supports (i.e., Christianity, scientific materialism, and economic materialism), Nelson (1987) has redeveloped Wallis's typology of affirming, accommodating, and rejecting orientations. Nevertheless, by showing that Weber's exemplary prophet does not produce a religious development that fits the sect-church continuum, Nelson has sought instead a cult-new religion continuum by which to measure change from dissident cult to dominant belief system.

In social science and the sociology of religion, cults are usually conceived of as small (e.g., Yinger). This alone presents a difficulty in applying the term to such large (at least widespread) and diffuse phenomena as the New Age and Neo-pagan movements. In actuality, each is composed of a heterogeneous combination of many different kinds of groups.[7] In fact, and although to a lesser extent with Neo-paganism, both movements include within their range of expression both cult- and sect-like organizations as well as charismatic leaders.

Both New Age and Neo-paganism, if they were to achieve durable stability and social acceptance as well as a unified structural organization, would conform to denominations (as understood by Wallis) rather than churches—being without central authority but embracing a large diversity of belief and expression and operating along democratic principles. Trying to analyze each movement according to a single type would be like attempting to reduce the full and fissiparous situation of Christianity to one sociological concept. If, however, we are forced to choose a single designation for the New Age and Neo-pagan phenomena each as a whole, New Age perhaps best conforms to Bainbridge and Stark's concept of the "audience cult"; Neo-paganism, to a combination of Bryan Wilson's thaumaturgical and manipulationist sects. On the other hand, the New Age movement might be understood in a generic but more limited sense similar to Beckford's (1985a) "*the* new religious movement"—having a collective impact although comprised of separate groups.

In our perusal of the church-sect typology and suggested alternatives, we find that *as tools* each conceptual schema affords some insight, analytical value, and perhaps predictive assessment when applied to the New Age and Neo-pagan phenomena.[8] For instance, virtually all New Age groups conform to Anthony and Robbins's understanding of monistic ideologies of meaning and morality.[9] New Age appears to accept "the ultimate illusory quality of the phenomenal world." Neo-pagan groups, on the other hand, do not: some being materialistically monistic; others, dualistically accepting of both spiritual and material realities. Moreover, though Anthony and Robbins are responsible for generating together the monistic-dualistic distinction, Robbins (1988b) criticizes the subsequent Anthony typology that has grown out of this understanding as dependent on "subtle clinical judgments" and as difficult to operationalize. Another "inadequacy" in the Anthony typology when approaching New Age as a whole is the distribution of its component members throughout the multilevel charismatic (e.g., Friends of Meher Baba, Johannine Daist Community, Sidha Yoga Dham of America), multilevel technical (e.g., Zen and Tibetan Buddhism [Naropa Institute], Raja Yoga, Sufi Order), unilevel charismatic (e.g., Rajneesh Foundation International, Divine Light Mission), and unilevel technical (e.g., Transcendental Meditation, *est*, Terry Cole Whittaker) breakdowns.

## Bryan Wilson

The overlap between New Age and Neo-paganism is most clearly evident when judged against the sectarian types delineated by Bryan

Wilson. Wilson is interested in the denominalization process that some types of sects undergo—a transformation from an exclusive collectivity with sharp boundaries and an indifferent or hostile attitude toward the secular society to a more tolerant association with an unclear self-conception and a general acceptance of the values and morality of the prevailing culture.[10] In these terms, it is obvious that New Age and Neo-paganism are closer to a pattern of denominational evolution if indeed either could be claimed to have ever been sects in the first place. Nevertheless, Wilson's sectarian classification helps to locate both movements in terms of types of mission and ideological or doctrinal character.

Although New Age and Neo-paganism reveal several elements that belong to other types of sects (e.g., the free-will optimism and efforts to alter both world and individual of the Conversionist sects, New Age's Adventist-like prediction of drastic alteration of the world, the Introversionist aspect of some New Ageism that seeks "higher inner values," or the Reformist goals of New Age and some Neo-paganism), both movements conform in general to the Thaumaturgical and, especially, the Gnostic/Manipulationist sects. New Age and Neo-paganism's effort to experience the supernatural, however, is less an attempt toward prediction or the purely miraculous as it is one for self-growth and empowerment. With its often less universalist response to the world, Neo-paganism is closer to the thaumaturgical sect than is New Age, but both movements are clearly manipulationist in "accepting in large measure the world's goals though seeking a new and esoteric means to achieve these ends."[11] In Wilson's terms, this constitutes a sort of "wishful mysticism." Certainly, in endeavoring toward an everyday achievement of worldly success, self-realization, health, material well-being, and happiness, both New Age and Neo-paganism conform to the manipulationist type of orientation[12]—one in which in addition "conversion is an alien concept" (Wilson, 1959:7), and yet, in so doing, both reveal their own mutual overlap.

## Rodney Stark and William Bainbridge

Whereas Wilson eliminates the "cult" concept in his typology, or subsumes it virtually under the manipulationist sectarian construct, Stark and Bainbridge (1985:25) stress the distinction of the cult from sect formation as the product of cultural innovation or importation. These authors recognize both sect and cult as "religious movements" rather than "religious institutions," that is, they exist in a relative tension with the socioeconomic environment. The most developed cult organization is termed the "cult movement"—an organization that is nevertheless "weak" in that it usually makes few demands on its members and manifests in essence in the form of a study group. In Stark and Bainbridge's language, the cult movement offers the most "general compensators."

More specific compensation is to be found in the "client cult" and the "audience cult," with the former being more organized than the latter. The client cult consists primarily of a relationship between patrons and a consultant. Adherents tend not to be organized into a social movement. While much of the New Age theater of activity is to be found in the specific acquisition of a human potential technique from a teacher or an occult service from a medium, channeler, or the like, in its broader manifestation, New Age is characterized more by Wallis and Bruce's "spiritual supermarket consumerism" or Bird's "conversion careering"[13] through which Stark and Bainbridge identify the "audience cult"—the least organized and most diffuse cultic form. New Age's lack of organized efforts toward recruitment or physical congregation apart from attendance of a lecture suggests its general conformity with the "audience cult." Neo-paganism, on the other hand, especially when organized into covens, groves, or some other ritualistically oriented collectivity, comes closer to the "cult movement." Nevertheless, aspects of both New Age and Neo-paganism fall throughout and beyond the range of Stark and Bainbridge's cult understanding, and this underscores an inherent weakness or limitation in their typological classification—at least as applied to New Age and Neo-paganism. Moreover, as Gerlach and Hine have pointed out, deprivation is at best a "facilitating condition," perhaps instrumental in the original cause of a movement but inadequate in explaining its subsequent development. In other words, Gerlach and Hine appear to contest the theory of religious compensators upon which Stark and Bainbridge's typological construction rests.[14]

## Peter Berger

Peter Berger (1954, 1958) suggests yet a further approach to the church-sect typology. He sees the sect as based on the belief of the spirit being immediately present—the church considering the spirit as remote. This analysis relates the inner meaning of belief-systems by the quasi-geographical location of the spirit; hence, the sociology of religion is to be seen as an "ecology of the sacred." In Berger's schema, the types of sect are understood as (1) Enthusiastic (Revivalist/Pentecostal; Pietist/Holiness); (2) Prophetic (Chiliastic; Legalistic); and (3) Gnostic (Oriental; New Thought; Spiritist). New Age and Neo-paganism would be sects according to Berger and primarily gnostic—though once again both movements reveal features that cut across the range of subtypes. Nevertheless, Hill (1973:93) finds that Berger's accounts "represent one of the few attempts to analyze sectarian phenomena in terms of Weber's original observations about them"—one that also suggests the category of *ecclesiola in ecclesia* as a valuable device for analyzing sectarian interpenetrations of church organizations, but Hill questions whether "*all* new sectarian movements could be attributed to a charismatic breakthrough" which he sees instead as only one important source of new religious movements as well as revivals of more institutionalized ones.

## Other contributions

The sociology of religion field is in fact rife with church-sect modifications or suggested alternatives. Among these are Bird's (1978; 1979b) threefold moral-accountability typology of devotee, discipleship, and apprenticeship—in which groups of these last constitute "the least religious" of the three types and generally do not form "compensatory movements." But here again New Age in particular cuts across all three types in that adherents may be devoted to a spiritual leader or truth, students of a spiritual discipline, or apprentices of some sorcerer or magic/science.[15]

Lofland and Richardson (1984) have developed a fivefold "corporateness" typology of the religious movement organization (RMO): clinics, congregations, collectivities, corps, and colonies. Lofland and Richardson focus on the degrees to which a set of persons actively promotes and participates in collective life. This analysis provides one possible means by which to bypass what Beckford objects to as an artificial distinction between general sociological organizational theory and socioreligious organizational theory which stems from application of the church-sect concept. Arguing that the terms "sect" and "cult" are not useful sociologically because they are imprecise, overgeneralized, and burdened with historical associations, Lofland and Richardson consider the RMO as a specific manifestation within the broader type of social movement organizations (SMOs), which also includes the political organization (PMO). Their five ideal-types are intended to identify and analyze organizational dynamics of which the RMO constitutes a particular mode of religious collectivity. Beckford himself has suggested a framework based on both "internal" bonding relationships and "external" modes of insertion into society.[16]

The main difficulty with all these conceptual analyses is that they may be helpful in describing features or groups within the overall New Age and Neo-pagan movements but not the amorphous nature of the movements themselves. Robbins (1988b:159) feels that "At present it does not appear that a single framework for the analysis of either all religious collectivities, new religious collectivities, or contemporary NRMs exists," though he cites Wallis's world affirming/rejecting/accepting types and the Anthony typology as suggesting that the so-called "value-oriented movements" might have "special characteristics and problems [that] require particular conceptual frameworks for their analyses."

## The cultic underground

The unclear sect-cult distinctions advanced by Glock and Stark, Nelson, and Stark and Bainbridge appear to reflect the very ambiguity involved with the sociological manifestation of the New Age and Neo-pagan movements themselves. In this sense, the concept of the "cult movement" developed by Nelson rather than that of Stark and Bainbridge perhaps comes closer in application to the movements' overall expression. Another and related approach is Campbell's (1972) notion of the *cultic milieu*—the permanent "cultural underground of society" where the chief organizational form is the "society of seekers." Nelson himself denies the reality of a single cultic milieu that may at best constitute a convenient sociological "catch-all" for pluralistically deviant belief-systems and practices.[17] The cultic milieu concept itself is similar to Judah's (1967) "American metaphysical tradition." The diffused collectivity of occult believers would comprise both what Marty (1970) distinguishes as the "occult underground" with its Gemeinschaft of structural totality (Wagner's [1983] "occult counterculture") and the mystical Gesellschaft's preference for option and structural freedom called the "occult establishment."[18]

I would suggest, in place of—or perhaps along with—the concepts of cultic milieu and counterculture, the notion of the "counter-cult," which shares with much mainstream religion man's inherent need to worship yet adheres to this-worldly values. Typically, prayer for the counter-cultist seeks such things as material well-being, wealth, health, offspring, professional advancement, etc. Judged from the viewpoint of the official theology in which it operates, it appears irrational or contradictory—often partaking of superstition (e.g., the worship of the Buddha in 'atheistic' Buddhism, the worship of the gods in world-denying Hinduism, worship of saints canonized or not in biblically iconoclastic Christianity, worship of Muslim saints in monotheistic Islam, etc., or such contemporary forms of hero worship as that of Elvis Presley).[19] Counter-cult behavior can be both deliberate and unconsciously automatic, but it is virtually universal[20]—occurring in both religious and secular forms (i.e., those occurring not within a recognized religious context). The important feature of the counter-cult, however, is that it is empirical and can be observed through devotional expression (venerational offerings, etc.), atavistic behavorial retention, vocabulary usage, and superstitious behavior. This devotional need/expression—both conscious and involuntary—I would argue underlies the cultic milieu or milieus from which in turn the metaphysical tradition, the occult underground or counterculture, and the occult establishment all arise.[21] And as the counter-cult represents a natural proclivity of the individual, it explains much of the attraction to NRMs generated among those within the more orthodox, mainstream religions as well.[22]

## Gerlach and Hine's concept of the SPIN

Hill (1973:81) suggests that "The whole problem of defining a religious organization by its *lack* of organization might be solved by referring to a *cultic milieu*." But Hill has here missed the mark and falls into the error made by most establishment perceptions of social change movements: it is not that there is a lack of organization but simply a different kind of organization than that known through the bureaucratic and hierarchical structures of the traditional establishment.

Robbins (1988b:166) comes close to this recognition when he attempts to explain cult controversy as arising in part because NRMs "tend to constitute highly diversified and multifunctional enclaves lying outside of the web of governmental supervision which increasingly enmeshes "secular" organizations and enterprises." Gerlach and Hine touch on this same point when they discuss governmental insecurity through not being able to find a single spokesperson who can speak for the movement (e.g., Black Panthers, Palestinian guerillas, etc.) as a whole. Gerlach and Hine first considered these movements for personal and social change to be acephalous or headless but later substituted the term "polycephalous" and finally settled on the expression "polycentric." They argue that leadership is often situation specific and that such movements appear to be leaderless because there is (1) a lack of agreement on movement goals and means, (2) no one who has a roster of individuals or knows about all the groups who consider themselves members, (3) no one who can make binding decisions on all or even a majority of movement participants, (4) no one who has regulatory powers over the movement, and (5) no one who can speak for the movement as a whole or can determine who is or is not a member (Gerlach, 1971:821f.). In such movements, a typical leader's position is precarious, dependent on a personal following and endorsed only through continual demonstration of its worth.

Gerlach and Hine argue that rather than a weakness, this polycephalous/polycentric quality enhances the strength of the diffuse movement through greater innovation and adaptability.[23] They define a movement as "a group of people who are organized for, ideologically motivated by, and committed to a purpose which implements some form of personal or social change; who are actively engaged in the recruitment of others; and whose influence spreads in opposition to the established social order within which it originated" (Gerlach and Hine, 1973:163). Apart from the question of "active recruitment" this definition covers the New Age and Neo-pagan movements as well. Even more applicable, however, is Gerlach and Hine's development of the concept of the segmented, many-headed, and networked organization.

Gerlach (1971:812) and Hine find the decentralized, segmented, reticulate social structure akin to the segmentary lineage systems of many African, Middle Eastern, and Asian tribal societies as well as the segmentation into competing sects of the (successful) Protestant movement. In their view, segmentation and competition (between both rival units and the polycephalous situation of leadership) constitute the key to the success of all movements of change. The noncentralized, many-celled organization is not subject to control, manipulation, or even prediction (Gerlach, 1971:815)—hence, the frequent antagonism against it that can be generated on both governmental and orthodox social levels.

The segmentary, polycephalous, and reticulate movement organization, or what Hine (1977) designates the Segmented Polycentric Integrated Network (SPIN), is perhaps the most accurate sociological construct applicable to the New Age, Neo-pagan and similar non-institutional, boundary-indeterminate movements. The proliferation of segmentation, which is a chief characteristic of these types of movements, is explained by Gerlach (1971:819f., 834) as resulting from (1) belief in personal power—the black liberation groups's "do your own thing" injunction, (2) pre-existing social separations, (3) personal competition, and (4) ideological differences. Gerlach describes a core or base—in the case of New Age and Neo-paganism, perhaps the cultic milieu or counter-cult residuum—from which a conservative-to-radical continuum of segments arises. On one end, there exists the "large bureaucratically organized national groups"; in the middle, various "more middle-range and conservative groups"; and on the radical end in which the belief that the existing system must be changed from without may dominate, one finds "distinct, often rival, units whose fissiparous nature tends towards the further production of "daughter cells" (Gerlach, 1971:817f.).[24]

The New Age movement, particularly in America, follows the general pattern of the Gerlach-Hine analysis with countless human potential, self-growth, and meditation groups on the "radical" side, and the opposite end of the continuum being represented in part through the New Age catalogues and registers that seek to circumscribe the movement as a whole—though even here one finds a degree of rivalry (e.g., differences of inclusion-exclusion between *The Whole Again Resource Guide* and *The New Age Catalogue*, etc.) Likewise, the segmented nature of contemporary paganism comprises a morass of local groups, covens, etc., with, on the other end of the scale, such 'national' organizations tying many of these units together yet remaining distinct from them: e.g., in the United Kingdom, the Pagan Federation or The Green Circle/Quest network; in the United States, Circle or CUUPS. Moreover, in my participation/observation of HOG, I have seen at least one 'daughter cell' proliferate from the older organization, namely, the Willow Grove.

But if the segmentary aspect of these non-bureaucratic movements or SPINs is an essential characteristic, the other is their virtually 'unbounded' reticulation. The network structure that helps to maintain a continuing functional viability among individuals and groups rests primarily on five types of (not exclusive) linkages: (1) ties of kinship, friendship, social relationship, etc., or personal associations based on similar experiences or ideological interpretation among members of different groups (for instance, I have often seen some of the same people attending HOG, Willow Grove, the Pagan Moon, the Pagan Federation, Quest Annual Conference, and the Talking Stick as well as St. James

Piccadilly)—as Gerlach and Hine (1968:27) express it: ". . . members come and go from one group to another, thereby forming links between all groups;"[25] (2) intercell leadership exchange or personal, kinship, and social ties among leaders and others in autonomous cells—ones that are facilitated by telephone, letter, newsletters, etc. (e.g., Vivianne Crowley gave a talk at the Quest Annual Conference of March 10, 1990; John Male, who heads a shamanic group in Kent, gave a lecture for the Talking Stick on June 6, 1990 and attended the Pagan Conference at ULU the weekend of May 5–7, 1990 as well as HOG on other occasions; the frequent interchange of speakers among Alternatives, Wrekin Trust, Findhorn, etc.); (3) the activities of traveling evangelists, spokespeople, ecoevangelists, evangelist-organizers, etc., as well as the movement of ordinary movement participants along the movement network (e.g., I have received and lodged visitors known through both PSA and CUUPS), (4) "in-gatherings" and large-scale demonstrations (e.g., Shan's Pagan Hallowe'en celebrations, the Pagan Moons, Marion Green's Quest Annual Conference, the Harmonic Convergence gatherings at Glastonbury Tor, etc.); and (5) the basic beliefs and ideological themes shared by traveling speakers, letters, word-of-mouth, discussions, lectures, workshops, individual and group interaction, publications, newsletters, books, and especially the increased communication system efficiency represented by desktop publishing. Gerlach (1971:823) notes that the very "variety of interpretation is the ideological basis for fusion." These external linkages—including the sharing of basic ideological beliefs—along with the collective perception of, and action against, a common opposition are all factors promoting cohesion. They constitute the integrating, cross-cutting links, bonds, and operations that form the reticulate structure and foster the segmentary movement's identity.

### Starhawk's circular structures of immanence

The 'grapevine' communication, the collection and distribution of intelligence, and the supporting activities characteristic of the SPIN are what Starhawk (1988:115) refers to as "structures of immanence" whose forms are "circular" in contrast to traditional hierarchical and bureaucratic structures whose basic form is the "ladder."[26] In Starhawk's (1988:121) terms,

> When a group is alive and thriving, coalitions are constantly forming, shifting, deepening, re-forming. When there is a great deal of crossover

among coalitions, they become the stitching that binds the group together as a whole.

In Starhawk's understanding, a healthy group is never stable but is perpetually changing, growing, and re-forming. And as they grow and combine, they form "metastructures," that is, small group networks by using "spokes" to join circles to other circles.

> Spokes are people chosen to speak for the group, to embody the group will and to connect it with other groups. . . . Spokes from many groups can meet to discuss issues and, if their groups empower them to do so, make decisions. (Starhawk, 1988:132)

In the social and personal change associations described by Starhawk, affinity groups form clusters—sending "spokes" to cluster meetings. Clusters in turn send delegates to an overall council that makes nonbinding decisions affecting the constituent groups.

Though networks of circles may be acephalous, Starhawk does insist that they often need a "center"—a person or small group of people, a physical meeting place, a periodic event, a telephone tree, a centrally located bulletin board, a radio station, a newspaper, a newsletter, a coffee house, a neighborhood bar, a festival, or a ritual. In whatever form, the "center" serves as the point for the collection and distribution of information to all circles or members of a group.

Starhawk argues that such structures are not inefficient—certainly no more so than the "amount of waste, theft and minor sabotage" that occurs daily in the lower levels of hierarchy. In Gerlach and Hine's terms, segmentation, ideological diversity, and proliferation of cells can produce rapid organizational growth, inspire depth of personal commitment, and be flexibly adaptive to rapidly changing conditions. Such adaptive functions are necessary for the SPIN or successful movement aiming to implement personal and social change because (1) they prevent effective suppression by the opposition, (2) there is a multipenetration of and recruitment from different socio-economic and subcultural levels, (3) adaptive variation is maximized through diversity, (4) system reliability is achieved through group duplication and overlapping—the failure of one does not harm the others, (5) competition among groups brings about an escalation of effort—also small groups permit face-to-face interaction between members, (6) social innovation and problem solving is promoted—fostering entrepreneurial experimentation, and

(7) selective adapting occurs—the maladaptive variant ceases to exist, and this information passes quickly through the reticulate network.

## The SPIN concept and the church-sect typology

The SPIN is a sociological construct that is applicable to the contemporary horizontal growth of NRMs; the church-sect typology fits more accurately the traditional hierarchical development of religious organizations. Both, however, may be used in conjunction to delineate the diversified range of religious collectivities confronting the sociologist of religion in the latter part of the twentieth century. For instance, Gerlach and Hine (1968:36f.) stress the role of real or perceived opposition in serving to intensify commitment, unify the local group, provide a basis for identification among groups, and maintain the linkages among organizational units in the reticulate structure of the movement as a whole, and they note in this context that Pope labeled the sect end of the sect-to-church continuum as one possessing a "psychology of persecution."

Related to group opposition is Moore's (1986:19) conclusions concerning "religious outsidership," which he sees as having frequently been a deliberate strategy developed by various religious movements in America to ensure continuity and distinct identity. "The creation of a consciousness of difference, a spirit alive and well in the 1960s, involved a group in inventing a dominant culture to set itself against . . ." Accordingly, "outsidership" in American religious history has frequently been a cultivated fiction that in fact places the group successfully and centrally within the religious mainstream. In fact, regarding pejorative labeling by the so-called Establishment, Moore (1986:115) states that "When Eddy's contemporaries called Christian Science an occult aberration, they were . . . saying that they did not like that aspect of their culture which explained its appeal." "Christian Science grew as a perfectly ordinary manifestation of tensions that were always present in American society" (Moore, 1986:124). Moore draws parallels with various post-1960 NRMs (e.g., TM, Meher Baba, etc.).

If Wallis's factor of deviance in his church-sect-denomination-cult typology were to be replaced with a determination of a group's real or perceived opposition, we might have a more viable analytical model for the range of religious collectivities today—one augmented by Bryan Wilson's typology of sects, Nelson's and Stark and Bainbridge's typologies of cults and Wallis's own typology of sects and cults (NRMs). If the basic four ideal-types were to be arranged in a continuum, I would picture the sequence as church-denomination-cult-sect—with the exclusiveness of church and sect membership, their greater boundary determinacy, unitary legitimacy, and dogmatic quality of ideological certitude placing them more to the fringes of the democratic core of current Western mainstream society.[27] Moreover, to the degree the pluralistically legitimate collectivity is opposed by its host society—or perceives itself as opposed, it conforms more to the cult-type. To the degree, on the other hand, that it is integrated with and undifferentiated from its surrounding environment and culture, it approximates the denomination.

Certainly within the vast networks or SPINs that make up the New Age and Neo-pagan movements, the concepts of cult and sect, etc., describe various constituent components, cells or collectivities. Starhawk's (1988:115) description of the circular structures of immanence as comprising clans, tribes, covens, collectivities, support groups, affinity groups, and consciousness-raising groups indicates that the contemporary SPIN is not composed exclusively of traditionally 'religious' groups. Gerlach and Hine, in fact, developed their concept of the SPIN through investigations of "change-oriented movements" in general —including communism, Mau Mau, Black Power, the new left, women's liberation, the counterculture, the Vietcong, Palestinian liberation, and the "participatory ecology movement" as well as both early Islam and the Pentecostal movement. The SPIN is pictured less as a 'religious' movement per se as it is one that aims toward personal and social change.

## The SPIN of SPINs

Marilyn Ferguson (1987:217), in her virtual handbook for the New Age movement, states that "The Aquarian Conspiracy is, in effect, a SPIN of SPINs, a network of many networks aimed at social transformation." I would take this concept further and identify what may be termed the contemporary "holistic movement" as a SPIN of SPINs that includes New Age, Neo-paganism, the ecology movement, feminism, the Goddess movement, the human potential movement, Eastern mysticism groups, liberal/liberation politics, the Aquarian Conspiracy, etc.—one that conforms as well to what Ruether (1980:842) designates as the liberal reformist, the socialist, and the countercultural romanticist trends of Western social movements. If the SPIN of SPINs concept is combined with the church-denomination-cult-sect typology as a special application within the SMO, i.e., the RMO—one expanded through the contributions of Wallis, Stark and Bainbridge, Bird, Lofland and Richardson, etc.—to analyze formations and changes among the NRMs and cells or segments that constitute the reticulate polycephalous structure comprising the holistic movement, we have a viable sociological tool that is applicable to contemporary late twentieth-century developments and study.

## Notes

1. See further, Lauer (1972), who presents an interactionalist process between any movement and its social environment as determinative of the movement's developmental direction. See also Wuthnow (1988:100–131) and his discussion of "special purpose groups."

2. Note, e.g., Langone and Clark as well as Anderson in Kilbourne (1985). See further, Kurtz (1986). For Robbins and Anthony (1981), the cult may be evocative of occultism.

3. Robbins (1988b:189) sees the "feedback model of deviance amplification" ("which delineates a spiraling process of mutually interdependent and escalating recriminations on the part of an increasingly alienated and extremist group and an increasingly hostile and persecutory environmental structure") occupying the middle ground between James Richardson's initially deformed organizational model of NRMs and Ofshe and Wallis's perspective emphasizing the initial privileges and immunities of new religious movements that foster their deviance and the outside hostile reaction to them. See further, Swatos (1981) who denies the validity of sect-cult distinctions on the basis of origins. He rejects "deviance" and "conventionality" as concepts involving a relativity of both position and value-judgment and argues, moreover, that cults are simply "religious collectivities" that become—or begin to become—"religious organizations" conforming to the church-sect typology only when they inaugurate "formal religious claims."

4. For Yinger, the cult is "small, short-lived, often local and built around a single dominant leader in contrast to the more typical sectarian feature of widespread lay participation." See Hill (1973:74), who discusses in addition David Martin's inclusion along with the factor of deviance, the cult's individualism as its "fundamental" criterion.

5. Undergoing a process entailing "an arrogation of authority." See further, Wallis (1974) and his discussion of the *centralized cult*.

6. Another criticism of the church-sect paradigm comes from Ellwood (1978), who finds an inherent limitation in its lack of historical perspective. Ellwood feels that use of diachronic rather than synchronic models emphasizes the tradition itself from which NRMs "emerge." Robbins (1988b) refers to

Ellwood, Moore, and others as providing "provocative quasi-historical analyses."

7. Both New Age and Neo-paganism are like Spiritualism, Theosophy, and New Thought, which, as Wallis (1974:316) states, "are not single groups, each recognizing a central source of authority; rather, each is a movement composed of a variety of groups which share a number of ideological themes but otherwise differ in many respects."

8. As Wilson (1982:104f., 112) explains, the 'ideal-type' is a construct by which key features and relationships are delineated for *comparative* (rather than classificatory) purposes. Explanations for salient discrepancies found among actual phenomena when measured against the type-construct can then more clearly become the sociologist's focus.

9. One exception, however, appears to be found in the dualistic school of thought represented by Terry Cole Whittaker.

10. According to Wilson (1982:98), a denomination is "a tolerant, world-accommodating religious movement that [has] abandoned most, if not all, of the distinguishing features of sectarianism."

11. Peter B. Clarke suggests "instrumentalist" sect as an alternative designation for Wilson's manipulationist sect. See further, Bird and Reimer (1982).

12. Or, alternatively, both movements—though especially New Age—may come closer to Wilson's "eighth basic supernaturalist" or base-line response since Wilson (1973:21) defines religious or sectarian deviance as "concern with transcendence over evil and the search for salvation and consequent rejection of prevailing cultural values, goals, and norms, and whatever facilities are culturally provided for man's salvation."

13. The religious market consumerism is referred to by Campbell (1972) as "consumer selectivity"; by Richardson et al. (1986) as "denomination switching"; by Shepherd (1979) as "serial adhesion."

14. For Wilson (1982:117f.), "relative deprivation remains too gross a category to explain sectarianism." Moreover, the subjective mental/emotional state of individuals upon which the thesis depends "leave it to be regarded as at best a plausible but untested, and perhaps untestable, hypothesis."

15. See also Beckford (1985a), who appears to expand Bird's three types to five based on internal bonding and commitment and ranging from devotee, adept, client, patron, and apostate.

16. Beckford's (1985a) external relationships are the anti-worldly refuge or retreat, the social transformatory revitalization mode, and the release approach of the HPM, etc.

17. Robbins (1988b) recognizes several "generative" cultic milieus including the evangelical Jesus movement, the psychedelic subculture, and the HPM.

18. For a different application of the German terms, see B. Wilson (1982:153f.).

19. On the religious dimension of the growing reverence for Elvis Presley, Christine King gave a talk on May 30, 1990 at the London School of Econom-

ics' Sociology of Religion Seminar entitled "Elvis: Religion, Myth and Fantasy" in which she linked the idea of medieval pilgrimages and popular culture. Neil Asher Silberman, in turn, ties the Elvis cult to the hero worship of antiquity ("Elvis: The Myth Lives On," *Archaeology*, July/August 1990:80). The ecstatic emotion found among the current fans and followers of Madonna, Sting, and other pop singers might be explored as further expressions of counter-cult expression.

20. Wilson (1982:65, 172) posits a contrast between "high culture" and "folk culture" in, for example, Asia's Theravada Buddhism and speaks of the persistence of local magic in some nominally Roman Catholic Latin American countries.

21. This contended counter-cult propensity in mankind is similar to Greeley's (1972; 1985) recognition that the human being inevitably makes his or her ultimate concerns into something sacred. Accordingly, Greeley considers such expressions as Marxism, nationalism, fascism, scientism, etc., as "religious movements."

22. For a related concept, refer to Ahlstrom's definition of "harmonial philosophy" (Moore, 1986:115–17).

23. Gerlach and Hine's argument appears to contrast significantly with what Robbins (1988b:108) notes for "Stark and Wilson [who] appear to concur in predicting that successful movements will be demographically and organizationally normal, i.e., possessing a population structure similar to that of the society and organized in terms of conventional units of social organization (e.g., families)." Robbins (1988b:132) also feels that "the economic or financial dimension of NRMs increasingly seems to be significant as a stimulus determining the direction of movement evolution."

24. This schismatic "strength" of the polycephalous social movement presents an alternative view concerning the institutional precariousness of pluralistically legitimate movements as understood by Wallis (1979a; 1984). Nevertheless, Wallis's study of the availability of means of legitimating authority —discussed above (Chapters 1 and 7)—represents an astute analysis of the mechanics of divisional tendency that is not only compatible with the Gerlach-Hine model of the SPIN but also with some developments and transitions occurring within the New Age and Neo-pagan movements.

25. For example, Starhawk (1988: xvii, xxiii) refers to her associations with Raving Coven (now disbanded), sister covens Holy Terrors and Wind Hags, the Matrix Affinity Group ("now also a coven"), the Social Change Trainers Core Group, the Abalone Alliance, The Livermore Action Group, and the Santa Rita Jailbirds. She has also been involved with the WomanEarth Feminist Peace Institute, teaches at Matthew Fox's Institute in Culture andCreation Spirituality in Oakland, California, and has addressed both the Unitarian Universalist General Assembly on behalf of CUUPS and Alternatives at St. James, Piccadilly.

26. Starhawk is essentially reformulating Hargrove's (1978) understanding of "transformative religion," characterized by openness and interpersonal rela-

tions and "integrative religions," which is specifically organized—often hierarchically—and stresses boundary maintenance.

27. See also Robertson's (1970b) comments on inclusive/exclusive membership as perhaps designating a measurable device to possibilities of perceived opposition.

# Bibliography

Academy of Parapsychology and Medicine. 1972. *The Dimensions of Healing.* Palo Alto, Calif.: APM.

Adler, Margot. 1986. *Drawing Down the Moon: Witches, Druids, Goddess-Worshippers, and Other Pagans In America Today.* Boston: Beacon Press.

Aidala, Angela A. 1984. "Worldviews, ideologies and social experimentation: clarification and replication of 'the consciousness reformation'," *Journal for the Scientific Study of Religion* 23.1:44–59.

Alexander, Brooks. 1978. "Holistic health from the inside." *SCP Journal* 2.1 (August):5–17.

Alexander, Jane. 1989. "The selling of the new age." *i-D Magazine* 75 (November):20–23.

Allen, Mark. 1978. *Chrysalis.* Berkeley, Calif.: Pan Publishing.

Anthony, Dick and Thomas Robbins. 1978. "The effect of detente on the growth of new religions: Reverend Moon and the Unification Church." Pp. 80–100 in *Understanding the New Religions*, ed. Jacob Needleman and George Baker. New York: Seabury.

———. 1982a. "Spiritual innovation and the crisis of American civil religion." *Daedalus* (Winter):215–34.

———. 1982b. "Contemporary religious ferment and moral ambiguity." In *New Religious Movements: A Perspective for Understanding Society. Studies in Religion and Society*, vol. 3, ed. Eileen Barker. New York: Edwin Mellen Press.

Anthony, Dick, Bruce Ecker and Ken Wilber. 1987. *Spiritual Choices: The Problem of Recognizing Authentic Paths to Inner Transformation.* New York: Paragon.

Argüelles, José. 1987. *The Mayan Factor: Path Beyond Technology.* Santa Fe, N.M.: Bear & Co.

Aron, Raymond C. F. 1970. *Main Currents in Sociological Thought* II. Garden City, N.Y.: Doubleday.

Bailey, Alice. 1944. *Discipleship in the New Age*—Vol. I. London: Lucis Press.

——. 1948. *The Reappearance of the Christ*. New York: Lucis Press.

——. 1954. *Education in the New Age*. London: Lucis Press.

——. 1955. *Discipleship in the New Age*—Vol. II. London: Lucis Press.

Bailey, Mary. 1978. "The Work of Triangles." Edited transcript of an address given at the Conference of the Spiritual Frontiers Fellowship in North Carolina, August 1978. London: Lucis Press.

Bainbridge, William Sims, and Rodney Stark. 1979. "Cult formation: three compatible models." *Sociological Analysis* 40.4:283–97.

——. 1980. "Client and audience cults in America." *Sociological Analysis* 41:199–214.

——. 1981. "The 'consciousness reformation' reconsidered." *Journal for the Scientific Study of Religion* 20.1:1–16.

Balch, Robert. 1985. "What's wrong with the study of cults and what can we do about it?" Pp. 24–39 in *Scientific Research and New Religions: Divergent Perspectives*, ed. Brock K. Kilbourne. San Francisco: Pacific Division, American Association for the Advancement of Science.

Barker, Eileen, ed. 1982. *New Religious Movements: A Perspective for Understanding Society. Studies in Religion and Society*, vol. 3. New York: Edwin Mellen Press.

——. 1984. *The Making of a Moonie: Brainwashing or Choice?* Oxford: Basil Blackwell.

——. 1989. *New Religious Movements: A Practical Introduction*. London: Her Majesty's Stationery Office.

Bartley, W. W., III. 1978. *Werner Erhard*. New York: Clarkson N. Potter.

Basil, Robert, ed. 1988. *Not Necessarily The New Age: Critical Essays*. New York: Prometheus Books.

Becker, Howard. 1932. *Systematic Sociology on the Basis of the Beziehungslehre and Gebildungslehre of Leopold von Wiese*. New York: Wiley; London: Chapman and Hall.

Beckford, James A. 1977. "Explaining religious movements." *International Social Science Journal* 29.2:235–49.

——. 1978. "Cults and cures." *Japanese Journal of Religious Studies* 5.4:225–57.

——. 1982. "The articulation of a classical sociological problematic with a modern social problem: religious movements and modes of social insertion." Paper read at the annual meeting of the Society for the Scientific Study of Religion in October, Providence, R.I.

——. 1983. "The restoration of 'power' to the sociology of religion." *Sociological Analysis* 44.1:11–32.

——. 1984. "Holistic imagery and ethics in new religious and healing movements." *Social Compass* 31.2–3:259–72.

——. 1985a. *Cult Controversies: The Societal Response to the New Religious Movements*. London and New York: Tavistock Publications.

——. 1985b. "New religious movements and healing." Pp. 125–38 in *Sick-*

*ness and Sectarianism: Exploratory Studies in Medical and Religious Sectarianism*, ed. Kenneth R. Jones. Aldershot, Hampshire: Gower Press.

———, ed. 1986. *New Religious Movements and Rapid Social Change*. London/Paris: Sage/Unesco.

———. 1987. "New religions: an overview." In *Encyclopedia of Religions*, ed. Mircea Eliade, Vol. X :390–394. New York: Free Press.

Bednarowski, Mary Farrell. 1989. *New Religions and the Theological Imagination in America*. Bloomington: Indiana Univeristy Press.

Bell, Daniel. 1977. "The return of the sacred? The argument on the future of religion." *British Journal of Sociology* 28:419–49.

Bellah, Robert N. 1967. "Civil Religion in America." *Daedalus* 96.1:1–21. (First published in 1964.)

———. 1969. "Religious evolution." Pp. 262–92 in *Sociology of Religion*, ed. Roland Robertson. Harmondsworth: Penguin.

———. 1970. *Beyond Belief*. New York: Harper and Row.

———. 1976. "The new religious consciousness and the crisis of modernity." Pp. 333–52 in *The New Religious Consciousness*, ed. Charles Glock and Robert Bellah. Berkeley: University of California Press.

Benson, J. Kenneth, and James H. Dorsett. 1972. "Toward a theory of religious organizations." *Journal for the Scientific Study of Religions* 10.2:138–51.

Berger, Peter L. 1954. "Sociological study of sectarianism." *Social Research* 21.4 (1954–55, Winter):467–85.

———. 1958. "Sectarianism and religious sociation." *American Journal of Sociology* 64.1 (July):41–44.

———. 1965. "Towards a sociological analysis of psychoanalysis." *Social Research* 32.1:26–41.

Berger, Peter L., and Brigitte Berger. 1976. *Sociology: A Biographical Approach*. Harmondsworth: Penguin.

Berger, Peter L., Brigitte Berger, and Hansfried Kellner. 1974. *The Homeless Mind*. Harmondsworth: Penguin.

Bird, Frederick. 1978. "Charisma and ritual in new religious movements." Pp. 173–89 in *Understanding the New Religions*, ed. Jacob Needleman and George Baker. New York: Seabury.

———. 1979a. "Charismatic cults: an examination of the ritual practices of various new religious groups." *Occasional Publications in Anthropology, Ethnology Series* 33:214–49.

———. 1979b. "The pursuit of innocence: new religious movements and moral accountability." *Sociological Analysis* 40:335–46.

Bird, Frederick, and William Reimer. 1982. "Participation rates in new religious and para-religious movements." Pp. 215–38 in *Of Gods and Men*, ed. Eileen Barker. Macon, Ga.: Mercer University Press.

Bletzer, June G. 1986. *The Doning International Encylcopedic Psychic Dictionary*. Norfolk, Va.: Doning.

Bloom, William. 1990. *Sacred Times: A New Approach to Festivals*. Forres, Scotland: Findhorn.

————, ed. 1991. *The New Age: An Anthology of Essential Writings*. London: Rider.

Bromley, David G., and Phillip H. Hammond. eds. 1987. *The Future of New Religious Movements*. Macon, Ga.: Mercer University Press.

Bromley, David G., and Anson D. Shupe. 1987. "The future of the Anticult Movement." Pp. 221–34 in *The Future of New Religious Movements*, ed. David G. Bromley and Phillip H. Hammond. Macon, Ga.: Mercer University Press.

Brooke, Anthony. 1976. *Towards Human Unity*. London: Mitre Press. (Reprint of talks given between 1965 and 1973.)

Bry, Adelaide. 1976. *60 Hours That Transform Your Life: est: Erhard Seminars Training*. New York: Avon.

Burr, Harold Saxon. 1972. *The Fields of Life*. New York: Ballantine.

————. 1975. *A Course in Miracles*. New York: Foundation for Inner Peace.

Burrows, Robert. 1984–85. "New Age Movement: self-deification in a secular culture." *SCP Newsletter* 10.5 (Winter):4–8 (I).

Bush, Jared. 1987. "Reincarnation—Fact or Theory?". *Prediction*, March.

Caird, Dale, and Henry G. Law. 1982. "Non-convention beliefs: their structure and measurement." *Journal for the Scientific Study of Religion* 21.2:152–63.

Campbell, Colin B. 1972. "The cult, the cultic milieu and secularization." Pp. 119–36 in *A Sociological Yearbook of Religion in Britain* 5, ed. Michael Hill. London: SCM Press.

————. 1977. "Clarifying the cult." *British Journal of Sociology* 28.3 September):375–88.

————. 1978. "The secret religion of the educated classes." *Sociological Analysis* 39.2:146–56.

Castaneda, Carlos. 1968. *The Teachings of Don Juan: A Yaqui Way of Knowledge*. Berkeley: University of California Press.

Choquette, Diane. 1985. *New Religious Movements in the United States and Canada: A Critical Assessment and Annotated Bibliography*. Westport, Conn.: Greenwood Press.

Clark, Elmer Talmage. 1937. *The Small Sects in America*. Nashville: Cokesbury Press.

Clark, Linda. 1972. *Help Yourself to Health*. New York: Pyramid House.

Clarke, Peter B., ed. 1987. *The New Evangelists: Recruitment Methods and Aims of New Religious Movements*. London: Ethnographica Publishers Ltd.

————, ed. 1988. "New Religious Movements." Pp. 905–66 in *The World's Religions*, ed. Stewart Sutherland, Leslie Houlden, Peter Clarke, and Friedhelm Hardy. London: Routledge.

Coleman, John, and Gregory Baum, eds. 1983. *New Religious Movements*. New York: Seabury Press.

Crowley, Vivianne. 1989. *Wicca: The Old Religion in the New Age*. Wellingborough, England: Aquarian Press.

Culpepper, Emily. 1978. "The spiritual movement of radical feminine consciousness.'' Pp. 220–34 in *Understanding the New Religions*, ed. Jacob Needleman and George Baker. New York: Seabury.

Cumbey, Constance. 1983. *The Hidden Dangers of the Rainbow*. Shreveport, La.: Huntington House.

Currie, R., A. Gilbert, and L. Horsley. 1977. *Churches and Churchgoers: Patterns of Church Growth and Decline in the British Isles Since 1700*. London: Oxford University Press.

Daly, Mary. 1973. *Beyond God the Father*. Boston: Beacon Press.

Das, Bhagavan. 1966. *The Essential Unity of All Religions*. Wheaton, Ill.: Theosophical Publishing House; originally published in 1932.

Dass, Baba Ram. 1971. *Be Here Now*. San Christobal, N.M.: Lama Foundation.

———. 1974. *The Only Dance There Is*. Garden City, N.Y.: Anchor Press/ Doubleday.

———. 1976. *The Only Dance There Is*. New York: Jason Aronson.

———. 1978. *Journey of Awakening: A Meditator's Guidebook*. New York: Bantam Books.

———. 1979. *Miracle of Love*. New York: E. P. Dutton.

Demerath, N. J., III. 1967a. ''In a sow's ear: A reply to Goode.'' *Journal for the Scientific Study of Religion* 6.1 (Spring):77–84.

———. 1967b. ''Son of sow's ear.'' *Journal for the Scientific Study of Religion* 6.2 (Fall):275–7.

Dezavalle, Jacques J. 1976. *Thoughts for a New Age*. New York: Vantage Press.

Dittes, James E. 1971. ''Typing the typologies: Some parallels in the career of church-sect and extrinsic-intrinsic.'' *Journal for the Scientific Study of Religion* 10.4 (Winter):375–83.

Dowling, Levi. 1907. *The Aquarian Gospel of Jesus the Christ*. Los Angeles: the author.

Durkheim, Emile. 1915. *The Elementary Forms of the Religious Life: A Study in Religious Sociology*. Trans. Joseph Ward Swain. London: Allen and Unwin; New York: Macmillan.

Eister, Allan W. 1967. ''Toward a radical critique of church-sect typologizing: Comment on 'Some critical observations on the church-sect dimensions'.'' *Journal for the Scientific Study of Religion* 6.1 (Spring):85–90.

———. 1972. ''An outline of a structural theory of cults.'' *Journal for the Scientific Study of Religion* 11.4 (December):320–31.

———. 1973. ''H. Richard Niebuhr and the paradox of religious organization.'' Pp. 355–408 in *Beyond the Classics?*, ed. Charles Y. Glock and Phillip E. Hammond. New York: Harper and Row.

———. 1975. ''Comment on 'Max Weber on church, sect and mysticism.' '' *Sociological Analysis* 36.3:227–28.

Ellwood, Robert S., Jr. 1973. *Religious and Spiritual Groups in Modern America*. Englewood Cliffs, N.J.: Prentice-Hall.

———. 1978. ''Emergent religion in America: an historical perspective.'' Pp. 267–84 in *Understanding the New Religions*, ed. Jacob Needleman and George Baker. New York: Seabury.

————. 1979. *Alternative Altars: Unconventional and Eastern Spirituality in America*. Chicago: University of Chicago Press.

————. 1983. "Asian religions in North America." In *New Religious Movements*, ed. John Coleman and Gregory Baum. New York: Seabury Press.

Ernst, Eldon G. 1978. "Dimensions of new religion in American history." Pp. 34–45 in *Understanding the New Religions*, ed. Jacob Needleman and George Baker. New York: Seabury.

Evans, Robert R., ed. 1973. *Social Movements: A Reader and Source Book*. Chicago: Rand McNally.

Evans-Wentz, W. Y. 1966. *The Fairy Faith in Celtic Countries*. Secaucus, N.J.: University Books.

Farrar, Janet, and Stewart Farrar. 1984. *The Witches' Way: Principles, Rituals and Beliefs of Modern Witchcraft*. Custer, Wash.: Phoenix Publishing.

Ferguson, Marilyn. 1987. *The Aquarian Conspiracy: Personal and Social Transformation in Our Time*. Los Angeles: J. P. Tarcher.

Fichter, Joseph H., ed. 1983. *Alternatives to American Mainline Churches*. New York: Rose of Sharon Press.

Fox, Selena. 1984. "Wiccan Shamanism." *Circle Network News* (Winter).

Foss, D., and R. Larkin. 1976. "From 'The Gates of Eden' to 'Day of the Locust': an analysis of the dissident youth movement of the 1960s and its heirs in the 1970s—the post-movement groups." *Theory and Society* 3:45–64.

————. 1978. "Worshiping the absurd: The negation of social causality among the followers of Guru Maharaj Ji." *Sociological Analysis* 39.2:157–64.

Funderburk, James. 1977. *Science Studies Yoga*. N.P.: The Himalayan International Institute of Yoga and Science.

Gardner, Martin. 1991. *The New Age: Notes of a Fringe Watcher*. Buffalo: Prometheus Books.

Garrett, William R. 1975. "Maligned mysticism: The maledicted career of Troeltsch's third type." *Sociological Analysis* 36.3 (Fall):205–23.

Gaskin, Stephen. 1974. *Hey Beatnik! This Is the Farm Book*. Summertown, Tenn.: The Book Publishing Co.

————. 1976. *This Season's People*. Summertown, Tenn.: The Book Publishing Co.

Gerlach, Luther P. 1971. "Movements of revolutionary change." *American Behavorial Scientist* 14.6:812–36.

Gerlach, Luther P., and Virginia H. Hine. 1968. "Five factors crucial to the growth and spread of a modern religious movement." *Journal for the Scientific Study of Religion* 7.1:23–40.

————. 1970. *People, Power, Change: Movements of Social Transformation*. Indianapolis: Bobbs-Merrill.

————. 1973. *Lifeway Leap: The Dynamics of Change in America*. Minneapolis: University of Minnesota Press.

Gilkey, Langdon. 1978. "Toward a religious criterion of religion." Pp. 131–37 in *Understanding the New Religions*, ed. Jacob Needleman and George Baker. New York: Seabury.

Glock, Charles Y., and Robert Bellah, eds. 1976. *The New Religious Consciousness*. Berkeley: University of Calif. Press.

Glock, Charles Y., and Phillip E. Hammond. 1973. *Beyond the Classics?*. New York: Harper and Row.

Glock, Charles Y., and Rodney Stark. 1965. *Religion and Society in Tension*. Chicago: Rand McNally.

Goleman, Daniel. 1978. "The impact of the new religions on psychology." Pp. 113–21 in *Understanding the New Religions*, ed. Jacob Needleman and George Baker. New York: Seabury.

Goode, Erich. 1967a. "Some critical observations on the church-sect dimension." *Journal for the Scientific Study of Religion* 6.1 (Spring):69–77.

———. 1967b. "Further reflections on the church-sect dimension." *Journal for the Scientific Study of Religion* 6.2 (Fall):270–5.

Goodman, Felicitas D. 1988. *Ecstasy, Ritual, and Alternate Reality: Religion in a Pluralistic World*. Bloomington: Indiana University Press.

Grad, Bernard. 1970. "Healing by the laying on of hands: review of experiments and implications." *Pastoral Psychology* 21.206 (Sept.):19–26.

Greeley, Andrew M. 1972/1985. *Unsecular Man: The Persistence of Religion*. New York: Schocken Books.

———. 1979. "Superstition, ecstasy and tribal consciousness." *Social Research* 37:203–11.

Green, Marion. 1987. *The Gentle Arts of Aquarian Magic*. Wellingborough, England: Aquarian Press.

Greil, Arthur L., and David R. Rudy. 1984. "What have we learned from process models of conversion? An examination of ten studies." *Sociological Focus* 17.4:306–23.

Griswold, Alfred W. 1934. "New Thought: a cult of success." *American Journal of Sociology* 40:309–18.

Gustafson, Paul. 1967. "UO-US-PS-PO: A restatement of Troeltsch's church-sect typology." *Journal for the Scientific Study of Religion* 6.1 (Spring): 64–68.

———. 1973a. "Exegesis on the gospel according to St. Max." *Sociological Analysis* 34 (Spring):12–25.

———. 1973b. "The missing member of Troeltsch's trinity: Thoughts generated by Weber's comments." *Sociological Analysis* 36 (Fall):224–26.

Gustaitis, Rasa. 1969. *Turning On*. New York: Macmillan.

Hadden, Jeffrey K., ed. 1977. "Review symposium: *The New Religious Consciousness*, edited by Charles Y. Glock and Robert N. Bellah." *Journal for the Scientific Study of Religion* 16.3:305–24.

Hadden, Jeffrey K., and Theodore E. Long, eds. 1983. *Religion and Religiosity in America: Studies in Honor of Joseph H. Fichter*. New York: Crossroad Press.

Hagler, Louise. 1978. *The Farm Vegetarian Cookbook*. Summertown, Tenn.:
The Book Publishing Co.

Hall, Manly Palmer. 1937. *Twelve World Leaders*. Los Angeles: Philosophers'
Press.

Halverson, Dean C. 1984–85. "Breaking through spiritual autism." *SCP Newsletter* 10.5 (Winter):12–16 (I).

Hammond, Phillip E., ed. 1985. *The Sacred in a Secular Age: Toward Revision
in the Scientific Study of Religion*. Berkeley: University of California Press.

Hargrove, Barbara. 1978. "Integrative and transformative religions." Pp.
257–66 in *Understanding the New Religions*, ed. Jacob Needleman and
George Baker. New York: Seabury.

Harper, C. L. 1982. "Cults and communities: the community interface of three
marginal movements." *Journal for the Scientific Study of Religion*
21.1:26–38.

Harris, Marvin. 1981. *America Now: The Anthropology of a Changing Culture*.
New York: Simon and Schuster.

Hartman, Patricia A. 1976. "Social dimensions of occult study: the Gnostica
study." *British Journal of Sociology* 27.2 (June):169–83.

Heelas, Paul. 1987. "Exegesis: methods and aims." Pp. 17–41 in *The New
Evangelists: Recruitment Methods and Aims of New Religious Movements*,
ed. Peter B. Clarke. London: Ethnographica Publishers Ltd.

————. 1988. "Western Europe: Self-Religions." In *The World's Religions*,
ed. Stewart Sutherland, Leslie Houlden, Peter Clarke, and Friedhelm Hardy.
London: Routledge.

Heline, Corinne. 1943. *Healing and Regeneration Through Color*. Santa Barbara, Ca.: J. F. Rowney.

Hexham, Irving, and Karla Poewe. 1986. *Understanding Cults and New Religions*. Grand Rapids, Mich.: William B. Eerdmans.

Hill, Michael. 1973. *A Sociology of Religion*. London: Heinemann.

Hiller, Harry. 1975. "A reconceptualization of the dynamics of social movement development." *Pacific Sociological Review* 17.3:342–59.

Hine, Virginia H. 1977. "The basic paradigm of a future socio-cultural system." *World Issues* (April/May). Center for the Study of Democratic Institutions.

Hinnells, John R. 1984. *A Handbook of Living Religions*. New York: Viking
Penguin; Harmondsworth, England: Penguin.

Houriet, Robert. 1971. *Getting Back Together*. New York: Avon.

Howard, John L. 1974. *The Cutting Edge: Social Movements and Social
Change in America*. Philadelphia: Lippincott.

Hunt, Dave. 1983. *Peace, Prosperity and the Coming Holocaust*. Eugene, Ore.:
Harvest House Publishers.

Inglis, Brian. 1969. *The Case for Unorthodox Medicine*. New York: Berkeley
Publishing.

Jayran, Shan. 1986. *Which Craft?* Whitstable, Kent: Whitstable Litho Printers
Ltd. (third printing, 1988).

Johnson, Benton. 1957. "A critical appraisal of the church-sect typology." *American Sociological Review* 22 (February):88–92.

————. 1963. "On church and sect." *American Sociological Review* 28 (August):539–49.

————. 1971. "Church and sect revisited." *Journal for the Scientific Study of Religion* 10.2 (Summer):124–37.

Jones, Prudence, and Caitlin Matthews. eds. 1990. *Voices from the Circle: The Heritage of Western Paganism*. Wellingborough, England: Aquarian Press.

Jones, R. Kenneth, ed. 1985. *Sickness and Sectarianism: Exploratory Studies in Medical and Religious Sectarianism*. Aldershot, Hampshire, England: Gower Press.

Joy, W. Brugh. 1978. *Joy's Way*. Los Angeles: J. P. Tarcher.

Judah, J. Stillson. 1967. *The History and Philosophy of the Metaphysical Movements in America*. Philadelphia: Westminster.

Juergensmeyer, Mark. 1978. "Radhasoami as a trans-national movement." Pp. 190–200 in *Understanding the New Religions*, ed. Jacob Needleman and George Baker. New York: Seabury.

Kanter, Rosabeth Moss. 1968. "Commitment and social organization." *American Sociological Review* 33.4:499–517.

————. 1972. *Commitment and Community: Communes and Utopias in Sociological Perspective*. Cambridge, Mass.: Harvard University Press.

Kaslow, Florence W., and Marvin B. Sussman, eds. 1982. *Cults and Family*. New York: Haworth.

Kerr, Howard, and Charles L. Crow, eds. 1983. *The Occult in America: New Historical Perspectives*. Chicago: University of Illinois Press.

Keyes, Ken, Jr. 1972; fifth ed. 1975. *Handbook to Higher Consciousness*. Berkeley, Calif.: Living Love Center.

————. 1982. *The Hundreth Monkey*. Coos Bay, Ore.: Vision Books.

Khalsa, Kirpal Singh. 1986. "New religious movements turn to worldly success." *Journal for the Scientific Study of Religion* 25.2:233–47.

Kilbourne, Brock K., ed. 1985. *Scientific Research and New Religions: Divergent Perspectives*. San Francisco: Pacific Division, American Association for the Advancement of Science.

King, Winston L. 1970. "Eastern religions: A new interest and influence." *The Annals of the American Academy of Political and Social Science* 387:66–76.

Kirpalvanand, Yogacarya. 1977. *Science of Meditation*. Kayavarohan, Gujarat, India: Sri Kayavarohan Tirth Seva Samaj.

Koebben, A.J.F. 1960. "Prophetic movements as an expression of social protest." *International Archives of Ethnography* 49:117–64.

Krishna, Gopi. 1971. *The Biological Basis of Religion and Genius*. New York: Harper and Row.

Kurtz, Paul. 1986. *The Transcendental Temptation: A Critique of Religion and the Paranormal*. Buffalo, N.Y.: Prometheus Books.

Lande, Nathaniel. 1976. *Mindstyles/Lifestyles*. Los Angeles: Price-Stern-Sloan.

Lasch, Christopher. 1976. "The narcissistic society." *New York Review of Books*, 30 September: 5–12.

Lattin, Don. 1989a. "Sect Gets Ready for Dark Days." *San Francisco Chronicle* 24 July: A1, A6.

———. 1989b. "Two Faces of the Spiritual Revival." *San Francisco Chronicle* 1 December: B3, B6.

Lauer, Robert H. 1972. "Social movements; An interactionist analysis." *The Sociological Quarterly* 13 (Summer):315–28.

Layard, Richard, and John King. 1969. "Expansion since Robbins." In *Anarchy and Culture*, ed. David Martin. London: Routledge and Kegan Paul.

Lewis, James R. 1991. *A Bibliography of Conservative Christian Literature on the New Age Movement*. Santa Barbara, Calif.: Santa Barbara Center for Humanistic Studies; Santa Barbara Center Occasional Paper No. 2 (Revised May 1991).

Lindsey, Robert. 1986. " 'New Age' Invades American Way of Life: Corporations Study Uses of the Occult; Critics Fear Efforts at Mind Control." *International Herald Tribune*, 3 October.

Lofland, John, and James T. Richardson. 1984. "Religious movement organizations: elemental forms and dynamics." In *Research in Social Movements, Conflicts and Change*, ed. L. Kriesberg. Greenwich, Conn.: JAI.

Lofland, John, and L.N. Skonovd. 1982. "Patterns of conversion." Pp. 1–24 in *New Religious Movements: A Perspective for Understanding Society*, ed. Eileen Barker. New York: Edwin Mellen Press.

Lovelock, James E. 1979. *Gaia: A New Look at Life on Earth*. Oxford: Oxford University Press.

Luckmann, Thomas, and Peter Berger. 1964. "Social mobility and personal identity." *European Journal of Sociology* 5:331–43.

Luhrmann, Tanya M. 1989. *Persuasions of the Witch's Craft*. Cambridge, Mass.: Harvard University Press.

Lukes, Steven. 1969. "Durkheim's 'Individualism and the intellectuals'." *Political Studies* 17.1:14–30.

MacLaine, Shirely. 1987. *It's All in the Playing*. New York and London: Bantam.

Mann, W. Edward. 1976. *Orgone, Reich and Eros*. New York: Simon and Schuster.

Marin, Peter. 1975. "The new narcissism: the trouble with the Human Potential Movement." *Harper's* 25 (1505):45–56.

Martin, David A. 1962. "The denomination." *British Journal of Sociology* 13 (March):1–14.

———. 1983. "A definition of cult: terms and approaches." Pp. 27–42 in *Alternatives to American Mainline Churches*, ed. Joseph H. Fichter. New York: Rose of Sharon Press.

Marty, Martin E. 1960. "Sects and cults." *Annals of the American Academy of Political Social Science* 332 (November):125–34.

————. 1970. "The occult establishment." *Social Research* 37.2:212–30.

McGuire, Meredith B. 1986. *Religion: The Social Context*. 2nd ed. Belmont, Mass.: Wadsworth.

————. 1988. *Ritual Healing in Suburban America*. New Brunswick, N.J.: Rutgers University Press.

McKinney, John C. 1966. *Constructive Typology and Social Theory*. New York: Appleton-Century-Crofts.

Melton, J. Gordon. 1978. *The Encylopedia of American Religions*, Wilmington, N.C.: McGrath.

————. 1982. "The revival of astrology in the United States: a perspective on occult religion in modern America." Photocopied. Evanston, Ill.: Institute for the Study of American Religion.

————. 1984. "Modern alternative religions in the west." In *A Handbook of Living Religions*, ed. John R. Hinnells. New York: Viking Penguin; Harmondsworth, England: Penguin.

————. 1986a. *Encyclopedia of American Religions*. Detroit: Gale Research Co.

————. 1986b. *Encyclopedic Handbook of Cults in America*. New York: Garland Publishing.

————. 1986c. *Biographical Dictionary of American Cult and Sect Leaders*. New York and London: Garland Publishing Inc.

————. 1987. "How new is new? The flowering of the 'new' religious consciousness since 1965." Pp. 46–56 in *The Future of New Religious Movements*, ed. David G. Bromley and Phillip H. Hammond. Macon, Ga.: Mercer University Press.

Melton, J. Gordon, and Robert L. Moore. 1982. *The Cult Experience: Responding to the New Religious Pluralism*. New York: The Pilgrim Press.

Melton, J. Gordon, Jerome Clark, and Aidan A. Kelly. 1990. *New Age Encyclopedia*. Detroit: Gale Research.

————. 1991. *New Age Almanac*. New York: Visible Ink Press.

Meyer, Michael R. 1976. *The Astrology of Relationship*. Garden City, N.Y.: Doubleday.

Michaelson, Johanna 1982. *The Beautiful Side of Evil*. Eugene, Ore.: Harvest House.

Miller, David L. 1974. *The New Polytheism: Rebirth of the God and Goddess*. New York: Harper and Row.

Montgomery, Ruth 1966. *A Search for Truth*. New York: Fawcett Crest.

————, with Joanne Garland. 1986. *Ruth Montgomery: Herald of the New Age*. New York: Fawcett Crest.

Moore, R. Laurence. 1986. *Religious Outsiders and the Making of Americans*. New York and Oxford: Oxford University Press.

Morgan, Robin. 1977. *Going Too Far*. New York: Random House.

Mosatche, Harriet S. 1984. *Searching: Practices and Beliefs of the Religious Cults and Human Potential Groups*. New York: Stravon Educational Press.

Motoyama, Hiroshi. 1981. *Theories of the Chakras: Bridge to Higher Consciousness.* Wheaton, Ill.: Theosophical Publishing House.

Needleman, Jacob. 1970. *The New Religions.* Garden City, N.Y.: Doubleday.

———. 1982. *Consciousness and Tradition.* New York: Crossroad.

Needleman, Jacob, and George Baker, eds. 1978. *Understanding the New Religions.* New York: Seabury.

Nelson, Benjamin. 1975. "Max Weber, Ernst Troeltsch, Georg Jellinek as comparative historical sociologists." *Sociological Analysis* 36.3:229–40.

Nelson, Geoffrey K. 1968. "The concept of cult." *The Sociological Review* 16:351–62.

———. 1969. "The Spiritualist Movement and the need for a redefinition of cult." *Journal for the Scientific Study of Religion* 8.1 (Spring):152–60.

———. 1987. *Cults, New Religions and Religious Creativity.* London: Routledge and Kegan Paul.

Niebuhr, H. Richard. 1957. *The Social Sources of Denominationalism.* 1929 Reprint. New York: Meridian.

Nisbet, Robert Alexander. 1966. *The Sociological Tradition.* New York: Basic Books.

Nock, A.D. 1933. *Conversion.* Oxford: Oxford University Press.

Nofziger, Margaret. 1976. *A Cooperative Method of Natural Birth Control.* Summertown, Tenn.: The Book Publishing Co.

Nyomarkay, Joseph. 1967. *Charisma and Factionalism in the Nazi Party.* Minneapolis: University of Minnesota Press.

Orr, Leonard, and Sondra Ray. 1983. *Rebirthing in the New Age.* Berkeley, Calif.: Celestial Arts.

O'Toole, Roger. 1976. " 'Underground' traditions in the study of sectarianism: Non-religious uses of the concept 'sect'." *Journal for the Scientific Study of Religion* 15.2:145–56.

Oyle, Irving. 1976. *Time, Space and the Mind.* Millbrae, Calif.: Celestial Arts.

Parker, William R., and Elaine St. John 1957. *Prayer Can Change Your Life.* Englewood Cliffs, N.J.: Prentice-Hall.

Parsons, Talcott. 1949. *Essays in Sociological Theory, Pure and Applied.* Glencoe, Ill.: Free Press; revised 1954.

———. 1965. "Introduction." Pp. *xix–lxvii* in Max Weber, *The Sociology of Religion.* Translated from the 1956 fourth edition by Ephraim Fischoff in 1963. London: Methuen.

Perkins, Lynn F. 1976. *The Masters as New Age Mentors.* Lakemont, Ga: CSA Press.

Perrone, Ed. 1983. *Astrology: A New Age Guide.* Wheaton, Ill.: Theosophical Publishing House.

Peters, Ted. 1991. *The Cosmic Self: A Penetrating Look at Today's New Age Movements.* San Francisco: Harper.

Popenoe, Cris, and Oliver Popenoe. 1984. *Seeds of Tomorrow.* San Francisco: Harper and Row.

Prebish, Charles. 1978. "Reflections on the transmission of Buddhism to America." Pp. 153–72 in *Understanding the New Religions*, ed. Jacob Needleman and George Baker. New York: Seabury.

Puryear, Herbert B. 1982. *The Edgar Cayce Primer: Discovering the Path to Self-Transformation*. London and New York: Bantam.

Rama, Swami [Rudolph Ballentine], and Swami Ajaya [Allen Weinstock] 1976. *Yoga and Psychotherapy, the Evolution of Consciousness*. Garden City, N.Y.: Doubleday.

Raschke, Carl A. 1980. *The Interruption of Eternity: Modern Gnosticism and the Origins of the New Religious Consciousness*. Chicago: Nelson-Hall.

Redekop, Calvin 1974. "A new look at sect development." *Journal for the Scientific Study of Religion* 13.3 (September):345–52.

Regush, Nicholas M., ed. 1977. *Frontiers of Healing*. New York: Avon.

Reisser, Paul C., Teri K. Reisser, and John Weldon. 1983. *The Holistic Healers*. Downers Grove, Ill.: InterVarsity Press.

Richardson, James T. 1983. "New religious movements in the United States: a review." *Social Compass* 30.1:85–110.

Richardson, James T., Jan van der Lans, and Franz Derks. 1986. "Leaving and labeling: voluntary and coerced disaffiliation from religious social movements." *Research in Social Movements* 9:97–126.

Robbins, Thomas. 1988a. "The transformative impact of the study of new Religions on the sociology of religion." *Journal for the Scientific Study of Religion* 27.1:12–31.

———. 1988b. *Cults, Converts and Charisma*. London: Sage.

Robbins, Thomas, and Dick Anthony. 1978. "New religious movements and the social system." *Annual Review of the Social Sciences of Religion* 2:1–28.

———. 1979. "Cults, brainwashing, and counter-subversion." *The Annals of the American Academy of Political and Social Science* 446 (November):78–90.

———, eds. 1981. *In Gods We Trust*. New Brunswick, N.J.: Transaction Books.

———. 1987. "New religions: new religions and cults in the United States." In *Encyclopedia of Religions*, ed. Mircea Eliade. Vol. X:394–405. New York: Free Press.

Robbins, Thomas, Dick Anthony, and Thomas Curtis. 1975. "Youth culture religious movements: Evaluating the integrative hypothesis." *Sociological Quarterly* 16.1: 48–64.

Robbins, Thomas, Dick Anthony, and James Richardson. 1978. "Theory and research on today's 'new religions'." *Sociological Analysis* 39.2:95–122.

Robertson, Roland, ed. 1969. *Sociology of Religion: Selected Readings*. Harmondsworth, England: Penguin.

———. 1970a. "The sociology of religion: problems and desiderata." *Journal of Religion and Religions*:109–26.

———. 1970b. *The Sociological Interpretation of Religion*. Oxford: Basil Blackwell.

————. 1977. "Church-sect and rationality: Reply to Swatos." *Journal for the Scientific Study of Religion* 16.2 (June):197–200.

————. 1981. "The manifest destinies of sects and nations." Photocopied paper read at the Conference on Conversion, Coercion, and Commitment, Center for the Study of New Religious Movements, 11–14 June 1981, at Berkeley, California.

Rosenblum, Art. 1974. *Unpopular Science.* Philadelphia: Running Press.

————. 1976: rev. ed. *The Natural Birth Control Book.* Philadelphia: Aquarian Research Foundation.

Rosten, Leo, ed. 1975. *Religions of America: Ferment and Faith in an Age of Crisis.* New York: Simon and Schuster.

Roszak, Theodore. 1969. *The Making of a Counter Culture: Reflections on the Technocratic Society and Its Youthful Opposition.* Garden City, N.Y.: Doubleday.

————. 1977. *Unfinished Animal: The Aquarian Frontier and the Evolution of Consciousness.* New York: Harper and Row.

————. 1978a. *Person/Planet: The Creative Disintegration of Industrial Society.* New York: Anchor Press/ Doubleday.

————. 1978b. "Ethics, ecstasy, and the study of new religions." Pp. 49–62 in *Understanding the New Religions,* ed. Jacob Needleman and George Baker. New York: Seabury.

Rowan, John. 1976. *Ordinary Ecstasy: Humanistic Psychology in Action.* London: Routledge and Kegan Paul.

Rudhyar, Dane. 1975. *Occult Preparations for the New Age.* Wheaton, Ill.: Theosophical Publishing House.

————. 1983. *Rhythm of Wholeness.* Wheaton, Ill.: Theosophical Publishing House.

Ruether, Rosemary Radford. 1980. "Goddesses and witches: liberation and countercultural feminism." *The Christian Century* (September 10–17): 842–47.

Russell, Peter. 1983. *The Global Brain: Speculations on the Evolutionary Leap to Planetary Consciousness.* Los Angeles: J. P. Tarcher.

Ryan, Alan. 1970. *The Philosophy of the Social Sciences.* London: Macmillan.

Satin, Mark. 1979. *New Age Politics: Healing Self and Society.* New York: Dell.

Schneider, Louis, and Sanford M. Dornbusch 1958. *Popular Religion: Inspirational Books in America.* Chicago: University of Chicago Press.

Scott, Gini Graham. 1980. *Cult and Countercult.* Westport, Conn.: Greenwood Press.

Shan. 1988. *Which Craft?: An Introduction to the Craft.* London: House of the Goddess.

Shepherd, William C. 1974. "Religion and the counter culture—a new religiosity." Pp. 348–58 in *Religion American Style,* ed. Patrick McNamara. New York: Harper and Row.

————. 1979. "Conversion and adhesion." Pp. 251–63 in *Religious Change and Continuity,* ed. Harry M. Johnson. San Francisco: Jossey-Bass.

Shupe, Anson D. 1981. *Six Perspectives on New Religions: A Case Study Approach*. New York: Edwin Mellen.

Simon, Justin. 1978. "Observations on 67 patients who took Erhard Seminars Training." *American Journal of Psychiatry* 135.6 (June):686–91.

Sinclair, John R. 1984. *The Alice Bailey Inheritance*. Wellingborough, England: Turnstone Press.

Skelton, Robin. 1988. *The Practice of Witchcraft Today*. Bury St. Edmunds, Suffolk, England: St. Edmundsbury Press.

Smith, Archie, Jr. 1978. "Black reflections on the study of new religious consciousness." Pp. 209–19 in *Understanding the New Religions*, ed. Jacob Needleman and George Baker. New York: Seabury.

Snook, John B. 1974. "An alternative to church-sect." *Journal for the Scientific Study of Religion* 13.2 (June):191–204.

Snow, David A., and Richard Machalek. 1984. "The sociology of conversion." *Annual Review of Sociology* 10:167–90.

Snow, David A., Louis A. Zurcher, and Sheldon Eckland-Olson. 1980. "Social networks and social movements: a microstructural approach to differential recruitment." *American Sociological Review* 45:787–80.

Spangler, David. 1975. *Festivals for the New Age*. Forres, Scotland: Findhorn Foundation.

———. 1976. *Revelation: The Birth of a New Age*. San Francisco: The Rainbow Bridge. Reprint, 1977. Forres, Scotland: Findhorn.

———. 1977. *Toward a Planetary Vision*. Forres, Scotland: Findhorn.

———. 1984. *Emergence: The Rebirth of the Sacred*. New York: Dell.

———. 1988. "Defining the New Age." *The New Age Catalogue*. New York: Doubleday.

Starhawk [Miriam Simos]. 1979. *The Spiral Dance: A Rebirth of Ancient Religion of the Great Goddess*. San Francisco: Harper and Row.

———. 1988. *Dreaming the Dark: Magic, Sex and Politics*. Boston: Beacon Press.

Stark, Rodney. 1981. "Must all religions be supernatural?". In *The Social Impact of New Religious Movements*, ed. Bryan R. Wilson. New York: Rose of Sharon Press.

———. 1983. "Europe's receptivity to religious movements." In *Religious Movements: Genesis, Exodus and Numbers*, ed. R. Stark. New York: Rose of Sharon Press.

Stark, Rodney, and William Sims Bainbridge. 1979. "Of churches, sects, and cults: preliminary concepts for a theory of religious movements. *Journal for the Scientific Study of Religion* 18.2:117–33.

———. 1980a. "Toward a theory of religion: religious commitment." *Journal for the Scientific Study of Religion* 19.2:114–28.

———. 1980b. "Secularization, revival, and cult formation." *Annual Review of the Social Sciences of Religion* 4:85–119.

———. 1980c. "Networks of faith: Interpersonal bonds and recruitment to cults and sects." *American Journal of Sociology* 85.6 (May):1376–95.

————. 1983. "Concepts for a theory of religious movements." Pp. 3–26 in *Alternatives to American Mainline Churches*, ed. Joseph H. Fichter. New York: Rose of Sharon Press.

————. 1985. *The Future of Religion: Secularization, Revival and Cult Formation*. Berkeley: University of California Press.

Stark, Rodney, and Lynne Roberts. 1982. "The arithmetic of social movements." *Sociological Analysis* 43:53–68.

Stein, Arthur. 1985. *Seeds of the Seventies: Values, Work, and Commitment in Post-Vietnam America*. Hanover, N.H.: University Press of New England.

Stone, Donald. 1976. "The Human Potential Movement." Pp. 93–115 in *The New Religious Consciousness*, ed. Charles Y. Glock and Robert Bellah. Berkeley: University of Calif. Press.

————. 1978a. "New religious consciousness and personal religious experience." *Sociological Analysis* 39:123–134.

————. 1978b. "On knowing how we know about the new religions." Pp. 141–52 in *Understanding the New Religions*, ed. Jacob Needleman and George Baker. New York: Seabury.

Straus, Roger A. 1979. "Religious conversion as a personal and collective accomplishment." *Sociological Analysis* 40.2:158–65.

Streiker, Lowell D. 1990. *New Age Comes to Main Street: What Worried Christians Must Know*. Nashville: Abingdon.

Stupple, David. 1975a. "Introduction: the occult experience." *Journal of Popular Culture* 8.4 (Spring):859–61.

————. 1975b. "The 'I AM' sect today: an *unobituary*." *Journal of Popular Culture* 8.4 (Spring):896–905.

Sutherland, Stewart, Leslie Houlden, Peter Clarke and Friedhelm Hardy, eds. 1988. *The World's Religions*, London: Routledge.

Swatos, William H. 1976. "Weber or Troeltsch?: Methodology, syndrome, and the development of church-sect theory." *Journal for the Scientific Study of Religion* 15.2 (June):129–44.

————. 1977. "Quo vadis: Reply to Robertson." *Journal for the Scientific Study of Religion* 16.2 (June):201–4.

————. 1981. "Church-sect and cult: bringing mysticism back in." *Sociological Analysis* 42.1:17–26.

Tarcher, Jeremy P. (n.d.). "The Real New Age Story." Los Angeles: J. P. Tarcher.

Tart, Charles, ed. 1972. *Altered States of Consciousness*. Garden City, N.Y.: Doubleday.

————. 1975. *Transpersonal Psychologies*. Garden City, N.Y.: Doubleday.

Tipton, Steven M. 1979. "New religious movements and the problem of a modern ethic." *Sociological Inquiry* 49.2–3:286–312.

————. 1982a. "The moral logic of alternative religions." *Daedalus* 111.1 (Winter):185–213.

————. 1982b. *Getting Saved From the Sixties*, Berkeley: University of California Press.

Tiryakian, Edward A. 1972. "Toward a sociology of esoteric cults." *American Journal of Sociology* 78:491–512.

————, ed. 1974. *On the Margin of the Visible: Sociology, the Esoteric, and the Occult.* New York: John Wiley and Sons.

Travisano, Richard. 1970. "Alternation and conversion as qualitatively different transformations." Pp. 594–606 in *Social Psychology Through Symbolic Interaction*, ed. Gregory P. Stone and Harvey A. Farberman. Waltham, Mass.: Ginn-Blaisdell.

Trevelyan, George. 1977/1984. *A Vision of the Aquarian Age: The Emerging Spiritual World View.* London: Coventure.

Troeltsch, Ernst. 1910.—cited in "Maligned mysticism: The maledicted career of Troeltsch's third type," by William R. Garrett. *Sociological Analysis* 36.3 (Fall, 1975):205–23.

————. 1931. *The Social Teaching of the Christian Churches.* Trans. O. Wyon. New York and London: Macmillan.

Truzzi, Marcello. 1972. "The occult revival as popular culture: Some random observations on the old and the nouveau witch." *The Sociological Quarterly* 13 (Winter):16–36.

Turner, Ralph R., and Lewis M. Killian, eds. 1957. *Collective Behavior.* Englewood Cliffs, N.J.: Prentice-Hall.

Vaughn, David. 1967. *A Faith for the New Age.* London: Regency Press.

Wagner, Melinda Bollar. 1983. *Metaphysics in Midwestern America.* Columbus: Ohio State University Press.

Wallace, A.F.C. 1956. "Revitalization movements." *American Anthropologist* 58:264–81.

Wallace, Robert Keith. 1971. "A wakeful hypometabolic physiologic state." *American Journal of Physiology* 221.3:795–9.

Wallis, Roy. 1974. "Ideology, authority, and the development of cultic movements." *Social Research* 41:299–327.

————, ed. 1975a. *Sectarianism: Analyses of Religious and Non-religious Sects.* London: Peter Owen.

————. 1975b. "Scientology: Therapeutic cult to religious sect." *Sociology* 9:89–100.

————. 1976. *The Road to Total Freedom: A Sociological Analysis of Scientology.* London: Heinemann.

————. 1979a. *Salvation and Protest: Studies of Social and Religious Movements.* London: Frances Pinter; New York: St. Martin's Press.

————. 1979b. "Varieties of psychosalvation." *New Society* 50.897–898:649–51.

————. 1979c. "The elementary forms of the new religious life." *Annual Review of the Social Sciences of Religion* 3:191–211.

————. 1980. "What's new on the new religions." *The Zetetic Scholar* 6:155–69.

————. 1981. "Yesterday's children: cultural and structural change in a new religious movement.'' Pp. 97–132 in *The Social Impact of New Religious Movements*, ed. Bryan R. Wilson. New York: Rose of Sharon Press.

———. 1982a. "The new religions as social indicators.'' Pp. 216–31 in *New Religious Movements: A Perspective for Understanding Society*, ed. Eileen Barker. New York: Edwin Mellen Press.

———. 1982b. "The social construction of charisma.'' *Social Compass* 29.1:25–39.

———. 1982c. "Charisma, commitment and control in a new religious movement.'' In *Millennialism and Charisma*, ed. R. Wallis. Belfast: The Queen's University.

———, ed. 1982d. *Millennialism and Charisma*. Belfast: Queen's University.

———. 1984. *The Elementary Forms of the New Religious Life*. London: Routledge and Kegan Paul.

———. 1985. "Betwixt therapy and salvation: the changing form of the Human Potential Movement.'' In *Sickness and Sectarianism: Exploratory Studies in Medical and Religious Sectarianism*, ed. R. Kenneth Jones. Aldershot, Hampshire, England: Gower Press.

———. 1986. "Figuring out cult receptivity.'' *Journal for the Scientific Study of Religion* 25.4:494–503.

———. 1988. "North America.'' Pp. 912–24 in *The World's Religions*, ed. Stewart Sutherland, Leslie Houlden, Peter Clarke, and Friedhelm Hardy. London: Routledge.

Wallis, Roy, and Steve Bruce. 1984. "The Stark-Bainbridge theory of religion: a critique and counter proposals.'' *Sociological Analysis* 45.1 (Spring): 11–27.

———. 1985. *Sociological Theory, Religion and Collective Action*. Belfast: The Queen's University.

Webb, James. 1974. *The Occult Underground*. La Salle, Ill.: Open Court.

———. 1976. *The Occult Establishment*. La Salle, Ill.: Open Court.

Weber, Max. 1947. *The Theory of Social and Economic Organization*. New York: Free Press.

———. 1948. "The sociology of charismatic authority.'' In *From Max Weber: Essays in Sociology*, ed. H. Gerth and C. Wright Mills. London: Routledge and Kegan Paul.

———. 1949. *The Methodology of the Social Sciences*. Trans. Talcott Parsons. New York: Free Press.

———. 1965. *The Sociology of Religion*. Translated from the 1956 fourth edition by Ephraim Fischoff in 1963. London: Methuen.

Welch, Michael R. 1977. "Analyzing religious sects: an empirical examination of Wilson's sect typology.'' *Journal for the Scientific Study of Religion* 16.2 (June):125–141.

Westley, Frances. 1978. " 'The cult of man': Durkheim's predictions and new religious movements.'' *Sociological Analysis* 39.2:135–45.

———. 1983. *The Complex of Forms of the Religious Life: A Durkheimian View of New Religious Movements*. Chico, Calif.: Scholars Press.

White, John, ed. 1972. *The Highest State of Consciousness*. Garden City, N.Y.: Doubleday.

White, John, and Stanley Krippner, eds. 1977. *Future Science*. Garden City, N.Y.: Doubleday.

Wiese, Leopold von, and Howard Becker. 1932. *Systematic Sociology*. New York: John Wiley and Sons.

Wilber, Ken. 1977. *The Spectrum of Consciousness*. Wheaton, Ill.: Theosophical Publishing House.

————. 1983. *A Sociable God: Toward a New Understanding of Religion*, Boulder. Colo.: Shambala.

Wilson, Bryan R. 1958. "The appearance and survival of sects in an evolutionary social milieu." *Archives de Sociologie des Religions* 5:140–50.

————. 1959. "An analysis of sect development." *American Sociological Review*, 24.1 (February):3–15.

————. 1961. *Sects and Society*. London: Heinemann; Berkeley, Calif.: University of California Press.

————. 1963. "Typologie des sects dans une perspective dynamique et comparative." *Archives de Sociologie des Religions* 16 (July–December):49–63; translated by Jenny M. Robertson and listed here as Wilson (1969a).

————, ed. 1967. *Patterns of Sectarianism*. London: Heinemann.

————. 1969a. "A typology of sects." Pp. 361–83 in *Sociology of Religion: Selected Readings*, ed. Roland Robertson. Harmondsworth, England: Penguin.

————. 1969b. *Religion in Secular Society: A Sociological Comment*. Harmondsworth, England: Penguin.

————. 1970a. *Youth Culture and the Universities*. London: Faber.

————. 1970b. *Religious Sects*. London: Weidenfeld and Nicolson.

————. 1973. *Magic and the Millennium*. London: Heinemann.

————. 1975. *The Noble Savage: The Primitive Origins of Charisma*. Berkeley: University of California Press.

————. 1976. *Contemporary Transformations of Religion*. London: Oxford University Press.

———— 1978. *Sects and Society: A Sociological Study of Three Religious Groups in Britain*. Westport, Conn.: Greenwood Press.

————. 1979. "The new religions: some preliminary considerations." *Japanese Journal of Religious Studies* 6(1–2):193–216. Pp. 16–31 in *New Religious Movements: A Perspective for Understanding Society*, ed. Eileen Barker. New York: Edwin Mellen Press.

————, ed. 1981. *The Social Impact of New Religious Movements*. New York: Rose of Sharon Press; Barrytown, N.Y.: The Unification Theological Seminary (Conference Series, no. 9).

————. 1982. *Religion in Sociological Perspective*. Oxford: Oxford University Press.

————. 1985. "A typology of sects." In *Religion and Ideology*, ed. Robert Bocock and Kenneth Thompson; translated by J. M. Robertson.

————. 1988. " "Secularisation": Religion in the modern world." Pp. 953–66 in *The World's Religions*, ed. Stewart Sutherland, Leslie Houlden, Peter Clarke, and Friedhelm Hardy. London: Routledge.

————. 1990. *The Social Dimensions of Sectarianism: Sects and New Religious Movements in Contemporary Society*. Oxford: Claredon Press.

Wilson, John. 1973. *Introduction to Social Movements*. New York: Basic Books.

————. 1979. *Public Religion in American Culture*. Philadelphia: Temple University Press.

Wuthnow, Robert. 1976. *The Consciousness Reformation*. Berkeley: University of California Press.

————. 1978. *Experimentation in American Religion*. Berkeley: University of California Press.

————. 1985. "The cultural context of contemporary religious movements." Pp. 43–56 in *Cults, Culture and the Law*, ed. T. Robbins, W. Shepherd, and J. McBride. Chico, Calif.: Scholars Press.

————. 1988. *The Restructuring of American Religion: Society and Faith Since World War II*. Princeton: Princeton University Press.

Yinger, J. Milton. 1946. *Religion in the Struggle for Power*. Durham, N.C.: Duke University Press.

————. 1957. *Religion, Society and the Individual*. London: Macmillan.

————. 1970. *The Scientific Study of Religion*. London: Macmillan.

————. 1982. *Countercultures: The Promise and the Peril of a World Turned Upside Down*. New York: The Free Press.

Young, Jock. 1971. *The Drug Takers*. London: McGibbon and Kee.

Young, Wendy Warren. 1987. "The aims and methods of 'est' and 'The Centres Network'." Pp. 131–147 in *The New Evangelists: Recruitment Methods and Aims of New Religious Movements*, ed. Peter B. Clarke. London: Ethnographica Publishers Ltd.

Zald, Mayer N., and Roberta Ash. 1966. "Social movement organizations: Growth, decay and change." *Social Forces* 44.3 (March):327–41; reprinted in *Social Movements: A Reader and Source Book*, ed. Robert R. Evans. Chicago: Rand McNally (1973).

Zaretsky, I.I., and M.P. Leone, eds. 1974. *Religious Movements in Contemporary America*. Princeton: Princeton University Press.

# Index

# About the Author

Michael York read for his Ph.D. degree in the Theology Department of King's College, University of London in the History and Philosophy of Religion Division, focusing on the sociology of religion and the sociology of new religious movements. He holds earlier degrees from San Francisco State University (Social Science: International Relations) and the University of California, Santa Barbara (English). He has also attended Purdue University, New York University, UCLA, and UC, Berkeley.

Dr. York currently directs the Academy for Cultural and Educational Studies (in London and Varanasi, India) and the Amsterdam Center for Eurindic Studies (in The Netherlands). He is a member of the Advisory Board for the Association of World Academics for Religious Education in Goleta, California. His current research interests are in the fields of the Sociology of New Religious Movements, Postmodernism, Indo-European Studies, and Indology.